EIGHTIES RINGWAY

Manchester Airpc

CW00816194

Part of the 'RINGWAY THROL

Written and researched by Mark Williams

Published by RINGWAY PUBLICATIONS
www.ringwaypublications.com

Ringway Publications

First published in Great Britain 2012

Copyright © Mark Williams 2012
Mark Williams asserts the moral right to be identified as the author of this work.

All rights reserved.
No part of this publication may be reproduced, stored in a retrieval system, or transmitted, in any form or by any means, electronic, mechanical, photocopying, recording or otherwise without the prior written permission of the publishers.

A catalogue record of this book is available from the British Library

ISBN No: 978-0-9570826-1-8

Printed and bound in Great Britain by
Beamreach (UK) Ltd
22 Pepper Street
Lymm
Cheshire
WA13 OJB
www.beamreachuk.co.uk

Contents

PHOTOGRAPH CREDITS

Front Cover:

23rd February 1980 - Seen on a cold, sunny afternoon in-between flights are B.737s G-AVRN & G-AZNZ of Britannia Airways, which went on to serve Britannia Airways until October 1993 and March 1985 respectively. The Boeing 737 had been the backbone of the airlines fleet since 1968, when they started to replace their Bristol Britannia's. In the background is the iconic Control Tower, opened by HRH Prince Phillip, the Duke of Edinburgh on the 23rd October 1962. The additional administration block was completed in 1970.

(Geoff Ball)

Back Cover:

February 1982 – This midweek shot depicts two contrasting markets. Firstly in the foreground, the three British Airways Tridents parked on Gates 44/46 & 48, are servicing the very busy Manchester-London Heathrow route. The main flight was operated by the Trident 3 in the centre, G-AWZE, whilst the Trident 2s either side were back-ups and would have departed after the main flight, mopping up any overspill from the main flight. In some cases, when it became apparent that two aircraft were needed, one would go ahead of the main flight once British Airways had made the necessary judgement at the time of check-in. Alternatively in the background are an Air Europe B.737 and a Dan-Air B.727, parked on the South Bay awaiting their next duties, but as this is the winter season, they would have been idle for most of the week.

(Rick Ward)

Acknowledgements

I would like to thank everyone who has contributed by supplying photographs, data, documents, information and encouragement.

I would also like to thank everyone who has visited our historic website, from the UK and across the world, particularly those who have participated by sharing their memories and photographs.

My eternal gratitude goes out to:

MANCHESTER AIRPORT ARCHIVE
Patsy McClements for allowing me access to their records, which included relevant documents, movement sheets, ATC Watch Logs and photographs and to Michael Hancock, Business Records Officer, for his helpfulness over the past eight years.

I would also like to mention his predecessor, Paul Isherwood, who sadly passed away in 2007. Without his support over the first twelve years of my research, this series of books would never have been written.

MANCHESTER CENTRAL LIBRARY
Particular thanks go to the Local Studies Department for arranging access to their archives over the last twenty years, which assisted greatly with missing movement's data.

RESEARCH/MOVEMENTS
To everyone who helped fill any gaps in my research, with special thanks to Geoff Ball, Ian Barrie, John Duffield (movements), Nik French, Chris Walkden (ATC logs), Paul Smith (supplying LAAS publications for reference), TAS (Winged Words for reference) and magazines for reference by the Cheshire Aviation Society and Air- Britain News.

PHOTOGRAPH CREDITS
To Ian Barrie, Manchester Airport Archive, Alec Rankin and Rick Ward for their wonderful pictures. Once again, Ringway Publications are proud and privileged to showcase Geoff Ball's exceptional photographs for everyone's enjoyment.

Mark Williams

Foreword by Gil Thompson
Manchester Airport Director 1981-1993

I wonder how many Mancunians recognise the significance of Balloon Street in downtown Manchester and how many are aware that from this site in 1785, Manchester's City Fathers had the courage and wisdom to authorise James Sadler to ascend in a hot balloon, watched by a crowd of 5,000 each paying half-a-guinea to observe the historic flight. One could say this epic event marked the beginning of Manchester's 'love-affair' with all the strands of aviation for which the North West subsequently became known and played such a key role in the economic development of the whole region. A major part of that was of course the opening of RINGWAY, as the airport was then called in 1935.

I was completely unaware of this unique aviation history when I first arrived in Manchester in 1974, in my new role as British Airways General Manager for the North of England. However, it did not take long to pick up and absorb the threads of history and to recognise the unexploited and massive potential the region offered in terms of airline passengers and air-cargo development opportunities. Indeed it was this background which prompted me to forego my airline career in 1981, in order to take up my new appointment as The Airport Director at Ringway, to succeed Gordon Sweetapple. Gordon deserves great credit for his major contribution to the successful development of Ringway in the 1970's and for providing me with such a valuable building block.

During the next decade the airport grew from a Regional Airport to one of the world's top twenty International Airports. How did we achieve this? I believe there were major decisions which brought about this unparalleled growth in traffic and profits. Firstly is the vital topic of the ownership. At the time of my appointment as the new Director, Ringway was owned and managed by Manchester City Council. This was recognised by the Council and management alike as an undeniable strength, but at the same time as a weakness. Let me explain. Airports were not 'profit makers' in the early eighties and therefore Ringway was most fortunate to be able to rely on the City Council to fund its development costs, as well as its running costs. Moreover Ringway was able to draw on the outstanding skills and advice from the Council's Officers in the vital fields of finance, engineering and architecture. However, these strengths were off-set by the unavoidable slowness in decision making. All initiatives and proposals had to be vetted by the relevant Council Sub-Committee, whose recommendations were forwarded to the City Council's full monthly meetings for approval. The City Council deserves full credit for recognising these shortcomings and for agreeing that Ringway should become a PLC (Public Limited Company), a status achieved in 1986 which made Ringway the first airport in Europe to become a PLC. This also empowered Ringway's Management Team to make commercial decisions in keeping with its agreed business plan.

I now turn to the second decision, which relates to Traffic Rights. In this regard it is not generally known that after the cessation of the Second World War, the UK Government bewilderingly signed an International Airline Traffic Rights Treaty, designating

London and Prestwick (Scotland) as the only gateway airports which foreign airlines could serve! In short, Manchester was completely excluded and denied any new foreign airlines. This was a situation we could not accept, so the Management Team coupled with the power of local MP's and members of the Manchester City Council, embarked on the most extensive and powerful lobbying campaign to overturn this discriminatory treaty. Our aim was to give Northerners the right to fly direct to their overseas destination, rather than being forced to fly to London to connect to another flight. The campaign succeeded, which enabled a great many foreign airlines to launch new routes into Manchester. In turn this produced a massive increase in passengers and cargo throughput.

Lastly, now that Ringway was able to compete with London on an equal basis, the Management Team embarked upon another campaign, a marketing initiative that was 'ground breaking' in the sense that it was designed to attract and incentivise new and existing airlines into launching new charters and scheduled routes from Ringway. The main thrust of this campaign was our proposal that Ringway would share the high risks as well as the costs of launching new routes with the airlines, which may lose money in the early stages of development. This strategy proved to be most profitable and successful indeed and for the first time, Ringway was able to offer its huge catchment area of over 20m people, the choice they had waited for and deserved – a selection of 150 worldwide destinations.

I count myself as the most fortunate man on earth to have been appointed to head-up the Ringway team, which produced this decade of growth and success. I see Ringway's continual growth as unstoppable, when one considers the most extensive network of rail services in Europe is feeding the airport and penetrating even further into its enormous catchment area.

I conclude by wishing my successors every success during the next decade and beyond.

Gil Thompson

Sir Gil Thompson

Gil Thompson, born in Belfast on the 1st March 1930, is married with two daughters. He resides in Bowdon, Cheshire and has engaged in a variety of Public Office activities and commercial posts over many years. He's a firm believer in keeping fit and enjoys jogging, bridge and golf and is a keen follower of sport, particularly soccer.

An airline man through and through, his career began in 1950 as a Management Trainee with British European Airways-Belfast, progressing to BEA Sales Executive Birmingham-England (1960), BEA Regional Manager Los Angeles-USA (1965), BEA Manager-Irish Republic (1967), BEA General Manager-USA (1969), British Airways General Manager-Scotland (1972), British Airways General Manager-North of England (1974), Chief Executive Manchester Airport (1981) and Vice President of Manchester Airport Plc (1993).

In recognition of his services to the airline industry, he was awarded Officer of the Most Excellent Order of the British Empire – OBE (1985), Mancunian of the Year (1985) and Conferral of Knighthood by H.M. the Queen (1993).

Other titles in the
'RINGWAY THROUGH THE DECADES' series

SEVENTIES RINGWAY 1970 - 1979

Coming Next

EIGHTIES RINGWAY 1985 - 1989

Visit our historic website
'RINGWAY THROUGH THE DECADES'
Covers all aspects of Manchester Airport from 1938 to the present day
www.ringwaypublications.com

All our products can be purchased from our on-line shop or through our stockists.

If you wish to contact us, we would be pleased to hear from you
via our website or by email:
info@ringwaypublications.com

1
Airport Diary 1980

January 1980

This month's passenger and movement figures were significantly up on last years, when the airport was plagued by industrial action; but freight was down on last January, when considerably more cargo than usual was handled, due to the docker's and transport driver strikes.

The Public Enquiry being held at Manchester Town Hall on the 12th February on the proposed runway extension, could last as long as two weeks. Although the ILS has already been relocated from the end of the runway and on to farmland to minimise any intrusion into local beauty spots on the South Side, up to 300 objections have already been received.

Over seventy MP's from the North West were shown proposals for the airport's £150m development plans up to 1995, which include a railway-link, station, second runway, freight terminal, second passenger terminal and new maintenance hangars. They were told that building work would only commence when passenger numbers exceeded 10m.

Brymon Airways will operate a once-weekly Manchester-Newquay flight again this summer, with one-way fares from £30 or from £49 return for an advanced purchase ticket.

British Airways used B.747s G-AWNH & G-BDPZ on Manchester-Prestwick-Toronto flights (BA080/1) & Manchester-Prestwick-Montreal flights (BA084/5) from 2nd-14th, which reverted thereafter to a three-weekly operation with SVC-10s as BA080/1. Other equipment changes on scheduled services included Air Malta (KM106): Austrian Airlines DC-9 OE-LDC (13th/20th/27th); KLM (KL153): NLM F.28 PH-CHD (13th); Lufthansa (LH074): B.727s D-ABCI (25th), D-ABKC (8th) & D-ABLI (11th); Sabena (SN617): Sobelair B.737s OO-SBQ (4th/14th) & OO-SBS (6th) and Swissair (SR842): DC-9-51 HB-ISW (3rd).

Although the weather was typically wintry with occasional fog, snow and lots of ice particularly over the first half of the month, the ILS still saw plenty of activity. RAF traffic identified included Hawks XX182 (2nd), XX232 (15th/16th), XX241 (28th) & XX294 (9th); Dominie XS730 (9th) and C-130s XV217 (15th) & XV291 (11th). Interesting civil ILS movements were Automobile Association Cessna 441 G-AUTO (16th), Air UK EMB-110 G-BGYS (16th), Invicta Britannia G-ANCF IM969 (17th) & BIA Herald G-BEYK (31st).

2nd British Airways B.747 G-BDPZ, ex-EI-ASJ leased from Aer Lingus since April 1979, operated Toronto flight BA081/0 daily until the 6th, when it positioned back to Heathrow.

3rd Sub-zero temperatures caused short and frequent closures at the airport for either de-icing or snow clearance. Poor braking action on the runway resulted in five scheduled flights inbound to Manchester diverting to Heathrow or Liverpool, amongst which was today's early-morning Lufthansa cargo flight, LH4072.

3rd The US Army made their only visit this year, when Beech C-12 73-22261 arrived at 1044 today on a round-trip from Hanau, Germany where the 104th Area Support Group are based. Hanau was massively targeted by an allied bombing raid in March 1945.

4th The ATC Watch Log recorded at 0725, that when British Airways flight BA5690 was leaving Stand 41 bound for Aberdeen, the pilot had to brake violently to avoid a catering truck crossing his path. He requested ATC pass on his complaint to the offending company!

4th Grumman AA-5 G-BFZO made a safe landing this morning, after declaring a full emergency with control problems.

4th Sobelair operated Brussels flight SN617/8 on behalf of Sabena several times during the month. B.737 OO-SBQ operated today/14th & B.737 OO-SBS on the 6th.

6th Southern International Viscount G-CSZB positioning in from Lydd at 2226, departed the following morning as DA6982 to Glasgow, taking oil workers back to Scotland.

7th The ATC Watch Log reported that at 1115, an unidentified aircraft appeared on the radar 15-miles to the east of the airfield and crossed the centreline without prior permission. It was believed to be a RAF Canberra, which was confirmed later when the airport received a telephone call at 1252 from a RAF Squadron Commander who admitted the incident and apologised for the error.

10th Liverpool based Vernair Transport Services operate a fleet of Beech Queen/King Airs for charter work and transporting workers to/from the BNFL Nuclear Plant at Dounreay, on the northeast coast of Scotland. Late in 1978 they acquired Shorts Skyvan G-AWWS for freight work, which diverted in at 1817 today from Beauvais, due to lack of customs at Liverpool.

12th January 1980 – Clyden Airways operated a Manchester-Dublin mail service from September 1978 to January 1981, with two Douglas DC-3s. EI-BDU is seen here having just arrived back at Ringway, after a failed attempt to land at Dublin due to fog. (Geoff Ball)

12th Dense fog seriously affected the Irish airports for most of the day. Amongst the various arrivals into Manchester were two Aviaco DC-9s: EC-CTU at 1439 (AO1744 from Tenerife) & EC-CTR at 1746 (AO1746 from Las Palmas) both Dublin diversions and Belfast diversion Balkan IL-18 LZ-BEK at 1216 (LZ925 from Sofia).

12th The cattle flights to Milan continued with Transavia B.737s PH-TVE today, PH-TVD (25th) & PH-TVC (31st). Britannia's G-ANCF & G-AOVF also operated a number of flights.

14th The airport was closed for a time during the morning, after ice formed on the runway, as the region was still suffering from the freezing conditions that started last month.

14th Cessna 402 N2715S, the company's current demonstrator, paid a visit from Cranfield at 1843 today, before departing for Dublin the following day.

15th A full emergency was declared by Manchester resident PA-28 G-BASI shortly after takeoff this morning with engine problems, but it managed a safe landing.

15th Two brand new C-130s passing through Manchester on delivery for the Yemen Air Force this month were in a similar, but slightly darker colour scheme, than those of the Royal Saudi Air Force. The first arrival was C-130H/1150 c/n 4825 today and the second, C-130H/1160 c/n 4827 was on the 29th. They were both delivered on the same routing of Gander-Athens, operated by Lockheed crews and the same Yemeni personnel.

15th Three BAe.125s passing through Manchester for customs clearance en route to Hawarden were HZ-DAC at 1227 today, HB-VFA (21st) & I-BOGI (27th), which had visited on several occasions previously under it former guise as HB-VAG.

16th EMB-110 G-BGYS operated a practice ILS this afternoon, from/to Leeds in basic Air Anglia colours with an Air UK tail, but it didn't land.

22nd Manchester's proposed new airline, Air Transcontinental, halted their recruitment drive due to financial difficulties. Their charter flights, due to commence on the 30th March, will take 250,000 holidaymakers abroad this year, initially with four Boeing 707s currently being operated by other airlines. A Boeing 747 will be added later, along with two Douglas DC-9-82s currently on order. Following talks, a decision on the feasibility of the airline operating from Manchester this summer is imminent and their spokesman stated 'They are confident their plans are still on course'.

23rd PA-31 Navajo G-LCCO operated by Lotus Cars, was noted in a very attractive all-black colour scheme today.

24th After five months of total inactivity, Boeing 707 N473RN was moved from its remote parking spot on the South Bay over to the North Side in preparation for possible departure, but it returned to the exact parking spot the following day!

25th British Cargo Airlines, newly formed last August by the amalgamation of Transmeridian and IAS, made the first of just two visits to Manchester today, when CL-44 G-AZKJ operated a cargo flight taking equipment to Umea, Sweden; but due to mounting debts they had ceased trading by March.

26th This month's only weather diversion from Heathrow was British Airways SVC-10 G-ASGH (BA066 from Nairobi), arriving at 0548 today. Later in the day Northwest Orient's first passenger B.747 to visit Manchester appeared, when N608US diverted in from Prestwick at 1716 (NW034A from Boston via Copenhagen).

26th Air Languedoc Metroliner F-GCFE, arriving at 1030 today, brought the French Rugby League team into Manchester from Rennes, for their match against Wales in Widnes.

26th B.707F G-BDEA made its final visit to Manchester today as a British Caledonian aircraft, operating cargo flight BR567 to Atlanta/Houston.

28th The first visit to Manchester of an Agusta 109 took place today, with the arrival of G-HELY owned by Barratt Homes, which replaces their Jet Ranger G-BEKH. The type, fully IFR equipped to fly on airways, can also make conventional ILS approaches.

28th Cessna 340 N98575 diverted in from Leeds at 1216 today. It was scheduled for maintenance there prior to its return to the USA, but the work was carried out by NEA at Manchester instead.

28th The collapse of Air Transcontinental was announced today, before it had even got off the ground! After the company was put into liquidation, their accountants blamed the airlines Middle Eastern financial backers for 'reneging on the deal'. The economy and political situation in Iran had influenced the last minute withdrawal of a promised cash injection. It was only last November that the airline announced ambitious plans to base a number of aircraft at Manchester and operate an extensive summer programme. After last-ditch efforts by several tour operators to save the airline had failed, they had no choice other than to go with alternative airlines. Prior to all this, Transasian Airlines as they were previously known, operated four Boeing 707s for lease-out to other airlines.

31st F-BTGV, arriving from Le Bourget today to transport Airbus wings out to their factory at Bremen, was the first Guppy to visit Manchester since 9th November 1979.

February 1980

This month's weather diversions caused by fog or snow were dominated by aircraft from Leeds, until Heathrow was affected on the 26th. From Leeds came numerous British Airways Viscounts, which will cease operating from Leeds and Manchester by the end of next month. Also from Leeds was a quantity of Air Anglia diversions, with three arriving on the morning of Saturday 23rd, including the first visit of one of their newly acquired Fokker F.28s.

Soviet travel firm, Intourist, will offer Inclusive Tours to Russia this summer, using Aeroflot. Prices starting at £290 will include tickets to the Olympic Games in Moscow. Also on offer are two-week holidays from Sunday 29th June, which includes the Black Sea resort of Yalta, a tour of Moscow and Leningrad and a three-night stay in the coal mining region of Donetsk, where holidaymakers will be given the opportunity to go down one of the mines.

Plans for work to commence on the £8m railway line, linking the airport and Manchester City Centre, have received a major setback following a report concluding that the line was a luxury and couldn't be justified on financial grounds. The plan to build a 3-mile link between the airport and Heald Green Station, linking the main Manchester-Wilmslow line, includes an underground station at the airport capable of handling an 8-car train. A southern link from this to Alderley Edge is also being considered, but in view of the study's findings, the City Centre link is likely to be relegated to the bottom of the GMC's transport shopping list!

Air Ecosse have applied to the CAA to operate a twice-weekday service between Manchester-Dundee, which they hope to commence on the 31st March.

British Airways saw the number of passengers using the Manchester-London Shuttle increase by more than 30%, since its introduction last November. More than 134,000 passengers used the service between November 1979 and February 1980.

NEA are using the most of the main South Side Hangar, No. 522, after converting the extreme eastern end into a maintenance bay and installing a plastic curtain from the floor to the false ceiling across their area. Barton Moss occupies the western end, previously used as offices by the North West Flying School, who are at the eastern end as they are now part of NEA. Apache Air Taxis, who occupy the middle space trading as Merlin Flying Services, are planning to acquire a BAe.125 for executive work.

Some old friends to Manchester, formerly operated by Biggin Hill-based Fairflight Charter, were lost after leaving for pastures new. Dove G-AROI, which had visited many times throughout the 1970's and made its last visit on 4th December 1978, was sold in Denmark and then quickly sold again to a buyer in the USA. Heron G-ANNO, delivered new in 1960 and operated by Fairflight Charter from 1974, made its last visit on 26th July 1978. It left Biggin Hill on the 12th for a new life in Thailand, along with a second Heron G-APKW, which had made its last visit on 11th November 1978. Two more Herons, G-ANSZ & G-AXFH, formerly operated by Norwich-based Peters Aviation, were sold to St. Lucia Airways during the month. G-ANSZ, which had been a frequent visitor throughout the 1960's operating to Oxford/Bournemouth for Morton Air Services, left on delivery on the 26th having made its last visit on 10th October 1978. This was followed by G-AXFH on the 1st March, which had last visited Manchester on 15th October 1977.

Air Bridge Carriers have taken charge of the weekly cattle flights to Milan again, although Invicta operated twice during the month with G-AOVF (4th) & G-ANCF (21st).

Equipment changes on scheduled services included Air France (AF964): Boeing 727 F-BOJE (2nd) & Air Charter SE.210 F-BJTH (13th); Air Malta (KM106): Austrian Airlines DC-9 OE-LDC (3rd/10th/17th/24th); KLM (KL153): NLM F.28s PH-CHD (9th), PH-CHF (16th) & first visit PH-CHI (14th) and Lufthansa (LH074): B.727s D-ABKJ (22nd/30th) & D-ABQI (31st).

RAF ILS traffic identified included Hawks XX170 (26th), XX172 (29th), XX175 (27th), XX179 (12th), XX190 (26th), XX240 (25th), XX244 (21st), XX245 (22nd) & XX290 (18th); C-130 XV305 (6th); Jetstreams XX494 (25th) & XX497 (26th) and Dominie XS739 (29th).

2nd Air France replaced the usual SE.210 Caravelle with Boeing 727 F-BOJE on Paris flight AF964/1, due to an increased load in connection with the England v France Rugby Union match in Paris.

3rd The Royal Saudi Air Force appears to be using Manchester for their transatlantic flights again, with six this month starting with westbound C-130H 466 today. Included with the rest were the first C-130E visits since last December, with the arrival of two of the rarer examples, 1609 (10th) & 455 (18th).

4th Cessna 404 G-BHGL, which was formerly operated by the French Air Force, suffered lightning damage on landing during its diversion from Leeds at 1435 today. After undergoing repairs with Northern Executive, it finally departed back to Leeds on the 24th.

6th British Airways took delivery of the first of twenty Boeing 737s due to arrive over the coming months, when G-BGDC touched down at Heathrow today.

9th Lear Jet EC-DEB arrived from Madrid at 1433 today, with a crew to take B.707 N473RN out to Madrid the following day.

10th February 1980 – After being stored at Manchester since August 1979, B.707 N473RN is ready to take to the skies again! It eventually departed to Madrid at 1510 today to its new owner, Transcargo, who operated it for two months before selling it on. Displaying Transcargo titles, it was still wearing its US registration, which was used as its call-sign. (Geoff Ball)

11th Executive movements were plentiful today: Falcon 20s F-BVPN & F-BRPK, Corvette F-BTTU & Lear Jet I-MABU would have been more than enough, but Manchester was also treated to three Danish aircraft: Rockwell 690 OY-ART, Beech 90 OY-AZV & PA-31 OY-ATP.

11th The French Government commenced their training flights again, with Corvette's F-BTTU today and F-BVPK (13th), which both made further visits during the month.

11th PA-23 Aztec G-AYLY currently owned and operated by Air UK, arrived in their full colours to night-stop, routing from Leeds to Blackpool, transporting their Managing Director around on a tour of various UK airports.

11th The Public Enquiry regarding the 800ft extension to Manchester's main runway began today. The scheme was backed by MP's and business/industry leaders from the North West and areas farther afield such as Humberside, Merseyside & Yorkshire. During the two-week enquiry, representatives from various airlines are expected to attend. These include British Airways, Northwest Orient & Laker Airways, whose Managing Director Freddie Laker said 'Plans to expand their Manchester operations and serve Los Angeles would not be possible without the extension'. During the enquiry, it was pointed out that it was Government policy for Manchester to become the major International gateway outside of the South East and the envisaged growth rate of 6% p.a. would result in 7.5m passengers passing through by 1990. Freight was forecast to rise from the present 33,000 tonnes a year to 55,000 tonnes by 1990 and staffing levels were likely to double to 11,000. The results of the enquiry are expected within six months.

13th Sabreliner N30IMC, arriving at 1901 today from Rotterdam, departed for Heathrow the following day. The executive-type Sabreliner has never been common to Manchester and today's appearance was the only visit by the type this year.

14th Light aircraft from Finland are very rare, but Beech 100 OH-BKA arrived from Staverton at 1252 to night-stop, before departing for Bournemouth the following morning.

15th The airport was put on standby for possible weather diversions from Dublin and Belfast and could receive up to five wide-bodied aircraft, but in the end just two arrived from Dublin. They were Manchester's Dublin flight BA844 returning after the weather showed no improvement and Aer Lingus B.747 EI-ASI at 1034 (EI104 from New York).

16th RAF C-130 XV302 (JWN17) arrived at 1628 today on three engines, en route Edinburgh-Lyneham, before departing the next day after repairs.

16th A dispute over airport loaders refusing to load bags containing 4½ tonnes of ballast onto a British Airways training flight, was finally settled today following the airport's promise to acquire new dustproof outer coverings for the bags.

20th CL-44-0 Skymonster N447T made its second visit today. Now operated by British Cargo, it arrived at 1824 to transport a 13½ tonne generator to Gran Canaria.

21st Martinair DC-10 PH-MBG arrived at 0323 today (MP5326 from Las Palmas), with an inbound load of 50 tonnes of tomatoes. This flight would normally be operated through Stansted, but the DC-10 was required at Manchester for a rather unusual outbound cargo. The Foreign Office had commandeered ten Bell Jet Ranger helicopters, which were ultimately bound for Rhodesia, to assist in the supervision of elections there. The charter company chose Manchester because of its central location, due to the helicopters arriving from all over the UK. They are due back early next month and those involved were G-AWJW–white/mustard 'Hissing Sid'; G-AWOL–white/orange; G-AZZB–white/mustard 'Captain Beaky'; G-BARX–white/red/dark blue; G-BASE–white/yellow stripes; G-BBFB–white/yellow stripes; G-BGYF–blue/white; G-AWLL–white/orange; G-BAKF–orange/yellow/white and G-WOSP–

yellow/black stripes. The last three were carrying 'Election Supervisors' and 'Dollar Helicopter' stickers. They all arrived by road late on the 21st/early 22nd already dismantled, except for G-WOSP, which flew in on the evening of the 20th and was dismantled in the South Side hangars. The main fuselages were loaded onto pallets in the Servisair freight sheds and then placed inside the DC-10, before the booms and rotors.

22nd February 1980 – Martinair DC-10F PH-MBG is seen here, still being loaded with its cargo of helicopters neatly packed away inside, before finally departing early the following morning. (Geoff Ball)

22nd Announced today was the news that Concorde will make its first commercial visit to Manchester on 27th April, when an Air France Concorde hired by the Renault motor company, flies company representatives in from Paris.

23rd February 1980 – XR442 arriving at 1224 today as 'Navy822', on a round-trip from RAF Northolt, is parked on the already busy Freight Apron. It was the only visit to Manchester this year by a Royal Navy Sea Heron. (Geoff Ball)

23rd British Caledonian's final Atlanta/Houston freighter, operated by B.707 G-BDSJ, arrived at 0458 today (BR567 from Gatwick) before departing at 0706 for its initial refuelling stop at Bangor. When the service started in April 1978, it was to Atlanta, but it extended to Houston in October 1979.

23rd Manchester received a number of fog diversions today. From Leeds were Air Anglia F.27s G-BAKL at 1202 (AQ821 from Amsterdam) & G-BDVT at 1154 (AQ201 from Edinburgh) and the first visit of the airlines first Fokker F.28, with G-WWJC at 1111 (AQ433 from Paris). From Newcastle were Dan-Air BAe.748s G-ARAY at 1204 (DA6835 from Rotterdam) & G-BFLL at 1210 (DA0074 from Glasgow) and the late evening Heathrow-Newcastle British Airways flight BA5458, normally operated by their newly delivered Boeing 737s but on this occasion a Trident 3, G-AWZF, was utilised. From Teeside was British Midland DC-9 G-BFIH (BD340 from Heathrow), on a rare diversion visit to Manchester.

25th The transition of aircraft into the newly combined airline, Air UK, continues. BAC 1-11 G-AXMU, arriving today to night-stop before its outbound charter to Cognac the following day (UK2207), was noted in BIA fuselage colours with the Air UK logo on its white tail.

26th A three month run of no Heathrow weather diversions finally ended today, on a grey and murky Tuesday morning when twelve arrived, plus one from Gatwick. The ATC Watch Log recorded at 0630 that visibility for both Heathrow and Gatwick was 100m and having already accepted five wide-bodied by 0715, there would be no stands available for any further wide-bodied arrivals, but this instruction was later rescinded. The first to arrive, B.747 G-BDXH at 0624 (BA050 from Johannesburg), was the 99th different B.747 to visit Manchester. The 100th aircraft would have been VT-EFO (AI102 from New York), had it not have ended up at Shannon, due to the lack of handling at Manchester! Qantas made their first appearance since 31st December 1978, with VH-EBG at 0635 (QF001 from Bahrain). British Airways B.747 G-AWNE at 1001 (BA070 from Toronto), had amongst its passengers the Austrian Olympic team, returning home from the Winter Olympics in Lake Placid after winning another stack of gold medals! Also arriving as a diversion was first visit Austrian Airlines DC-9-51 OE-LDL at 1036 (OS451 from Vienna), which had been on its way to Heathrow to collect the Austrian team and take them back to Vienna, but as both aircraft had diverted in, the team simply boarded the DC-9 at Manchester instead. Manchester's emergency services were put on standby when Lufthansa A.300 D-AIAC (LH050 from Dusseldorf) diverted in as a full emergency at 0929. In addition to being low on fuel, after holding for Heathrow due to the weather, it had also shut down one of its engines. Unfortunately for Manchester, this was to be the last major weather diversion session this winter.

26th German Air Force Transall 50+07 made its first visit today, bringing in a spare engine and a Lufthansa maintenance crew. They worked overnight in the South Bay to change the engine of broken A.300 D-AIAC. As well as being the first visit of a German Transall since 50+79 arrived on Wednesday 28th July 1976, it was also the last visit of a German Air Force Transall to Manchester.

28th An Air Ecosse EMB-110 (WG901 East Midlands-Edinburgh), requested a diversion after declaring a full emergency with one engine on fire; but due to the visibility at Manchester it eventually diverted to Liverpool instead.

29th Eastern Airways DC-3 G-AMPO arrived at 1659 today, to take Manchester Utd down for their following days match with Ipswich. They returned on the evening of 1st March, having been thoroughly beaten 6-0, but at least they had the consolation of arriving back in vintage-style onboard G-AMPO again!

March 1980

Hopes are still high that the £8m rail-link to Manchester Airport is still alive, despite last month's devastating report saying it couldn't be justified financially. Council and business leaders agree it's needed, to relieve the pressure on the surrounding roads, currently handling the airport's freight. A visit has been arranged for the Chairman of British Rail to see the suggested route for himself next month.

Car parking will increase from 1st May, but a short-stay of up to 30-minutes will remain at 10p. Multi-storey charges for 3-hours will rise to 80p, 24-hours from £1.90 to £2.30, 7-days from £8 to £9.50 and 14-days from £16 to £19. Daily rates for the main surface car park will rise from £1.30 to £1.50 and the perimeter car parks from £1.10 to £1.30. The Airport Committee was informed that the increases would bring in an extra £290,000 per year. Food will also cost more, when the Airport Catering Services raise their prices by 10.5%.

Equipment changes on scheduled services included Air Malta (KM106): Austrian Airlines DC-9 OE-LDC (2nd/9th/23rd); KLM (KL153): DC-8 PH-DCT (15th/21st/22nd) & NLM F.28 PH-CHD (8th) and SAS (SK539): DC-9-21 OY-KGF (4th).

RAF ILS traffic identified included Hawks XX161 (5th), XX172 (10th), XX185 (17th), XX238 (19th), XX244 (31st), XX294 (18th), XX295 (11th) & XX298 (6th); C-130s XV184 (13th), XV200 (12th), XV213 (17th) & XV303 (14th) and Bulldog XX616 (5th). Civil ILS traffic included BAe.748s G-BCDZ (6th/21st) & G-AVXJ (7th); Air UK EMB-110 G-BGYV (11th) and Dove G-ASMG (17th). BAe.748 G-BCDZ made several test flights out of Woodford and BAe Dove G-ASMG performed an ILS (17th). Although this aircraft has operated for Hawker-Siddeley/BAe for many years, it's never landed at Manchester! Finally, Air UK EMB-110 G-BGYV appeared on a test flight from Blackpool (11th).

1st March 1980 – New airline, Orion Airways, will commence IT operations from Manchester on the 28th. Their first B.737 to be delivered, G-BGTV, is seen here on a crew training exercise prior to entering service. (Geoff Ball)

1st Cessna 182 D-EEXF, arriving at 1432 today from Dusseldorf, was clearing customs en route to Blackpool.

3rd LOT operated a charter from/to Warsaw, when Tupolev TU-134 SP-LHD arrived at 1722 today (LO3235/6), before departing on the 5th.

4th Dan-Air's G-BEBA, was the first BAe.748 to visit Manchester in their new livery, the one with the red and blue 'go faster' stripes up the fuselage.

4th SAS used their first DC-9-21 'hot-rod' of the year, when OY-KGF operated afternoon Copenhagen flight SK539/40. The type is the short version of their standard DC-9, series -41.

4th Cessna 150 N96IL, owned by the Lakenheath Aero Club, operated from/to Lakenheath today. It finally departed Manchester on the 7th, after an aborted attempt on the 6th, when it returned with engine trouble. Cessna 172 N14496, also owned by the Aero Club, arrived on the 7th with the essential screwdriver for the repair!

4th On its arrival at Manchester, Royal Saudi AF C-130H 1612 (RSF604 from Milan-Malpensa) requested the attendance of the fire brigade, due to a fire in the No.3 engine. A spare engine was brought in by C-130H 469 on the 9th and following an engine change, it finally left on the 12th.

6th Berlin-based Dan-Air B.727 G-BEGZ positioned in to operate DA3014/5 to/from Funchal today.

7th Martinair DC-10 PH-MBN returned from Harare, via Lusaka today, with the Jet Rangers taken out at the end of last month. After unloading, the helicopters were dispatched to their respective owners by road.

7th TAG Aviation HZ-NOT on a return flight to Le Bourget today, was the first of two Falcon 10s making their first visits this month. The second was N8200E (16th) and other biz-jet first visits were Citation's 550 HB-VGR & 551 G-JRCT (27th) and Lear Jet 35 D-CCHB (24th).

12th Six airport workers were taken to hospital today, following a radiation scare after a 240lb container containing dioxide powder was accidently dropped, whilst being unloaded off Northwest Cargo B.747F N617US. The uranium from the United States was destined for the BNFL factory at Springfield, near Preston.

15th KLM used DC-8 PH-DCT on this morning's KL153/4 and again on the 21st/22nd.

18th Lego Citation 500 OY-DVL arrived at 0815 today from Billund. Although the company now have a new Citation 550, OY-GKC, they are still operating the older example.

18th Bristow's Jet Ranger, G-BEWY, made numerous visits during the month, but today it was seen operating from a field outside of the airfield's boundary on the South Side.

19th French Air Force Transall No.61 arrived at 1143 today on a training flight (FM0138 from Lyneham), before departing to Edinburgh the following afternoon. Another was operated by Noratlas No.87/64-KA, routing Edinburgh-Bournemouth as FM0401 (27th).

21st Now that Alidair and Guernsey Airlines have merged, Viscount G-ARIR operated a return charter from/to Guernsey today, in full Alidair colours with Guernsey Airlines titles.

23rd Northwest Cargo B.747F N618US operated a charter on behalf of the computer company, ITT, from/to New York today (NW2711).

23rd DC-9 OE-LDC operated Air Malta KM106/7 for the final time this evening, before returning to Austrian Airlines at the end of the month.

24th Air Charter B.727 F-BPJV made its first visit today, positioning in from Paris-Orly to operate an outbound charter to Basle (SF104), before returning on the 27th.

24th Citation 550 HB-VGR made its first visit today, operating from/to Heathrow. This aircraft, was originally delivered through Manchester last August as G-BFLY, but was sold shortly afterwards.

24th Noted during the day making its first appearance for a while was GKN's IFR equipped helicopter, Bolkow 105 G-BCRG. Barratt's Agusta 109 G-HELY, which is also IFR equipped, remains a frequent visitor to Manchester, as does their Cessna 421, G-OAKS.

24th Numerous Royal Saudi AF Hercules aircraft arrived throughout the month. C-130E 451 was due in from Gander today but when the pilot realised they would arrive during the night-time closure, he proceeded to divert to Liverpool where the aircraft became unserviceable upon arrival!

25th NEA took delivery of their latest acquisition, Cessna 421 Golden Eagle G-TLOL, which departed later in the day for attention with Rogers Aviation at Cranfield.

26th The De Havilland Dove, a type once common to most airports, is increasingly rare nowadays. The first one to visit Manchester this year was Exeter based G-ATAI, which night-stopped from/to Exeter today.

28th March 1980 – After surviving several near-misses and reincarnations since their inception in 1965, this was the final year of operations for Invicta. Britannia G-ANCF is seen here amidst a showery backdrop, which along with their other Britannia G-AOVF, was heavily involved in the transportation of cattle until their demise in October 1980. (Geoff Ball)

28th New airline Orion Airways operated their first flight out of Manchester today, with their first aircraft to be delivered, B.737 G-BGTW, which departed for Mahon at 0833 as KG919. It first appeared last month on crew training flights along with G-BGTV, which was the first to land on 1st March, whilst performing a number of circuits and touch-and-goes.

28th Transamerica DC-8 N4865T, arriving at 1014 today from Toronto, was on a charter carrying cattle destined for various locations throughout the UK.

28th Another Saudi Air Force Hercules with technical trouble, was C-130H 1603, arriving at 1137 today (RSF906 from Gander). The following day it made two unsuccessful attempts to depart for Jeddah. It returned to Manchester the first time with hydraulic/control problems and the second, after declaring a full emergency at 1153 with a flight control problem. Fortunately it made a safe landing, before finally leaving on the 31st.

28th Cessna 402 N2719L, arriving at 1616 today with an oil pressure fault, was on delivery en route Reykjavik-Nice. After attention by NEA, it departed for Nice on the 31st, ultimately bound for Dar es Salaam.

31st British Airways operated their final scheduled Viscount flight through Manchester today. G-AOYN operated the last Isle of Man rotation (BA5578/9), with the outbound flight carrying 68 passengers and the return flight just 17. The final inbound Aberdeen flight (BA5699) operated by G-AOHT, carried 32 passengers and both aircraft positioned out to Cardiff the next day. Apart from a small number being retained for services within Scotland, most of the airlines remaining Viscounts will be withdrawn from service by the end of the year.

31st British Airways BAC 1-11 G-BFWN departed for Heathrow today, after being Manchester based for the winter. This aircraft eventually returned to Cyprus Airways, from whom it was leased, as 5B-DAJ.

31st The airport played host to an exhibition of business aircraft, organised by the charter specialists, London Executive Aviation, who recently opened an office in Manchester. The range available for charter, held on stands 42/44, were EI-BGL Rockwell 690 Commander, G-ARGR Viscount, G-AYFT PA-30 Twin Comanche - Merlin Flying Services, G-AYLJ PA-31 Navajo – NEA, G-BFFI PA-31 Navajo Chieftain - Merlin Flying Services, G-BFVX Beech 90 King Air – Vernair, G-BGOE Beech 76 Duchess, G-LEAR Lear Jet-NEA, G-OSRF Cessna 421 Golden Eagle – NEA, G-POST EMB-110 Bandeirante - Air Ecosse and G-VRES Beech 200 Super King Air – Vernair.

April 1980

Passenger numbers, movements and freight all showed healthy increases this month, compared to last April, when the airport was blighted by industrial action.

The following airlines made changes to their summer schedules: Air France Paris flight AF964/1 remains a SE.210 operation for the time being, but is retimed to 1755/1835. Air Malta will operate up to three-weekly during the summer. British Airways Aberdeen service will be operated by BAC 1-11s, Nice has been reintroduced and Amsterdam now operates twice-weekday. There are no Viscounts or SVC-10s scheduled from May and B.747s will operate Montreal/New York and Toronto services via Prestwick. A new twice-weekly Manchester-New York direct service operated by B.707s (BA183/2) will be introduced from 15th May. Tickets for the first eight flights will be sold at £25 less than their other three New York flights, which route via Prestwick. The discounted return fare of £184 will be offered on a first-come-first-served basis. Cyprus Airways will operate twice-weekly to Larnaca during the summer. SAS will operate their Copenhagen passenger flight six-weekly, with four proceeding onwards to/from Dublin. Aer Lingus, Lufthansa & Swissair cargo flights will all operate from Liverpool until October, due to further runway work.

Equipment changes on scheduled services included KLM (KL155): NLM F.28 PH-CHD (3rd); Lufthansa (LH074): B.727s D-ABHI (2nd), D-ABKJ (9th) & D-ABSI (30th); SAS (SK539): Douglas DC-9-21s SE-DBO (10th/29th), SE-DBR (17th) & (SK541): DC-9-21 SE-DBS (28th) and Swissair (SR842): DC-9-51 HB-ISK (18th).

RAF/Royal Navy ILS traffic identified included Hawks XX296 (25th) & XX297 (30th); C-130s XV196 (18th) & XV297 (17th); Royal Navy Jetstream XX488 (17th); BAe.125s XW791 (14th) & XX507 (3rd/8th/11th) and Nimrod XV260 (23rd). Civil ILS traffic included BAe.125 G-5-11 (6th) and Corvettes F-BTTU (28th) & F-BVPK (26th/28th). RAF Hawk XX297 actually performed a touch-and-go (30th) and the French Government Corvettes now prefer ILS approaches, rather than touch-and-goes or full stop landings. Finally, British Caledonian DC-10 G-BEBM operated a tea-time training flight from/to Gatwick (14th).

1st Air UK took over the Manchester-Isle of Man service from British Airways, operating three-times-daily and today's first flight was flown by Herald G-BCZG.

3rd Austrian Airlines commenced their new three-times-weekly service (OS471/2) between Manchester-Vienna today, with Douglas DC-9 OE-LDB operating the first flight.

4th The second Viscount route relinquished by British Airways, Manchester-Guernsey, was taken over by Guernsey Airlines. Initially operating once-weekly, they increased to five-weekly from May and Viscount G-BDRC was used on today's first flight. Advance purchase midweek return fares are being offered from £63 and weekend returns from £69.

6th Two Robins visiting the airport, F-BXMK today and F-GCAI (22nd) were in connection with the sale of Manchester resident PA-39 G-AZMW, in France. F-BXMK brought in the new owners of G-AZMW & F-GCAI brought in a spare crew to take G-AZMW back on the 23rd.

7th Passing through on delivery today was Austin Airways BAe.748 C-GQWO, en route Reykjavik-Nice, ultimately bound for the Reunion Islands on lease to Air France. Formerly LV-PGG, it's an ex-Argentinean presidential machine. Although it's converted to a standard passenger layout, it was also transporting a quantity of parts, including a spare engine.

8th Due to a shortage of aircraft, Britannia Airways is using Air Belgium B.737 OO-ABB on a short term lease, which made regular visits to Manchester last year as A4O-BG. It operated BY991B inbound from Munich at 1427 today, before positioning out to Brussels.

9th BAe.125 N605W arrived at 1318 today from Hawarden to clear customs, before returning back to its Copenhagen base.

9th Mount Cook BAe.748 ZK-MCF arrived from Nice at 1417 today, for its regular summer lease to Dan-Air as G-AYYG. It departed for Teeside on the 12th, after being re-registered and undergoing maintenance checks with Dan-Air Engineering.

9th Ralleye EI-BGU, arriving at 1937 today from Dublin, stayed until the 12th. It was still in the colours of its former owner, the French airline Air Inter.

9th The ATC Watch Log recorded a bizarre entry at 2330. 'Sky lit up as if daytime, with slight flickering effect for duration of approximately 2-3 seconds'. The incident was also noted by Liverpool and East Midlands Airports and similar reports came in from Yorkshire and Scotland. The bright lights were also witnessed as far away and far apart as Germany and North Carolina, yet Heathrow and London ATC saw nothing. Several telephone calls on the subject were received by the airport and national newspapers, including the Daily Express.

10th Queens Flight BAe.748 XS790 (Kitty 2) was taking the Duchess of Gloucester back to RAF Benson, but due to its late return, the airport had been closed in readiness for the night-time runway work. Following negotiations, it was agreed that the work wouldn't commence until the aircraft had departed.

11th Air Florida commenced a once-weekly Manchester-Miami charter, operated by their sole DC-10, N1035F, so the chances of getting bored of seeing it this summer are very high!

11th More Royal Saudi AF C-130Es appeared during the month, passing through to/from the Lockheed factory for modification or maintenance. Today, 1606 was returning eastbound from Marietta via Gander (RSF806) and then onwards to Jeddah.

12th Cessna 404 C-GTLH, arriving at 1555 today from Nice en route for Prestwick, was ultimately bound for Canada.

12th British Airways Copenhagen flight BA994, was forced to return to Manchester fifty-two minutes after takeoff, due to a faulty undercarriage warning light. Emergency crews were on standby after a full emergency was declared, but it made a safe landing before being towed onto a stand, where the passengers were transferred to a replacement aircraft.

14th Over 300 holidaymakers flew out on the inaugural charter to Miami. Organised by tour operator Intasun and flown by Laker Airways Douglas DC-10 G-BGXF (GK061), it returned the following morning as GK062. The occasion was attended by the Lord Mayor of Manchester and TV character Selwyn Froggitt, alias actor Bill Maynard. The flight, breaking new ground in the holiday market, is so popular with North West tourists that 38,000 have already booked the four-times-weekly flights. Laker Airways also applied to the CAA to commence Skytrain services to Miami from Prestwick, Manchester & Gatwick, but were only given the go-ahead to operate from Gatwick.

14th Belgian Air Force Merlin CF-01 arrived at 1021 today (Belgian AF 51), from RAF Lyneham to Brussels. Six Merlin's in total were ordered to replace their ageing Pembroke's.

15th April 1980 – Immaculate Convair CV-580 N5590L is parked on the South Bay, after diverting in with a fuel fault. It was operated by Chevron until August 1987 and then sold to the Northrop Corporation. It was sold again in Zaire as 9Q-CRS in 1994, but it crashed in April 1997. (Geoff Ball)

18th Martell's Falcon 20 F-BTML positioned in from Liverpool today and parked up for the weekend before departing on the 21st to Cognac. It then appeared daily until the 24th, night-stopping each time, in connection with the Grand National at Aintree they were sponsoring.

18th Tradewinds operated a rare freight charter through Manchester. Having recently disposed of their CL-44 fleet, with the last to leave being G-AWGS, they now operate just two B. 707Fs, G-BFEO & G-WIND, with the latter operating an inbound freight flight from Helsinki as IK4887 today.

18th The first of two British Aerospace BAe.125s to visit Manchester this month was G-BFAN, arriving from Hatfield at 1821 today, before departing for Frankfurt the following day. The second, G-BBCL, operated from/to Dunsfold on the 24th.

21st BAe.125 9Q-CFW arrived at 0929 today to clear customs from Ostend, en route to Hawarden.

22nd PA-31T OE-FDH called in for fuel at 1331 on its delivery flight from Reykjavik-Vienna.

22nd The ATC Watch Log recorded a telephone call at 1800 today, from a Macclesfield resident, complaining that an aircraft just passed over his house around 200ft. Further investigation concluded it was a Nimrod on a test flight out of Woodford (Avro 4), which should operate no lower than 2,000ft, so Woodford was promptly reminded of that fact!

18th April 1980 – Who nowadays wouldn't give their right-arm to fly in one of these? Well, in 1980 several football teams had the pleasure and the privilege of travelling on this classic aircraft. Vintage Eastern Airways DC-3 G-AMPO is seen here about to depart, with Manchester Utd onboard again, this time transporting the team to Norwich for the following days match. It returned them late on the 19th, after beating Norwich 2-0. (Geoff Ball)

24th Army Air Corps Gazelle XZ347 diverted in at 1832 today, en route to RAF Topcliffe, when the Pennine weather became too precarious for the flight to continue.

25th Dan-Air was involved in another airline disaster, ten years after Comet G-APDN was lost on approach to Barcelona on 3rd July 1970. Boeing 727 G-BDAN operating flight DA1008 departed Manchester at 0922, en route for Tenerife-Los Rodeos Airport, with 146 passengers and crew onboard. After an uneventful flight, the pilot contacted Tenerife North Approach Control at 1314 to report they were at FL110 (11,000ft), 14-nautical miles from the 'TFN' VOR/DME. ATC cleared him onward to radio beacon 'FP' for an approach to Runway 12. Once he had reached 'TFN', he was further cleared to descend to FL60 (6,000ft). When the pilot was overhead 'TFN', ATC instructed him to join a non-standard holding pattern over the 'FP' beacon. The instruction was accepted, even though the holding pattern was not a published procedure and the crew had no charts for it. However, the aircraft did not pass over the beacon, but passed south of it instead, entering the holding pattern the wrong way. It had incorrectly turned left towards the South East and into an area of high ground, where the minimum safe altitude was 14,500ft. About a minute after the pilot informed ATC he was entering the hold, he was instructed to descend to FL50 (5,000ft). It wasn't until the aircraft was descending towards FL50 that its GPWS (Ground Proximity Warning System) came into operation and warned the pilot he was too low. The crew reacted swiftly at this point, by climbing quickly, with the engines on full power and initiating a steep turn to the right. Unfortunately, due to thick cloud they had no visual awareness of their surroundings and the aircraft struck a mountain and disintegrated, spreading debris over a wide area and instantly killing everyone onboard. The official investigation concluded that the crash was caused by the pilot not taking into account the altitude at which he was flying and by taking the aircraft into an area of high terrain, he had failed to maintain a safe height and that when the aircraft was on its descent to Tenerife North approach, it flew into high terrain after entering a holding pattern the wrong way. The disaster marked the greatest loss of life in an accident to a British-registered aircraft at the time.

25th The ATC Watch Log recorded that Air Malta flight KM106 declared a full emergency at 2047 today, with a suspect nosewheel. Although the aircraft landed safely, it was unable to exit the runway until locking pins had been inserted into the nosewheel to prevent the risk of collapse.

27th April 1980 – Air France Concorde F-BVFB, the first of three Air France special charter flights during 1980, is seen here about to depart back to Paris-Charles De Gaulle. (Geoff Ball)

27th On a warm Sunday morning, Manchester Airport was swamped with visitors ready to witness the arrival of the first commercial Concorde flight. The event caused overflowing car parks and gridlocked roads, when hundreds of cars parked illegally on verges and double yellow lines. One youth even ended up in hospital, after falling 20ft from the roof of the multi-storey car park, onto an adjoining roof. Fortunately for the 13 year old, he was not seriously injured. Up to 40,000 turned up to watch Air France Concorde F-BVFB arrive at 0956 (AF4906 from Paris), before departing back to Paris at 1147 as AF4907, routing from/to Paris via the Irish Sea and the North Atlantic on both sectors, in order to reach its supersonic speeds. The Concorde had been chartered by the French car company, Renault, as a special thank you to its 200 UK dealers. The 100 southern dealers were flown out to Paris yesterday, to catch today's Concorde flight into Manchester and the 100 northern dealers were flown out on Concorde to Paris for an overnight stay, before returning to Manchester on the scheduled Paris-Manchester flight.

29th Another French Air Force Noratlas appeared on its customary training flight (FM0401 Lyneham-Bournemouth), but unfortunately it was 87/64-KA, the same aircraft that had already visited on the 27th March.

29th Mooney PH-MTA, owned by the Fokker aircraft company, operated from/to Amsterdam today.

29th The second executive jet to be based at Manchester arrived in the form of BAe.125 G-AZVS. Purchased by Merlin Air, it was previously operated by Lease Air of Humberside. In addition to its executive duties, it will also be used as an air ambulance.

30th Fifteen years of continuous SVC-10 operations from Manchester came to an end today, when G-ASGA operated the last scheduled flight from/to Manchester. The outbound (BA081 Manchester-Prestwick-Toronto) carrying 51 passengers, returned the following day (BA080 Toronto-Prestwick-Manchester), before finally positioning out to Heathrow at 1422.

30th RAF Hawk XX297 operating as 'FLN09' performed a touch-and-go this afternoon, rather than a straight forward ILS approach and overshoot, which made him liable for a landing charge!

May 1980

The last few days of May were affected by a dispute involving Servisair ground staff, which lasted into June. Some airlines continued as normal, but Laker Airways operated out of East Midlands and Transamerica, Wardair, SAS, Spantax, Trans Europa & Air Malta all operated from other airports, including Liverpool.

British Airways now operate a three-times-weekly B.747 service to Prestwick/Toronto (BA080/1) and three-times-weekly to Prestwick/New York (BA184/5). In addition, BA182/3 will operate twice-weekly direct to New York from the 15th, with B.707s.

Air Ecosse were finally granted permission to operate their twice-weekday service between Manchester-Dundee. After several delays, the flights finally started on the 9th June.

The following airlines have summer IT programmes from Manchester: Air Malta, Aviaco, Aviogenex, Balkan, Inex-Adria, JAT, LOT, Spantax, TAP, Tarom & Trans-Europa; as do a variety of UK operators: Air Europe, Air UK, Britannia Airways, British Airtours, Brymon Airways, Dan-Air, Laker Airways, Monarch Airlines & Orion Airways. Airlines operating regularly to the USA/Canada this summer are Air Florida (Miami), CP Air (Toronto & Vancouver), Laker Airways (Los Angeles, Miami, New York & Toronto), Transamerica (Los Angeles & New York) and Wardair (Calgary, Edmonton, Toronto & Vancouver).

Equipment changes on scheduled services included Air Malta (KM106): Monarch B.707 G-BHOX (14th); Lufthansa (LH074): B.727s D-ABCI (21st), D-ABKE (23rd) & D-ABKP (13th) and Swissair (SR842): DC-9-51 HB-ISV (23rd).

RAF ILS traffic identified included Hawks XX162 (28th), XX239 (27th), XX240 (29th), XX292 (13th) & XX309 (27th) and C-130s XV188 (29th), XV200 (2nd), XV202 (29th), XV220 (15th), XV295 (1st) & XV300 (14th). British Airways operated a crew training flight with L.1011 Tristar 200 G-BGBC (19th).

1st Today's arrival of Bristow Bell 206 G-BBOS, was the first of seventeen different civil helicopter visits this month, including non-UK example Bell 206 EI-AWA from Macclesfield (16th). Apart from the Jet Rangers, three different Bell 47s this month were G-BBVP (9th) & G-BEHK (12th), both on pipeline inspection work and G-BHBW, which was fitted with crop-spraying booms (30th). Four different Squirrels which also arrived were G-BGIL (9th), G-BFNC (13th), G-BGHG (18th) & G-BHIV (21st). Enstrom Shark G-BGWS made its first visit (10th), Barratt Homes Agusta 109 G-HELY was also around (10th) and the final helicopter type worthy of note was Hughes 369 G-BDOY (30th).

2nd Eastern Airways DC-3 G-AMPO appeared on another football charter today, bringing Ipswich Town up for their following day's game with Manchester City, which the travellers lost 2-1.

2nd Transamerica began a transatlantic summer programme today, with first time visitor B.747 N741TV positioning in from Zurich at 1228, to operate the first Los Angeles flight, via Gatwick the following morning. Their second B.747, N742TV, made its first visit a week later. They also used DC-10s N101TV, N102TV & N103TV for summer flights to New York. Formerly TIA, the airline was no stranger to Manchester, as they operated transatlantic charter flights during the 1960's with Boeing 727s & Douglas DC-8s, which continued into the 1970's with DC-8s & DC-10s. In 1979, they operated their first regular summer programme from Manchester, with weekly flights to New York.

3rd Executive Express, operators of a fleet of Cessna 404s & 421s, made numerous visits during the month transporting Britannia Airways flight crews from/to Manchester. Aircraft used included Cessna 421s G-BRIT & G-BBSV (3rd), Cessna 404 G-IANT (10th) & Cessna 404 G-BEMX (12th).

5th Due to an aircraft shortage, Britannia Airways will base a Transavia Boeing 737 at Manchester for the summer season. It will position in from Amsterdam on Monday's, operate various IT flights until Thursday and then position back to Amsterdam. They will be flown by Transavia crews, with Britannia Airways cabin crew. The first, PH-TVE, positioned in from Amsterdam today as HV9993, to operate BY570A out to Corfu.

5th B.707 G-BHOX, leased by Air Malta for the summer season, made its first appearance today as KM734/5 in full Air Malta colours. Recently acquired by Monarch Airlines, this aircraft is no stranger to Manchester, as it's been in before as 9G-ACN & G-TJAB.

7th Gulfstream 2 N1PG owned by Proctor & Gamble, made its first visit to Manchester today, arriving from Heathrow.

8th RAF Puma XW237 arrived from Shawbury to night-stop, before departing to a school in Audenshaw for demonstration purposes the following morning.

8th Air UK commenced a once-weekly trooping flight from/to Osnabruck until the 25th September, with BAC 1-11 G-AXOX operating today's first flight (UK2554/3).

14th Wardair B.747 C-FDJC (WD421) bound for Vancouver, managed to close the airport from 1339 to 1420 today after reporting 'The surface of the runway had disintegrated on its departure'. Following this all operations were immediately suspended, until temporary repairs had been carried out.

14th Things didn't go too well for Northwest B.747F N616US (NW923 from Amsterdam). The pilot reported possible damage to his undercarriage on landing at Manchester and although no debris was found on the runway, it was considered serious enough to delay the aircraft's outbound departure to New York for 24-hours. When it eventually left the following day at 1622, it managed to lift up a temporary layer of asphalt newly laid on the runway during the work in progress!

15th An unidentified RAF Canberra (BQL80), was in the vicinity between 1400 and 1600 today, undertaking a photographic survey.

16th The ATC Watch Log recorded receiving a telephone call at 1615 today from Barton Moss Engineering, advising that due to unpaid debts of £6,000, they had impounded PA-28 G-BCPP. The aircraft, which arrived from Liverpool yesterday for maintenance, is currently residing in Hangar 522 and as a precaution, the propeller, seats and parts of the radio have all been removed!

17th British Airtours are basing a B.707 & B.737 for the summer. G-BGJF positioned in to operate their first B.737 IT flight from Manchester (KT868 to Venice) today and from the 29th, an aircraft swap will take place on Thursday's MAN-Monastir-MAN flight, KT816/7.

18th Inex-Adria DC-9 YU-AJX, leased by the airline for the summer, made its first visit to Manchester today. The ex-Ozark aircraft which still operates in their basic colours, made its last visit on 26th September operating JP552/3, before returning to the USA on 20th October.
18th The ATC Watch Log records that considerable inconvenience and extra work has been caused by Shells refusal to take their refuelling trucks over to the South Side. The Freight Apron was blocked during the morning by Guppy F-BTGV and Stand 48 was being used for the refuelling of light aircraft, where the additional restriction of a time limit was imposed by the marshaller. It went on to say that if Shell persists, there will be significant problems at the weekend when the majority of light aircraft operate, especially now that summers approaching and traffic increases sharply.
18th Beech 90 N1857A arriving at 1700 today, night-stopped whilst on its delivery flight, en route Reykjavik-Nice.

19th May 1980 - CL-44 EI-BGO made its first visit today, operating an inbound freight flight (QT3036 from Baghdad), before positioning out to Larnaca the following day. This aircraft was operated by Aer Turas until its withdrawal in January 1986. (Geoff Ball)

19th Army Air Corps Gazelle XX375 arrived from Otterburn today, before departing for a local site in Hazel Grove. The month also saw visits by the RAF, Royal Navy & Royal Marines.
19th Chevron Oil's Twin Otter C-GCSC arrived from Nice to night-stop today, before leaving for Keflavik the next morning and returning home after a spell operating in the Sudan.
19th British Airways operated a training flight through Manchester today for the first time in a while, with newly delivered Tristar 200 G-BGBC, from/to Prestwick.
19th As if the Canadian Twin Otter wasn't enough for today, also passing through was Mooney C-GMWJ at 1339, routing Belfast Harbour-Doncaster. The pilot was given a 'stiff talking to' by ATC, after crossing the main runway for the South Side without permission, when an aircraft was already on short finals.
20th Royal Saudi AF KC-130H 457, a tanker variant, made its first visit to Manchester today, en route from the Lockheed factory at Marietta, Georgia for modification.
27th Passengers arriving at the airport today, found their flights delayed, diverted or cancelled, due to a 24-hour strike by ground workers. Eighty Servisair employees had walked out during the morning, over a pay row that had been simmering for several weeks. The men,

whose jobs included aircraft cleaning, toilet servicing and the push-back of aircraft, have already rejected a 19% pay offer and are seeking pay parity with their British Airways counterparts. Britannia Airways were unaffected, as they used their own ground handling staff. Because there were no push-back crews or vehicles available, the ATC Watch Log recorded that permission had been given to Orion Airways flight KG967 to use reverse thrust to push itself from its stand, which was an extremely rare event!

22nd May 1980 – The Spanish-manufactured CASA 212, a rare aircraft at Manchester, is seen here on the first visit of a Costa Rican registered aircraft, the first visit of type and the only visit of type during the 1980's. Servicos Aereos Nacionales TI-SAB, arriving at 1707 today, was passing through on delivery to Costa Rica. It was on its way to night-stop at Glasgow, when strong headwinds forced it to make a fuel stop. Unfortunately this aircraft was involved in a fatal accident in January 1990. (Geoff Ball)

28th Yesterdays 24-hour strike by Servisair ground staff escalated into an indefinite one, after Britannia Airways carried out ground work normally done by Servisair staff. The dispute also spread to Glasgow, Edinburgh, Newcastle & Belfast, but the affects were minimal. Manchester's action resulted in flights being diverted to Liverpool, which delayed passengers by a couple hours. The strikers are considering arbitration, as suggested by their company.

29th Visits by British Airways Viscounts are rare now that Manchester has no flights operated by the type, but Viscount G-AOYM arrived on this morning's Glasgow flight (BA920), after the usual BAC 1-11 had gone tech at Glasgow. It positioned out later in the morning to Edinburgh.

29th Devon WB533, operated by the Royal Air Force since 1949, made its final visit to Manchester at 1743 today (RR7533 from RAF Cranwell). It was sold to a private operator in 1984.

30th Another RAF Devon flight, was VP952 arriving at 0822 today (RR7555 Waddington-Coltishall). Having been delivered in 1947, it was making its last visit to Manchester before being withdrawn and later preserved in 1984.

30th Cessna 152 G-BHDR routing Blackpool-Duxford strayed off the areas low-level-route and appeared on the approach radar as unidentified traffic, crossing the Runway 24 approach at 2-miles. This forced inbound Belfast flight BA5493 to break off its approach and Inex-Adria flight JP580 to enter the hold until the Cessna was diverted back onto its original course. The pilot of the Cessna had apparently got lost and he was reported to the CAA.

31st The continuing Servisair dispute caused a Laker Airways flight to Los Angeles (GK045) to be switched to Gatwick and the 300 passengers being taken by road in order to board it! Also affected was an inbound Laker Airways flight from Miami (GK062), which diverted to Liverpool. Although Servisair and the union held talks with a conciliation officer from ACAS (Advisory Conciliation & Arbitration Service), a meeting is yet to be arranged between the two sides.

June 1980

June 1980 - Car parking at Manchester Airport has become a serious issue, since hundreds of panicking motorists have been abandoning their cars on double yellow lines, grass verges and even on the hard shoulder of the M56 motorway, in a desperate bid to catch their flights after failing to find a parking space! Although 550 more parking spaces were made available last winter, parking facilities are still grossly inadequate. In order to address the problem, the Airport Authority is relooking at the plans for the second multi-storey car park, which is due for completion by 1983. (Manchester Airport Archive)

Equipment changes on scheduled services included Austrian Airlines (OS471): DC-9-51 OE-LDO (26th); KLM (KL155): NLM F.28 PH-CHD (15th); Lufthansa (LH074): Condor B.727 D-ABIN (4th) and Swissair (SR842): DC-9-51s HB-ISU (11th) & HB-ISW (4th).

RAF ILS traffic identified included Hawk XX172 (16th/17th); C-130s XV187 (19th), XV201 (9th), XV202 (17th), XV205 (24th), XV206 (26th), XV222 (9th) & XV302 (3rd); Dominie XS735 (6th) and Canberra XH567, which also overshot en route from Woodford to Warton as 'Blackbox Delta' (6th). British Aerospace BAe.125 G-OBAE performed four ILS approaches (9th).

1st LOT commenced their twice-weekly service between Manchester-Warsaw today. Flights will operate on Fridays and Sundays, with fares starting at £154 for an advanced purchase return ticket. The first flight was operated by TU-134 SP-LHD today (LO287/8).

1st Air Malta has operated year-round scheduled flights between Manchester-Malta since 1974. They were once-weekly until 1978, when they became twice-weekly during the summer, but from today the frequency has increased to three-times-weekly for the summer, in addition to the five-weekly and three-fortnightly charter flights.

2nd RAF Wessex XR525 arrived at 0732 today from Ballykinler, Northern Ireland (COK60) and departed the following morning for Shawbury.

2nd NEA Islander G-BNEA left for its new home in Holland today, carrying dual marks G-BNEA & PH-PAR. This means that the only Islander still owned by NEA is G-AZGU, which has recently been refurbished and is up for sale.

4th Lufthansa operated 'short' Condor B.727 D-ABIN on the scheduled LH074/5 today.

4th Aer Lingus flights resumed today, after four days of action by their maintenance staff.

4th Flights returned to normal today, following a meeting of the Servisair employees who'd been on strike for eight days. Although mediation is continuing with ACAS, they've been offered a 21% pay increase, putting them in line with their British Airways counterparts.

4th Austin Airways BAe.748 C-GOUT arrived at 2251 today from Reykjavik for maintenance with Dan-Air, prior to its lease to Maersk Air for the summer season.

6th The Rothmans Aerobatic Team, consisting of the five specialist Pitts Special aircraft, arrived in formation at 1639 today from Ronaldsway. They stayed overnight, in preparation for their participation in the following days Barton Air Show.

6th The ATC Watch Log reported that the pilot of PA-34 G-AZJB, Davyhulme MP Winston Churchill, had tried to circumnavigate the night-time runway closure, by requesting to use Runway 28. He was declined however, as it can only used for light aircraft during the daylight hours.

7th Today is the annual Barton Air Show, taking place on a Saturday instead of a Sunday. The usual suspects using Manchester as a base prior to their departure for the show included the Battle of Britain Memorial Flight Lancaster PA474, Spitfire P7350 & Hurricane LF363 and Sea Fury TF956 from Yeovilton. Others arriving for the event were RAF Hawk XX232 which was the first to land at Manchester and two Jaguars, XX113 which performed at Barton & XX763 as the standby. The Red Arrows had a prior engagement and were unable to attend for the first time.

7th Brymon recommenced their weekly Saturday service to Newquay today, with Herald G-ATIG (PM044/7) operating the first flight.

7th The RAF operated several trooping flights to Gibraltar this month with C-130s XV293 (RR4540) & XV303 (RR4541) today and XV209 (RR4542) & XV300 (RR4543) on the 21st.

9th Air Ecosse commenced a twice-weekday service from Manchester to Dundee, timed to connect with scheduled flights to/from the Continent. This gives the Tayside area a fast throughway to Europe and direct access for businessmen to/from Northern England. Fares start at £29 one-way and today's first flight was operated by EMB-110 G-CELT (WG700/1).

10th Martinair DC-9F PH-MAO operated a freight charter from/to Amsterdam today (MP6001/2).

12th Today's arrival of Army Air Corps Lynx XZ192 at 2103 (Army 670) from Belfast, was a first visit of type. Ultimately bound for West Germany, it departed for Lydd the following morning.

13th A pair of Swedish Cessna 172s, SE-IBX & SE-IMF, arriving from Birmingham today stayed for the weekend, before departing for Ostend on the 15th.

13th Tonight saw the arrival of the first British Airways B.737 into Manchester, when G-BGDC diverted in from Newcastle at 2213 (BA5458 from Heathrow).

14th The bad weather affecting Yorkshire and the North East yesterday, continued into today and as a result Manchester received several diversions. JAT B.707 YU-AGI (JR2226 from Dubrovnik) & Tarom TU-154 YR-TPI (RO719 from Constanta) diverted in from Newcastle and Dan-Air Viscount G-BCZR (DA372 from Jersey), Air UK Herald G-BEYF (UK372 from Ronaldsway) & Air Languedoc Metroliner F-GBTO, all diverted in from Leeds.

14th The ATC Watch Log recorded at 1537 today, that a number of complaints had been received by the airport and Middleton Police, regarding the activities of a BAe.748 and a Nimrod from BAe Chadderton allegedly operating at heights of less than 500ft. Another batch of complaints received on the 18th July from residents in the Blackley, reported a Nimrod flying at heights between 200ft-500ft.

15th The second commercial visit of Concorde took place today, with the arrival of F-BVFB at 1235 (AF4916 from Paris), with 99 passengers onboard. It was three hours late due to a technical hitch forcing its initial return to Paris, having reached North Wales with one of the four engines using too much oil. The flights organised by Woodcock Travel of Sheffield, costing £275-£330 per person, included champagne onboard and accommodation in Paris.

17th A near-miss in the Oldham area with a F-4 Phantom at around 4,500ft, was recorded by the pilot of inbound BAC 1-11 BA5493 from Belfast.

18th Northwest Orient B747F N619US (NW923 Manchester-New York) returned to Manchester with engine trouble soon after departure.

18th The very final visit of a Comet took place this afternoon, when G-BDIW operated on behalf of Laker Airways (DA8672 from Gatwick), before positioning out the next afternoon to Dusseldorf. It's very final service was the 31st October operating Frankfurt-Gatwick, although it also flew an 'enthusiast's special' on the 9th November. It was flown to Lasham the following day for permanent withdrawal and eventually sold to a museum in Germany in December.

18th Citation 500 PH-CTE, arriving at 1550 today, brought a number of Dutch Government officials into Manchester.

18th Jodel F-BIQY, arriving at 2101 today from Le Touquet, was en route to its new base at Barton. It was accompanied by C.172 G-BCVJ acting as its radio ship and they both departed to Barton on the 20th.

19th The ATC Watch Log recorded the following at 0635: 'The cleaning lady still working in the Tower using a very noisy vacuum cleaner has made ATC on the front desk impossible. Cleanings been cancelled so it can be taken up with the contractors, as it could lead to a dangerous situation'!

19th It was revealed that the Servisair strike caused sixty-eight aircraft, including thirteen wide-bodied, to divert to Liverpool between 27th May and 3rd June, involving 13,508 passengers.

19th The Captain of British Caledonian flight BR986 to Gatwick, complained in the strongest possible terms 'That he was nearly hit twice by two separate MIAA luggage trailers, whilst taxiing out for departure'!

20th Due to an aircraft shortage, JAT is leasing two Hapag-Lloyd Boeing 727s, D-AHLL & D-AHLM, for the summer. Flights JU208/7 & JU206/9 were operated by D-AHLM today and by D-AHLL the following week. From then on they could both be seen on a regular basis each Friday, until their programmes finished on the 24th October.

23rd B.747 G-AWNC was the first British Airways aircraft to be painted in their rebranded 'British' titles. It was rolled out at Heathrow today and made its first visit to Manchester as such on the 1st July.

25th Cessna Citation 550 G-BPCP made its only visit to Manchester today, arriving at 1421 from Birmingham, as it was written-off in a landing accident at Jersey in October.

26th The pilot of Laker Airways BAC 1-11 flight GK206 got the fright of his life today, when on finals for Runway 06 at 0656. He was at 2,500ft and established on the ILS when he reported hearing another aircraft on finals at the same height, but the other plane was actually talking to Heathrow Tower! As Heathrow and Manchester Tower share the same frequency it can be a common occurrence, but only under certain weather conditions.

26th Outbound Northwest Orient B.747F N629US (NW923) was carrying a varied cargo, including two RB-211 engines and a couple of Maserati racing cars.

28th Beech 60 G-BFDR was held on the runway for inspection after bursting a nosewheel tyre on landing. No debris was found and it managed to taxi over to the South Side.

29th Aeroflot operated the first of a series of fortnightly Sunday charters today, with TU-134 CCCP 65770 (SU2241/2 from/to Moscow-SVO).

July 1980

1st July 1980 – Both of Saudia's brand new C-130H Hercules, HZ-HM5 & HZ-HM6, are seen here having arrived at Manchester during the morning from Dover AFB, Delaware, on their delivery flight direct from the factory. They stayed overnight, before proceeding onwards to Jeddah. (Geoff Ball)

Pegasus Holidays will offer direct flights from Manchester to St Lucia and Antigua from December, operating on Mondays throughout Christmas/New Year and then fortnightly until April 1981. Prices from £389 for a week's self-catering in St Lucia include free water sports.

Strikes have been affecting TAP/Air Portugal since the end of last month. The weekly Monday flight TP9552/3 to Faro was cancelled for the first three weeks, the weekly Thursday flight TP9524/5 was cancelled on the 7th and the following week it was operated by Laker B.707 G-BFBZ, before reverting back to normal. The weekly Sunday flights TP9218/20 & TP9221/19 were operated by Euralair B.737 F-GCSL (6th) & Laker B.707 G-BFBZ (13th/20th), before normal operations resumed the following week.

Equipment changes on scheduled services included Lufthansa (LH074): B.727s D-ABHI (8th), D-ABKD (19th), D-ABKG (27th) & Condor B.727 D-ABIL (1st); LOT (LO287): IL-18 SP-LSI (20th) and Swissair (SR842): DC-9-51s HB-ISL (9th) & HB-ISU (18th).

RAF ILS traffic identified included solitary Hawk XX231 (31st) and C-130 XV181 & RAE Comet XV814 from Farnborough as MPDXA (28th).

2nd The first of three Canadian Air Force C-130 flights appeared today, when 130320 (CAM515) arrived to night-stop routing Trenton, Ontario en route for Lahr, Western Germany. Others following the same routing were 130325 (CAM516-4th) & 130321 (CAM517-6th).

4th Besides JAT, Inex-Adria is also operating other aircraft on their own flights. Berlin-based Dan-Air B.727s G-BEGZ, G-BFGM & G-BFGN all operated Friday's JP584/5 flight from/to Split during the month and continued until the 18th September, when the airlines DC-9s took over again.

6th The French airline Aerotour, operated two outbound flights to Nice today, with SE.210 F-BUFH (FV3514 & 3515) and a further flight with SE.210 F-BVSF (FV211) on the 8th. The return flights took place on the 8th with SE.210 F-BVSF (FV210 & FV211) twice and SE.210 F-BYAT (FV3517). EAS SE.210 F-BYCO also operated an inbound flight from Nice (EY1460) on the 10th.

8th July 1980 – B.707 N5038 made its second appearance at Manchester today, routing from/to Heathrow, having previously visited in July 1978. Owned and operated by industrial giant Dresser Industries, who own a large plant in Wythenshawe, Manchester, it served with the company until 1983, when it was sold to Boeing for spares. (Geoff Ball)

8th French Air Force Transall F.98/61-ZP, arriving at 1644 today, was operating a crew training flight from Prestwick to RAF Lyneham.

9th Kar-Air Douglas DC-8 OH-KDM positioned in from Oslo at 0828 today, to operate an outbound charter to Helsinki (KR3333/4). Another Kar-Air charter took place on the 29th, with Finnair SE.210 OH-LSF operating KR3335/6.

11th Although JAT continues to operate the two Hapag-Lloyd B.727s, D-AHLL & D-AHLM, Douglas DC-9 YU-AJL was used on today's JU206/9 and B.727 D-AHLL operated JU208/7.

11th The pilot of British Airways BAC 1-11 flight BA849 inbound from Dublin at 1632 today, reported hearing a loud bang on touchdown, possibly a burst tyre. A visual inspection of the runway and the aircraft confirmed his suspicions!

12th Brymon Airways used British Air Ferries Herald G-BDFE on their scheduled Newquay flight, BC044/7 today. It was the second of two Heralds bought by the airline in 1975, with the first being G-BCWE. G-BDFE had previously operated in Canada, initially in a VIP configuration shuttling pop groups, politicians and football teams up and down the country, but by 1980 it had certainly lost that status! A further decline took place when it was sold in Zaire in 1984, where it operated for a further two years before being finally broken up in 1987.

13th The fortnightly Aeroflot flights continued with TU-134s CCCP-65780 today and CCCP-65815 (27th), both operating as SU2241/2.

14th The second Army Air Corps Lynx to land at Manchester was XZ333 (Army 241), on a flight from/to RAF Middle Wallop today as 'Army 333'.

17th Alidair Viscount G-ARBY was written-off today, in a crash landing in a field near Exeter on a flight from Santander. It's been operating for Guernsey Airlines this year and was a regular visitor to Manchester in the 1970's.

18th Air New Zealand DC-10 ZK-NZR arrived at 0807 today (BA074 from Montreal), bound for Heathrow. It was carrying an additional number of Manchester bound passengers, who hadn't made it onto Manchester's own Montreal flight (BA084).

19th Dan-Air BAe.748 G-ARMX had left for Aberdeen after maintenance with Dan-Air, when it arrived back at Manchester at 1708 on a full emergency after shutting down one of its engines, due a fire warning light.

20th LOT flight LO287/8 from/to Warsaw was operated by Ilyushin IL-18 SP-LSI today, rather than the usual Tupolev TU-134.

23rd Another RAF Devon making its final visit to Manchester this year was VP977 at 1012 today, on a round-trip from RAF Northolt as RR1784. Delivered to the RAF new in 1949, it was sold to a private owner in 1984.

25th Sabena B.737 OO-SDL (SN618) outbound for Brussels at 1938, aborted takeoff due to a bird-strike. Following an inspection, two dead birds were found on the runway.

25th Jersey European Twin Otter G-OJEA arrived to night-stop on delivery from Reykjavik. It departed to Jersey the following afternoon.

27th Mooney SE-GXS routing southbound from Prestwick, requested a diversion into Manchester, after declaring a full emergency with a major electrical fault. The aircraft made a safe landing and departed for Oxford the following afternoon.

29th A warm and sunny Manchester did not reflect the weather elsewhere, as twenty-two diversions arrived over the course of the day, mainly from Leeds and mostly standard fare. There were also diversions from Luton, Humberside & East Midlands as well as VC-10 XV104 at 0651 (RR2104 from Washington), which was the only arrival from RAF Brize Norton.

29th July 1980 – The CAA's two BAe.748s used for the calibration and flight checking of Navigational Aids and ILS systems throughout the UK, were frequently at Manchester. G-AVXI is seen here about to depart for Stansted. This and their other aircraft, G-AVXJ, were both operated until they were withdrawn in 1998. (Geoff Ball)

August 1980

Equipment changes on scheduled services included British Airways (BA183): SVC-10 G-ASGA (4th); Lufthansa (LH074): B.727s D-ABFI (10th/17th), D-ABKH (20th), D-ABRI (5th) & Condor B.727 D-ABPI (8th) and LOT (LO287): IL-18s SP-LSE (1st/22nd) & SP-LSF (24th).

RAF ILS traffic identified included Hawks XX164 (21st), XX183 (21st) & XX238 (20th); C-130s XV184 (7th), XV200 (12th), XV203 (11th), XV206 (4th), XV295 (11th), XV303 (20th) & XV307 (12th) and Nimrod XV256 (19th). RAF Nimrod XV256 performed an ILS approach on a test flight from Woodford (19th), as did BAe.748 G-BCDZ (26th). The last ILS visitor of the month was another unidentified RAF Jaguar, (NVE 39) at 1632 (27th).

1st Inex-Adria continued using Berlin-based Dan-Air B.727s on flight JP584/5 during the month, utilising G-BEGZ, G-BFGM & G-BFGN.

2nd Two early morning diversions were British Caledonian DC-10 G-BFGI at 0722 (BR232 from Atlanta) originally due into Gatwick and RAF VC-10 XV108 at 0915 (RR2105 from Gander), which was due into RAF Brize Norton. Two that didn't make it were Cathay Pacific B.747 flight CX201 from Hong Kong/Bahrain and Northwest Orient B.747 flight NW044 from Minneapolis, which ended up at Prestwick as the runway hadn't reopened at that point.

2nd Exactly two weeks since the last Dan-Air BAe.748 incident, G-BEKG was also returning to Aberdeen after maintenance, when it too was forced to return to Manchester after declaring a full emergency at 1014 today, with one engine shut down. It managed to leave for Aberdeen three hours later at 1301.

3rd An unusual visit to Manchester today, was made by LeVier Cosmic Wind G-BAER. The type, a small single-seat racer, was originally built with the aim of winning the American Goodyear Trophy in 1947. It was a new competition, set up after the war consisting of a number of air races across the USA. Only six of the aircraft were ever made, the first three between 1947 and 1948 and the rest over the next 24 years. The last one ever built was today's arrival, which was actually designed and built in the UK in 1972 by Lockheed's Chief Test Pilot, Tony LeVier and a group of Lockheed engineers.

4th British Airways used SVC-10 G-ASGA on today's New York BA183/2. It positioned up from Heathrow to operate BA183 Manchester-New York direct, before returning the following morning as BA182. Although it was an aircraft substitution, it was the last SVC-10 to operate on Manchester's transatlantic flights.

6th Having been commonplace in June, Maersk B.720 OY-APV didn't visit Manchester at all last month, but it appeared today operating for Air Malta. It showed up again on flights KM752/3 (11th) and KM750/1 & KM712/3 (13th).

6th Amongst the numerous Saudi Air Force C-130s passing through, was KC130H Tanker 456, bound for maintenance at Marietta. Another Tanker, KC-130H 457, travelled in the opposite direction (RSF129 Stephenville-Milan-Jeddah) on the 15th.

7th Dutch AF F.27 C-1 brought a member of the Dutch Royal family, Princess Margriet, into Manchester for a shopping trip today.

8th Another Condor B.727, D-ABPI, appeared today operating Lufthansa Frankfurt-flight LH074/5. It had previously visited in September 1978, but as a Lufthansa aircraft.

9th Brymon Airways used British Air Ferries Herald G-BCWE on their scheduled Newquay flight, BC044/7. The first of two Heralds bought by BAF in 1975, it was used by the airline until 1983, before being eventually sold in Guatemala in 1988. The second was G-BDFE and both formerly operated in Canada.

9th Another French Jodel on its way to its owners at Barton was F-BLDG, arriving from Cambridge at 1712 today to clear customs.

10th Of the four Aeroflot charters arriving at Manchester this month, the following three were first visits: TU-154s CCCP-85440 today, CCCP-85381 (17th) & IL-62 CCCP-86506 (31st).

12th Pan American/National DC-10 N82NA operated for Air Florida from/to Miami as NA198/9 today, in full National colours. Pan American had acquired National Airlines earlier in the year, but they still operated under their own flight-codes and livery.

14th RAF Puma XW225 (LYD 85) called in at 1440 today for fuel, bound for its base at Odiham.

15th The pilot of Laker Airways DC-10 G-GFAL (GK026 from New York) reported to New York ATC that his undercarriage had been damaged on departure and that when he was closer to Manchester, he'd be declaring a full emergency. However, once he entered UK airspace, he stated that he would be diverting to Gatwick, where he made a safe landing.

16th Another British Airways B.737 showing up this month was G-BGDJ, positioning in from London today to operate BA5216/5221 to/from Jersey, before returning to Heathrow.

19th Beech 55 HB-GEC appeared for some brief attention from NEA, before departing for Fairoaks within ninety minutes of arrival.

27th British Airways B.747 G-AWND (BA299 Chicago-Heathrow), diverted in at 0929 today, due to all traffic routing through the Daventry sector (roughly in the Leicester area), being suspended between 0850 and 0940.

27th NEA's sole remaining Islander, G-AZGU, has been active during the month and showing signs it's about to be sold, as the registration has been alternating between G-AZGU & 8R-GFI.

27th August 1980 – Former British Midland B.707 N37681 is showing clear signs of its previous operator, PIA, having recently arrived three days earlier for storage. It was formerly N730PA, before being sold to Donaldson International in May 1970 as G-AYXR, but after they ceased trading in 1974, it was transferred to BMA who operated it on a lease-out basis until April this year. It was then sold to International Air Lease of Miami, who converted it into an all-cargo configuration. It finally left Manchester on 31st December for Lasham, where it remained until 1983, before springing to life again and departing for the USA, which was quite remarkable as the writer had witnessed it in a very sorry state, parked up at Lasham in March 1982 seemingly going nowhere! (Geoff Ball)

28th Two consecutive summers of overnight closures came to an end today, during which time 235,000 tonnes of asphalt has been used to strengthen the runway and fill in the hump, at an overall cost of £131m. The 150ft runway width has been extended to include 75ft of paved shoulders on each side and Category III lighting has been installed. Cat III status will be granted next month, subject to a full inspection of the necessary facilities, which will make Manchester's runway the most technically advanced in Europe.

29th Aviaco DC-8 EC-CQM operated a student return charter today, from/to Madrid as AO8434/5. It was one of a batch of six second-hand models, purchased between 1973 and 1975. They are being replaced with ex-Iberia DC-8 'stretched' versions and a complete listing of the last visits of the original Aviaco DC-8s and their subsequent fates are as follows:

EC-ARB, 30/10/76, sold 10/77	EC-ARC, 29/10/78, sold 11/78
EC-ASN, 01/08/80, sold 10/81	EC-ATP, 31/08/78, sold to Spanish Air Force 01/80
EC-AUM, 28/05/82, sold 12/83	EC-CQM, 29/08/80, sold 04/85

31st The South Side operators, particularly NEA, are finding business very hard going at the moment. Maintenance work has slowed right down and some members of staff are on short-time working. The current economic climate has caused them to close down the North West Flying School, make the staff redundant and put their aircraft fleet up for sale.

September 1980

Special half-price fares between the UK and Germany will introduced by Lufthansa on the 1st November. The fly 'n' save fares will cut prices by almost 50% between London and nine German cities, including Manchester-Frankfurt. Tickets can be used on any day of the week, but passengers must pay in advance and stay between six nights and one month. As an example of price, a Manchester-Frankfurt return ticket will cost £101, compared to the normal economy return price of £193.

British Airways are introducing a new standby fare of £77 single between Manchester-New York on the 1st October, which they claim is the lowest across the Atlantic. It will apply to all five of their Manchester flights, in a bid to compete with the oncoming threat of Laker Airways. A new pond-hopper fare of £90 single between Manchester-New York, bookable nine days before departure, will also be offered.

Following on from their success in introducing Miami as a new holiday destination, American holiday specialists, Jetsave, are adding weekly flights to Puerto Rico from next April. Operated by Transamerica Boeing 747s, the 14-day vacations starting at £195, include flights and self-catering accommodation. They anticipate carrying at least 25,000 holidaymakers to San Juan in the first six months, on flights from Manchester and Gatwick.

Britain's third largest holiday firm, Horizon, are adding an extra 10,000 holidays for next year, which means Manchester will become the main departure point for the Midlands-based firm, accounting for a third of the 337,000 holidays on the market. Demand for next year has been strong and tour operators anticipate bumper bookings, despite this year's economic gloom, strong pound, high accommodation costs and the summer blockades of the French Channel ports!

Regardless of strong objections by local residents and environmentalists at last February's Public Enquiry, the airport has been given the go-ahead for the 800ft extension of Runway 06/24. Land covering 131 acres will be compulsory purchased, to extend the main runway to 10,000ft. The Public Enquiry Inspector said it will help shift the burden of heavy air traffic from London and bring great benefits to the airport and the region. He added that although it couldn't be predicted how much extra traffic would be created; he was impressed by Manchester's consistency to make a profit over many years, unlike most other regional airports. The airlines reacted favourably to the news, but hope that the work due to start next March, won't interfere with normal runway operations.

A report conducted by ABTA (Association of British Travel Agents), shows that Manchester has the dearest car parking charges outside of London and is more expensive than the other provincial airports. The cheapest summer parking is £1.30 per day at an offsite car park, bookable in advance and the airport's surface car parks cost £1.50 per day or £10.50 per week, which drops to £1.30 per day in the winter. Birmingham's cheapest charge is 85p per day or £5.95 per week, Liverpool is 80p per day or £5.60 per week, Leeds-Bradford is 80p per day or £5.60 per week and East Midlands is 75p per day or £5.25 per week.

Equipment changes on scheduled services included Finnair (AY032): DC-9 OH-LYH (5th/8th/12th) & OH-LYI (14th); Lufthansa (LH074): B.727s D-ABLI (16th), D-ABRI (18th) & Condor B.727 D-ABIR (24th) and SAS (SK541): DC-9-21 SE-DBS (29th).

RAF ILS traffic identified included Hawks XX180 (19th), XX187 (25th), XX224 (11th) & XX309 (26th); C-130s XV185 (17th), XV199 (30th), XV220 (18th), XV298 (5th) and Andovers XS643 (30th) & XW750 (25th). Civil ILS traffic included BAe.125 G-5-16 in green-primer (17th)

& Fords Gulfstream 1 G-ASXT from Liverpool (18th). An unidentified Jaguar (EHK 39) caused a number of complaints, due to the excessive amount of power used on the climb-out (15th).

1st RAF VC-10 XR808 (RR2700) arriving from Brize Norton today, was operating an outbound trooping flight to Dusseldorf.

2nd The German Air Force operated a flight from/to Cologne with a very rare type, the Hansa Jet 16+01, which arrived at 0959 today operating as DCN9282.

5th The ATC Watch Log recorded the following at 1244 today 'The Captain of British Airways flight BA942 Manchester-Geneva pushing back off Stand 24, reported that the loaders loading a Douglas DC-10 on Stand 22 next door were fighting and could we report this immediately, as it was a disgraceful sight for his passengers to see!' The incident between the two Servisair personnel was reported to their superiors and they were dealt with accordingly!

7th Aeroflot operated their final charter of the season today, with TU-134 CCCP-65785 (SU2241/2).

7th Yet another Jodel bound for Barton passed through Manchester today, when F-BLDH arrived at 1518 from Deauville to clear customs, before leaving for Barton later in the afternoon.

8th Aer Turas Britannia EI-BBH hasn't been a particularly regular visitor to Manchester, but it operated a livestock charter today from/to Dublin. The aircraft was delivered to the airline in September 1975 and operated until November 1981.

8th Smurfit's new Lear Jet, G-JJSG, made its first appearance at Manchester today, from/to Shannon. It replaces G-BBEE, which made its last visit last month on the 30th August, before being eventually sold in the USA.

9th The latest example of light aircraft operators adopting call-signs, was Scholl's Beech 90 N14CP, arriving at 1001 today from Leavesden as 'Clog 434'.

9th The only Argosy to visit so far this year was G-BEOZ, diverting in at 2339 today (AK118 from Saarbrucken), originally bound for Liverpool.

13th British Airways operated a number of charters over the weekend in conjunction with NATO's Operation Crusader. Outbound trooping flights to Brussels and Dusseldorf were operated by L.1011 G-BBAF today; B.747 G-AWNM (14th); L.1011 Tristars G-BEAK & G-BEAM, B.747 AWNM and SVC-10 G-ASGL (15th), with some making several flights a day.

14th Two further RAF trooping flights, VC-10s XV102 (RR2726) & XR808 (RR2727), operated to Gutersloh today in connection with Operation Crusader.

14th British Air Ferries Herald G-BEBB positioned up from Southend today, to operate a charter to Reims the following morning (VF1452). This aircraft has recently returned off lease from Nile Valley Aviation of Egypt.

14th Sterling SE.210 OY-STH positioned in from Gothenburg to operate an outbound charter today, departing at 2008 to Ibiza as NB2573.

18th The military version of the Dove, the Devon/Sea Devon, appears to be an endangered species judging by the amount making their last visits to Manchester this year. Royal Navy Sea Devon XJ347, operating as 'Navy 827' from/to Hawarden today, was also its last visit. After being sold early in 1982, it reverted to its original civil marks of G-AMXT.

18th Swiss-airline CTA SE.210 Caravelle HB-ICO arrived at 1516 today, operating RU471 from Athens. A further flight from/to Geneva was operated by HB-ICO as RU198/9 on the 22nd.

19th Air Ecosse used Twin Otters on their scheduled flights twice this month, G-STUD today and newly acquired G-MAIL on the 26th.

20th British Airways Manchester services appear to have escaped the airlines recently announced cuts, after achieving their targets. Flights to Belfast, Aberdeen & London are all carrying more passengers than the year before, but the European services showed a slight decrease. They are looking to save £20m, with Gatwick, Heathrow & Birmingham most likely to be affected.

20th Royal Saudi Air Force C-130H MS-019, which operates as a survey and medical support aircraft, made its first visit today arriving at 1852 from Montreal. It's in a VIP type colour scheme, consisting of a grey underside, green cheatline and a white roof and tail with a green Saudi flag.

23rd Even on a weekday, huge numbers of spectators turned up to see the third commercial visit of Concorde. F-BTSD arriving at 1021 today (AF4698/9 from/to Paris) was of particular interest, as onboard was super-salesman John Gibson. The aircraft had been chartered in his honour by his employer, the window firm Coldshield, after winning their national sales competition by turning over £93,000 worth of business during the 13 week contest. After landing at Manchester, he and 100 salesmen were treated to lunch at the airports Excelsior Hotel.

23rd French Air Force Transall F.159/61-ZY, arriving at 1106 today, was operating a crew training flight from Prestwick to Lyneham. Another, Noratlas F.167/64-BX, operated as FM0107 Brize Norton-Bournemouth, on the 25th.

23rd A rare type to visit Manchester was the executive MS.760 Paris, but I-FINR arrived at 1553 today from Cologne, before its departure for Geneva the following day. The type had last visited in March 1979 when there was flurry of French Ministry examples.

23rd Air Bridge Carriers Merchantman G-APES recently returned to service after a five month rebuild, during which time it received a bold new colour scheme. It positioned in from East Midlands late this evening, to operate a cattle charter to Milan the following morning.

25th This month's Canadian Air Force CC-130 flights were 130325 (CAM515-today), 130322 (CAM516-27th) & 130320 (CAM517-29th).

26th Today saw the first visit of a Cargolux aircraft since CL-44 TF-LLI arrived on 28th July 1976. DC-8F TF-BCV was operating a freight charter to Australia and amongst the cargo on this 'Noah's-ark' style flight were sheep, cattle, horses, zebras, chinchillas and a goat.

26th British Airways started returning troops to Manchester today, after their latest NATO exercise in Germany, with most aircraft making several return journeys. B.747 G-AWND, L.1011 Tristar G-BBAH & SVC-10 G-ASGK operated today and B.747 G-AWNN & L.1011 G-BBAH on the 27th. RAF flights were operated by VC-10s XR807 (RR2766) & XV103 (RR2759/2763), both on the 27th. The two British Airways SVC-10s that have visited this month, G-ASGK & G-ASGL, had been taken out of storage at Prestwick and specially reactivated for these trooping flights.

26th This evenings interesting arrivals were Norwegian Cessna 404s LN-AEL from Oslo and LN-MAT from Kristiansand, which both departed for Oslo on the 28th and Gulfstream 2TT N365G at 1917 from Shannon.

28th There were several fog diversions from the South East today, starting with three British Airways B.747s: G-AWNH at 0630 (BA006 from Anchorage), G-AWNF at 0656 (BA174 from New York) & G-AWNK at 0701 (BA032 from Abu Dhabi), plus B.707 G-AXXY at 0643 (BA272 from Philadelphia) and SVC-10 G-ASGA at 0634 (BA120 from Dhahran). Others included British Caledonian DC-10 G-BFGI at 0622 (BR366 from Kano), Transamerica DC-8 N4869T at 0636 (TV869 from New York), TWA B.747 N53116 at 0718 (TW754 from Boston) and Canadian Gulfstream 2 C-GSLK diverting in from Luton at 0808. Manchester could have seen many more diversions, had the apron space not been limited by the work in progress and the airports own flights, which are considerable on a summer Sunday! In contrast, Prestwick received nine wide-bodied diversions and Air Jamaica DC-8 6Y-JII.

29th Crossair of Switzerland started a weekly flight transporting Air Florida crews from Brussels and returning another crew to Zurich using Metroliners, with HB-LLA operating today's first service.

October 1980

Since British Airways launched their Manchester-London Shuttle service twelve months ago, it's recorded a 21% increase in passengers and carried over 486,000. Currently operating eight-times-daily in each direction, the lowest fare is £33 one-way for a guaranteed seat, or £15 for a standby ticket.

Arrowsmith Holidays who are part of the Laker group, plan to introduce 298-seat Airbus A300s from Manchester between April and October next year, when 200,000 holidays will be offered, which is 50,000 more than this year.

Laker Airways are planning to launch Skytrain services from Manchester to New York & Los Angeles, after receiving the go-ahead from the CAA, although other airlines such as British Airways have one month to appeal the decision. They will be the first airline operating Manchester-Los Angeles, with one-way fares starting at £101. Subject to availability, single tickets to New York will be offered at £78 for their basic walk-on seat-only Skytrain service, which doesn't include meals and drinks. Bookable Skytrain fares including meals and drinks start from £134 to Los Angeles and £92 to New York. Three-weekly services between Manchester-New York are planned for the winter, compared to the four-weekly flights via Prestwick currently operated by competitor British Airways, who've 'tweaked' their fares in readiness to compete.

Cutbacks in Government spending are threatening Manchester Airport's £150m expansion plans. If passed, a bill due to return from the Lords and then back to the Commons for amendment purposes, could severely restrict the ability of municipally owned airports to use their own revenue to fund development programmes. If it becomes law without the amendments, Manchester Airport will have to compete for any available cash, not only with other provincial airports, but also with Manchester City Council and the Metropolitan Councils.

The number of plane spotters parking on roads and streets in and around the airport has reached unacceptable levels, but despite numerous complaints by residents, the police have taken no action so far. It's reported there are so many enthusiasts in the area, particularly at weekends, that one hot-dog seller in particular was doing a roaring trade! To combat the problem, the Airport Authority has been asked to consider providing a special parking area for viewing purposes.

Due to high maintenance costs, British Airways have now withdrawn their four Trident 1Es. The last flight on 30th September was operated by G-AVYC (BA5457 Newcastle-Heathrow) and their last visits to Manchester and subsequent fates are as follows:

G-ASWU, 08/08/79, last service 01/08/80 (EDI-LHR), scrapped at LHR 05/81
G-AVYB, 07/07/79, last service 31/08/80 (BA5455 NCL-LHR), scrapped at LHR 05/81
G-AVYC, 05/07/79, last service 31/07/80 (BA5457 NCL-LHR), scrapped at LHR 05/81

G-AVYE, 09/10/79, withdrawn 08/80, flown 04/81 to Wroughton for preservation

Equipment changes on scheduled services included Austrian Airlines (OS471): first visit DC-9-51 OE-LDM (2nd); Finnair (AY032): DC-9 OH-LYH (5th/8th/10th/12th); Lufthansa (LH074): B.727s D-ABKA (24th) & D-ABKD (17th) and Swissair (SR842): DC-9-51 HB-ISU (17th).

Military ILS traffic identified included RAF Hawks XX177 (31st), XX234 (10th), XX312 (9th); C-130s XV206 (2nd/31st), XV292 (30th), XV296 (29th), XV298 (20th), XV301 (30th) & XV307 (17th); Andover XS643 (1st); BAe.125 XW789 (16th); RAE aircraft Comet XS235 (14th/17th) & BAC 1-11 XX105 (14th) and Canadian Air Force C-130E 130315 (23rd) overshooting as 'CAM410' en route to Prestwick.

1st It threatened to be a very busy morning for diversions, with the arrival of three DC-10s. Two from British Caledonian were G-BFGI at 0557 (BR362 from Lagos) & G-BEBM at 0603 (BR232 from Atlanta) and the other was Laker Airways G-BELO at 0651 (GK040 from New York). British Airways B.747 G-BDPZ appeared at 0708 (BA120 from Dhahran), but nothing else arrived after this short burst.

1st Dove G-ARUM operated by the National Coal Board from new in 1961, visited Manchester for the final time today, staying for twelve minutes from Edinburgh to Stansted. It was sold in February 1984 as G-DDCD.

2nd October 1980 – Another interesting CV-580 visitor this year was N328VP, owned by American evangelist group, The Way International. It arrived at 0126 today as a fuel divert, originally destined for Dublin. It departed to Paris Le Bourget on the 6th and returned to Manchester on the 10th from Inverness. Originally delivered in 1962 as a corporate aircraft for ESSO as N200A, it was operated by The Way International from 1977-1989. (Geoff Ball)

2nd A fuel strike in Ireland caused a considerable amount of Irish traffic to route through Manchester up until the 12th. The majority were Aer Lingus flights and all their types were seen (BAC 1-11s/B.707s/B.737s & B.747s). Several Transamerica flights also routed through Manchester, along with flights by Aviaco, Air Portugal, Inex-Adria & TAP.

4th Cessna 210 N5252Y, arriving at 0857 today from St. John's, Newfoundland, was on its delivery flight. Operating under call-sign 'UNR102', it departed later for Brussels.

5th As Kar-Air's DC-6 was away for maintenance until the 15th, DC-9 OH-LYH operated all Finnair cargo flights until its return.

6th Five British Airtours Boeing 707s made their last visits to Manchester during the month. The first was today, when G-ARRC operated KT993/2 from/to Corfu, before being withdrawn at the end of the month. It was flown Gatwick-Stansted on the 3rd November for storage, then sold in March 1981 to French-airline Europe Air Service for scrap.

7th Northern Executive Aviation are now licensed to carry out full maintenance and servicing on executive jets, after providing similar services for light aircraft for the last 20 years.

11th An early morning fog diversion to Manchester was RAF VC-10 XV104 at 0931 (RR2328 from Washington). The emergency services were alerted to a nosewheel problem, which may have prevented the aircraft from clearing off the runway, but all was normal once it had landed.

12th Former NEA Islander, G-AZGU, finally left for Reykjavik on the first leg of its lengthy delivery flight, bound for Guyana. Its sale as 8R-GFI ends NEA's ten-year association with the type.

13th In contrast to the 1st, there was a variety of diversions today, mainly from Heathrow. Of note were B.747 VT-EDU at 0900 (AI116 from New York), Air New Zealand DC-10 ZK-NZQ at 0906 (BA074 from Montreal), B.747 N741PA at 0929 (PA106 from Washington) which declared a fuel emergency and ex-National DC-10 N82NA at 0909 (PA098 from Miami). The record for the highest number of wide-bodied aircraft on the ground at Manchester was broken today, from ten to eleven. Of these, eight were diversions and three scheduled aircraft: B.747 G-BDPV, DC-10 G-BGXF & DC-10 G-GSKY.

13th Royal Saudi Air Force C-130H 1601 (RSF136 from Gander) remained on the runway for several minutes, after bursting two tyres on landing and taxiing off the runway very slowly!

13th Coincidentally, two British Airtours B.707s made their final visits to Manchester today. The first, G-ARRA (KT993/2 from/to Corfu) was flown Gatwick-Stansted on 5th November, before being withdrawn and sold in March 1981 to French-airline Europe Air Service for scrap. The second, G-APFG (KT491 from Tenerife) which departed the following morning for Palma as KT690, was withdrawn by the end of the month and flown Gatwick-Stansted on 3rd November for storage. It was later purchased by Aviation Traders, to be used as a ground trainer at Stansted.

14th Beech 200s EI-BIP & EI-BFW combined to operate Clyden Airways mail flight CE100/1.

17th British Airways B.737 G-BGDN, operating the inbound BA5221 from Jersey before positioning to Heathrow, was the third British Airways B.737 to visit Ringway so far this year.

17th Air Malta flight KM750 with 138 passengers onboard, landed 16-hours late at 1244 today, after being grounded in Paris due to a bomb hoax. It was overflying France when ATC advised the pilot there was a bomb onboard. After landing at Paris, the passengers spent the night in a hotel whilst the plane was thoroughly searched, but nothing was found.

18th Manchester resident PA-28 G-BCGD made a forced landing in the Northwich area today, following an engine failure. Luckily there were no injuries to the occupants onboard.

18th Twin Otter C-FCSF arriving at 2228 today from Nice, night-stopped on its way back to Canada. It departed the following morning at 1151, initially bound for Glasgow.

20th British Airtours B.707 G-APFO was another aircraft making its final visit, arriving at 1102 today from Corfu as KT993, before positioning to Gatwick as KT993P at 1358. It was withdrawn in November and flown to the USA in March 1981 for scrapping.

21st EL AL commenced a once-weekly charter from/to Tel Aviv via Gatwick, with a third of the 466 seats being offered to Manchester passengers. Boeing B.747 4X-AXF operated today's inaugural flight as LY5315/6.

22nd The last of the five British Airtours B.707s making their final visits to Manchester was G-APFF at 1834 today (KT899 from Corfu), before positioning out to Gatwick as KT899P at 1930. It was flown from Gatwick to Stansted early next month, withdrawn from service and flown to Boeing Field for scrapping in May 1981. This left just G-APFJ as their only B.707 still operating, although some ex-British Airways examples were received the following year.

25th Britannia Airways B.737 G-AXNB, which has been converted into a cargo aircraft, positioned in from Luton today to operate an outbound cattle flight to Milan-Malpensa.

25th Maersk BAe.748 OY-APT arrived at 1832 today from Copenhagen for maintenance with Dan-Air Engineering. It had passed through originally on the 4th June as C-GOUT and left in full Maersk colours.

26th Dan-Air Viscount G-BGLC arrived today for maintenance. It was devoid of all Dan-Air titles by the 29th and two days later it was registered as VP-WGB with Air Zimbabwe. On the same day it made a return trip to East Midlands on a training detail, before its delivery flight via Bari on the 2nd November.

29th The Government's proposed bill restricting local airports from using their own revenue for expansion purposes is likely to be dropped, following the Lords rejection of the bill.

29th Exactly five months since the last visit, another British Airways Viscount, G-AOYG, arrived this morning operating from/to Glasgow. In similar circumstances to the last Viscount, this was also deputising for a sick BAC 1-11.

29th Invicta made their final visit to Manchester today, when Britannia G-ANCF night-stopped from/to Milan on their final cattle charter (IM366/7). It was also the airlines very final flight, as they ceased operations on the 31st. For the record their other Britannia, G-AOVF, last visited Manchester earlier in the year on the 1st August.

30th Worthy of note was today's brief visit by the British Airport Authorities Rockwell 680, G-BFGB. It would normally have no business visiting a council-owned airport, but it brought BAA Chairman, Sir Norman Payne, in for a meeting with the airports management.

31st Beech 200 N86DA was on the ground at Manchester for eleven minutes today. It carried the serial 'RSAF 029' on the fin and was routing Hawarden-Glasgow.

November 1980

British Airtours have a winter programme out of Manchester for the very first time, with a single based Boeing 737 operating to various IT destinations.

Several airlines made changes this month. Air France retained their evening flight timings on a six-weekly operation, Air Malta returned to a once-weekly flight, Air UK operate twice-daily to Ronaldsway except for Sundays and British Airways will operate a once-weekly B.747 flight to Toronto (BA073), returning the following morning (BA072). Their New York flights will operate five-weekly with two direct using B.707s, but Montreal has been dropped completely. Cyprus Airways reverted to once-weekly service again for the winter, Guernsey Airlines have a weekly Friday departure to Guernsey (GE710) returning on Sundays (GE711), Northwest Orient will operate three-weekly throughout the winter and Lufthansa & Swissair have restored their cargo flights after the summer night-time runway closures. Winter IT flights are operated by Air Europe, Air Malta, Aviaco, Britannia Airways, British Airtours, Dan-Air, Laker Airways, Monarch Airlines & Orion Airways and Transatlantic flights are operated by Laker Airways (Miami) & Wardair (Toronto), both weekly.

Equipment changes on scheduled services included LOT (LO287): IL-18 SP-LSF (17th); Lufthansa (LH074): B.727s D-ABKD (17th), D-ABDI (22nd), D-ABFI (23rd) and first visit Condor B.727 D-ABIQ (6th).

Military ILS traffic identified included RAF Hawks XX162 (10th), XX178 (4th), XX182 (5th), XX186 (5th), XX231 (10th), XX232 (3rd) & XX295 (6th); C-130s XV181 (18th), XV183 (4th), XV197 (27th), XV210 (26th), XV213 (3rd), XV301 (14th) & XV306 (5th); Jetstreams XX494 (12th) & XX499 (21st) and Royal Navy Jetstream XX475 as 'Navy 572' (24th).

November 1980 – This is a typical view of the cafeteria in the main terminal. The main windows, which are just out of shot, offer panoramic views of the apron. A major refurbishment of this area began in 1987. (Manchester Airport Archive)

1st Air UK F-27 G-BDVS brought in Norwich City FC for a First Division league match with Manchester City. City's win of 1-0 was their first of the season.

2nd Army Air Corps Scout XV138 and Puma XW231 called in twice during the day, routing Hereford-Teeside both times.

4th The first Nord 262 to visit Manchester for a while, was F-BPNS on a training flight from/to Gatwick today.

5th Amongst the Hawks appearing for practice ILS approaches during the day was a Red Arrows example, 'Red 02', performing a practice ILS in the morning.

6th Red Arrows Hawk 'Red 02' appeared again this morning for a practice ILS approach to Runway 06, but on this occasion it broke off to the right and made a run across the British Airways hangars, down the taxiway past the end of the piers with 'full smoke' on! None of this had been approved by ATC and the pilot was consequently told so - and in such terms! Coincidentally, there were only two more Hawk visits for the rest of the month.

6th Lufthansa passenger flight LH074/5, operated by Condor B.727-100 D-ABIQ, was also the very last visit of a Lufthansa/Condor 'short' Boeing 727 to Manchester. All Lufthansa & Condor B.727-100s had gone by 1982 and the last Lufthansa example to visit was D-ABIA on 2nd June 1979. For the record, the very first Boeing 727 to visit was also a Lufthansa aircraft when B.727-100 D-ABIC diverted in from Heathrow as LH220 on 7th March 1965.

6th Bristol Britannia's are becoming an endangered species these days, but remarkably two made first visits to Manchester this month. Katale Aero Transport 9Q-CDT arrived at 1418 today, in an unadventurous white scheme, to take a quantity of cotton bales out to Zaire via Djerba. More colourful was Redcoat's G-BHAU, arriving at 1458 on the 12th, to operate the regular cattle charter now mainly operated by B.737 G-AXNB.

7th Laker Airways B.707 G-BFBS positioned in from Gatwick early evening, to operate a return flight to Tenerife the following day as GK303/4.

8th Laker Airways B.707 G-BFBS arrived at 1919 today (GK304 from Tenerife) and remained parked until the 10th, when it operated GK309 outbound to Las Palmas.

9th Royal Saudi Air Force KC-130H Tanker 456 arrived at 0830, routing back to Jeddah via Milan (RSF138), after further modification work at the Lockheed factory, Marietta.

10th The Royal Navy sent Wessex XT764 into the region, as part of their Navy Presentation Team. It was based at Manchester until the 17th, during which time it operated demonstrations at various local schools. When it was operating in the Stockport area on the 13th, local residents made several complaints about its 'unusually low altitude'.

10th Laker Airways B.707 G-BFBS, arriving at 1906 today (GK310 from Las Palmas), was the aircrafts final operational flight with the airline. It was towed over to the South Side area on the 25th and parked on Runway 10/28 with B.707 N37681 for two days, before being taken back to the North Side for some attention.

14th Brymon Airways Twin Otter G-BFGP arrived with Southampton FC to play a First Division League match with Manchester City the following afternoon. They were 'on a bit of a roll' and easily beat Southampton 3-0.

14th The Royal Saudi Air Force sent another Tanker through Manchester this month, which was also a first visit, when KC-130H/459 routed from Milan-Malpensa to Gander today (RSF139), bound for the Lockheed factory for modifications.

19th Eastern Airways DC-3 G-AMPO operated a freight charter to Bergen today.

20th Two French Air Force Noratlas aircraft sent through Manchester on training flights were 139/64-IE today and 162/64-II (24th), both operating FM0403 Brize Norton-Bournemouth.

24th Clyden Airways were suffering from equipment problems again, so from today and for the remainder of the month, they used Air Atlantique DC-3 G-AMCA.

25th Europe Air Service SE.210 F-GCJT made its first visit this morning, operating a round trip from Paris-Orly. Three other French registered aircraft also arriving today were Brit Air EMB-110 F-GBLE, Rockwell 690 F-GCJY & Cessna 421 F-BUYB.

17th November 1980 – Polish national airline LOT, introduced a twice-weekly schedule to Warsaw this year. Tupolev TU-134s were the regular type operating the service, but Ilyushin IL-18s were also used occasionally and today was such an occasion, when SP-LSF operated flight LO287/8. (Geoff Ball).

26th Trust House Forte's newly acquired BAe.125, G-HHOI, brought Sir Charles Forte up from London today, to open a new hotel near Haydock.

26th Vintage Army Air Corps Beaver XP771, which was delivered new in February 1961, operated from/to Belfast today as 'Army 405'.

28th So far, this month had been dominated by cold and sunny, but breezy weather, which meant few diversions, but British Airways B.737 G-BGDO bucked the trend when it diverted in as 'Speedbird 5458' from Heathrow, due to fog at Newcastle.

28th Brymon Airways Twin Otter G-BFGP made its second visit in two weeks this evening, bringing in Southampton FC again for the following day's match with Manchester Utd, ending in a 1-1 draw.

December 1980

This month saw just two more diversions than the last month, six in total and nothing of note. Again there was only one airliner, British Airways B.707 G-AYLT (BA084 from Prestwick) on the 20th. It's thought the unseasonal weather patterns of continual low pressure and no anti-cyclones has been caused by the eruption of Mount St. Helens (Washington State) earlier in May, which was responsible for discharging vast quantities of ash into the atmosphere.

Plans for the 800ft extension of Runway 06/24 have been given financial approval by the Government and although the £10m scheme is of regional and national importance, no Government funding will be made available to help with the cost. This means the Airport Authority will have to use its own money to pay for the work, or borrow it if necessary. It also means that work can commence on other major developments, including more aircraft parking, car parks and offices. The runway work due to start next March, is already out to tender.

Air Portugal will commence scheduled services from Manchester from the 13th May next year. A twice-weekly flight between Manchester-Lisbon will provide the city's first direct link with Portugal. The proposed Wednesday and Saturday flights, operated by Boeing 727s, will also give onward connections to South Africa and South America.

Due to the success of their once-weekly flight to Newquay this summer, Brymon Airways will increase the service to twice-weekly next summer. The single fare costs £35 and an advance purchase ticket costs £57 return.

Air France have made drastic cuts to their SE.210 Caravelle fleet this year, their Manchester service will be operated by Boeing 727s from next March. The following Caravelle's made their last visits to Manchester this year:

F-BHRD	02/04/80, withdrawn 04/80	F-BHRX	31/03/80, withdrawn 04/80
F-BHRE	11/02/80, withdrawn 03/80	F-BJTF	21/03/80, withdrawn 03/80
F-BHRK	27/03/80, withdrawn 04/80	F-BJTR	07/09/80, withdrawn 12/80
F-BHRU	24/08/80, withdrawn 09/80	F-BJTS	26/02/80, withdrawn 12/80
F-BHRV	16/12/80, withdrawn 12/80	F-BLKF	14/10/80, withdrawn 11/80

This leaves the remaining examples still in service going into 1981:
F-BHRF/F-BHRH/F-BHRI/F-BHRY/F-BJTE/F-BJTL/F-BJTP & F-BOHA.

Spantax operated two weekly flights during the summer, with Convair CV-990s serving Las Palmas on Mondays (BX727/8) and Palma on Thursdays (BX787/8). All twelve of their CV-990s are up for sale and their last visits and subsequent fates are as follows:

EC-BJC	17/10/79, withdrawn 11/79	EC-CNF	13/10/80, withdrawn 12/82
EC-BJD	25/09/80, withdrawn 04/83	EC-CNG	16/10/80, withdrawn 04/82
EC-BTE	06/10/80, withdrawn 10/81	EC-CNJ	11/09/80, withdrawn 03/81
EC-BXI	31/07/80, withdrawn 06/81		

This left five aircraft which continued to visit: EC-BQA/BQQ/BZO/BZP & EC-CNH.

Equipment changes on scheduled services included Air France (AF964): Air Charter SE.210 F-BJTG (30th); Austrian Airlines (OS471): DC-9-51 OE-LDL (4th) and LOT (LO287): IL-18 SP-LSB (8th).

RAF ILS traffic identified included RAF Hawks XX163 (6th), XX166 (6th), XX181 (5th), XX225 (5th/7th), XX226 (12th) & XX312 (12th) and C-130s XV181 (1st), XV213 (3rd), XV219 (11th) & XV223 (18th). Civil ILS traffic included BAe.125 N169B on a test flight from Hawarden (2nd) and Ford Motor Co's Gulfstream 1 G-BRAL which arrived from Liverpool (11th).

1st Manchester's Airport Director, Gordon Sweetapple, has brought forward his retirement and will leave his post next year. This gives his successor the chance to work alongside him on the restructuring of the airport's management. Mr Sweetapple, who has filled the position since 1974, plans to move into aviation consultancy work.

1st Omani Royal Flight Gulf 2 A4O-AA brought a number of visitors into Manchester today, ultimately bound for Harrogate.

3rd Today saw the arrival of Noratlas 163/64-BY, the first of six French Air Force training flights during the month, all routing Brize Norton-Bournemouth. The others were Noratlas 32/64-BY (4th), Noratlas 141/64-IJ (9th) sporting a desert style camouflage, Noratlas 167/64-BX (10th), Noratlas No.183 (11th) and Noratlas 110/64-BV (15th).

7th British Airways B.747 G-AWNA operating BA072 Toronto-Manchester-Heathrow, was taxiing out for its flight to Heathrow, when the pilot reported that Lear Jet G-JJSG which was parked in the South Bay, was positioned too close to the taxiway. An inspection of the aircraft revealed it was locked up, so apart from warning other aircraft of the obstruction, nothing could be done!

7th Citation 550 N45EP arrived at 1825 today to clear customs, en route to Liverpool.

8th Redcoat Britannia G-BHAU paid another visit to Manchester, arriving at 1512 today, operating an inbound cargo flight from Malta as RY639.

10th The police contacted Manchester ATC at 1225 today, to report that workmen had dug up a suspected unexploded bomb on the new West Apron extension. It was confirmed later that the object found on the old western dispersal site near the Romper Public House was definitely a bomb.

12th The best executive jet visitor of the year, appeared on this very windy Sunday afternoon. Westwind YV-388CP was on its delivery flight initially bound for Prestwick, when it diverted in at 1442 due to strong headwinds en route, before departing the following morning for Goose Bay.

12th Laker Airways other B.707, G-BFBZ, arrived at 1503 today (GK099P from Gatwick) for storage, joining its sister-ship G-BFBS & BAC 1-11 G-AVBX.

15th Another batch of three Canadian Air Force CC-130Es arriving during the month were 130327 (CAM515-today), 130325 (CAM516-17th) & 130321 (CAM517-19th), all routing Trenton-Lahr.

17th Experts are examining the damaged engines of an Air Europe B.737, after flying into a flock of seagulls. It was 50ft above the runway, when it was forced into an immediate return to Manchester. More than sixty dead gulls were removed from the runway and the flight, AE934 bound for Malta with 113 passengers and crew onboard, was delayed for three hours until a replacement aircraft was flown up from Gatwick.

18th BAe.748 C-GYMX called into Manchester for fuel at 1328 today, en route Nice-Reykjavik. It was on delivery for Bradley Air Services, in full Air Pacific of Fiji livery. (Manchester Airport Archive)

17th After 25 years of service with the RAF and Royal Navy, the Westland Whirlwind has been effectively retired from front-line service, but three RAF squadrons are still using the type. Two are based in Cyprus and the third is a Search & Rescue squadron based at RAF Chivenor, who re-equipped with Wessex aircraft from December 1981. The last Whirlwind examples to visit Manchester were RAF XJ435, which overshot on 30th October 1978 and the last to actually land was RAF Rescue XP395 on 27th September 1978. Both aircraft were scrapped in the late 1980s.

18th RAF C-130 XV223, which overshot at 1120 today as Evergreen 47, has the notoriety of being the first of a number of RAF C-130s to be stretched at the Lockheed factory at Marietta, Georgia, in December 1979. This adds an extra 8′ 4″ to its overall length, which boosts cargo carrying capacity by 40%, or enables the aircraft to carry an extra 28 paratroopers or 36 infantry. Work on the remainder of the fleet will be carried out at Marshalls of Cambridge.

23rd BAe.748 G-BCDZ, arriving at 1118 today from Woodford for attention with Dan-Air Engineering, will be leased to German operator DLT until their own aircraft are delivered.

23rd Army Air Corps Scout XW799, arriving at 1218 today, was routing Middle Wallop-Belfast as 'Army 383'.

26th Boxing Day saw the arrival of Army Air Corps Beaver XV271 at 1321 from Waddington to Belfast, as 'Army 402'.

31st B.707 N37681 finally left for Lasham today, after having two of its engines refitted.

First/Last Arrivals & Departures 1980

First arrival:	B.737 G-BGNW/BY413BV from Luton at 0058
First departure:	Cessna 401 G-AWSF to Belfast at 0422
Last arrival:	Trident 3 G-AWZH/BA4532 from Heathrow at 2140
Last departure:	EMB-110 G-FMFC/WG779 to Dundee at 1910

Airport stats 1980 (+/- % on previous Year)		
Scheduled Passengers	4,423,970	+25.6%
Freight & Mail (Tonnes)	27,659	+9.3%
Movements	83,251	+11%

2
Airport Diary 1981

January 1981

It's being claimed that the British Airways Manchester-Heathrow Shuttle is taking business away from Manchester. The results of a survey carried out over two weeks last autumn, showed that of the 4,532 passengers questioned, 67% were using the service to catch flights from London to other destinations. In light of this, the airport has backed calls from a number of local councillors to hold urgent talks with the airline operators, particularly British Airways, to discuss the possibility of more direct foreign flights from Manchester.

British Airways will cease its direct flights to New York (BA183/2) from the 11th, as the service will revert to three-weekly via Prestwick (BA184/5), but still with Boeing 707s.

The future of Dan-Air's network of UK City-Link services is in the balance, after decreasing passenger numbers and high airport charges are making it uneconomical. A summer review of the Newcastle-Manchester-Birmingham-Cardiff-Bournemouth City-Link service could result in frequency cuts, use of smaller aircraft and even abandonment.

Olympic Airways announced plans to fly from Manchester. Details are still being finalised, but they expect to operate scheduled services into Manchester for the first time by March 1982. A spokesman for the airline said their existing routes from Athens to Europe will be extended to link Manchester directly with the Greek capital.

Equipment changes on scheduled services included <u>Austrian Airlines (OS471):</u> DC-9-51 OE-LDO (11th); <u>Lufthansa (LH074):</u> B.727s D-ABKA (21st), D-ABHI (23rd), D-ABPI (24th) & D-ABRI (4th/26th) and <u>SAS (SK539):</u> DC-9-21 OY-KGE (12th).

RAF ILS traffic identified included RAF Hawk XX299 (6th) and C-130s XV186 (27th) & XV297 (26th). The only civil ILS traffic was BAe.125 5N-AVJ from/to Hawarden as 'Newpin 42' (27th). Overall there was little ILS traffic, probably due to the persistent cloud conditions.

2nd A rare visit this morning of a British Airways Viscount (or British as they are now known), took place when G-AOYP operated from/to Glasgow as 'Speedbird 6642'.

3rd Laker Airways operated its inaugural Manchester Skytrain service today, when DC-10 G-BGXG departed to Miami as GK071 and returned the following morning as GK072. Further services to Los Angeles & New York will be added in March.

6th The last of EL AL's Tel Aviv flights (LY5315/6), was operated today by B.747 4X-AXB on its first visit. The flights will restart in April as LY5317/8 with Boeing 707s, operating direct from/to Tel Aviv, rather than via Gatwick.

7th Iscargo Electra TF-ISC arrived at 2037 today from Reykjavik, with 10 tonnes (282 boxes) of cod and haddock destined for Fleetwood Fish Market, due to the blockading of Fleetwood Port by local fishermen. Following a flurry of publicity more flights were promised, but after the same Electra returned on the 13th with another load of fish, it was the last flight.

8th Beech F.90 G-BIED, routing from Keflavik on a delivery flight to Eagle Aviation, was a first visit of type. The aircraft, which differs from a standard Beech 90 as it has a T-tail, departed later for Leavesden to be used as a company demonstrator.

8th British Airways were quick to counteract claims made earlier in the month, that their Shuttle service was taking passengers away from their own direct European flights from Manchester. At an Airport Authority meeting, they stressed that traditionally 70% of passengers flying from Manchester-London are business travellers, connecting with worldwide International flights. They added that since the Shuttle was launched, the main growth was in carrying day-trippers to the capital and the level of passengers travelling to London for connecting flights was now less than 60%. It was also reported that the service, used by 493,500 passengers last year, up 18% on the previous year, was the most successful air route in Europe.

13th Laker Airways, the parent company of local tour operator Arrowsmith, sent in one of their new Airbus A.300s, G-BIMA. It departed to Palma the following morning on the first of two demonstration flights, for the benefit of travel agents and various management staff. Amongst the passengers were Arrowsmith's Commercial Manager, the Chairman of the Airport Authority and Manchester Airport's Director, Mr Gordon Sweetapple. The aircraft returned later in the evening and operated a second flight on the 15th.

15th The airport was closed from 0830 to 0930 today, for extensive de-icing of the main runway.

16th Orion Airways latest B.737 made its first visit to Manchester today, when G-BHVG arrived from East Midlands as KG913F.

17th Swissair DC-9-32 HB-IFO made its final visit to Manchester today, operating SR842/3. It was sold this March to Texas International as N534TX.

18th Royal Saudi Air Force C-130H 1619 went tech on arrival at 1539 today (RSF901 from Milan), before finally departing on the 24th after an engine change.

20th A mass meeting of 300 British Airways engineers, maintenance men and ground staff was held last night, to discuss a pay claim made by their Heathrow counterparts and whether to support their 24-hour strike on the 23rd January. However, it was announced today that Manchester's workers had rejected the proposal and refused to support the strike.

20th Irish airline Clyden Airways have ceased trading and last evening's flight, operated by DC-3 EI-BDU, proved to be their final one. The mail flights between Manchester-Dublin, which they've operated since September 1978, have been taken over by Eastern Airways DC-3s. The first today was operated by G-AMYJ and G-AMPO was also used during the month. Both of Clyden Airways DC-3s were sold. EI-BDT reverted to its original registration of G-AMPZ and EI-BDU was bought by Aces High of Duxford as G-AKNB, after a long period in storage.

21st Swiss biz-jets are not particularly common to Manchester, but this month saw three different examples, all Lear Jets. HB-VGH arrived today in a particularly striking all-red colour scheme, with white stripes along the fuselage, HB-VFZ (7th) and HB-VGC (14th/29th/30th) which was a first visit.

22nd Transamerica DC-8 N870TV positioned in at 0456 today, operating as TV870 from Riyadh. It was transporting various animals, ultimately bound for New Zealand and Australia. The aircraft, chartered by a Chorley-based company specialising in the import and export of livestock, was nick-named the 'Noah's Ark' by airport staff. The inventory consisted of eighty-five dogs, thirteen cats, eight heifers, six horses, two bulls and two rabbits. They were mostly pets, on their way to their owners who'd already emigrated to Australasia. The rest were racing/hunting horses and pedigree cattle for breeding purposes. Servisair staff and an Australian veterinary official worked all night, making sure the animals were well enough to make the 13,000 mile, 42-hour journey. As an example of price, the average fare for a dog is £500. The quarantine time is one month for the New Zealand bound animals and ninety days for those travelling to Australia. The DC-8 eventually left at 2100, routing Edmonton-Los Angeles-Honolulu-Fiji, before reaching its unloading points in Auckland, Sydney & Adelaide.

22nd RAE BAe.748 XW750 called in for fuel today (Nugget 89), en route to Brize Norton.

22nd A new biz-jet type making its first visit to Manchester was the Falcon 50, when PH-ILR arrived at 0916 today. Owned by the electrical company Philips, who have a factory in Bramhall, Stockport, it operated from/to Eindhoven where the company is based.
22nd Royal Saudi Air Force C-130H 1615 arrived from Milan today (RSF802), with a spare engine for C-130H 1619, which hadn't moved since its arrival on the 18th.
23rd A 24-hour strike by British Airways ground staff at Heathrow starting this morning, affected their Manchester-Heathrow service, but all other Manchester flights continued as usual.
25th Aztec PA-23 G-FOTO, a specialist aircraft fitted out for air photography, arrived to undertake photographic work at BAe Woodford today.
26th Rockwell 690 OO-MRU brought in a party of Federal Aviation Authority officials from Frankfurt today, to carry out an airfield inspection.
26th British Airways started using an alpha-numeric call-sign system for the first time, seven years after last experimenting with it, only this time it proved to be more permanent. Today's flights began with Trident 3 G-AWZG operating the outbound Shuttle-flight (BA4403) as Shuttle R3S, departing at 0731. The first inbound flight under the new system was Trident 3 G-AWZA operating Shuttle M2N (BA4402), arriving at 0834. Although it was slow to catch on initially, it would eventually be adopted on a wider scale throughout the industry, particularly during the 1990's, when a seemingly random sequence of numbers and/or letters were used, specially designed to avoid confusion with similar sounding flight-numbers.
27th A particularly murky evening saw the arrival of two Heathrow diversions, starting with the first visit to Manchester of an Air Malta B.737, when PH-TVE appeared at 2001 (KM104 from Malta). The airline has leased three Boeing 737s from Transavia, until their recently ordered aircraft are delivered. The second was British Airways B.707 G-AWHU at 2124 (BA178 from New York).
30th The grey and murky weather covering the UK for most of the week turned into dense fog today, especially in the South East, when Heathrow & Gatwick sent twenty-six diversions into Manchester. Of the seventeen arrivals between 0431 and 1345, all but five were wide-bodied. Up until 0830 the writer was tracking the arrivals on his radio, but due to the low cloud, none could be seen. After I'd been at work for a few hours, I telephoned my friend who worked at the airport to find out what I'd missed between 0900 and 1345. Up to this point the highlights were three first visits, with the first being Yemen Airways B.727 4W-ACH at 1317 (IY524/5), diverting in from Gatwick. It had arrived from Sanaa via Rome, but rather than waiting for a weather clearance at Gatwick, it departed back to Sanaa via Rome again. Alitalia A300 I-BUSB at 1344 (AZ282 from Rome) was the second first visit and the third was Pan American B.747 N740PA at 0906 (PA002 from New York). Other notables were the second visit of a Kuwait Airways B.747 to Manchester, with the arrival of 9K-ADB at 0855 (KU102 from New York), but unfortunately this aircraft had visited previously on 10th November 1978. Air Portugal made a rare diversion visit when B707 CS-TBE arrived at 1242 (TP450 from Lisbon). The airport went quiet for more than two hours before the diversions started up again and the first of the next batch was British Airways B.747 G-AWNE arriving at 1616, which had already diverted into Manchester during the morning (BA072 from Toronto). It had attempted a return to Heathrow during the afternoon, only to be thwarted when their visibility fell below its landing limits again. Only nine more diversions arrived between then and 2102, mainly due to facilities being overstretched. The record for the highest number of wide-bodied aircraft on the ground at Manchester at the same time was broken today, from eleven to twelve. By the time I got back from work, the cloud had lifted

sufficiently enough to see the arrivals. British Airtours B.707 G-APFJ made its final visit to Manchester at 1706, arriving as KT102P from Frankfurt and the others included LOT TU-134 SP-LHA at 1713 (LO281 from Warsaw), Gulf Air L.1011 A40-TX at 1717 (GF017 from Bahrain), the first visit of a Nigeria Airways DC-10 with 5N-ANN at 1853 (WT800 from Kano) and finally Concorde G-BOAD, making its fourth visit at 1905 (BA194 from New York). The last two aircraft could be heard on Approach 119.4 at the same time, landing within ten minutes of each other. By the time the last two aircraft had landed, Gatwick was no longer accepting traffic and Heathrow was only accepting Category 3 equipped aircraft. Manchester could have handled so many more, but was unable to for several reasons, including the fact that as it is now officially a CAT 3 airport, the availability of parking stands for diverted aircraft has been greatly reduced, due to the introduction of new procedures safeguarding the movements of aircraft on the ground during periods of low visibility. Another reason was the apron construction work on the Western Side, which took Stand 27 at the end of Pier C out of use, a situation which also applied to the end of Pier A. Remote parking areas such as the South Bay are at present being taken up with aircraft staying overnight. Last night alone there were twenty-three. Access to the apron in front of Dan-Air and Fairey is also restricted, due to the construction of the new apron, which will be fully available in November and provide parking for up to six B.747s.

30th Aviaco DC-9 EC-CGQ, operating AO1626/7 from/to Malaga today, displayed a badge proclaiming it as 'The Official Carrier for the World Cup 1982'.

30th Amongst today's diversions was Boeing 737 F-GCGR, en route to Shannon. Now owned by TAAG of Angola, it arrived in their colours after a recent repaint at Lasham. Prior to this, it was operated by the French airline, Aerotour, until they ceased trading on the 5th November 1980.

31st The South East was still affected by fog during the morning, but Manchester was unable to accept any more diversions for the reasons given yesterday, except for British Airtours B.737 G-BGJG (KT457 from Faro) arriving just after midnight. Two that ended up diverting to Prestwick were Sudan B.707 ST-AFB (SD128 from Rome) and Zambia Airways B.707 9J-AEL (QZ704 from Lusaka). As the South East fog began to clear, yesterdays diversions started leaving for Heathrow or Gatwick in the afternoon, but Birmingham was affected all day and Liverpool from the early evening.

February 1981

A new freight centre at the airport, with a throughput capacity of 250,000 tonnes per year, could be operational within five years. The plans, to be presented to the Airport Committee, are broadly in line with a consultant's report prepared in 1973. The new centre, which could be built with private funds, is aimed at stemming the decline in cargo over recent years. The drop in freight from 46,000 tonnes in 1974, to 25,000 last year, was mainly due to the night-time closures for the runway work completed last August. Currently more than 16,000 tonnes of cargo are being collected from Manchester each year, then roaded to Heathrow for onward transport by air.

The Airport Authority wants detailed engineering studies to be carried out on the proposed rail-link between the airport and Manchester City Centre. They have urged Greater Manchester Council to apply to the Government and the EEC for the funds to finance it. Following a recent technical study concluding the line may not be viable, British Rail have floated the idea of a loop from the main Manchester to London line. It's hoped local MP's will form part of the delegation due to present itself to the Department of Transport, to argue the case for the rail-link. In support of the plan, they will refer to the airport's continuing expansion and the fact that Manchester has been designated as the major British airport outside of London.

British Airways announced 110,000 passengers had flown the Manchester-London route in the last three months, an 8% increase on last year. Their Northern Division Manager said contributing factors were the use of Tridents being able to land in thick fog and the lack of serious weather problems. The gentleman making these comments was destined to become the new Airport Director!

British Airways sold two Boeing 747s to TWA during the month, when G-AWNI became N17125 & G-AWNK became N17126. G-AWNI last visited Manchester on 15th October 1979 (BA278) & G-AWNK on 28th September 1980 (BA032), both as diversions.

Air UK withdrew a number of Heralds from service last November and stored them at Norwich. Their last visits to Manchester were G-APWH 06/09/80 (scrapped 04/82), G-ASBG 02/07/80 (scrapped 09/84) and G-AVEZ 05/09/80.

Equipment changes on scheduled services included Austrian Airlines (OS471): DC-9-51 OE-LDO (15th) & MD-81 OE-LDS (12th) and LOT (LO287): IL-18 SP-LSF (26th).

RAF ILS traffic identified included RAF Hawk XX223 (23rd), C-130 XV306 (12th) & Jaguar XX841 (20th). The only civil ILS traffic was Dove G-AREA (11th). Lossiemouth-based RAF Jaguar XX841 showed up for a practice overshoot (20th), which was a change from the usual Coltishall examples and two unidentified RAF Hawks arrived in formation (26th).

1st Laker Airways BAC 1-11 G-AVBX was brought out of storage during the morning to operate flight GK305 to Palma, but after departing at 0823, it declared an emergency and returned after shutting down one engine. Co-incidentally another Laker Airways BAC 1-11, G-AVBW, which also arrived this morning for storage, taking the place of the resurrected G-AVBX, was immediately pressed into service to operate the delayed flight. As soon as it arrived back at 1919 (GK306 from Palma), it was towed back to keep the two B.707s company again, while the broken BAC 1-11, G-AVBX, was ferried to Gatwick later that afternoon as GK099P. Another one of their BAC 1-11s, G-ATPK, has recently been sold.

1st With the exception of Saturdays, Eastern Airways continued with their nightly mail flights during the month, operated exclusively by DC-3 G-AMYJ.

2nd British Airways recently acquired an all-cargo B.747, G-KILO, which made its only visit today, diverting in at 0713 due to strong winds at Prestwick. Manchester was its elected alternate, as Heathrow's weather was also marginal. Delivered in September 1980, it served with the airline for less than two years, before being sold to Cathay Pacific in March 1982.

4th Manchester was hit by a 24-hour strike, when 900 manual workers walked out at 1800 today. The dispute over back-pay had been brewing for several days, since semi-skilled engineers started a work-to-rule and overtime ban ten days ago. Seventy work-shop employees had staged a one-day stoppage, which didn't affect flights, but when the union discovered the management had carried out some of the work, the jobs were then blacked. The airport became a huge bus and coach terminus, where hundreds of passengers were transferred to other airports such as Birmingham, Liverpool & Leeds to catch their flights.

5th Flights resumed this evening after the 24-hour strike. The first arrival was British Airways BAC 1-11 G-BBMG at 1757 (BA9710P), positioning in from Birmingham.

6th Brussels based Beech 200 N84MD, operated by McDermott Drilling, made a lunchtime visit to Manchester before departing at 1707 today.

9th Air Ecosse has commenced two late evening flights as part of the Post Office Datapost service. WG917 & WG919, both operated by EMB-110 Bandeirantes, will operate Monday-Friday to Stansted, returning in the early hours.

12th The McDonnell Douglas MD-80, which claims to be the world's quietest airliner, made its first appearance at Manchester this evening, with the arrival of Austrian Airlines OE-LDS. It was operating Vienna flight OS471/2, which was technically for demonstration purposes. The MD80 is a new stretched version of the DC-9 family and although the type won't be regularly used on the service, it could be an occasional aircraft substitution. The current type on the route is the DC-9-32, capable of carrying 97 passengers, while the MD-80 carries up to 135.

12th Queens Flight BAe.748 XS789, arriving at 2336 today from Nice, had the Duke of Edinburgh onboard. The aircraft departed the following afternoon to Luxembourg, again with Prince Philip.

15th Royal Saudi AF KC-130H 459 arriving at 0844 today was returning from the Lockheed factory at Marietta, Georgia, after modification work.

17th A cold and cloudy morning saw the arrival of four Heathrow diversions. One from Lufthansa was B.727 D-ABKT at 0913 (LH040 from Hamburg) and three from British Airways were B.747s G-BBPU at 0930 (BA072 from Toronto) & G-BDXG at 0740 (BA054 from Nairobi) and B.707F G-ASZG at 0738 (BA3602 from Abu Dhabi).

18th Air Languedoc EMB-110 F-GBMF arrived at 1539 today from Birmingham, with the French Rugby League team for their match with England at Leeds on the 21st.

19th The second Saudi AF KC-130H this month was 1620, arriving at 0820 today on its delivery flight routing from Marietta, Georgia, via Dobbins AFB to Jeddah, before its departure on the 21st.

22nd Cold winds and grey days have been the norm this month and today was no exception. Due to the Midlands being affected by snow all day, Falcon 10 N90DM diverted in from Birmingham during the morning and six more arrived in the afternoon, amongst which were Air Portugal B.707 CS-TBF at 1303 (TP8451 from Faro), Aviaco DC-9 EC-CGO at 1437 (AO1088 from Palma) and Transeuropa SE.210 EC.BIB at 1712 (TR116 from Palma). Another batch of diversions arriving in the evening were British, apart from PA-31 OE-FSK from Brussels, after being unable to land at East Midlands.

23rd Due to the unavailability of fuel at Dublin, Mooney D-ECMF arrived from there at 1521 today to upload fuel, before continuing onwards to Amsterdam.

25th Over the past eighteen months Lufthansa have been gradually disposing of their early B.737-100 series, although they still make the occasional appearance on Frankfurt flight LH074/5. This service is mainly operated by their B.737-200QC aircraft (QC-Quick Change), as they are quickly converted from passenger to cargo configuration, or vice versa. They have a quantity of B.737-200s on order and the first of these appeared today, when D-ABFS operated LH074/5 on a rare day when the operational runway was 24, which made a pleasant change from the constant easterly winds during the month!

25th Gulfstream 1 N720G arrived at 1758 today from Glasgow, for overnight attention with Dan-Air Engineering.

26th Transamerica N870TV, which arrived from Edmonton at 0722 today on a cattle charter, night-stopped before positioning out to Luxembourg in the early hours.

26th Lear Jet 25 I-DEAN made its only visit to Manchester today, night-stopping whilst on delivery routing Reykjavik-Rome.

27th Aurigny Airlines made their first visit to Manchester today, when Twin Otter G-BFGP brought Southampton FC in for the next day's Division One match against Liverpool. The aircraft night-stopped, before positioning over to Liverpool the following day at 1452 in preparation to return the team home after the match, which they lost 2-0.
27th Laker's second A300, G-BIMB, performed a fly-past of the Tower today before landing, after positioning up from Gatwick prior to being based at Manchester. But ironically, its first service was a flight on behalf of Dan-Air, DA1202/3 to/from Milan.

March 1981

Work on extending Manchester's main runway length from 9,200ft to 10,000ft, which will start on the 16th and be completed by December 1982, is not expected to disrupt everyday operations. The extension means that aircraft previously carrying weight penalties will be able to increase their payload by 10,000 kilos, or carry extra fuel for a further 500-mile range.

Applications have been flooding in for one of Britain's most prestigious airport positions, the job of Manchester Airport Director. Several industrialists are willing to take a pay cut for the £25,000 a year post, attracting candidates from as far afield as the Middle East and America. It's understood that forty-four names will be selected for initial consideration, before being cut down to twelve, then short-listed to six. The position becomes vacant in June, following the resignation of Gordon Sweetapple, the Airport's Director since 1974, who joined Manchester from Liverpool Airport in 1969 as Deputy Director.

Saudi Air Force KC-130H 1621 was due through Manchester on delivery today, but after sustaining tail damage en route, it was forced to divert to Shannon before flying onto Cambridge for repairs.

Air France is withdrawing the SE.210 Caravelle from its Manchester-Paris service this month, after operating the route almost interruptedly since 1961. To mark the end of the aircrafts service, Cresta Travel is offering a £150 'Champagne-Farewell-Weekend' to Paris, flying out on the final departure on the 27th. The trip includes return flights, a champagne dinner, accommodation at the deluxe Meridien Hotel in central Paris, a half-day sightseeing tour and a gourmet dinner on the River Seine. The Boeing 727, which takes over the route from the 29th, will increase capacity from 86 to 160 seats. Interesting facts about the Caravelle are as follows:

(a) Air France put the SE.210 Caravelle into service on the 6th May 1959, operating from Paris to Istanbul. Since then it's flown 1,419,766 hours, over 84,181,750 passenger miles and carried more than 48m passengers.

(b) On the 22nd May 1964, the actor Roger Moore was the 8-millionth passenger to fly on an Air France SE.210 Caravelle.

(c) On the 21st August 1964, SE.210 F-BHRX created a new record for a commercial flight by flying London Gatwick-Paris Orly, in just 33-minutes.

Equipment changes on scheduled services included Aer Lingus (EI9216): B.707F EI-ANO (4th); Sabena (SN617): Sobelair B.737 OO-SBT (6th) and SAS (SK539): DC-9-21OY-KGF (3rd).

ILS traffic went berserk this month, producing lots of movements and variety. Military traffic identified mainly involved RAF aircraft: Hawks XX241 (31st), XX242 (17th) & XX295 (19th); C-130s XV197 (3rd), XV202 (3rd) & XV211 (10th); Dominie XS712 (17th); Jaguars XX139 from Lossiemouth (17th) & XX842 from Coltishall (25th); Bulldog XX636 (8th) plus RAE Andover's XS641 (27th) & XS643 (26th/27th/30th) and Royal Navy Jetstream XX482 (4th).

Civil ILS traffic noted included BAe.748 G-11-5 (12th), DLT BAe.748 D-AHSA (14th) & Corvette F-BVPK (25th). Three BAe 748s appeared on test flights from Woodford from the 12th-16th, but the only one of interest was D-AHSA, which will be the first aircraft for German operator DLT. RAF C-130s XV197 & XV202 were of the stretched variety and RAF Bulldog XX686 appeared over from Woodvale. RAE Andover XS643 made numerous visits from the 26th-30th, supplemented by XS641 (27th). RAF Hawks were plentiful, but mainly unidentified and there were also various Cessna's from the Lancashire Aero Club.

2nd Lear Jet D-CEPD made its first visit, arriving at 1735 today from Oran, Algeria, on an ambulance flight. Lear Jet F-GCLE, which was also from Oran, operated a further hospital flight the following day.

3rd Corvette SE-DED was also a hospital flight, arriving from Graz, Vienna, before departing to Vasteras at 1116 the following morning.

4th An Air Canada DC-8 was due into Manchester today on a livestock charter, with a valuable load of Canadian Holstein & Hereford cows and bulls, destined for breeding farms as far afield as Aberdeen and Leicester; but British Airways advised they wouldn't be able to clean the aircraft. The unions said the flight couldn't be handled at Manchester, after the trouble caused by the airline arranging for the jet to be cleaned by a specialised cleaning firm, rather than the airport's in-house company. In the end the flight was cancelled and operated through Prestwick instead.

4th This evenings Aer Lingus mail/freight flight EI9216/7, operated by Boeing 707 EI-ANO, was the penultimate visit of an Aer Lingus B.707 to Manchester. It's been seventeen years since the first one, EI-AMW, arrived in August 1964.

5th Loganair Twin Otter G-BGPC made its first visit to Manchester today, positioning in to operate an outbound charter to Enniskillen the next morning. It returned the following evening with a second Loganair Twin Otter, G-RBLA, which were both inbound from Enniskillen.

5th Beech 200 G-IPRA, arriving from Alicante today, was on another medical flight. It was carrying a patient with suspected Legionnaires Disease, who unfortunately died prior to touchdown at Manchester.

5th This evenings Air UK Isle of Man flight (UK564/5) was operated by F.27 G-BHMW. The type has now replaced Heralds on their twice-daily flights.

9th ATC services were withdrawn at most UK Airports, including Manchester today, as part of an ongoing civil service dispute with the Government. The airport was closed all day and the only arrival was Britannia Airways G-AZNZ at 2210, positioning in from East Midlands. The strike, involving 500,000 civil servants, is over the Government's refusal to increase their 7% offer, as the unions want 15%. In addition to the shortage of ATC staff, the strike was also supported by CAA workers, including Customs & Immigration staff, switchboard operators and weathermen throughout the country.

10th The only Heathrow diversion this month was Finnair DC-9-51 OH-LYW at 1115 today (AY831 from Helsinki), arriving at Manchester due to the ATC delays.

11th British Airways used B.737 G-BGDO on this evening's Aberdeen flight, BA5699.

12th Sabena continue to operate their antique Cessna 310s for crew training purposes. OO-SEB appeared today and OO-SEG on the 16th, both from/to Brussels. These aircraft were sold soon afterwards by the airline and were replaced by a number of Embracer EMB-121 Xingu's.

13th After an absence of ten years, the skies over the UK will reverberate to the sound of the radial engines from a Bristol 170 Wayfarer! ZK-EPH arrived at Stansted today, after undertaking an 87-hour ferry flight from Australia. Purchased by Instone Air Line, the aircraft will eventually become G-BISU, available for general and ad-hoc freight charters. In an overall grey colour scheme, with a blue cheatline and red sea horse logo on the tail, it's titles are carried under the wing on the lower fuselage.

14th A strike by a hundred Dan-Air maintenance and engineering workers over a six-month pay freeze, has been made official by their unions. The engineers, who are members of the Amalgamated Union of Engineering Workers and the Electricians & Plumbers Unions, say their pay is well behind the rates paid to similar workers in the North West. So far, flights have been unaffected by the strike which started on the 6th, but the action could be stepped up if the airline fails to negotiate.

16th French Air Force Noratlas 179/64-BP, arriving at 1101 today as FM0403, was on a training flight from Brize Norton to Bournemouth.

16th The only Sabreliner visit last year was N30IMC and today, exactly a year to the day, it arrived at Manchester again operating a flight from Heathrow to Gothenburg.

19th The two-week strike by Dan-Air maintenance men employed at Manchester was stepped up today, by the walkout of sixty more semi-skilled workers. This particular action was taken to make the management and the union negotiate a settlement.

20th BAF Herald G-BEYF arrived during the afternoon (VF1532 from Southend), with Ipswich Town FC for tomorrow's game with Manchester Utd. The match ended in victory for the home team 2-0 and the aircraft departed the following evening at 1858 as VF1533. Incidentally, it was carrying 'Occidental of Libya Inc' titles on the fuselage.

21st March 1981 – British Airways Trident 1 G-ARPR made its final visit to Manchester today, operating a back-up Shuttle flight. It was withdrawn later in the month, as were several others during the year. On 10th June 1965, this aircraft made the world's first fully automatic landing of a commercial airliner carrying fare-paying passengers, operating Paris-London flight BE343. (Manchester Airport Archive)

20th Cessna 425 G-BJET made a first visit of type today, arriving from Leeds. Currently owned by Gatwick Air Taxis, it was the first Cessna 425 on the UK register.

20th The inaugural Laker Skytrain service to Los Angeles, operated today by DC-10 G-BGXG (GK045), returned the next day as GK046. This followed the previous night's celebrity launch held at the Golden Garter, Wythenshawe, where copious amounts of food and alcoholic beverages were consumed. More than 1,000 travel agents were invited, including the writer, who was a travel agent at the time. The star-turn was the comedian Mike Yarwood, who apologised for not being able to impersonate Sir Freddie Laker; just before the man himself made a grand entrance onto the stage riding a bicycle! To add extra glamour to the occasion Laker's associate company, Arrowsmith Holidays, had flown 600 orchids in from Madeira for especially for the event. Sir Freddie had previously stated that bookings for the Manchester-Los Angeles Skytrain flights were high enough for him to consider increasing the frequency from the initial once-weekly operation.

22nd Prince Charles was the pilot of Queens Flight BAe.748 XS790, arriving at 1705 today from Aberdeen, for a quick stop before continuing to RAF Benson.

23rd The dispute involving Dan-Air engineers took a further step backwards, with no resolution in sight. From today, the action caused the rerouting through Liverpool of the Datapost and Eastern Airways mail flights. GPO personnel wouldn't cross the picket line and although the flights resumed on the 30th, the dispute wasn't resolved until the 6th April.

24th Royal Saudi AF KC-130H 458 passed through Manchester today, en route Milan-Gander (RSF146) and stayed until the 26th, on its first visit since 4th February 1975.

25th Another rare executive type, the Morane-Saulnier MS.760 Paris, made an appearance this evening, when early production F-BLKL arrived from Toulouse. It stayed overnight and departed for St. Nazaire the following morning.

26th The inaugural Laker Skytrain service to New York from Manchester was operated by DC-10 G-AZZC today (GK021), before returning the following day as GK022. Frequencies will be increased during the summer, to up to three flights weekly.

27th Air France F-BOHA operated the final SE.210 Caravelle service today, on Manchester-Paris flight AF964/1, as they are being removed from the airlines service. They have used the type since the 1st June 1961, when F-BHRD inaugurated the new Manchester service. The remaining aircraft making it into the 1980's were withdrawn by April 1981 and made their last visits to Manchester as follows:

F-BHRF 10/03/81, F-BHRH 12/02/81, F-BHRI 19/03/81, F-BHRY 26/03/81, F-BJTE 16/03/81, F-BJTL 24/03/81, F-BJTP 27/02/81, & F-BOHA 27/03/81.

30th Frankfurt-based FAA run-around Rockwell 690 OO-MRU arriving at Manchester this morning, had its visit cut short when the passengers made a hasty retreat to Luton, to investigate the recent crash-landing accident of Jetstar N267L.

30th British Airways G-ASGL operated a SVC-10 charter from Heathrow today, as 'Speedbird 9050', as part of a 'SVC-10 Farewell-tour', organised by Gold Star Travel. They were booked-up weeks in advance and special arrangements were made for checking-in. Passengers reported to a conference room on the 9th floor of a British Airways building in the maintenance area, where they were ticketed and served refreshments, before being transported by bus to the SVC-10 hangar for boarding. The aircraft was towed to the runway, past the British Airways brass band, before taking off at 12.30. It made a low pass over the Rolls-Royce factories at Derby where the engines were built, before heading for Manchester to perform an ILS approach at 1325 and flying to Prestwick to perform another ILS. Whilst cruising down the Irish Sea, the passengers enjoyed a champagne lunch, before dipping over Bristol-Filton and Farnborough and landing back at Heathrow.

April 1981

British Airways reduced their Manchester-London service from eight to seven daily flights in each direction, as the loss of a daily rotation was offset by the increased use of the larger Trident 3, rather than the 99-seat BAC Super 1-11. From this month, the flights being dropped are the inbound BA4482 at 1640 and the outbound BA4523 at 1920.

British Airways had retired their final SVC-10s from service by the end of last month. It's thought that apart from G-ASGC, all fourteen would be sold to Lansa of Honduras based at Miami, operators of charters to the Caribbean and South America, but after the deal fell through they were sold to the RAF, mainly for spares. The SVC-10 served BOAC and later British Airways, for 17 years. The type's flown 562m miles and carried more than 13m passengers without a fatality, although two aircraft were lost along the way. G-ASGN was blown up by hijackers on 6th September 1970 and G-ASGO was destroyed in a hi-jacking at Amsterdam on 3rd April 1974. A complete listing of the SVC-10s last visits, final flights and fates are detailed below:

G-ASGA 05/08/80, final revenue flight 03/81
G-ASGB 04/12/79, final revenue flight (Beirut-LHR) 02/10/80
G-ASGC 11/10/79, sold to Duxford Air Museum 04/80
G-ASGD 12/02/80, final revenue flight (Amsterdam-Heathrow) 25/03/80
G-ASGE 04/03/80, final revenue flight 04/80
G-ASGF 11/12/79, op. very last SVC-10 scheduled flight (BA064 Larnaca-LHR) 29/03/81
G-ASGG 02/09/79, final revenue flight (Gutersloh-LHR) 26/09/80
G-ASGH 26/02/80, final revenue flight 03/80
G-ASGI 26/02/80, final revenue flight (Amman-LHR) 30/03/80
G-ASGJ 18/03/80, final revenue flight (Cairo-LHR) 31/03/80
G-ASGK 26/09/80, final revenue flight 03/81
G-ASGL (30/03/81), final flight 30/03/81
G-ASGM 23/10/79, final revenue flight 04/80
G-ASGP 08/01/80, final revenue flight (Cairo-LHR) 29/09/80
G-ASGR 01/04/80, final flight 04/80

Airlines making changes to their summer schedules were Air France operating Paris flight AF964/1 six-weekly with B.727s and Air Malta operating twice-weekly during the summer, in addition to numerous charter flights. British Airways reintroduced schedules to Malta twice-weekly and Nice once-weekly, New York is once-weekly with B.707s via Prestwick (BA184/5), Toronto twice-weekly with B.747s (BA082/3) supplemented between 24/06-11/09 with a further twice-weekly B.707 flight via Prestwick (BA082/3). Brymon Airways recommenced a once-weekly schedule to Newquay, Cyprus Airways will operate twice-weekly to Larnaca during the summer and Guernsey Airlines to operate up to six-weekly flights. Laker Airways will operate Skytrain flights to Los Angeles twice-weekly and four-weekly to Miami and New York. SAS will operate the Copenhagen passenger flight six-weekly, proceeding onwards to/from Dublin on three of the flights, with cargo flights being operated by Fred Olsen Electra's from May. Finally, Swissair are introducing the Douglas DC-9-51 on passenger flight SR842/3 from June.

A £1.6m scheme to extend the eastern wing of the Booking Hall has been approved by the Manchester City Finance Committee. Manchester City Council also gave the go-ahead for a badly-needed 170-room hotel at the airport, but engineers employed by the same body blocked the proposal due to some access problems. The main stumbling block to the proposed site, close to the main terminal on Outwood Road, is the link-road crossing the route of the proposed southern section of the Manchester outer ring road. Manchester City Council, who will make the final decision, have been told to withhold permission until a study on alternative road schemes is completed.

Equipment changes on scheduled services included Austrian Airlines (OS471): DC-9-51 OE-LDL (23rd) and Lufthansa (LH074): B.727 D-ABKM (1st).

RAF ILS traffic identified included Hawk XX241 (2nd); C-130s XV184 (8th), XV205 (15th) & XV307 (1st); Dominie XS730 (7th) and Jaguars XX139 & XX832 (9th). Civil ILS traffic noted included BAe.125s G-ASNU (3rd) & G-5-13 (14th); Corvettes F-BVPK (6th/9th) & F-BVPT (10th); Dove G-ARHW (15th) and British Air Ferries Herald G-BEYG (15th). The month saw plenty of ILS traffic up until the 15th, but there was nothing after that. The two RAF Jaguars, en route from Laarbruch in Germany to Lossiemouth, performed practice diversions with BAe.125 G-5-13, observed in primer (9th).

April 1981 - Guernsey Airlines started operations from Manchester in April 1980, with Viscounts. Although they continued to use the type, this year they also took delivery of two Shorts SD-330s, G-BITV & G-BITX, which is pictured above. (Geoff Ball)

1st Alkair EMB-110 OY-ASY arrived at 1923 today from East Midlands, to operate an outbound Ford charter to Cologne.

2nd Early morning fog produced British Caledonian B.707 G-BDLM (BR358 from Banjul), diverting into Manchester from Gatwick at 0828.

2nd Light aircraft operators Executive Express have been operating morning weekday flights on behalf of Orion Airways, rotating their crews from/to East Midlands.

2nd A much publicised event took place today, when ALIA B.747 JY-AFB made its first visit to Manchester, diverting in at 1821 with 368 passengers and 14 crew. It was over the East Coast operating RJ261, routing Amman-Amsterdam-New York, when a note was handed to a member of the cabin crew saying there was a bomb onboard. The Captain decided to divert to Manchester, after dumping over 4,000 gallons of fuel. Upon landing, he parked outside the fire station, where the aircraft was evacuated and searched. Once the all-clear was given five hours later, the flight continued onto New York, minus a seventeen year old American male passenger! The student, who later admitted to planting the bomb hoax note, was part of a group from the Church of God Christian School in Virginia, who'd been touring religious sites in the Middle East. He and several others had been drinking and he claimed their game of writing notes had simply got out of hand. He was tried by Manchester Magistrates and convicted to three months in prison, but this became a temporary measure after the case was transferred to Manchester Crown Court, where the sentence was increased to six months. Under British law a minor can only be imprisoned for special reasons and it was decided these were exceptional circumstances!

3rd RAE Andover XW750 performed several touch-and-goes during the morning, on a training flight from/to Bedford, despite the visibility being a mere 200m.

3rd Aviaco recently acquired DC-9 EC-BIP from Iberia, which made its first visit as such this evening, operating AO1079 to Palma.

3rd Cessna 425 G-BJET, arriving from/to Gatwick today, was operated by Gatwick Air Taxis. It's owned by Davyhulme MP, Winston Churchill, who regularly flies it himself.

4th Laker Airways BAC 1-11 G-AVBW left for Gatwick today, after spending equal time between storage and operational duties since 1st February. From this month, the airline will cease using BAC 1-11s from Manchester, in favour of Airbus A300 & DC-10 aircraft, which will be used on this year's summer programme.

5th The dispute by Dan-Air engineers ended this evening, after pressure from airport hands, saying they would black Dan-Air flights from tomorrow unless a solution was found. A mass meeting of 200 maintenance men accepted Dan Air's improved offer of a pay freeze until July rather than September, followed by a 5% pay increase.

5th British Airways introduced the concept of Club Class on their European flights, after phasing out First Class and Economy. Passengers now have the choice of Tourist or Club Class. The new Club Class offers the same benefits as the old First Class service, at a slightly higher cost than the old Economy fare and the Tourist Class offers a no-frills budget flight.

5th Swissair DC-9-32 HB-IFP made its final visit to Manchester today, operating SR842/3 before being sold later in the month to Texas International as N535TX.

6th Transavia B.737 PH-TVR, arriving at 0835 today (HV9993 from Amsterdam), is on lease to Britannia Airways. Its first service was to Heraklion as BY445A and it was present at Manchester almost daily until the 2nd May.

6th All flights between Manchester-Belfast were grounded today, after a walkout by 200 ground staff at Belfast Airport.

6th Following today's return to work by Dan-Air engineers, the first aircraft arriving for attention was BAe.748 G-ATMJ the following day.

6th The Shorts Skyvan type was never a regular visitor to Manchester, but Shorts company liaison aircraft G-ASZJ, which was built in 1964, arrived this afternoon from/to Belfast Harbour as 'Short 4'.

6th LOT'S Monday Warsaw flight, LO287/8, was cancelled today and for the rest of the month, so Heathrow flight LO281/2 operated via Manchester with IL-62s. The first was operated by SP-LBC today and the 13th, the flight on the 20th was cancelled and the following week's flight was operated by SP-LBD. Manchester's Friday flight, LO287/8, continued as normal.

8th Three months after its last visit, Iscargo Electra TF-ISC arrived at 2221 today (KJ821 from Reykjavik), transporting more fish bound for Fleetwood docks.

9th This month's Canadian Air Force CC-130Es were 130317 (CAM515-today) and 130314 (CAM516-11th). The customary third, CAM517, should have operated on the 13th, but it was cancelled due to technical problems.

9th Overnight fog caused practically the whole of Liverpool's postal operation to divert into Manchester this evening and overnight. Flights involved were three Air Ecosse, four Dan-Air, two Euroair and one each from Air Bridge Carriers, Air Atlantique & Express Air Services.

10th The four month search for a new Airport Director came to an end today, when Manchester Airport appointed a man literally from under their noses! The new Director, Gil Thompson, is currently North of England Manager for British Airways. His office on the 6th floor of the Airport Control Tower is directly under the 7th floor office he will move into on the 1st June, taking over from Gordon Sweetapple, who is joining an aviation consultancy firm. Mr Thompson, who lives in Bowdon, has been an airline man since 1950, when he joined BEA at Belfast Airport. Of all the developments planned for Manchester Airport, he sees the projected direct rail-link as the most important.

10th PA-23 Vecta Geronimo N4422P, a conversion of a standard PA-23 Apache, made the first of three visits this year, calling in at 1530 from Belfast before leaving for Cork.

11th Tomorrows Rugby League International between England and France was the reason today for two Air Languedoc aircraft, EMB-110 F-GBMF and Metro F-GCFE, from/to Toulouse.

12th Britannia Airways have also leased Air Belgium B.737 OO-ABB, which has been based at Gatwick. It positioned up this morning as BY579AF, to operate BY579A to Corfu.

13th Orion Airways B.737 G-BHVI made its first visit today, operating KG922/1 from/to Mahon. It was carrying an inscription proclaiming it was the '737th 737 to be built'!

14th French Air Force Transall 48/61-MT, arriving at 1132 today as FM0159, was on a training flight from Glasgow to Lyneham.

15th Beech 95 N72588, which was previously operated as SE-FNF, called in at 1326 today from Shannon, en route to Bremen. This aircraft was based at Manchester from 1964-1969, as G-ASZC and flown by local businessman Eric Raffles as 'Raffles 1'.

15th BAF Herald G-BEYG was operating VF1523 today, when it performed an ILS at Manchester, en route from Liverpool to Southend.

16th Laker Airways DC-10 G-GFAL was en route from New York to Manchester as GK026 today, when the pilot reported he may have damaged or lost a wheel on departure from New York. He considered the situation serious enough to re-route into Gatwick for immediate attention.

17th Cessna 182 G-GEAR, which is unique for having a retractable undercarriage rather than a fixed arrangement, arrived from Liverpool today, before departing for Bodmin.

20th Eastern Airways DC-3 G-AMYJ was operating the outbound mail flight to Dublin, when it returned to Manchester with engine trouble. It was under repair with NEA, parked up on the South Side until it left for Dublin on the 24th, during which time DC-3 G-ANAF operated the flight instead.

23rd British Air Ferries Herald G-BEYH made its first visit today, positioning in at 0807 from Southend, to operate an outbound flight to Hamburg as VF1562. It returned from Hamburg as VF1563 on the 25th.
23rd Sir Freddie Laker flew into Manchester today, to promote the airlines Skytrain service to New York. His £78 single walk-on fare is less than British Airways cheapest fare of £99. Laker Airways now run DC-10 services from Manchester to Miami four-weekly, Los Angeles two-weekly and New York will increase to four-weekly. He will also open his first travel agency outside of London next month, in Piccadilly Gardens, Manchester, called Laker North which is in direct competition with his other firm, Arrowsmith's.
24th Due to financial difficulties this year, Merlin Air Services sold BAe.125 G-AZVS back to its former operator Eastern Airways, which arrived this evening as EN4407 from Cologne.
25th Air UK F.27 G-BAUR brought Norwich City FC up for a Division One match with Manchester Utd (UK8611/2), which ended as a 1-0 victory for United. Another arrival in connection with the match was Vernair's new Beech 200, G-VRES.
27th British Airways B.737 G-BGDI arriving at 2050 today, was on its first visit operating BA5619 (Aberdeen-Heathrow), due to the cancellation of the Manchester-Aberdeen flight.
28th Dan-Air's last Viscount, G-BCZR, arrived at 0814 today for attention, prior to its delivery to Air Zimbabwe as VP-WGC. It departed for Harare on the 3rd May, via Bari.
29th Industrial action affected Manchester again today, this time between 0730 and 1400. Most of the ATC staff required for the early watch stayed away, but enough showed up to operate a limited service of around 70%.
30th Fast Air PA-31 PH-JGM arrived at 1239 today, to take a large piece of machinery to an industrial plant in Antwerp.

May 1981

There was further industrial action by ATC staff, which affected all UK airports, but some ATC staff at Manchester defied instructions and managed a restricted service during the following strike periods: 1400-2130 (7th), 1400-1730 & 2130-0730 (14th/22nd) & 1400-2130 (29th). The airport was shut down completely when there was no ATC cover at all between 1730-2130 (14th) & 2130-0730 (29th/30th), when most flights operated from Liverpool & Birmingham. The times of the action were altered at short notice, in order to maximise disruption and the month ended with no resolution in sight.

Merlin Air Services, an air charter company based at the airport, have gone into receivership with debts of £105,000. They blamed steep rises in fuel costs and the reduction in executive air travel for their predicament, but a phoenix did rise from the ashes when a new version of the company, Grosvenor Aviation Services, was established later in the month.

The following airlines have summer IT programmes from Manchester: Air Malta, Aviaco, Aviogenex, Balkan, EL AL, Inex-Adria, JAT, LOT, Nor-Fly, Spantax, Tarom, TAE, Trans-Europa & WDL; as do a variety of UK operators: Air Europe, Air UK, Britannia Airways, British Airtours, Dan-Air, Laker Airways, Monarch Airlines & Orion Airways. Airlines operating regular flights to the USA/Canada this summer are Air Florida (Miami), CP Air (Edmonton, Toronto & Vancouver), Transamerica (Los Angeles & New York) and Wardair (Calgary, Edmonton, Toronto, Vancouver & Winnipeg).

Equipment changes on scheduled services included Air France (AF964): B.747s N28366 (28th) & N28899 (26th); Air Portugal (TP458): B.707s CS-TBI (30th) & CS-TBT (23rd); Austrian Airlines (OS471): DC-9-51 OE-LDL (15th) & British Caledonian BAC 1-11

(3rd/8th/10th/15th/24th); KLM (KL155): DC-8 PH-DEG (13th); Lufthansa (LH074): B.727s D-ABKF (20th) & D-ABKQ (8th); SAS (SK539): DC-9-21 SE-DBP (26th) and Swissair (SR842): DC-9-51 HB-ISP (31st) & HB-IST (22nd).

RAF ILS traffic identified included Hawk XX305 (5th); C-130s XV177 (20th) & XV292 (1st); Jetstream XX498 (11th) and Mosquito RR299 (30th). ILS traffic was well down on the previous month, but there were still items of interest including the RAF Jetstream performing two ILS approaches in the morning and an unidentified F-4 Phantom overshooting at 2123 (19th). Morane-Saulnier MS.733 Alcyon G-SHOW and Boeing Stearman G-THEA were also seen in formation just after 1900 (30th).

1st Morning flights between Manchester-London were cancelled today, due to a half-day strike by Heathrow ATC. The stoppage, which also affected Gatwick and Stansted, was part of an ongoing series of walkouts in support of the civil servants pay claim. Five diversions made it to Manchester, but most other flights went to airports nearer Heathrow. The inbound crews of the two diverted British Airways B.747s, G-AWNE (BA012 from Dubai) & G-BDXD (BA054 from Nairobi), went out-of-hours on arrival and there were considerable delays returning the aircraft back to Heathrow, as new crews were needed to fly them back. TWA also diverted in two flights, B.747 N93108 at 0835 (TW770 from Chicago) & L.1011 N31019 at 0908 (TW708 from New York), which was the first visit of a TWA Tristar. The morning's diversions were rounded off by Kuwait Airways Boeing 747 9K-ADA (KU102 from New York).

1st Transavia B.737 PH-TVR, which has been based at Manchester throughout April, operated for the final time today. Arriving at 2337 (BY499B from Malaga) before positioning to Amsterdam the following evening, it was replaced by Eagle Air B.737 TF-VLK, which arrived from Luton on the 2nd as VL737 to operate the following day as BY579A to Corfu.

4th May 1981 – The highlight of the month was Korean B.747 HL-7452 operating as SV8364 from/to Jeddah. Delivered to Korean Airlines in June 1980, it was then leased to Saudia from February-June 1981 and is seen here operating a freight flight on behalf of Saudia, transporting more than 100,000 kilos of dried cement to Jeddah for the construction of a chimney. It should have been on the ground for two hours, but in the end it took eight hours to be loaded! A repeat flight was planned, but after today's chaotic events it was cancelled! This aircraft went on to serve Korean Airlines until 2004. (Geoff Ball)

2nd Due to a significant increase in bookings, Transamerica are operating a weekly Saturday flight from/to New York with a Douglas DC-8 and N4869T was used on today's first flight.

2nd Gulfstream 2 F-BRUY arrived from Heathrow at 1207 today, with the Aga Khan onboard for a race meeting at Haydock, before leaving for Paris-Le Bourget.

2nd Swissair DC-9-32 HB-IFS, operating SR842/3, was the first of six making their final visits to Manchester this month. It was sold to Texas International as N536TX the following month.

3rd Austrian Airlines are leasing BCAL BAC 1-11 G-AWYS, which made its first visit to Manchester today, operating OS471/2 in full BCAL colours with a large Austrian Airlines logo.

4th RAF C-130 XV203 (RR5606) arrived at 1257 today, operating a trooping flight from Gutersloh.

7th Although advance warnings were given of the latest ATC strike, due to take place between 0730-1400 today, the timings were changed last night to 1230-2230, but luckily it had a limited impact on flights.

10th PA-44 Seminole G-BGTF, operating from/to Coventry today, was on demonstration to various South Side operators.

11th McAlpine Aviation BAe.125 G-BSHL made its first visit to Manchester today (RM554A/B from/to Luton), bringing in Trust House Forte's management for the topping out ceremony on the ACS flight catering building extension near Ringway Road.

11th Biggin-Hill based Fairflight Charter has entered the jet age, a far cry from their days of operating Doves and Herons. Their Lear Jet, G-ZONE, made its first visit today operating an ambulance flight as FC822 from Annaba in North East Algeria.

12th In amongst some early morning fog diversions was British Caledonian B.707F G-BDSJ at 0609 (BR552 from Tripoli), on its last visit to Manchester. It was sold in October to Uganda Airlines as 5X-UBC for passenger operations.

12th Viscount G-APEY made its first visit to Manchester with its new owners today, operating outbound as VF5040 to Stavanger. It's one of several former British Airways aircraft purchased by British Air Ferries. Other Viscounts bought by BAF so far are G-AOHM, G-AOHV, G-AOYN, G-AOYJ, G-AOYP, G-APEX and G-AOHL as a cabin ground trainer only.

13th The lunchtime KLM Amsterdam flight KL155/6 was operated by first time visitor DC-8-63 PH-DEG, due to the morning flight (KL153/4) being cancelled for technical reasons.

13th Air Portugal commenced their twice-weekly Manchester-Lisbon service today. The first flight was operated by B.727 CS-TBL and the last two Saturday flights of the month were upgraded to B.707s with CS-TBT (23rd) & CS-TBI (30th).

14th Swissair DC-9-32 HB-IFY made its final visit to Manchester today, operating SR842/3. Its final service for Swissair was 6th September, before being sold in October to Texas International as N544TX.

14th World Airways DC-10 N106WA made its first visit to Manchester today, operating an outbound flight to Orlando on behalf of Air Florida.

15th Another bout of ATC industrial action at Heathrow produced just one diversion into Manchester today – but it was a good one! Nigeria Airways DC-10 5N-ANR arrived at 2107 (WT800 from Kano), on its first visit to Manchester.

16th PA-31T Cheyenne N2565X was on delivery, when it arrived at 1430 today from Reykjavik, before departing for Stansted.

16th A 10lb block of ice narrowly missed Saturday afternoon shoppers at Stockport's busy market today, when it fell from a unidentified landing aircraft and shattered a stall canopy!

16th May 1981 – Nor-Fly first appeared at Manchester on 28th April 1976, with CV-440 LN-KLK. They continued making occasional visits up until 1985, when they merged with Partnair, another Norwegian charter airline. In 1981 they operated a regular weekly charter between Manchester-Bergen and CV-580 LN-BWG pictured here was in charge of today's flight on a wet Saturday afternoon. (Geoff Ball)

17th Swissair DC-9-32 HB-IFN made its final flight into Manchester today, operating SR842/3. Its final service for Swissair was 14th June, before being sold in July to Texas International as N545TX.

17th Twin Otter C-FCSG, owned by Chevron Oil, was on delivery when it called into Manchester for fuel at 1620 today from Keflavik. It was later outbound to Nice and ultimately bound for Africa.

18th Air Florida returned to Manchester for the first flight of their summer programme, which is far more extensive than last years, operating from a variety of UK and European airports. Although they still operate DC-10 N1035F, they have also acquired two ex-Transamerica DC-10s. N102TV made its first visit as an Air Florida aircraft today, but it's unlikely that the other, N101TV, will put in an appearance as it has first-class seating and will be used primarily on the airlines new scheduled route between Gatwick-Miami.

19th With the assistance of specially trained sniffer-dogs, Customs Officers discovered £250,000 worth of cannabis, concealed in the hollowed out legs of wicker furniture, flown in from Ghana over a week ago.

20th Britain's new short-haul feeder-liner, the British Aerospace BAe.146, was rolled out at Hatfield today and G-SSSH made its first flight from there on 3rd September. It's the first major British airliner to be produced since the BAC 1-11 in 1963.

21st The promotional launch of Leyland's latest truck, the T-45, was responsible for a number of interesting visitors. Euralair B.737 F-GCLL (EK3060/1 from/to Paris-CDG) & Brit-Air EMB110 F-GBRM (from/to Le Havre) arrived today. British Air Ferries Viscount G-APEX

(VF5102/3 from/to Amsterdam) arrived yesterday and another Euralair B.737, F-GCSL appeared the following day.

21st All of British Airways Manchester Shuttle services were cancelled today, due to more industrial action by ATC staff at Heathrow.

23rd Brymon Airways started their twice-weekly Manchester-Newquay service with Herald G-ATIG operating today and Twin Otter G-BGMD on Wednesday's flight on the 27th.

24th Swissair DC-9-32 HB-IFG made its final visit to Manchester today (SR842/3) and its final service for Swissair on 12th July, before being sold the following month to New York Air as N543NY.

26th Air France used B.747 N28899 on scheduled flight AF964/1, due to increased outbound passenger numbers, in connection with Liverpool's participation in the European Cup Final in Paris on the 28th. A further B.747, N28366, was used on the 28th to bring the extra passengers back on AF964. These were the first Air France passenger B.747s to visit Manchester, although a cargo variant, F-BPVV, had called in on 7th November 1978. Incidentally these aircraft remain American registered, as they are only on lease to Air France.

26th Swissair DC-9-32 HB-IFR also made its final visit to Manchester today (SR842/3). Its final service for Swissair was the 2nd August, before being sold in September to Texas International as N537TX.

26th The only British registered Merlin, G-IIIB, arrived for demonstration to NEA today. It remained on the UK register until late 1982, when it was sold in Zaire.

27th RAF Devon VP965 arrived at 1721 today, on a round-trip from RAF Cranwell.

28th Another Swissair DC-9-32, HB-IDR, made its final flight into Manchester today (SR842/3). Its final service for Swissair was the 30th August, before being sold in September to Texas International as N542TX.

29th The airport's management are keen to avoid a repeat performance of the events this time last year, when plane-spotters swamped the car parks. They've asked enthusiasts not park in the main terminal building this Bank Holiday, as it's not only the busiest weekend of the year; it's also the weekend of the Barton Air Show. The show always attracts extra visitors, as participating aircraft tend use the airport as a preparation base for their displays. In order to address the problem, spotters are being asked to park on the site of the old Jacksons Brickworks on Moss Lane.

29th ATC staff sprang a nasty surprise on the airport at the end of their latest batch of strikes, by extending the action due to end at 2130 today, to 0730 the following morning.

30th Dan-Air's latest purchase, HS.748 G-BIUV, arrived after a marathon delivery flight. Its full routing was Suva-Noumei-Brisbane-Mount Isa-Darwen-Denpasar-Singapore-Bangkok-Calcutta-Delhi-Karachi-Dubai-Kuwait-Larnaca-Corfu-Marseilles-Jersey-Manchester. It had stopped off at Jersey for fuel, due to strong headwinds. The aircraft, ex 5W-FAN, was still in basic Air Polynesia colours when it entered Dan-Air's hangar the following day.

31st Today was the day of the annual Barton Air Show, but aircraft arrivals in preparation for the event were virtually non-existent, compared to previous years, as most were still at Blackpool after yesterdays air show. Having said this, Manchester did receive Lancaster PA474, Vintage Pair Meteor WF791 & Vampire XH304 and RAF C-130 XV291, which was in connection with the Red Devils Parachute Team.

31st The Red Arrows wanted to run up Runway 06 (easterly direction) on their way to Barton to begin their display, but once they had over flown the end of R.06, they were refused clearance by ATC. They were turned due to the other traffic and because R.24 was in use and their request would have caused maximum inconvenience all-round. After holding for a while over Northwich, they were eventually vectored straight to Barton, much to the leader's annoyance!

31st Transamerica DC-8 N872TV, was operating another livestock flight inbound from Edmonton, before positioning out to Turin later on. Another flight due to be operated by Flying Tigers this month, was cancelled because of goat's disease in Australia and paperwork issues with officials.

June 1981

The major news this month was Northwest Orient's decision to withdraw their Manchester-New York cargo service and operate it from Gatwick from September. They say it will help rationalise their UK operation, currently involving freight and passenger services from Prestwick and a passenger service from Gatwick. Due to a bilateral agreement, they can't operate transatlantic passenger services from Manchester and any request for change would result in the whole agreement having to be renegotiated. Another airline withdrawing is Eastern Airways, who operated their last Manchester-Dublin mail-flight on Thursday 28th May. From the 1st of this month, this flight will be part of the postal network operating from Liverpool.

Equipment changes on scheduled services included Air Portugal (TP458): B.727-200 CS-TBY (17th); Lufthansa (LH074): B.727 D-ABKB (27th); SAS (SK539): DC-9-21 LN-RLO (2nd) and Swissair (SR842): now operating as a daily DC-9-51 with the following DC-9-32s - HB-IDO (28th), HB-IFH (5th) HB-IFL (7th) & HB-IFX (6th).

ILS traffic identified included RAF Hawks XX165 (24th), XX225 (16th), XX237 (16th), XX249 (25th), XX290 (15th) and XX292 & XX305 (24th); RAF C-130s XV185 (11th) & XV186 (2nd); RAF Nimrods XV147 (10th) & XV254 (3rd) and RAE BAC 1-11 XX105 (9th). Civil/miscellaneous ILS traffic noted included Corvette F-BVPT (10th), Cessna 172 EI-BCK (18th) and Battle of Britain Memorial Flight Hurricane LF363 & Lancaster PA474 (22nd).

The most interesting aircraft to not actually land at Manchester was probably an unidentified USAF HH-53 helicopter, a type better known as the Jolly Green Giant, which overflew the airfield on the 8th. These aircraft are used by the USAF for long-range combat search & rescue and are the military version of the Sikorsky S-61 Sea King. Others of interest were the Battle of Britain Memorial Flight Lancaster PA474 and Hurricane LF363, overshooting en route to the Woodford Air Show on the 22nd.

1st RAF Rescue Wessex XT604 (Rescue 22), which called in at 0559 today for fuel from/to Valley, was assisting in the search of Cessna 150 G-BACD. It had crashed in bad weather the previous evening and was eventually located on high ground in Burnthill, near Accrington.

6th PA-28RT F-GCTI was competing in a Paris-New York Air Race, until it developed engine trouble and diverted into Manchester today. It was routing from Paris Le Bourget to Stornaway when the problems started, but after receiving attention at NEA it was able to depart the following afternoon, having retired from the race.

6th Swissair DC-9-32 HB-IFX made its final visit to Manchester today (SR842/3). Its final service for Swissair was the 20th December, before being sold later the same month to Texas International as N538TX.

6th Euroair started a series of flights transporting Air Florida crews today. An EMB-110 Bandeirante arrives on Sunday evenings from Prestwick and departs the following day to Amsterdam.

6th June 1981 - Inex-Adria have a 'new' standard DC-9 for the summer, in the form of all-silver YU-AJY. It made numerous visits during the season and its final appearance at Manchester was the 26th August, operating JP350/1. It had also operated for the airline last summer, under its former identity of YU-AJX, in a basic Ozark colour scheme. (Geoff Ball)

7th Swissair DC-9-32 HB-IFL made its final visit today, operating SR842/3. Its final service for Swissair was 14th November and it was sold in September 1982 to New York Air as N541TX.

7th A plane load of passengers expecting to fly out at 2130 last night, were still stranded at a Manchester Airport hotel, more than 24-hours after Air Malta flight KM765 should have taken off. After checking-in, the passengers were given seven different takeoff times and three different reasons for the delay. Today, airline officials insisted the aircraft was still in Malta due to technical reasons and after an anxious wait by the passengers, it finally left at 0056 on the 8th.

11th Sabena recently took delivery of five Embraer EMB-121 Xingu's for crew training purposes, which will eventually replace their Cessna 310s. The first of these to visit Manchester was OO-SXE, arriving at 1135 today, routing Liverpool-Brussels.

12th Air Europe is leasing Boeing 737 N54AF from Air Florida for the summer. It operates almost exclusively out of Gatwick, but it made its first visit to Manchester today, arriving at 0722 as AE420P from Gatwick.

12th A new dispute broke out today between civil servants and the CAA, over allegations of strike-breaking by Air Traffic Controllers. The civil servants, currently in dispute with the Government, are blaming the CAA for bringing the controllers in, but the CAA claimed that the controllers turning up for normal duty were not involved in the strike. A strike was already set for 0730-1400, but after the walkout was extended until 0730 the following morning, the airport was completely closed between 1730-0730, at very short notice. Action by air traffic staff at Heathrow is estimated to have cost British Airways £20m so far and the airline is facing yet another day of chaos, when a 14-hour strike by controllers at the main ATC flight centre at West Drayton commences.

12th Passengers onboard Laker A.300 G-BIMB (GK315 to Mahon) had an unexpected surprise when they went to claim their bags at their destination – as there weren't any! For reasons unknown, their luggage had failed to be loaded onto the aircraft and although some bags were put on a later flight, the rest didn't arrive until the following day.

12th The last of the original batch of Boeing 707s delivered to BOAC in 1960, G-APFJ, made its final flight today to RAF Cosford for preservation. It initially routed Gatwick-Brize Norton to wait for suitable easterly winds before proceeding to Cosford, where it made two dummy approaches to their short runway, before landing with less than 250m to spare. It had made its last visit to Manchester earlier in the year, on the 30th January, operating for British Airtours as Gatwick diversion KT102P.

15th Transamerica are now terminating their inbound weekly Los Angeles-Manchester-Gatwick flight at Manchester, meaning that another aircraft arrives at Manchester to return the Gatwick-bound passengers. Dan-Air BAe.748 G-ATMI was used today and others during the month for this purpose were Air UK BAC 1-11 G-AXMU (22nd) & Air UK BAC 1-11 G-AXBB (29th). These flights continued until October, when the Los Angeles flights ended for the summer.

15th CAA engineers at Manchester were due back at work this afternoon, following a 17-hour strike over a pay claim. The men are responsible for the maintenance of radar, radio and other installations used by ATC.

15th Over 4,000 passengers were affected when Manchester closed overnight for a further ten hours, because of the ongoing ATC action. Although this particular stoppage began at 1400, some controllers refused to stop work in support of the civil service pay claim and kept operations running near to normal until 2130, but when there was nobody to man the Tower overnight, the airport was closed between 2130-0730.

16th Passengers bound for Italy and Greece were subjected to severe delays today, due to a 24-hour strike by Italian ATC, the second in three days. Delays built up during the day as airlines tried to find alternative routes avoiding Italian airspace. Flights to Greece started routing via Yugoslavia, but this option soon became saturated and subjected to severe delays as well!

16th Air Ecosse rationalised their Manchester postal flights by operating WG918/9 for the final time today, but WG916/7 continues. They also changed type from EMB-110s to Twin Otters.

17th Aer Lingus B.737 EI-ASC, operating cargo flight EI9217 bound for Dublin, declared a full emergency twenty minutes after takeoff, having shut down one of its engines.

17th The second major incident of the day involved a bomb scare for Orion Airways. Boeing 737 G-BGTY (KG1014 to Malta) was held up for more than two hours, following a telephone warning, taken when the aircrafts one-hundred passengers were preparing to board. It was eventually parked on Taxiway 3 adjacent to the fire station, where it was thoroughly searched by police and security staff, but when nothing was found it finally left at 0924.

18th Another ATC strike at West Drayton caused the delay of some Manchester flights to Heathrow and Gatwick. Further action later in the day saw a limited operation at Gatwick and a complete closure of Heathrow from 1800-2130, which was the reason for British Airways L.1011-200 G-BHBO (BA222 from Amman) diverting into Manchester at 1828 today, on its first visit.

20th Alidair Viscount G-ARIR operating Guernsey Airline flight HW1731/2 today, was its very last flight prior to withdrawal and being scrapped at East Midlands in March 1982.

22nd There had been little of interest so far this month with regards to executive jets, but today was the exception, when Falcon 10 I-CHIC arrived to night-stop from/to Milan.

24th Apart from L.1011 G-BHBO on the 18th, the only other diversion of interest this month was TWA B.747 N93109 (TW700 from New York), arriving at 0807 today after declaring a full emergency, with a fire warning light in the baggage hold. The indication proved to be a faulty one, but as a spare part had to be flown in to repair the problem, the 312 passengers made their onward journey to London by train.

25th Lufthansa also operated a training flight this month, when Beech 90 D-ILHD performed a touch-and-go today, routing Shannon-Elstree. It was their first training flight since 19th May 1977, when D-ILHA made a 40 minute stay en route from Edinburgh to Stansted.

26th Another stoppage took place at the West Drayton ATC centre today, when controllers withdrew their labour from 0730-1430. As ATC engineers were also involved in a 24-hour strike, considerable delays and cancellations built up throughout the day. There was some good news however on the continual strike, regarding a Government announcement due to be made next week, on the setting up of an independent body to look into civil service pay. Ministers hope this will bring the industrial action to a halt, now in its 16th week!

27th June 1981 – Parked on the old cross runway 02/20, are ex-Laker Airways B.707s G-BFBS & G-BFBZ. They arrived in December 1980 and eventually left this September. Also in this shot is company BAC 1-11 G-AVBW which is also in storage, but it regularly re-enters service when required. The airline currently doesn't have enough work for their three BAC 1-11s, particularly since the introduction of the Airbus A.300. (Geoff Ball)

27th The first of Inex Adria's recently acquired MD-80s, YU-AJZ, made its first visit to Manchester today, operating JP676/7.

28th A first visit of type today was Rockwell 100 N9906S, routing Zurich-Bournemouth, sporting winglets with '1000' written on them.

29th A new airline to Manchester, German operator WDL, commenced a series of IT flights to Dusseldorf today with Fokker F-27s. D-BAKA was the first and they will operate until 14th September.

July 1981

Following a report ahead of December's renewal of the duty-free contract, the Airport Committee claimed a new system of running the airports major concessions, such as duty-free and catering, could benefit thousands of passengers as well as the airport. One option was to form partnerships with the companies running the concessions. The duty-free shop, once described as 'a licence to print money', is currently run by Finnegan's of Wilmslow, who won a three year contract in December 1978. After their bid to pay the airport a minimum of £9m over the next three years was accepted, a row erupted following claims that the airport could have made an extra £1m, had they gone with Grand Metropolitan's rival bid.

Announced during the month was the news that American tour-operator Jetsave will use British Airways on a variety of flights from Manchester next year, to destinations including Miami, Orlando, New York & Los Angeles. CP Air may also operate a programme from Manchester next year, rather than for Jetsave.

A new Flying School called Ravenair, formed from the ashes of the defunct North West Flying School, have set up on the South Side. They are currently operating the former NWFS PA-38 examples G-BGBY, G-BGEK & G-BGEL.

Air France announced they will operate B.707s four-times weekly on the scheduled AF964/3, to cover for their B.727s deployed on IT work, but alas this never happened!

Equipment changes on scheduled services included Austrian Airlines (OS471): DC-9-51 OE-LDM (5th) and SAS (SK539): DC-9-21 SE-DBO (22nd).

RAF ILS traffic identified included Hawks XX173 (2nd) & XX245 (10th); C-130s XV187 (2nd/6th) & XV299 (22nd); Andover XS643 (2nd/3rd); Wessex XT674 (1st) and Dominies XS714 (7th) & XS738 (6th). ILS traffic wasn't restricted to military types as frequent visits were made by Lancashire Aero Club Cessna 150s/152s and Cessna 172 EI-BAS also had a go (31st). RAF Rescue Wessex XT674 appeared in RAF camouflage, with yellow rescue patches on the tail (1st). The 24ILS runway was taken out of service (21st) to facilitate its relocation during the runway extension work. Under normal summer conditions, it would have been a good idea but unfortunately it was cloudy, foggy, or raining torrentially!

3rd A further batch of Canadian Air Force CC-130Es arriving during the month were 130327 (CAM515-today), 130314 (CAM516-5th) & 130328 (CAM517-7th).

3rd A lightning strike by Air Traffic Controllers resulted in the airport closing from 1845-2145, when more than 28 flights and 2,000 passengers were diverted to other airports.

4th The airport was closed from 0200-0400 today, due to further action by ATC staff.

6th The Argosy is becoming increasingly rare to Manchester, as the only three still operating in the UK are Air Bridge Carriers G-APRL, G-APRN & G-BEOZ, but having said this two visited during the month. The first today was G-BEOZ, operating from East Midlands to Nantes (AK364/5) and the second G-APRN (11th), operated a Liverpool mail flight (BD998F/AK720) via Manchester instead, due to the ATC industrial action. Another British-registered Argosy, G-APRM, which has operated for Rolls-Royce since 1970 and only ever visited Manchester once on the 9th June 1976, was withdrawn from service early this year. An Argosy familiar to Manchester towards the end of 1976, was OTRAG' 9Q-COA, which had been fully overhauled and converted by Dan-Air Engineering, but it was scrapped at East Midlands earlier this year in May.

6th The French Air Force operated a training flight today with Nord 262 No.56 (FA055 Dinard-Edinburgh), which returned on the 8th routing Edinburgh-Amsterdam.

7th Isle of Man based Rockwell 680 N71AF made its first visit today, arriving at 0833 from Biggin Hill, before departing later for Ronaldsway.

7th July 1981 – Balkan operated the Ilyushin IL-18 on their 1970 & 1971 summer IT flights, but since then they've been rare visitors to Manchester. Today however saw the arrival of the only one this year, when Balkan IL-18 LZ-BEP (LZ8509/10) appeared at 1836, operating inbound from Plovdiv, with a choir taking part in the annual Welsh Eisteddfod in Llangollen. It's seen here threading its way through the work in progress, about to depart for Sofia. (Geoff Ball)

10th Due to industrial action, flight operations were subjected to delays and cancellations from 2130 today, up until 0730 the following morning. There was also total closure of operations between 0200 and 0400 on the 11th.

11th Polish Airline LOT began a short series of late-night IT flights to Krakow today, with Ilyushin IL18s, which were operated until 30th August.

11th Laker Airways BAC 1-11 G-AVBW departed at 1521 today for Cherbourg (GK4843P), after a period of storage.

12th Aeroflot also began a short series of fortnightly flights to Leningrad. Unlike last year, when they used TU-134s/TU-154s & IL-62s, this year they operated TU-154s on all the flights up until they finished on the 6th September.

14th Douglas DC-9-51 OH-LYX, operating a charter from/to Helsinki (KR3011/2) today, was making its first visit. SE.210 Caravelle OH-LSF also operated from/to Helsinki (KR3011/2) on the 30th.

14th Cornwall based Bell 206 G-LRII was a long way from home, arriving from Liskard this afternoon at 1738, before eventually departing south again at 1845, initially bound for Chesterfield.

14th A first visit of type by the single-engine Maule Lunar Rocket, a high wing monoplane with a 4-seat cabin which made its first flight in 1971, was made today when G-NHVH arrived from Exeter at 1749, before departing back to Exeter the following day at 1905.

15th Inex Adria MD-80 YU-ANA, the second of the airlines three aircraft ordered, made its first visit today, operating JP676/7. It made its final visit on the 10th October also operating JP676/7, as unfortunately it was involved in a fatal air crash later in the year on 1st December.

14th July 1981 – BAe.748 G-AYYG, seen here in basic Mount Cook colours, was operating DA059 Newcastle-Bournemouth. The City-Link flights were taken over by Twin Otters of Metropolitan Airways in March 1982, when the BAe.748s became uneconomical to operate. (Geoff Ball)

15th Dan-Air leased B.727 YA-FAW from Ariana Afghan Airlines for the summer, which made its first visit today, positioning up from Gatwick to operate DA2832/3 to/from Rhodes as G-BIUR.

31st July 1981 – The top military movement of the month was today's visit of Upper Volta Air Force BAe.748 XT-MAN. The aircraft had been worked on at Prestwick and then flown to Manchester in preparation for its delivery flight the following day, before eventually departing on the 2nd August. Upper Volta was renamed Burkina Faso in 1984. (Geoff Ball)

17th Ivory Coast registered aircraft are not exactly common to Manchester, but PA-31 TU-TLU arrived at 2046 today and stayed for three hours, operating from/to Bordeaux.
18th Also uncommon to Manchester are Italian-registered light aircraft, but Beech 55 I-MAWW arrived at 1221 today, operating from/to Milan-Malpensa.
19th Enstrom F.28 G-BFFN, arriving at 1605 today to clear customs, was en-route Oxford-Dublin.
24th Beech 76 G-BGLD arrived at 1451 today from Leavesden, to operate a demonstration flight for NEA, before departing back to Leavesden at 1752. Someone must have been impressed by the visit, as the aircraft became a Manchester resident on the 1st September.
27th A forgotten souvenir left on British Airways BAC 1-11 G-BGKF, operating flight BA995 from Copenhagen and onwards to Birmingham, caused a full scale security alert today. The package found underneath a seat, prompted bomb disposal experts to be brought in from Liverpool and at one point there were fifteen fire appliances and a fleet of ambulances standing by. Ninety minutes later a remote sniffer device revealed that the parcel, wrapped in brown paper, contained nothing more than a harmless card table!

August 1981

The recent industrial action by ATC and civil service staff came to an end this month, but further disruption was then caused by ATC strikes from the other side of the Atlantic. The Professional Air Traffic Controllers Organisation (PATCO) declared a strike on the 3rd for better pay and working conditions, including a 32-hour week, but the action was in violation of US law. Strikes by Government unions were banned and the President, Ronald Reagan, declared it a threat to national safety and commanded that PATCO order its members back to work. When only 1,300 of the 13,000 strikers returned, those who stayed away were issued with the ultimatum that unless they returned within 48-hours, they would be sacked. True to his word on the 5th August, Reagan fired the 11,345 Air Traffic Controllers who'd ignored the order and banned them from working for the Federal Aviation Authority for life. The FAA initially claimed that staffing levels would return to normal within two years, but it would actually take closer to ten years. The mass sackings not only impacted on US internal flights, but also on all air travel from/to the USA from the rest of the world. Needless to say services from Manchester to America and Canada were hit by severe delays, especially during the first few weeks of the strike action.

A working party has been set up to discuss the need for a new freight village to replace the existing fragmented facilities, in the wake of Northwest Orient's recent announcement of transferring their cargo operations from Manchester to Gatwick.

The first week of the month was notable for the weather, when the regions hot and humid spell was temporarily broken by heavy and frequent thunderstorms on the 3rd. Another hot spell was broken on the 5th/6th by thunderstorms, producing 4½ inches of rain in a 24-hour period.

Equipment changes on scheduled services were Austrian Airlines (OS471): DC-9-51 OE-LDN (20th) & MD-81 OE-LDR (28th) and SAS (SK539): DC-9-21 SE-DBO (22nd).

Due to the relocation of the 24ILS to the other side of the River Bollin, there were just three ILS visitors, RAF BAe.748 XS791 (14th), RAF Jetstream XX490 (21st) and a very interesting visitor in the shape of US Army OV-10 Bronco 17010. The type, a turboprop light attack and observation aircraft, has been in use since the late 1960's and this particular aircraft was carrying out a photographic exercise in the Burtonwood area, when Manchester ATC persuaded the pilot to do an ILS. For the record, when it overshot at 1715 its call-sign was 'Hawk 21' (4th). Finally, CAA BAe.748 G-AVXJ was helping to recalibrate the ILS into its new position (25th).

2nd Now the summer season is in full swing, Romanian airline Tarom have three weekend flights operated by TU-154/IL-62 aircraft; but today and the following week, Boeing 707 (YR-ABA) was used on the morning RO711/2.

2nd Air Malta flight B.720 9H-AAO (KM106 from Malta) landed on three engines today, but for reasons unknown the pilot declined to declare an emergency.

3rd Transamerica are still terminating their weekly inbound Los Angeles flight at Manchester, so other aircraft are being used to fly the passengers back to Gatwick. Today it was Air UK BAC 1-11 G-CBIA, but from the 10th the following British Air Ferries Heralds were used: G-BDFE (10th), G-BEBB (17th) & G-BEYH (24th).

4th August 1981 – With the summer season in full swing the Airport Authority has a hard enough time dealing with its own flights, let alone any unexpected ones, but Manchester handled an extra fourteen weather diversions today, nine of which were wide-bodied. This morning scene is dominated by six Laker Airways aircraft, four of which were diversions. Laker ceased trading on the 5th February 1982. (Manchester Airport Archive)

4th Due to the unseasonably foggy weather, a general hold state was in force for Heathrow and Gatwick at 0613 today. Manchester was in a position to accept four wide-bodied aircraft, plus six narrow-bodied, on the basis that most would be parked on remote stands without refuelling capability, where the passengers would be disembarked by bus. In the end, Manchester received fourteen early morning diversions from Heathrow and Gatwick and even one from Amsterdam, with the arrival of KLM Douglas DC-8-63 PH-DEK operating a Surinam Airways flight (PY764 from Paramaribo). After landing it became so hot onboard, that two passengers fainted! Also of note was the first visit of Cathay Pacific to Manchester, when

Boeing 747 VR-HIC diverted in from Gatwick at 0836 (CX201 from Hong Kong/Bahrain). British Airways at Manchester were only able to handle two diversions: B.747 G-AWNP at 0709 (BA174 from New York) & Qantas B.747 VH-EBD at 0654 (QF001 from Bahrain). British Caledonian pitched in with two Douglas DC10s: G-BEBM at 0617 (BR366 from Kano) & G-BHDH at 0620 (BR381 from Hong Kong/Dubai), plus Boeing 707 G-BDLM at 0728 (BR212 from Lusaka). Laker Airways diverted four flights into Manchester: DC-10 G-AZZD at 0733 (GK032 from Toronto), DC-10 G-BBSZ at 0800 (GK020 from New York), DC-10 G-GFAL at 0817 (GK454 from Las Palmas) & Airbus A.300 G-BIMC at 0849 (GK602 from Berlin), on its first visit to Manchester. Finally, Zambian B.707F 9J-AEQ diverted in from Heathrow at 0738 (QZ1920 from Lusaka), making its first visit as a Zambian aircraft, as it had been in previously as our own Pelican G-BPAT. Incidentally, Pelican Cargo ceased operating during the month. The record for the highest number of wide-bodied aircraft being on the ground at the same was broken this morning, from twelve to thirteen.

5th Beech F.90 G-BIED, arriving at 1002 today, was on delivery from Fairoaks to its new owners, United Biscuits. The type is basically a Beech 90 King Air, with a T-tail. Although it won't be based at Manchester, it will be a regular visitor, as United Biscuits have a factory in Stockport. It replaces the company's previous run-around, Beech 200 G-HLUB, which has been sold.

6th The local area saw torrential rain over a 24-hour period and although London didn't see as much, it did suffer from violent thunderstorms late morning and early afternoon. Due to this, Heathrow suspended flights for a short period at lunchtime and as a result Manchester received four diversions in between thunderstorms of its own! These were British Airways B.747 flights: G-AWNL at 1248 (BA295 from Miami) & G-BDXJ at 1239 (BA286 from San Francisco); Air India B.747 VT-EGA at 1230 (AI107 from Kuwait) and N93105 at 1244 (TW760 from Los Angeles). The last three aircraft were making their first visits and B.747 VT-EGA was the 200th different wide-bodied aircraft to visit Manchester.

6th Yorkshire was also affected by severe weather later in the day, resulting in Gulfstream 2 A4O-AA inbound to Leeds from Larnaca, diverting into Manchester instead.

7th Royal Marines Gazelle XX399 diverted into Manchester at 1251 today (Marines 399), on a flight from Blackpool, having originally been flight planned into Woodford.

8th Swissair DC-9-32 HB-IDO operating SR852 Zurich-Dublin, diverted into Manchester this lunchtime, declaring a medical emergency due to a passenger giving birth in-flight!

10th BAe.125 9Q-CCF, arriving at 0946 today from Brussels, was en route to Hawarden for maintenance when it passed through Manchester to clear customs.

12th Transatlantic flights started to move again today, after Canadian ATC agreed to end their boycott. Their strike had closed the Gander Air Traffic Centre in Newfoundland, which controls all flights to/from the USA and Canada. The Canadian controllers took action after claiming the US ATC system was unsafe, because of their strike. They later agreed to return to work on condition that the Canadian Government set up a fact finding team to assess the safety of US airspace.

13th Bristow Helicopters Bell 206 G-BBOS, arriving at 1739 today from Melton Mowbray, was piloted by its owner Sir Alan Bristow. Tragically, later the same the day one of the company's Wessex helicopters, G-ASWI, lost power whilst routing from a gas field in the North Sea to a landing site at Bacton, Norfolk.

13th The French Air Force operated Transall F.36/61-MC on a training flight today (FM0158), routing Edinburgh-Lyneham.

16th August 1981 – Despite its extensive summer programme and having up to three Boeing 737s based at Manchester this year, Air Europe B.737 N54AF pictured above, only visited three times during its summer lease from Air Florida. (Geoff Ball)

20th Lear Jet G-ZEAL owned by Air Ecosse, made its first and only visit of the year, arriving at 0116 today from Ibiza on an ambulance flight.

21st The only VC-10s to look forward to nowadays are the RAF examples, with today's arrival of XV104, operating from/to Belfast as RR2369A/B.

22nd The new turbo-powered regional airliner, Dash-7, made its first visit today when Brymon example G-BRYC arrived at 0954, on a crew training detail from Cardiff to East Midlands. The type first appeared in the UK in 1978, debuting at the Farnborough Air Show.

24th August 1981 – Tupolev TU-134 DDR-SCO, which served with East German operator Interflug from 1978-1990, is one of sixteen different aircraft to visit Manchester between 23rd October 1977 and 22nd December 1988. Today's flight, arriving at 1223 operating Gatwick-Leipzig as IF7427, was their first from Manchester since October 1977. (Geoff Ball)

23rd Spantax CV-990 EC-CNG, which operated a sub-charter for Air Europe (AE677/6) from/to Palma today, was one of only two visits of a CV-990 Coronado this year.
25th Air UK Herald G-AVPN, arriving at 1231 today from Gatwick as UK8211, was carrying a Muslim religious leader and his entourage. They proceeded to the airport coach park, where they met up with a hundred followers who had arrived by coach. An impromptu prayer meeting took place, before they returned to Gatwick onboard G-AVPN again.
28th The second Embraer EMB-121 Xingu on the UK register, was G-XING operated by CSE Aviation, which arrived at 1418 today routing Liverpool-Oxford.
29th Two Pitts Specials, G-WREN & G-ROLL, belonging to the Marlborough Aerobatic Team, gave a short display at Manchester prior to their arrival from Barton. They departed for another display at a private function at Styal, before flying on to Leicester.
30th US Army Beech C-21 18043 arriving at 1422 today from Sembach AFB, Germany, as 'Lord 32B', was in connection with the following days C-141 visit.
30th TAE SE.210 EC-CUM, which has been a regular visitor to Manchester this summer, made its last visit today operating JK404/5. It returned to Sterling, from whom it was leased, in September.
31st Bank Holidays rarely produce interesting visitors, but today's military arrival was spectacular and a first visit of type! USAF C-141B Starlifter 40629 appeared from Charleston AFB, South Carolina, with ninety troops in full combat gear, who were transported onwards to RAF Burtonwood on two corporation buses. As the aircraft was also carrying a hazardous cargo, it was parked on Taxiway 3, close to the Fire Station. The C-141, which was first delivered to the USAF in 1965, served as a strategic carrier of troops and cargo. In 1977 a major programme was undertaken to 'stretch' the C-141 by a further 23ft, after which it was referred to as variant C-141B.
31st An uncommon type to Manchester was the Metroliner, a 19-seat twin turboprop airliner. European Air Transport example OO-JPI arrived at 1448 from Brussels. Formerly operated by Sabena, it had visited previously in April 1978.
31st RAF Wessex XT604 called in for fuel at 1739 today as 'KHC803', en route for Ronaldsway.

September 1981

Manchester Airport made a new record by carrying 685,845 passengers last month, a 16% increase on the same time last year, but the national trend is an overall decline of 1%.

British Airways announced that ninety engineers will be made redundant at Manchester, due to the closure of their maintenance base and termination of their Prestwick-Manchester-New York service. The unions are sceptical that money would be saved by transferring the maintenance of the Super 1-11 fleet to Heathrow. The cuts, which are part of the airline's attempts to stem enormous losses currently running at £200 a minute, include the overall loss of 9,000 jobs, a pay freeze, closure of some passenger routes and the possible sale of dedicated cargo aircraft. It's hoped the cutbacks will be achieved through voluntary redundancies, but if the target isn't reached by next June, redundancies will be imposed to reduce the workforce from 52,000 to 43,000.

Further to the announcement made earlier in the year by Olympic Airways, their plans to fly from Manchester have been finalised. From next April, they will operate three-times weekly to Athens via Brussels, with Boeing 727s.

Tour operators experienced a last minute rush of holiday bookings this month and as the writer was an employee of a local travel agency, he experienced it first-hand. Upon my arrival at work one Monday morning, I was greeted by a well-to-do couple sat on their suitcases outside the shop. Their brief was simple, 'they wanted to go anywhere, immediately and money was no object!' Although this seemed like an easy request, it actually wasn't, but after an hour of telephone calls they settled on a £3,000 two-week holiday in Barbados, flying out of Heathrow that afternoon! In order to meet the extra demand for holidays, Manchester put on more IT flights. Spantax laid on an extra two flights, Aviaco were up to eight-weekly and another Spanish IT airline, Trans Europa, also introduced eight flights a week to Palma.

British Caledonian sold all seven of their BAC 1-11-200s to American-operator, Pacific Express Airlines, which will be delivered to their new owners over the next six months. Originally nine were delivered brand new to British United in 1965, but two left the fleet early under different circumstances. G-ASJA was sold to Marshalls of Cambridge in 1970 and G-ASJJ crashed shortly after takeoff at Milan in January 1969.

Not strictly to do with Manchester Airport, but of interest nevertheless, was the scrapping of ex-RAF Comet XK659, which began at Pomona Docks at the end of the month. The aircraft was struck off charge by the RAF and sold to a company called Compass Catering. It made its last flight from RAF Wyton to Manchester Airport on 13th May 1974, where it was dismantled and taken by road to Pomona Docks, Salford to be converted into a bar/restaurant called 'Westward Ho'. Due to cash problems the company folded and sadly the Comet was destined to become a pile of metal by early next month!

RAF ILS traffic identified were C-130s XV179 (22nd) XV187 (18th) & XV307 (7th); Dominie XS737 (11th) and Gazelle XW906 (18th).

1st Today's arrival of Citation SE-DDE at 1537 from East Midlands to Stockholm, marked an incredible month of biz-jet movements. Twenty-five different aircraft visited in total, with a wide range of types from various countries.

2nd The downside or the upside, depending on your point of view, of the fine weather currently being experienced by the UK, is the likelihood of overnight fog and this morning was such an occasion. Although the London area was affected, only one diversion arrived into Manchester, but it was worth waiting for! N611US was the second passenger Northwest Orient B.747 to visit, diverting in from Gatwick at 0828 (NW044 from Minneapolis). The writer saw it passing overhead on his way to work, against the backdrop of a clear blue sky.

2nd Air Ecosse EMB-110 G-DATA made its first visit today, operating WG756. There was nothing particularly remarkable about this flight, except for the aircraft's colour scheme! It was painted in an overall pillar-box red, with bright yellow titles of 'Post Office Special Services' and 'Datapost' all over it, even on the upper wing surfaces and Air Ecosse was written up the tail.

3rd It was the Midlands and the South East's turn to be affected by fog this morning. Of the fourteen diversions arriving into Manchester, only a few were of interest including two British Caledonian DC-10s: G-BHDH at 0815 (BR232 from Atlanta) & G-BHDI at 0916 (BR268 from St. Louis) and British Airways B.737 G-BGDI at 0909 (BA5601 from Aberdeen).

4th Due to fog affecting the southern airports again, Manchester received eighteen diversions between 0542 and 1043. Unlike yesterday, there was plenty of variety, much to the delight of the writer, who was lucky enough to be off work and saw all the arrivals! There were three Laker Airway's DC-10s: G-AZZC at 0818 (GK020 from New York), G-BELO at 0542 (GK448 from Gatwick) & G-GSKY at 1020 (GK052 from Berlin); two British

Caledonian flights: B.707 G-ATZC (BR214 from Lusaka) making its last visit and DC-10 G-BHDH at 0822 (BR232 from Atlanta) and British Airtours L.1011 G-BHBP at 0801 (KT885 from Malta). Making their first appearance at Manchester since October 1975 was Luxair, with first visit B.737 LX-LGH at 0834 (LG401 from Luxembourg). A first visit of type was British Airways L.1011-500 G-BFCC at 1043 (BA9421 from Heathrow), which is noticeably different to other Tristars as the variant has a much shorter fuselage. This flight was originally positioning from Heathrow to Gatwick, but was unable to return to Heathrow when the weather fell below limits. Other diversions included Yemen Airways B.727 4W-ACH at 0837 (IY524 from Rome), South African Airways B.747 ZS-SAN at 0922 (SA226 from Sal Island), Pan American B.747 N741PA at 0925 (PA002 from New York), KLM DC-8 PH-DEH at 0957 (KL115 from Amsterdam), Alitalia B.727 I-DIRU at 1017 (AZ458 from Rome) and Kenya Airways B.707 5Y-BBI at 1040 (KQ414 from Frankfurt). One that didn't make it was Braniff B.747SP flight BN602 Dallas to Gatwick, which diverted to Frankfurt. All the passengers who were diverted into Manchester were transported onwards by train or coach.

5th The ATC Watch Log recorded at 1840 today, that Servisair and the police had received reports that TU-154 LZ-BTT (LZ905 from Varna) had struck the roof of a house on short final. According to the Tower Controller, the aircraft carrying 150 passengers appeared to be making a normal approach; yet local residents insisted it was off-course. Following an inspection, a police report stated there was no damage to the aircraft, but there was a hole in roof of the house!

6th September 1981 – Today's arrival of Aer Turas Britannia EI-BBH from/to Dublin on a livestock charter, also marked the very final visit of a Bristol Britannia to Manchester. This aircraft was one of several ex-RAF aircraft, released onto the civil market in immaculate condition and led to temporary surge in the amount of Britannia activity in Europe, but by the early 1980's most had been withdrawn from use or had been sold to other operators such as Aerocaribbean (Cuba), or some smaller carriers in Zaire. EI-BBH had been withdrawn from use by December and sold by Aer Turas in spring 1982. (Geoff Ball)

6th Northwest Orient operated their last cargo flight out of Manchester today, when B.747F N629US arrived from Prestwick, before departing to Amsterdam as 'Northwest 922' at 0037. The ceasing of these flights accounted for the major drop in this month's freight figures, compared to September last year. When no other carrier came forward to replace

Northwest Orient, by the end of the month all of Manchester's transatlantic cargo was being taken by road to either London or Prestwick.

6th CSE of Cranfield is the distributor for all Cessna types in the UK. Their current Cessna 404 demonstrator, N6768V, arrived from Leicester today, before departing onward to Inverness. It made the return trip to Inverness-Leicester on the 8th.

6th September 1981 - Aeroflot operated a fortnightly charter flight between Manchester and Leningrad during the summer. TU-154 CCCP-85242, seen here making its first visit to Manchester, was the 13th different Aeroflot TU-154 to visit since 1st July 1976. (Geoff Ball)

8th The Lockheed Jetstar which first flew in 1957 was the largest biz-jet on the market for many years, seating up to ten passengers. Distinguishable by the four engines mounted on the rear of the fuselage, the type had never been a common visitor to Manchester, probably because none had ever been registered to a European country. Only five different visits by the Jetstar had been made since 1970 and they were all American registered. The fact that the last one to visit was N7782 on the 25th August 1978, made it all the more remarkable that two arrived this month. The first, N100GL, arrived from Gander today, before departing for Shannon on the 11th.

11th Aurigny Airlines Twin Otter G-BIMW made its second visit today, arriving from Southampton with the local football team for tomorrow afternoon's Division One game with Manchester City. The aircraft returned the team the following evening, after a 1-1 draw.

12th British Midland, whose mainstay business over many years was the leasing out of its Boeing 707s; appear to be using them for their own purposes. They've been granted a service to New York from Birmingham/Belfast starting next year, but having said this, today's visit of B.707 G-BFLD was to operate Palma flight BY556A/B on behalf of Britannia Airways.

12th The RAF operated a number of outbound C-130 trooping flights today. XV303 (RR6414 Lyneham-Brussels), XV191 (RR4436 Lyneham-Hanover & RR4477 Hanover-Brussels) and XV187 (RR4437 Lyneham-Hanover & RR4438 from/to Hanover). Others were VC-10 XV104 (RR2397) Brize Norton-Belfast & RR2398 Belfast-Brize Norton (14th) and C-130s XV306 (RR4450A), XV292 (RR4603), XV178 (RR4451), XV213 (RR4452) & XV214 (RR4457), all routing Hanover-Lyneham (26th).

13th Liverpool-based Cessna 182 G-HUFF arrived at 0953 today, to clear customs en route from Liverpool to Dublin.

14th Swiss airline CTA operated an outbound charter to Geneva today, returning on the 16th, with SE.210 HB-ICQ both ways. This aircraft and their other SE.210, HB-ICO continued in the airlines service until 1988.

18th RAF Gazelle XW906 overshot at 1239 today, en route from Shawbury to Woodvale and again at 1545, on its way back to Shawbury.

19th An old friend returned today, when BAC 1-11 N1543 arrived at 1417 from Luton, before departing for Edinburgh. It was a Manchester 'resident' from October 1978 to April 1979.

20th DC-8F TF-FLE arriving at 0904 today (SV8457 from Dhahran), was carrying an outbound load of cargo bound for Riyadh, destined for the Saudi Royal Family.

21st Worldways Canada Boeing 707 C-GRYN operated a Toronto flight on behalf of Wardair today (WB320/1). This airline 'rose from the ashes' of the original Ontario Worldways, which ceased trading late last year.

22nd Two Laker Airways Boeing 707s, stored at Manchester since last year, suddenly sprang to life this month when they departed to Gatwick. G-BFBZ, present since 12th December 1980 left today and G-BFBS present since 10th November 1980 left on the 25th, both as GK099P. Each aircraft did one last approach and overshoot, before setting course for Gatwick. They were destined for Worldways of Canada, but after the deal fell through neither aircraft saw further service and eventually made their way to Lasham to be withdrawn.

23rd September 1981 – In a busy month for biz-jets, BAC 1-11 N825AC, which made its first visit to Manchester today on a flight from Luton, is seen here parked on the Domestic Pier. Delivered new to American Airlines in 1966, the aircraft only served them for five years, before being stored initially and then sold to a private owner. (Geoff Ball)

23rd In addition to today's BAC 1-11, Gulfstream 2 N442A also appeared from Luton, before eventually departing for Edinburgh. Both of these aircraft are operated by Saudi Arabian petroleum company, Aramco. Another biz-jet, Ingersoll-Rand Falcon 50 N1871R, departed for Dusseldorf today, following its arrival from White Plains, New York on the 20th.

23rd BAe.125 G-BFSO, one of two operated by the diamond company De Beers, made its first visit to Manchester at 1332 today from Heathrow, before departing later for Shannon. It appeared again the following day, operating in the opposite direction. Their other aircraft was G-BFSP and both operated for the company until 1985.

25th A further batch of Canadian Air Force CC-130Es appearing during the month were 130323 (CAM515-today) and 130321 (CAM516-27th), but CAM517, the third flight that normally operates was cancelled.

26th September 1981 – Only two USAF C-135s have visited Manchester and both arrived in successive months. On a gloomy Saturday afternoon, C-135C 61-2669 appeared at 1324 as 'Trout 99' from Pisa. It was carrying a high ranking US Air Force General and departed to Andrews AFB, Maryland. Known as the 'Speckled Trout', as well as transporting senior military leaders, it's also a communications aircraft. It's designated as a C-135C and although it's based on the Boeing 707, it's actually shorter, with a narrower fuselage. The first US military B.707 to visit was VIP aircraft VC-137 58-6970 on 4th October 1978. (Geoff Ball)

27th Today is Sunday and the weather is a mixture of sunshine and heavy showers. In the afternoon the writer heard an aircraft call up on his radio on approach, with the call-sign 'DCN2975'. I knew from experience this was a German Air Force call-sign, but I didn't know which aircraft to expect and waited patiently for it to pass over. When it I saw it was 11+02, the second Jetstar of the month, which was carrying a number of German military VIP's, I rang my friend Brian and we agreed to go the airport so we could both get photos of this great looking aircraft.

27th Another final visit was Kar-Air Douglas DC-6F OH-KDA, operating AY032 for the last time. It arrived from Helsinki/Heathrow at 0705 today, before departing for Helsinki at 0837. From the 30th, the service will be operated by Douglas DC-9s.

28th French Air Force Noratlas 87/64-KA arrived at 1205 today as FM0403, on a training flight from Evereux to Bournemouth.

28th Following on from last month's visit of Beech F.90 G-BIED, now owned and operated by United Biscuits, another aircraft in their possession, Beech 200 G-UBHL, made its first visit arriving from Denham at 1037 today.

October 1981

British Airways firmed-up their intention to cut routes and aircraft to save money. Cut by the end of the month were Heathrow-Thessaloniki, Zagreb & Valencia; Gatwick-Frankfurt; Glasgow-Copenhagen and Manchester's New York service. To be cut next March are Heathrow-Sofia, Bucharest & Luxembourg; Gatwick-Zurich & Dusseldorf and Birmingham-Brussels, Zurich & Milan. Their cargo B.707s will be sold by the end of the month and their sole all-cargo B.747 will be gone by next March.

New direct air links between Manchester-Montreal are a distinct possibility, following recent talks between airport officials and a delegation from Montreal Airport and Canadian airline representatives. The route's not been served since British Airways withdrew in December 1980.

Thomson Holidays, Britain's biggest tour operator, will offer cut-price deals to entice more people to take winter breaks, with prices from £69 for a week on the Costa Blanca. Allowing for inflation, this makes a holiday cheaper than in 1970. They will also offer budget air fares to thirty-three destinations from sixteen UK airports, with return fares from Manchester to Alicante from £64.

Equipment changes on scheduled services included Air Portugal (TP458): B.707 CS-TBB (31st); Austrian Airlines (OS471): first visit MD-81 OE-LDP (25th) and Lufthansa (LH074): B.727s D-ABKA (25th) & D-ABKN (29th).

RAF ILS traffic identified included Hawks XX166 (21st), XX236 (8th), XX250 (20th), XX290 (19th), XX294 (15th) & XX308 (23rd); C-130s XV181 (30th), XV199 (2nd), XV210 (1st) & XV213 (16th); Andovers XS596 (13th) & XS641 (14th); Dominie XS737 (11th); Canberra WH902 (16th); Tornado ZA555 (26th) and RAE Devon XA880 (27th). Civil ILS traffic noted included Corvettes F-BVPK (21st) & F-BVPT (28th/29th); PA-28 G-AVSA (7th) and Cessna 152 G-BHRB (23rd/30th). The RAF Canberra overshooting at 1118 as 'Tarnish 09' was noted in green primer. The first appearance of a RAF Tornado at Manchester was ZA555/Tarnish 09 (26th), noted in green primer on a test flight out of Warton at 1201.

2nd Cessna 172RG G-PARI, arriving at 1039 today on a daytrip from its Scottish base at Inverness, was notable as unlike other Cessna 172s, it had a retractable undercarriage.

2nd The weekly cattle charters to Milan recommenced after several months, with the first flight being operated by Merchantman G-APES today. The flights are being operated by Air Bridge Carriers, who last operated them on a regular basis in 1979.

3rd New operators, French-airline Corse Air, made their first visit to Manchester. They have purchased a number of ex-Aerotour SE.210s to operate IT/charter flights from France to points throughout the Mediterranean and today's arrival of SE.210 F-BYAT was taking race-goers to Paris, for the prestigious Prix de L'Arc de Triomphe, before returning the following evening. The aircraft, which was formerly I-DABG with Alitalia, operated for Corse Air until its withdrawal in December 1983.

3rd Another visitor arriving to take outbound passengers to the Prix de L'Arc de Triomphe in Paris was Lear Jet F-GCMS, which was also making its first visit.

4th CP Air Douglas DC-8 C-FCPO made its last visit today for the airline, arriving from Edmonton as CP866 at 1155, before departing to Prestwick at 1317. Their first aircraft to visit Manchester was Douglas DC-8-43 CF-CPF on the 24th May 1964, when they were known as Canadian Pacific Airlines, but made no further visits! Since then they've been regular visitors, particularly from 1976 onwards, but from this winter they will concentrate on operating Boeing

747s & Douglas DC-10s into the UK. A complete listing of the last visits and subsequent fates of the DC-8s are detailed below:
C-FCPG 13/07/79, withdrawn 03/80
C-FCPH 22/10/78, withdrawn 11/80
C-FCPJ 11/10/79, withdrawn 11/81
C-FCPL 26/10/80, sold as N29180 12/81
C-FCPM 12/09/80, sold as HK-3125X 04/82
C-FCPO 04/10/81, sold to Worldways Canada 03/83
C-FCPP 05/09/81, sold to Worldways Canada 03/83
C-FCPQ 28/09/81, sold to Worldways Canada 03/83
C-FCPS 24/08/81, sold to Worldways Canada 03/83
C-FCPT 01/09/77, sold September 1977

6th Morane-Saulnier MS.760 Paris F-BLKL made its second visit of the year today, operating from/to St. Nazaire.

7th British Airways B.707 G-AYLT operated the final Manchester-New York flight today, arriving at 1149, before positioning out to Heathrow at 1310. The final outbound flight operated at 1247 on the 2nd (G-AYLT-BA185 to Prestwick/New York), which brought the service, operated since 7th May 1954 to an end. This was also the last visit of a British Airways B.707. Their first B.707 to visit was BOAC example G-APFD, on a training flight on 25th May 1960. The last remaining British Airways B.707s made their last visits as follows:
G-ASZF, 02/12/79, last service 31/03/82, sold to DAS Cargo as 5N-ARO in 05/83
G-ASZG, 17/02/81, last service 14/11/81, sold to Tratco as LX-FCV in 05/83
G-ATWV, 13/10/78, withdrawn 10/81, sold to West African Cargo as 9G-ACX in 01/82
G-ATZD, 20/05/81, sold to Jamahiriya Air Transport as 5A-DJV in 05/83
G-AVPB, 16/03/81, transferred to British Airtours in 04/81
G-AWHU, 12/06/81, last service 24/05/82 (BA154 Cairo-LHR), sold as 9Q-CKI
G-AXGW, 12/08/81, sold to Alymeda as 7O-ACO in 12/81
G-AXGX, 28/04/78, leased to Qatar Government as A7-AAC in 03/81
G-AXXY, 09/09/81, last service 27/03/82 (BA154 Cairo-LHR), to British Airtours 04/82
G-AXXZ, 05/08/81, last service 27/03/82 (BA236 Damascus-LHR), leased to Zambia Airways
G-AYLT, 07/10/81, last service 31/10/81 (BA154 Cairo-LHR), sold to GKN as 9Q CLY

7th Transamerica B.747 N742TV (TV400 from Los Angeles) arrived over six hours, due to the aircraft originally operating the flight having to make an emergency return landing at Los Angeles, with undercarriage trouble.

7th Korean Airlines B.707F HL-7427 arrived at 1914 today (KE9679 from Maastricht) to operate an outbound livestock charter, before leaving for Seoul the following afternoon via Fairbanks, Alaska. Unfortunately, this aircraft had visited before on 7th February 1979.

8th BAe.125 G-ASNU arrived from Newcastle at 0810 today and departed for Hatfield at 0844. It's currently the second oldest flying BAe.125 in the world, having first flown in 1964 and although it remained on the UK register until 1991, it never came to Manchester again. As a final postscript regarding this particular aircraft, it received notoriety when it was hijacked in 1967 whilst transporting the Congolese President, who'd been overthrown in a coup and sentenced to death in his absence. Although it remains unclear where the aircraft was actually heading at the time, the plane was diverted to Algeria.

9th Due to changeable weather, there were few diversions this month, but Spantax CV-990 EC-BZP diverted in for fuel at 2007 today (Las Palmas-Dublin as BX229).

10th Citation 500 G-DJHH gave a demonstration to Grosvenor Aviation today, operating from/to Brough.

12th When Cessna 172 G-BCHK was operating out of Barton today, on a photographic detail of Altrincham, it frequently found itself directly under the Manchester flight path around 1-mile out. The pilot of Britannia Airways flight BY102B inbound from Reus found this too close for comfort and after opting to overshoot at 1330, he requested that Manchester approach remove the aircraft from the approach track!

15th RAF BAe.125 XW791 arriving at 1549 today (RR1668 from/to Northolt), was carrying the head of the Royal Navy, the First Sea Lord and several high ranking members of the Admiralty.

16th Today saw the second visit to Manchester of a USAF C-135 in as many months, when VC-135B 62-4127 arrived at 1437 from RAF Wittering, before its departure for Heathrow. Converted as a VIP aircraft, it served with the 89th Military Air Wing based at Andrews AFB, Maryland.

17th October 1981 – A classic line up of three Aviogenex TU-134s, YU-AHX, YU-AHY & YU-AJA, all of which continued operating into Manchester until the 28th October 1989, when YU-AHX operated the final Aviogenex TU-134 flight out of Manchester. (Alec Rankin)

20th Dan-Air Boeing 727 G-BHNE (DA2573/2 from/to Palma), made its first visit to Manchester today, eighteen months after being delivered to the airline.

21st Agusta 109 G-HWBK made its first visit to Manchester at 1353 today, on a fuel stop, transporting a heart transplant team from Papworth Hospital, Cambridgeshire to Davyhulme Hospital. It called in again, on its return flight back to Papworth Hospital.

21st T-Tailed PA-32 Lance PH-WWG arrived at 1709 today, on a freight flight from/to Amsterdam.

23rd Having arrived two days earlier, Royal Saudi Air Force C-130H 468 left for Cambridge today with its No.1 engine feathered, before returning the following day and departing for Milan. Feathering the engine means that the pilot adjusts the angle of the propeller, so it slices through the air easily to eliminate drag.

24th The airport had been affected by a 2-hour stoppage by baggage loaders last night, following the suspension of three men refusing to load a British Caledonian flight. Before the situation was resolved, three aircraft diverted to Liverpool, but by today the suspensions had been lifted and normal working was resumed.

24th Two aircraft diverting into Manchester this afternoon, due to the unavailability of customs at Liverpool, were Ralleye EI-BHD at 1325 and Cessna 172 EI-BAS at 1418.

25th TAE SE.210 EC-CMS, which has been a regular visitor throughout the summer, made its last visit to Manchester today operating JK404/5. The following month it returned to Sterling, from whom it was leased.

27th Air Florida Boeing 737 N54AF, which has been on lease to Air Europe, made only its third but final visit today (AE827 from Ibiza), before departing to Palma as AE844. It was also its last day in service for Air Europe, prior to its return to the USA.

29th Having arrived from Deauville, Metroliner F-GCFE was lined up on the runway ready for departure for Kirkwall, when customs contacted ATC to refuse him permission to depart. They insisted he return to the apron, as he hadn't cleared customs inbound, but the pilot said he had. When customs were notified of the situation, they ordered the pilot to report to their office in person before departure, but when he and his crew were unwilling to do this, customs backed down and sent a representative out to the aircraft with the relevant paperwork to sign. They finally departed at 1045, fifty-five minutes later than intended.

31st Transamerica operated the penultimate flight of their summer programme, with DC-10 N103TV (TV200 from Miami), before positioning out to San Antonio, Texas on the 2nd November. They won't be operating for Jetsave next year, as the tour operator's USA/Canada programme will be operated by British Airways, except for some of the Canada flights which will be operated by Air Canada.

November 1981

Tour operators Cosmos will offer a 24% increase in holidays from Manchester next year, with Corsica, Algarve, Barbados & Vancouver as new destinations.

Direct charter services will be offered to Orlando for the first time from next May, by Jetsave, using British Airways for the nine hour flight. Their flights to New York, Los Angeles, San Francisco, Toronto & Hawaii due to operate next year, are part of the biggest North American travel programme ever run by the company. For an extra £99 on top of the regular fare, flights will offer First Class with sleeper seats, champagne and a four-course meal.

To satisfy increasing demands from holidaymakers, Tunis Air is considering direct air services between Manchester-Tunis. Of the 155,000 passengers flying to Tunisia last year, over 25,000 were from the North West, but direct flights didn't happen until 1983 with just one flight a week, although the long term aim was to operate two or three a week.

Airlines making changes this month were Air Malta operating twice-weekly (Fri/Sun) with B.737s and Austrian Airlines twice-weekly (Thur/Sun). British Airways are operating to Frankfurt via Birmingham, Malta & New York have been permanently dropped from the schedules and Toronto continues once-weekly, originating from Heathrow (BA073/2). Cyprus Airways reverted to once-weekly again for the winter. Finnair will operate a three-weekly cargo schedule, with one on Saturday evenings. Guernsey Airlines have twice-weekly flights (Fri/Sun) from/to Guernsey. KLM maintain the daily morning Amsterdam flight (KL153/4), whilst the lunchtime (KL155/6) operates Mon-Fri and they have added a Sunday lunchtime flight (KL157/8). Laker Airways will operate Skytrain flights once-weekly to Los Angeles and Miami and four-weekly to New York. LOT terminated their scheduled flights on 30th October and winter IT flights are being operated by Air Europe, Air Malta, Aviaco, Britannia Airways, British Airtours, Dan-Air, EL AL, Laker Airways & Orion Airways and transatlantic flights by Laker Airways (Barbados & Toronto) and Wardair (Toronto).

Equipment changes on scheduled services included Lufthansa (LH074): B.727 D-ABKH (6th) and SAS (SK539): DC-9-21s LN-RLL (23rd/26th), LN-RLO (12th) OY-KGF (17th), SE-DBR (30th) & SE-DBS (10th).

ILS traffic identified included Hawk XX291 (26th); C-130s XV177 (11th), XV199 (12th), XV298 (14th); Gazelle XZ934 (13th) and Bulldog XX688 (30th). The only civil ILS traffic of note was Agusta 109 G-OAMH operated by Alan Mann Helicopters (27th). There was an unidentified RAF Jaguar 'EEP39' (3rd) and RAF Gazelle XZ934 overshot at 1315 'EXL53' from Shawbury (13th).

1st The last remaining TAE SE.210 Caravelle, EC-DFP, which has been a regular visitor to Manchester throughout the summer, made its last visit today operating JK404/5. Like the other two operated by the airline, this aircraft also returned to Sterling during the month.

4th A local news item simmering since April, regarding the takeover of the Laurence Scott & Electromotors Group in Openshaw earlier in the year, came to a head today. Problems started when the out-going owners informed the workers that the factory was superfluous to the new-owners requirements and would close. After being told they would only receive the minimum redundancy pay, they went on strike and occupied the factory. The eight month sit-in dragged on with no resolution in sight until today, when bailiffs smashed their way in and retook the factory, aided by a considerable police presence. The new owners also sent in two helicopters, Bell 206 Jet Ranger G-BBOR and Squirrel G-BGIF, which landed on the factory roof to help with the recovery of goods. G-BBOR had already carried out a dummy run the day previously and both aircraft had refuelled at Manchester before carrying out the raid! Such was the outrage of the trade unions and various MP's that this drastic action had been taken, questions were asked in the House of Commons, which led to a re-enactment of the whole event being carried out by the Civil Aviation Authority on the 27th, with Bell 206 G-AYCM. It was also reported that the helicopters would not have been allowed to refuel at Manchester, had the airport known about the raid.

4th Aviaco now operate the longer DC-8-63s, previously operated by Iberia. EC-BMZ arrived at 1245 today (AO1962A from Gatwick) to operate a charter to Palma on behalf of a number of travel agents and the return flight on the 6th took place with DC-8 EC-BSD.

5th Foreign registered helicopters are uncommon to Manchester, but the airport saw two this month. The first was Hughes 369 EI-AVN, arriving at 1514 today from Sywell, before departing for Liverpool. The second was Bell Long Ranger D-HBBZ on the 14th, newly owned by Alton Towers Helicopters; it made frequent visits during the month from/to Alton Towers.

7th British Airways Toronto flight BA073 was operated for the first time today by one of the airlines Rolls-Royce powered B747s, G-BDXF.

8th Due to a strike by EL AL, the weekly Tel Aviv charter LY5317/8, was operated by British Midland Boeing 707 G-BFLE today, in basic Air Algerie colours. On the 15th the flight was operated by British Caledonian B.707 G-AXRS, which is currently on lease to Monarch.

9th In an uninspiring month for executive jets, there was a first visit today with the arrival of Falcon 20 OO-VPQ at 0900 from/to Antwerp, which had visited previously as F-BVPQ.

7th November 1981 – Seventeen different Pan Am Boeing 747s had visited Manchester since the first, N770PA 'Clipper Queen of the Pacific', arrived in October 1971. Today's rare non-diversionary appearance of N659PA (PA8280 from Miami) was the eighteenth. Finishing off the Transamerica Miami programme, it stayed overnight before positioning out to Rome. This aircraft served with the airline until 1989, when it was sold to Evergreen International. (Geoff Ball)

12th Falcon 50 N150BG arriving at 1404 today from Amsterdam, left the following afternoon for Gander after performing a local flight. This executive type is becoming more regular to Manchester.

21st November 1981 – A new airline to Manchester operating a short series of IT flights to Monastir was Tunis Air. They operate four Boeing 737s, but these flights were operated exclusively by TS-IOE & TS-IOF. Up to this point, they had only made two visits, both with Boeing 727s. (Geoff Ball)

21st November 1981 – C-130 F-GDAQ which operated for SFAIR as a French-registered aircraft from 1981-1987, is seen here in its colourful livery, having arrived from Bordeaux to transport a generator to Frobisher Bay, Canada. This was a first visit to Manchester of both the airline and the aircraft. (Geoff Ball)

27th Aurigny Airlines Twin Otter G-BIMW arrived at 1824 today with Southampton FC, ahead of the following afternoons Division One match with Liverpool. The team were transferred to Anfield by coach the next morning and the aircraft positioned over to Liverpool at 1917 to take them back to Southampton. They were glorious in victory after winning 1-0 and inflicting the second home defeat of the season on Liverpool.

December 1981

Aberdeen recorded a temperature of 15°c on the 3rd, but the month ended as one of the coldest and snowiest of the century. The transformation started when the wind changed to a northerly direction bringing snow showers into Scotland, but the chilling weather didn't reach central and southern parts of the UK until the 7th/8th, when the temperature fell below freezing and heavy snow fell widely. Exceptionally cold winters are generally characterised by long spells of dry and sunny weather, with occasional snowfalls, but this month's snow was heavy and widespread. A further snowstorm on the 11th saw the South worst hit, when roads and railways were paralysed and London recorded over a foot of snow in the suburbs. On the 13th a fierce blizzard sweeping across England, Wales & Northern Ireland and persisting over much of Scotland & Northern England, resulted in the Yorkshire Dales being buried under 3ft of snow. Even HM the Queen was affected, when she was stranded in a Cotswold pub! Sea defences were breached along the Bristol Channel and some homes in Somerset were without electricity for five days. Further snow affected the West Country on the 16th, Northern Scotland on the 17th and central & Eastern England on the 21st/22nd. High winds creating chaos in our coastal waters on the 19th, caused the Penlee lifeboat to capsize off the Cornish coast during the rescue of seamen off the crippled cargo ship, the Union Star, on a day when sixteen souls were sadly lost from both ships. A fine and frosty Christmas Day was followed by another belt of snow, crossing the UK eastwards on the 27th, but then a general thaw settled in. During the brief interlude between snowstorms on the 11th & 13th, most of England was gripped by a severe frost. The temperature at RAF Shawbury in Shropshire reached as low as -22°c at daybreak and it climbed no higher than -12°c during the afternoon of the 12th, before plummeting to -25°c in the early hours of the 13th.

The Government's approval of £41m worth of improvements for municipally-owned airports next year, meant that Manchester would be able to lengthen the main runway extension, build additional aircraft stands and make terminal improvements.

A number of British Airways Tridents made their last visits to Manchester during the year, now the type's on a slippery-slope to being phased out completely. The remaining Trident 1s are being used exclusively for Shuttle operations, Trident 2s mainly for Domestic and European services and the occasional Shuttle service, whilst Trident 3s are used on Shuttle and Domestic/European services. Details of their last visits, final flights and fates of those withdrawn this year are as follows:

G-ARPD 25/04/81, last service 30/04/81 (BA4953 Glasgow-LHR), withdrawn 04/81
G-ARPR 21/03/81, last service 31/03/81 (BA4815P Edinburgh-LHR), withdrawn 04/81
G-AVFC 27/09/81, last service 23/10/81 (BA711 Moscow-LHR), withdrawn 10/81
G-AVFH 20/02/81, last service 24/10/81 (BA5615 Aberdeen-LHR), withdrawn 10/81
G-AVFI 04/03/81, last service 11/09/81 (BA821 Dublin-LHR), withdrawn 09/81
G-AVFK 21/10/81, withdrawn 12/81

Spain's national airline, Iberia, will introduce a direct service to Madrid and Malaga next year, commencing on the 28th March. These flights will open up additional routes connecting through Madrid, giving access to the airlines extensive Domestic services to all points in southern Spain, Canary Islands and their long-haul services to Latin America and Africa.

Manchester's cattle flights to Milan continued throughout the month. Aircraft used were Air Bridge Carriers Merchantman G-APEJ & G-APES making frequent visits and a specially converted Britannia B.737, G-AXNB, was also involved.

Equipment changes on scheduled services included Air Portugal (TP458): B.707 CS-TBG (12th); Austrian Airlines (OS471): DC-9-51s OE-LDK (10th), OE-LDM (6th) & OE-LDN (3rd/17th); Lufthansa (LH4072): B.707F D-ABUA (24th); SAS (SK539): DC-9-21s LN-RLL (15th), SE-DBO (8th) & SE-DBR (1st) and Swissair (SR842): first visit MD-81 HB-INK (11th) & DC-9-32 HB-IFH (16th).

RAF ILS traffic identified included Hawks XX164 (18th), XX293 (21st) & XX313 (23rd); Nimrods XV232 (2nd) & XV246 (16th) and Dominies XS731 (2nd) & XS737 (16th). The two Nimrods performed practice ILS approaches prior to their landing at Woodford, an unidentified RAF Bulldog out of RAF Woodvale overshot (5th) and there were two unidentified RAF Jaguars (1st/16th).

1st Euroair are using their two EMB-110 Bandeirantes, G-HGGS & G-LATC, to transport Laker Airway's crews from/to Gatwick. The flights usually take place on Tuesdays and Sundays (weather/Bank Holidays permitting) and G-HGGS operated today as EZ751/2.

1st British Airways operated the first of a series of flights to Nice this month, on behalf of British Leyland with L.1011 Tristars. G-BBAG operated the first outbound flight today and the others were G-BBAG (3rd), G-BBAI (5th) & G-BBAF (7th). The inbound flights were G-BBAG (3rd), G-BBAI (5th) & G-BBAF (7th).

1st German registered Bell Long Ranger D-HBBZ owned by Alton Towers, had been a common visitor last month, but its only visit this month was today. This was due to the weather and because it was away taking up British registry, before eventually becoming G-JLBI.

3rd Jetstream G-BBYM diverted into Manchester at 1830 today, en route to Heathrow, declaring a full emergency following an electrical failure affecting its navigational capability.

5th French airline Minerve made its first visit today, with the arrival of SE.210 F-BRGU at 0943, on a night-stopping charter from/to Toulouse. It brought the French Rugby League team into Manchester for a match against Great Britain at Hull the following afternoon.

7th AA-5 Traveller G-BGPH, arriving from Blackbushe at 1701 today, was forced to stay an extra ten days due to the severe weather. It was parked outside the South Side hangars and covered by so much snow and ice, that it tipped onto its tail and was virtually submerged in a snow drift!

7th Korean Airlines B.707F HL-7427 made another visit today, positioning in at 2122 (KE9579 from Stockholm) to transport seventy cattle to Sharjah, via Frankfurt the following day.

8th A cold spell starting at the weekend, began to pay off today, as far as weather diversions were concerned. The morning produced a small number from Heathrow & Gatwick, due to snow and although Manchester had some of its own, it wasn't enough to affect operations. British Airways sent in two B.747s: G-AWNL at 1049 (BA072 from Prestwick) & G-AWNB at 1053 (BA276 from Shannon), which had previously diverted into their respective airports and set off back to London, only to be turned away again. Air Florida Miami-Gatwick flight QH200 operated by a regular to Manchester, Douglas DC-10 N1035F, also diverted in. Pan American produced the first of their newly delivered Tristar 500s, when N503PA diverted in from Gatwick at 1109 (PA090 from Houston), on a relatively new operation in direct competition with British Caledonian, who already operate the route.

9th A more organised band of snow caused short but frequent closures at Manchester today, mainly for de-icing and snow clearance. The first closure from 0850-0955, was after Trident 1 G-ARPH landed and reported that braking action on the last third of the runway was non-existent. The next from 1145-1225, was for extensive de-icing after a fresh snowfall swiftly froze and the third from 1700-1735 for snow clearance was undertaken by a single sweeper, as the other had broken down. The final closure around 1840 followed a heavy snowstorm around 1800. The airport should have only closed for an hour, but in the end it was 0615 the following morning before it reopened again.

9th In between the frequent short closures due to the wintry weather, British Midland Viscount G-AZLR diverted into Manchester at 1037 today (BD502 Ronaldsway-Liverpool).

10th The airport finally reopened at 0615 this morning, after heavy overnight snow. Due to fog in the south, it wasn't long before Manchester started receiving diversions, beginning with Laker Airways Douglas DC-10 G-GSKY at 0731 (GK020 from New York). Despite difficult handling conditions and the airport closing for further snow clearance between 0900 and 0930, Manchester received thirty diversions from a variety of airports including Heathrow, Gatwick, Brize Norton, Birmingham, Northolt, Liverpool, RAF Valley and even Dublin! Pan American diverted in a second L.1011 Tristar 500, when N501PA made its first visit at 1123 (PA090 from Houston). Other Tristars making their first visits were two Saudia diversions from Heathrow: HZ-AHP at 1135 (SV175 from Paris) & HZ-AHM at 1958 (SV189 from Jeddah). Boeing 747s of note were South African Airways ZS-SAM at 1000 (SA9224 from Abidjan) and Qantas VH-EBO at 1214 (QF001) & Cathay Pacific VR-HKG at 1523 (CX201) which both arrived from Prestwick due to handling problems there. There were also two British Airways examples: G-AWNJ at 1152 (BA072 from Montreal) & G-AWNL at 1204 (BA295 from Miami). British Caledonian pitched in with three Douglas DC-10 diversions from Gatwick: G-BEBM at 1157 (BR364 from Paris), G-BEBL at 1314 (BR666 from Salvador) & G-BHDJ at

1844 (BR334 from Tripoli). Two Birmingham diversions arriving within ten minutes of each other were Martinair DC-9F PH-MAO at 1439 (MP2337 from Amsterdam) & Spantax DC-9 EC-CGZ at 1441 (BX811 from Madrid). Up to this point, the record for the most wide-bodied aircraft on the ground at once was thirteen on 4th August 1981, but this was broken three times today. At 1517 it stood at fourteen, but when Cathay Pacific B.747 VR-HKG arrived, which incidentally suffered a bird-strike on landing, it was raised to fifteen. Two Laker DC-10s departed before three more wide-bodied aircraft arrived: DC-10 G-BHDJ, Laker A.300 G-BIMC & Saudia L.1011 HZ-AHM, which upped the total to sixteen. Other arrivals of note were Lear Jet HB-VGH diverting in from RAF Valley at 1008 & BAe.125 YU-BMA diverting in from Luton at 2014. Luckily I was off work and didn't miss anything, but my friend Brian did and after filling him in on the day's events, he picked me up his yellow 1973 Ford Escort Mk.1 (STU817L) and we set off for the airport. The terraces had long since closed by the time we got there around 8pm and after precariously driving up to the top floor of the multi-storey, we saw stands and aprons packed with diverted aircraft. While we were there, BAe.125 YU-BMA arrived in the dark, but when nothing else turned up we didn't hang around!

10th December 1981 – This shows the line up on the International Pier around 2100. Note the lit-up British Caledonian DC-10, G-BHDJ, has the newer style titles on the fuselage, as does B.707 G-BDLM in the foreground. (Geoff Ball)

10th With Manchester handling such large numbers of aircraft and more than 5,000 diverted passengers, some flights had to be turned away, but overall the airport did a remarkable job! The Qantas B.747, the Pan American L.1011 and the Laker DC-10, G-BGXE, were all parked on the newly constructed Stands, 30/31. The first aircraft to use Stand 30 was Qantas VH-EBO, but it should have been BA B.747 G-AWNL, but the pilot refused it, as it had no hydrant refuelling facilities. He then proceeded to block the taxiway for a considerable time until Stand 12 was made available for him. British Airways caused further problems by refusing to handle any more diversions after 2pm, which affected Air Rhodesia B.707 VP-WKR (RH124 from Harare) bound for Gatwick. He was originally intending to divert to Birmingham, but when their weather fell below limits the pilot requested a diversion into Manchester. He'd reached as far as Congleton beacon at FL60 (6,000ft), when he was refused permission due to the handling issues, so he proceeded up to Prestwick. Later in the evening Nigeria Airways DC-10 RP-C2003 (WT800 from Kano) had also reached FL60 on its descent into Manchester, when he too was refused by British Airways and diverted to Liverpool instead. Braniff B.747 N601BN (BN602 from Dallas) was talking to Servisair at one stage about a possible diversion into Manchester, but due to a short closure for snow clearance, he ended up at Newcastle. Two Pan American B.747 flights were also due, but they managed to beat the weather and land at Heathrow. An Olympic Airways Airbus A.300 (OA259 from Athens), which had reached Daventry beacon on its way to Manchester, made an abrupt 180° turn and diverted to Brussels, presumably because British Airways refused to handle it.

11th December 1981 – The lull before the next wave of extreme wintry weather! Manchester was calming down after yesterday's activity and although the airport was suffering from major handling problems due to the weather and the amount of diversions already received, more were accepted today. In the foreground is Zambia Airways B.707 9J-AEL, which arrived the previous morning as QZ702 and seen in the background is the only visit of Garuda Indonesia, when B.747 PK-GSD arrived later the same morning. (Geoff Ball)

11th The airport was closed from 0720-1015 for snow clearance, but seven more diversions still managed to arrive during the morning, including some of interest. Another Cathay Pacific B.747, VR-HIB appearing at 1137 (CX201 from Bahrain) on its first visit, meant there were two Cathay B.747s on the ground at the same time, as yesterdays still hadn't left. Aviaco DC-8 EC-BSD arrived at 1044 (AO4420 from Madrid), but the highlight was the one and only visit to date of Indonesian-airline Garuda, when B.747 PK-GSB which had been flight-planned into Manchester two hours earlier, arrived at 1251 (GA882 from Paris); Orion Airways B.737 G-BHVH diverted in from Luton at 1452 (KG618 from Malta) and Swissair DC-9-51 HB-ISL diverted in at 1748 (SR804Q from Zurich) due to snow at Heathrow.

11th The wide-bodied record was broken again, when our own Laker Airways New York flight GK026 operated by DC-10 G-GFAL, landed at 1315. From 1315-1431 the figure stood at seventeen and for the record they were British Airways B.747s G-AWNJ & G-AWNL;

BCAL DC-10s G-BEBL, G-BEBM & G-BHDJ; Laker Airways DC-10s G-BGXE, G-BGXF & G-GSKY; Saudia L.1011s HZ-AHM & HZ-AHP; Pan American L.1011 N501PA; Garuda B.747 PK-GSB; Qantas B.747 VH-EBO; Cathay Pacific B.747s VR-HIB & VR-HKG and South African B.747 ZS-SAM.

11th December 1981 - Today's arrival of the second Cathay Pacific, VR-HIB, caused major problems, as it was parked on Stand 14 at the end of the International Pier in such a way, there was insufficient room for other wide-bodies to pass it on the taxiway, the only one available for departures off Runway 24. This meant that wide-bodied aircraft had to enter the runway at the 06 end, back-track the runway and exit at the end, before turning around for departure off Runway 24, which caused considerable delays to outbound traffic. It was another five hours before VR-HIB was removed, only for it to block another taxiway at its narrowest point, where no aircraft whatsoever could pass it! (Manchester Airport Archive)

11th Due to the weather in the South, two interesting 'diverted' flights, Air Lanka L.1011 4R-ALF and an Alitalia A.300 (AZ304 from Rome) which were flight-planned into Manchester, failed to show as at that point the airport had been closed because of the snow.

11th The only Canadian Air Force CC-130E flight this month was today's visit of 130308 (CAM515), as CAM516 (13th) & CAM 517 (15th) were both cancelled due to the weather.

11th I'd been tempted over the last few months to replace my ageing King Sonic aircraft radio, after seeing a good range in my local Hi-Fi shop, Fairbotham & Co. Earlier in the year I'd bought a new Sharp hand-held aircraft radio from them and was now being hypnotised by a Regency Scanner in the shop window. A scanner would save the wear and tear on my wrist, from continually tuning up and down the frequencies, as it could be pre-programmed. Today was the day I finally decided to make the £200 purchase and after asking about its specifications and what it was capable of, I handed over my hard earned cash and couldn't wait to try it out. After setting it up I didn't like it, maybe I didn't give it enough of a chance, but I couldn't get used to it and after a few hours I realised what a fabulous yet simple radio my five-year old King Sonic was! I regretted buying the scanner and packed it up, hoping to get my money back. Luckily the shop gave me a full refund and that was the last of my adventures with an aircraft scanner - for another ten years at least!

11th December 1981 – Loganair SD-330 G-BGNA was new to the airline in 1979. Originally destined for Liverpool, it's seen here having diverted into Manchester (BD512 from Belfast). It was leased to Manx Airlines from June 1981 - June 1983. (Geoff Ball)

11th The Captain of BCAL BAC 1-11 G-ASJH, which brought flight BR985 in from Gatwick two days ago, had made several requests to return to Gatwick, but was still stuck with his aircraft. Due to the severity of the weather at both ends and the precarious conditions, he'd been dissuaded from leaving. After accepting his predicament he sent a crew member out to buy him some clean underwear! By early evening, after giving up all hope of leaving, he made plans to return to the hotel, which was bizarre as at that point things were moving again and operations in London told him in no uncertain terms 'To get the aircraft back to Gatwick post-haste!'

11th British Aerospace BAe.125 demonstrator G-OBAE arrived at 1637 today from Frankfurt to night-stop, before departing to Luton at 1117 the following day.

11th The first visit of a Dan-Air B.737 took place today, with the arrival of G-BICV as DA1035P, after originally diverting into Liverpool due to snow clearance at Manchester. It positioned over at 1743 and as there were no International stands available, it parked on the Domestic Pier before departing for Palma as DA1034.

11th Manchester's weather had deteriorated by the evening, with dropping temperatures, intermittent snow showers and ice forming on the taxiways. Numerous works vehicles were engaged in repositioning diverted aircraft, snow clearing, de-icing and snow sweeping. Laker flight GK212 arriving from Tenerife at 2157 got stuck in compacted snow and slush whilst attempting to clear the runway, but finally got clear by reversing and moving forward again.

11th Swissair used an MD-80 for the first time, when HB-INK operated this evening's SR842/3 Zurich flight, instead of the usual smaller Douglas DC-9-51.

11th December 1981 - Saudia L.1011 Tristar HZ-AHP & Lear Jet HB-VGH, seen here possibly parked on the old disused runway, were two of thirty fog diversions from the previous day. The fact that the airport handled any diversions at all was utterly remarkable, considering the snow and freezing conditions that had prevailed for the last three days. (Manchester Airport Archive)

11th December 1981 – This shot perfectly illustrates how bad the weather's been. Having arrived the previous evening, Saudia L.1011 HZ-AHM is seen here taxiing precariously for its departure for Heathrow. Note the snowplough and the snow still on the fuselage. Despite the clear blue sky, the conditions were very cold and extremely hazardous and more snow was on the way! (Geoff Ball)

11th December 1981 - Further overnight snow only added to the already hazardous conditions. These three British Caledonian DC-10s had great difficulty moving, once they were readied to leave. Compacted snow and ice around the wheels made it virtually impossible and with the airports de-icing rigs in constant demand, it proved to be a very challenging day for both airline and airport staff! (Manchester Airport Archive)

12th The airfield's control vehicle reported at 0400 that 'Cathay B.747 VR-HIB is stuck and under tow at the end of the East-link taxiway and taxiway 2'. He went on to describe the taxiway as 'Littered with snowballs like rocks'. The Senior Airfield Operations Controller was informed, but due to industrial problems he was unable to clear them. By 0600 the airport was affected by such dense fog that a Lufthansa cargo flight, B.737 D-ABCE, requested a follow-me vehicle whilst taxiing out for departure, as he thought he was lost! Despite all this more diversions arrived, including two British Airways aircraft from Heathrow, twelve hours apart: Trident G-AVFB at 1100 & B.747 G-BDXG at 2344 (BA282 from Los Angeles). Of the four diversions from Liverpool, the highlight was the first visit of a British Midland F.27, with the arrival of G-BLGW at 1502 (BD582 from Heathrow).

13th Overnight temperatures of -13°c made it the coldest December night at the airport since 1950. Following the early morning diversion of British Airways L.1011 Tristar G-BGBC (BA128 from Dhahran) from Heathrow, it was Manchester's turn to be affected by bad weather. There were no arrivals after 1147 and due to snow and a crosswind, the airport was closed completely by 1300.

14th The airport remained closed and there were no movements, apart from two flights given special permission to depart, which were Laker Airways BAC 1-11 G-AVBY at 1113 (GK535P to Gatwick) & Air UK Herald G-AVPN at 1426 (UK8003 to Southend). After reopening at 1615, operations were short-lived, as it was closed again from 1726-1801 to remove a snow plough blocking the runway.

15th Severe icing on the runway and taxiways closed the airport from 0030-1235.

15th Today saw the last visit of a Martinair DC-9 to Manchester, when DC-9F PH-MAR operated a round trip from Amsterdam, arriving at 1823 (MP6641/2). This aircraft was sold in October 1982, whilst their other freighter, PH-MAO, made its last visit later in the year on the 29th December (MP6643/4 from/to Amsterdam), before being sold as N502MD in April 1983. Finally, their sole passenger DC-9, PH-MAX, was transferred to KLM during the month.

16th Due to fog in the Midlands, there were two highlights amongst this morning's four diversions. The first was JCB's latest executive-toy, BAe.125-700 G-TJCB, diverting in from East Midlands at 1126. Delivered earlier this year in March, it replaces BAe.125-600 G-BJCB. The second was NLM F.27 PH-KFL (HN495 from Rotterdam) as a Birmingham diversion at 0950.

17th Local farmers came to the rescue today, by providing additional help in keeping the airport operational. The airport's snow and ice clearing machinery struggled with the Siberian-style weather and after all their de-icing methods had failed; the farmer's tractors were able to break the ice causing major hazards on the stands and taxiways,

18th Fokker F.27 G-BDVS (UK560 from Ronaldsway) got its nosewheel stuck in a snowdrift after landing, when turning off the runway onto an exit taxiway. The airport had to close from 0850- 0930, in order to take off the passengers and pull the aircraft clear.

20th Manchester received two Laker diversions, when snow closed Gatwick for spell this afternoon. DC-10 G-BGXE arrived at 1333 (GK002 from Los Angeles) & BAC 1-11 G-AVBW at 1428 (GK4956 from Milan).

20th BAe.125 G-BJOY, currently owned by Air Europe's 'top-brass', was operating from/to Gatwick this afternoon, when it made its first visit and stayed overnight.

21st The airport was closed for the second time in a week, to remove a broken down snowplough from the runway, this time from 1700-1725 today.

24th Due to an increased cargo load, Lufthansa used German Cargo Boeing 707F D-ABUA on today's LH4072/3, which operated later than usual.

24th Considering the amount of wintry weather that's been around for more than two weeks, the chances of seeing a white Christmas were very high! The airport was closed for snow clearance from 0925-1050 today and it snowed periodically up to mid-afternoon, but there was no snow on Christmas Day itself. However, the next batch of chilly weather to sweep across the country arrived on the 27th.

26th Further fog in the South East produced more diversions, but only two of interest. The first, Cathay Pacific B.747 VR-HKG at 0938 (CX201 from Bahrain) was the airlines third visit of the month and the second was first time visitor BWIA Tristar 500 9Y-TGJ at 0833 (BW900 from Bridgetown), which replaces the B.707 on their Heathrow flights.

27th Another belt of snow affecting the UK produced twenty-one diversions from Heathrow, Gatwick, Stansted, Luton, Birmingham & East Midlands, with most arrivals from 1900 onwards. Amongst them was Sudan Airways on their first visit since October 1978, with B.707 ST-AFB at 1911 (SD128 from Frankfurt). Busy Bee B.737 LN-NPB diverted in from Stansted at 2050 (BS335 from Malmo), on its first visit. Both of Monarch Airlines newly acquired Boeing 737s diverted in from Luton, with G-BMON at 2237 (OM048 from Berlin) & G-BJSO at 2323 (OM223 from Malta), as the type will eventually replace the airlines ageing B.720s. Also of note was British Airtours B.737 G-BGJG at 2143 (BA475 from Malaga), diverting from Gatwick in full British Airways colours.

28th Another diversion by Norwegian airline Busy Bee was F.27 LN-NPH, arriving from Stavanger as BS5261, after being unable to land at Norwich due to the snow.

First/Last Arrivals & Departures 1981

First arrival:	B.737 G-BJFH/AE935 from Malta at 0030
First departure:	B.737 G-BGNW/BY073A to Luton at 0745
Last arrival:	B.737 G-DDDV/AE581 from Alicante at 2329
Last departure:	B.737 EI-ASE/EI273 to Dublin at 2158

Airport stats 1981 (+/- % on previous Year)		
Scheduled Passengers	4,875,164	+10%
Freight & Mail (Tonnes)	82,379	-1%
Movements	32,535	+18%

3
Airport Diary 1982

January 1982

The first few days of the New Year were relatively mild, compared to last month's arctic weather, but the combination of heavy rain and melting snow led to serious flooding along the Yorkshire Ouse, Severn and the Trent. Arctic winds swept southwards across the country between the 3rd and 5th, then heavy snow fell across Central & Eastern Scotland and the North East. Snow at Braemar, Aberdeenshire, was 40cm deep on the morning of the 5th and at Balmoral Castle nearby, snow was on the ground continuously for fifty-six days from the 4th December 1981. The greatest disruption occurred on the 8th/9th, when an Atlantic depression moved into the South West approaches and heavy snow accompanied by gale force easterly winds produced one of the most severe blizzards of the century across southern England, Midlands, Wales & Ireland. Throughout the snowfalls lasting over thirty-six hours, temperatures between -2 and -4C made the snow dry and powdery enough to drift freely in the wind. Transport services were completely dislocated over a wide area and millions of commuters failed to get to work in London for two days running. When South Wales was isolated for three days, troops were brought in to deliver essentials and help clear the roads. Worst hit were Gloucestershire, Monmouthshire & Glamorgan, where levels snow lay over 60cm deep and drifts were 6m high. Milder air reached Cornwall and South Devon, but heavy rain falling on frozen ground in mid-Devon, South Somerset & West Dorset created extensive glazed ice. Following the blizzard the cold tightened its grip, when on the morning of the 10th the temperature fell to -26.1c at Newport in Shropshire, breaking the new record set for England just four weeks earlier. Braemar in Scotland recorded -27.2c on the same morning, equalling the UK's all-time record set way back in 1895. The afternoon maximum temperature at Braemar of -19.1c was another new record. As far south as Wiltshire, daytime temperatures struggled to reach freezing and only reached -10c in many places on the 13th, when freezing fog blanketed many areas. Warmer weather did return towards the end of the month and the rest of the winter was reasonably mild and snow-free and as a consequence of this change, the winter quarter of December 1981-February 1982 ranked only as the ninth coldest in the 20th century, but had the cold weather have continued, average temperatures could have been on a par with the infamous winter of 1962-63.

Air Canada's summer flights to Toronto and Vancouver on behalf of Jetsave have been cancelled, so alternative flights with British Airways will be offered to those who have already booked.

Due to a rail strike extra mail flights were operated throughout the month, mostly by British Air Ferries, but some were operated by Loganair. On most days from the 14th two late evening flights were operated by Heralds G-BCZG & G-BDFE, from/to Gatwick.

The Manchester-Amsterdam route will see four-daily return flights from April. The two each from British Airways and KLM represents more services than ever on an International route from Manchester and an extra midday flight on the Manchester-Paris service brings the total to six a day.

Equipment changes on scheduled services included Austrian Airlines (OS471): DC-9-51 OE-LDK (21st); Lufthansa (LH074): B.727s D-ABDI (12th) & D-ABKH (15th); SAS (SK539):

DC-9-21 LN-RLL (11th/18th), LN-RLO (25th), SE-DBR (12th/14th/21st) & SE-DBS (5th) and Swissair (SR842): DC-9-32 HB-IFU (20th).

RAF ILS traffic identified included RAF Hawk XX313 (15th), Dominies XS711 (27th), XS734 (11th) & XS738 (14th) and Andover XS641 (19th/21st). Civil ILS traffic consisted of Citation 500 PH-CTB (26th), Corvette F-BTTU (26th) and BAe.748 G-BDVH overshooting at 1328 as 'Avro 2' (28th).

1st The New Year was ushered in by dense fog, which affected operations at Manchester to such an extent that only one aircraft arrived all day. For the record this was Orion Airways B.737 G-BGTV, diverting in from East Midlands at 0055 (KG730 from Malta).

2nd Transeuropa's late evening charter, operated by SE.210 EC-CYI (TR1290/1 from/to Palma), was the Spanish airlines last visit to Manchester. Their assets were taken over by Aviaco, following years of financial trouble.

3th The ATC Watch Log recorded at 1300 today, that an object had been observed being thrown down from the pier above Stand 46, to a passenger walking out to board a British Airways Trident. The incident was reported as a possible security breach, but following a police investigation, the item was revealed as nothing more than a belt!

4th Helicopter Bell 206 Long Ranger G-LRII was a long way from its base, arriving at 1325 today from Liskard, before returning there later in the day via Exeter.

5th Falcon 50 N880F was forced to make a fuel-stop at 0856 today, en route from Goose Bay to Amsterdam, due to strong headwinds.

5th Royal Navy Sea Devon's are dwindling in numbers and today's arrival of XK895 at 1513 as 'Navy 518' from RAF Culdrose to Prestwick, was one of only two visiting Manchester during the first part of the year.

5th French Cessna 421s F-BUTD & F-GAPR, arriving during the evening from Le Havre within ten minutes of each other, departed for Leeds the following morning in a similar fashion!

6th The airport had been virtually closed on New Year's Day, due to dense fog and since then the temperature has remained close to freezing. It was closed again today for runway de-icing between 1627-1642 and 1718-1727.

8th Overnight blizzards brought heavy snow up to 9" deep and most areas dropped well below freezing. Gatwick and Birmingham were closed and Heathrow struggled to stay open with one operational runway. Manchester remained open through cold winds and frequent snow showers, up until British Airways BAC 1-11 G-BGKG (BA901 from Paris) arrived as the last flight at 1308. Liverpool was closed for a time during the morning and sent in three diversions, as did Gatwick with Laker Airways DC-10 G-BGXF at 1002 (GK012 from Miami) and British Caledonian DC-10s G-BHDH at 1029 (BR246 from Houston) & G-BGAT at 1034 (BR254 from Dallas). Most other Gatwick International and long-haul traffic diverted to either Heathrow or Stansted.

8th Douglas DC-9 PH-MAX, formerly operated by Martinair, made its first appearance at Manchester as a KLM aircraft on this morning's KL153/4. It was purchased as a replacement for PH-DNZ, which made its last visit on the 14th November last year, before it was sold.

9th Manchester reopened at 0920 today, after an 18-hour closure due to snow. The problem was further exasperated during the night, when the wind changed direction and blew the cleared snow back onto the runway. Laker DC-10 G-BGXE (GK064 from Prestwick) was the first diversion, followed by eleven more between 1534-1922, mostly British apart from World Airways DC-10 N112WA at 1657 (WO033 from Frankfurt) from Gatwick on its first visit. It would normally operate Frankfurt-London-Baltimore, but after dropping off London-bound passengers at Manchester, it continued onwards to Baltimore. There were also two Heathrow diversions: Air Portugal Boeing 727 CS-TBV at 1238 (TP450A from Lisbon) & MEA Boeing 720 OD-AFL at 1620 (ME201 from Beirut), the first visit of an MEA aircraft since B.720 OD-AFP also diverted in on 20th December 1975.

9th On a personal note, before the severe weather set in I'd arranged to spend a couple of days at Heathrow (8th/9th), staying with an old school friend now living and working in London. I'd travelled down on an early morning National Express coach from Manchester (8th), but on the morning of my departure, the weather wasn't looking too good. It was snowing and although there wasn't too much on the ground, it didn't bode well for my journey south! It was windy and bitterly cold and it got worse the further south we went, before eventually arriving at Heathrow at 3.30pm. By now the light was fading under a leaden sky, it was snowing and very windy. I foolishly made my way to the Queens Building hoping to do some spotting, but understandably it was closed. I then made my way up a multi-storey car park, which was sheer madness, as it was cold and windy beyond belief! I quickly gave up for the day and headed to my friends at Willesden, hoping for some warmth and comfort, which was wishful thinking! He shared a bedsit with five students, which was cramped, chaotic and freezing as they had no heating - even in this weather! After a cold and uncomfortable night, I decided to cut my visit short and head back home after another trip to the airport. I caught a couple of buses to Heathrow, where it was cold and windy again, with even more snow than yesterday. The Queens Building was closed again, so I ventured off to the Terminal Three car park. Once at the top, I saw the worst conditions I'd ever seen as a spotter. It was snowing heavily and the cloud was so low, the view was almost non-existent. The visibility was so poor I could only see the aircraft right in front of me and the active runway was totally obscured. Snow was ankle deep in some places and it was bitterly cold with a fierce wind. I braved it for an hour and logged very little, although aircraft seemed to be landing and departing, which was really surprising considering the weather! I caught the coach back to Manchester at 5.00pm and didn't thaw out until the following morning! As a final testament to Heathrow, the British Airport Authority and their ten snow-brush machines did an incredible job in keeping the airport running!

12th Fog affected Manchester all day, particularly in the morning and evening, when flights were cancelled or diverted to other airports, but even so, twelve diversions still managed to arrive from Liverpool due to their all-day fog. There were several of interest, including Jersey European Twin Otter G-OJEA at 0115 (JY862F from East Midlands) on its first visit since being delivered through Manchester in July 1980 and the first of only two Argosy visits during the year, when G-APRL diverted in at 0221 (BD998F from Belfast). Aer Turas CL-44 EI-BGO also diverted in during the afternoon from Cologne. The evening brought in another Liverpool diversion, with Heavylift Shorts Belfast G-BEPS as NP603 from Cologne, the first civil-registered Belfast to appear at Manchester. Heavylift purchased a number of these ex-RAF types in the late 1970s and this particular aircraft was the first to be converted for the airline. Beech 100 D-IMSH was also from Liverpool, arriving just before our visibility dropped beyond the capability of most aircraft. Three further arrivals, EI-BGO, G-BEPS & D-IMSH, were operating car-part charters on behalf of Fords. One that didn't make it was Air India flight AI503, bound for Birmingham. It made it as far as Congleton before giving up, when the visibility dropped below his landing requirements and he eventually diverted to Gatwick.

15th RAF BAe.125 XX507 arrived at 0900 today (RR1545 from Northolt), with the Prime Minister, Margaret Thatcher. She attended a local engagement before departing back to Northolt at 1626.

15th The largest executive visitor of the month was Boeing 727 N4002M. Operated by the Fluor Corporation, it arrived at 0903 today from Amsterdam, before departing for Stansted the following morning.

15th More fog across the UK brought in twenty-four diverted flights from airports such as East Midlands, Birmingham, Liverpool & Leeds and the only diversion from Heathrow, Kuwait Airways B.747 9K-ADC at 1059 (KU102 from New York) on its first visit. Aer Lingus BAC 1-11 EI-ANE diverting in at 1928 (EI764 from Cork) from Birmingham was the only other non-British arrival. British Airways Viscount G-AOYO arriving at 1953 (BA5665 from Edinburgh) was the only other diversion of any significance, as it was the final arrival of a British Airways Viscount. The seven currently operating will all be withdrawn from service in March.

15th Beech 90 N702US arrived at 1340 today to night-stop, on a delivery flight from Reykjavik to Geneva.

15th British Airways BAC 1-11 G-AVMU (BA953 from Dusseldorf), with 97 passengers onboard, burst two tyres on landing. After failing to clear the runway fully, the airport had to be closed between 1730 and 1900.

17th Birmingham was affected by fog again and today's highlight was Air India Boeing 707 VT-DSI at 1807 (AI515 from Moscow). They commenced a twice-weekly Birmingham-Bombay service, via Moscow, Amritsar & Delhi on the 3rd January and this aircraft last visited Manchester as far back as 25th September 1970. Gatwick was also affected by fog during the morning and again in the evening, but the only diversion from there was Laker Airways DC-10 G-GFAL at 1954 (GK454 from Palma), as Heathrow, Stansted & Bournemouth seemed to be the main beneficiaries.

20th Two Heathrow diversions making it into Manchester this morning due to fog, were British Airways B.747 G-AWNC at 1020 (BA274 from Boston) & Kenya Airways B.707 5Y-BBJ at 1040 (KQ214 from Rome). Most aircraft diverted to Gatwick and a few made it to Birmingham.

21st A two-day rail stoppage on the 13th & 14th, saw a 65% increase in passengers using British Airways/British Caledonian London flights, compared to the same time last week.

22nd Thurston Aviation PA-23 G-AZHA inbound from Glasgow at 2350 today, made a heavy landing due to a sudden gust of wind, which caused a burst nosewheel tyre and bent propeller tips on the left engine. Although the damage was slight, the runway was closed for over an hour before the aircraft was towed away for attention at NEA, before departing back to Glasgow on the 24th.

24th A very grey, overcast Manchester saw the arrival of ten diversions between 0527 and 1828, on a day when the airport was initially prepared for up to five wide-bodied and ten narrow-bodied aircraft. The first was Dublin diversion Aer Lingus B.737 EI-BEB at 0527 (EI6577 from Malaga), followed by B.737 EI-ASL at 0755 (EI9529 from Paris). Gatwick produced four diversions: British Caledonian DC-10s G-BEBL at 1023 (BR246 from Houston) & G-BHDJ at 0611 (BR366 from Kano), Cathay Pacific B.747 VR-HID at 0959 (CX201 from Bahrain) on its first visit and Braniff B.747 N601BN at 0931 (BN602 from Dallas), which seemed to be on its way to Prestwick at one point. Two Heathrow diversions arriving within ten minutes of each other were Air India B.747 VT-EBN at 0910 (AI112 from New York) and the first visit of a Boeing 747SP, with the arrival of South African Airways ZS-SPA at 0920

(SA236 from Sal Island), in the revised colour scheme of English writing on the port side and Afrikaans on the starboard side. Finally, there were two evening diversions from Birmingham: Aer Lingus B.737 EI-ASL at 1828 (EI272 from Birmingham) and another visit from Air India with B.707 VT-DSI at 1729 (AI515 from Moscow).

24th January 1982 – Braniff International who began in 1928, started operations from the UK in 1978, with their Dallas-Gatwick service. Although Manchester was declared as their No.1 diversionary airport, today's arrival of B.747 N601BN, seen here returning to Gatwick, was the last of only three visits. They also operated a DC-8 military charter in 1978 from Manchester, but they ceased trading later this year in May. (Geoff Ball)

26th Two USA bound PA-23 Aztec's, N40375 & N200RD, en route from Madrid to Stornaway today, diverted in after N200RD developed engine problems. It declared a full emergency with oil low pressure, but after receiving attention with NEA, they continued on their way on the 1st February.

26th WDL Fokker F.27 D-BOOM, arriving at 2311 today as WS111, was operating a freight charter from/to Frankfurt.

28th Flying Tigers DC-8 N790FT made its first visit today, operating another Australia bound livestock flight, originally to be operated by a Korean Airlines Boeing 707F. Due to its late arrival into Manchester by several hours and having to be thoroughly cleansed at Stansted, the crew had gone 'out of hours'; so it departed the following day at 1527 routing Manchester-Keflavik-Anchorage-Fiji-Adelaide.

February 1982

Manchester's landing charges will increase by 9% from the 1st April, as will car parking and access to the spectator terraces by 20%. As the demand for car parking currently outstrips supply, it's hoped that increased coach services from the North will bring less cars to the airport. In a bid to attract new airlines, a 50% rebate scheme on off-peak operations will be offered from April.

Due to the continuing rail-strike, 2-3 extra mail flights are still being operated by British Air Ferries Heralds most evenings, but they seemed to have stopped by the 19th. Aircraft used were G-BAVX & G-BDFE in full BAF colours, G-BCZG in basic BAF colours with no titles and G-BEYE in 'Agloco' titles, belonging to the Libyan oil company from whom it was leased.

The last Lufthansa Boeing 737-130 to visit, D-ABEY, operated LH074/5 for the final time on the 24th. The Frankfurt service will continue to be operated by the B.737-200QC and the B.737-230ADV, a type the airlines been receiving over the past twelve months. They received twenty-two B.737-130s from December 1967 to February 1969 and the first one to visit Manchester was D-ABES on 1st July 1969, on commencement of their Manchester-Frankfurt passenger service. The -100 series was slightly shorter in length than the more successful -200 that followed. In 1970, when Boeing only had orders for a mere thirty 737 aircraft, serious consideration was given to closing down production altogether, but they continued mainly due to Boeing's Supersonic Transport project being cancelled, which freed up the funds to carry on. A full breakdown of their final visits is detailed below:

D-ABEA	26/04/1981	D-ABEB	10/06/1981
D-ABEC	19/05/1981	D-ABED	21/08/1981
D-ABEF	31/05/1981		

All of the above were sold to Far Eastern Air Transport

D-ABEG	05/04/1981	D-ABEH	04/10/1981
D-ABEI	01/06/1981	D-ABEK	15/04/1981
D-ABEL	30/07/1981	D-ABEM	13/06/1981
D-ABEN	11/10/1980	D-ABEO	03/07/1980
D-ABEP	12/10/1981	D-ABEQ	27/12/1981
D-ABER	05/10/1980	D-ABES	07/12/1980
D-ABET	11/06/1981	D-ABEU	20/07/1981
D-ABEV	14/04/1981	D-ABEW	10/02/1982
D-ABEY	24/02/1982		

All of the above were sold to People Express.

Equipment changes on scheduled services included Air Portugal (TP458): B.727-200 CS-TBX (27th); Austrian Airlines (OS471): DC-9-51 OE-LDK (21st); Lufthansa (LH074): B.727s D-ABDI (12th), D-ABKH (15th) & Condor B.737 D-ABHD (26th); SAS (SK539): DC-9-21 LN-RLL (11th/18th), LN-RLO (25th), SE-DBR (12th/14th/21st) & SE-DBS (5th) and Swissair (SR842): DC-9-32 HB-IFU (20th).

RAF ILS traffic identified included Hawks XX181 (25th), XX237 (1st), XX299 (8th), XX305 (18th), XX309 (1st) & XX310 (1st); C-130 XV179 (25th); Dominie XS738 (4h) and RAE Comet XS235 from/to Boscombe Down as 'MPRHM' (18th). Civil ILS traffic included Corvette F-BVPK (2nd) and British Aerospace BAe.125 G-BFAN from/to Hawarden (15th).

1st The most notable military visitor of the month was today's arrival of French Navy Nord 262 No.70 at 1336, on a training flight from Cardiff to Edinburgh. It made a further visit on the 3rd, this time from Glasgow to Munster.

1st The trend of British out-of-sequence registrations, shows no sign of slowing down. This was demonstrated by Partenavia P.68 G-SVHA (registered in 1981) arriving from Humberside, before departing for Ostend later on. The 'SVHA' stands for Sullom Voe Harbour Authority in the Shetland Isles, well known for its major oil terminal.

4th There were only two Royal Navy Sea Heron visits to Manchester this year. The first, XR442 arriving at 1524 today as 'Navy 719' from/to Yeovilton, had previously operated for the Queens Flight, before the unit re-equipped with BAe.748s in the late1960's.

5th This was the day Sir Freddie Laker's world came crashing down! A.300 G-BIMA had left Manchester at 0910 (GK211 to Tenerife) with a full load, but it was ordered back half way into its journey. When it eventually landed at 1138, its alcohol content had been cleared out by the passengers and crew! This was possibly the final landing anywhere of a Laker Airways aircraft. Another, DC-10 G-BGXF, was being readied for departure (GK063 bound for Prestwick/Miami), but the passengers were eventually offloaded and told to return their duty-free goods and collect their baggage. There was also a BAC 1-11, G-AVBW, parked on the South Bay, which had flown the writer back from Malta less than two weeks ago. All three aircraft were removed to the new apron area and effectively impounded by the Airport Authority, who placed blocks of concrete in front of them. Most Laker passengers stranded abroad were brought home courtesy of Britannia Airways. Whilst the repercussions of the collapse would be felt for months to come, the majority of IT flights were picked up by other operators, but the transatlantic flights were another matter, as no interest was shown in taking them over. According to Manchester Airport's figures, Laker had been carrying approximately 9% of the airports traffic, 2% of which were flights to the USA & Canada.

6th February 1982 – Yesterday's demise of Laker Airways saw DC-10 G-BGXF & A.300 G-BIMB impounded on the West Apron - a sad end for such a pioneering and ambitious airline! (Geoff Ball)

6th British Caledonian acquired two 'new' BAC 1-11s, the first of which, G-BJRT, visited today (BR952 Edinburgh-Gatwick). The second, G-BJRU, made its first visit on the 13th March, operating the same flight. Bought from German-airline Hapag-Lloyd, both had visited Manchester previously as D-ALFA (G-BJRT) & D-ANUE (G-BJRU).

10th In the wake of the Laker crash, the airport's management team have been working hard at selling Manchester's services They've been busily contacting British and American airlines to persuade them to step in and as a result a number are actively considering bidding for Laker's transatlantic services next week, after they've been revoked. Laker carried more than 130,000 passengers from Manchester last year, of which 65,000 were to Miami, 27,000 to Los Angeles and 40,000 to New York.

11th The second Royal Navy Sea Heron to visit within seven days was XM296, arriving at 1524 today (Navy 729 from Wyton), before departing the following morning for Prestwick.
11th Air Atlantique DC-3 G-AMPO arrived at 1813 today from Jersey, before departing later in the evening for Bristol.

11th February 1982 - SAS operated eight shorter Douglas DC-9-21s, which were commonplace this year. At the airlines request, McDonnell-Douglas specifically designed this series, with more powerful engines, stronger wings and a shorter fuselage, than the original Series -10. The first were delivered to SAS in 1968. (Geoff Ball)

15th Manchester received two early morning Heathrow diversions, British Airways B.747 G-AWNC at 0528 (BA006 from Anchorage) & TWA B.747 N53110 at 0706 (TW700 from New York). The TWA aircraft went tech with a thrust reverser problem, before eventually leaving the following day at 0715.
16th Citation 551 G-BJIL, operated by Mining Company Rio Tinto Zinc, arrived at 0808 today from Biggin Hill. It was on its first visit, night-stopping, before departing for Haugesund the following morning. It served the company until 1984, when it was sold in the USA.
17th PA-31 Navajo G-NMAN, owned and piloted by the pop singer Gary Numan, arrived from Edinburgh at 1745 today. He gained notoriety for his near-death experience last month, when his aircraft crash-landed on a Southampton motorway. It was widely reported that he was the pilot, but on that particular day he was in fact a passenger. Customs & Excise prevented the aircraft from being moved from the crash-site, until they had classed it as an imported item, which took several days!
18th A very rare RAF military type, the Percival Pembroke, paid a visit to Manchester today, when XK884 operated from/to RAF Wildenrath as RR8020. The type, which entered RAF service as far back as 1953, is still used by No.60 squadron based at RAF Wildenrath, Germany.
18th Twelve months after British Airways introduced an alpha-numeric system for ATC purposes, Dan-Air introduced their own today, to be used on all their flights, except for IT and Charters. As far as Manchester's concerned, the change affected the following City-link flights

until the 25th March, when the routes were taken over by Metropolitan Airways who reverted back to using the flight numbers:
DA051 - Newcastle-MAN-Cardiff-Bournemouth (Tue/Thu), new call-sign DA'B6EE
DA052 - Bournemouth-Birmingham-MAN-Newcastle (Tue/Thu), new call-sign DA'B6EF
DA058 - Bournemouth-Cardiff-MAN-Newcastle (Tue/Thu), new call-sign DA'B6EL
DA059 - Newcastle-MAN-Birmingham-Bournemouth (Tue/Thu), new call-sign DA'B6EM

19th BAe.125 N400KC, operated by multi-national health care company Kimberley-Clark, made its first visit to Manchester arriving at 0936 today from Newcastle, before departing in the afternoon for Heathrow.

21st The airport staged a practice disaster today, so the police, fire, ambulance and other emergency services could deal with a 'bomb situation'. In a realistic re-enactment, dozens of police and firemen rushed to the airport at midday, after being alerted to a bomb onboard a Britannia Airways B.737, heading to Belfast from Munster, Germany. As soon as they were notified of the aircrafts imminent arrival 'Operation Firecracker' triggered into action. The 'practice plane' landed safely and the passengers were quickly disembarked and transferred onto two airport coaches, before the 21lb device exploded. The 'bomb' had been taken onboard by a covert 'passenger', hidden inside his hand luggage. Four hours into the practice, the scenario was that of the 127 passengers, 14 were dead, 76 were injured and being treated at Wythenshawe and Withington Hospitals and the remaining 37, including 6 children were uninjured. To add realism to the event, a Britannia Airways B.737 was used for some of the time. After the exercise, airport and emergency services chiefs scrutinised the operation to see where improvements could be made. It brought to light that evacuating passengers had been allowed to take their belongings with them, which could have included the bomb! In view of this finding, rules on what passengers could and couldn't take with them during a 'bomb scare' evacuation would be tightened up.

22nd Citation 501 G-BIZZ, arriving at 1302 today from Reykjavik, was on delivery to Vickers Engineering. It departed the following day for Cranfield and will eventually be based at Barrow.

23rd A flurry of Liverpool diversions this evening were Genair EMB-110 G-RLAY at 2047 (ZA406 from Gatwick), Air Ecosse EMB-110 G-CELT at 2146 (postal flight WG926 from Dublin) & NLM Fokker F.27 PH-KFH at 2104 (BD590 from Heathrow), which is currently on lease to British Midland.

24th Heathrow was affected by dense fog until early afternoon, but unfortunately so was Manchester during the morning. Although a number of diversions were received, the toll could have been so much higher. There were some interesting arrivals however, including four British Airways B.747s: G-AWNO at 0853 (BA014 from Muscat), G-AWNN at 1008 (BA256 from Bridgetown), G-BBPU at 1016 (BA274 from Boston) & G-AWNB at 1125 (BA295 from Miami). Another TWA B.747, N93105, arrived at 0937 (TW770 from Chicago) and Lufthansa chipped in with Airbus A.300 D-AIBC at 1004 (LH030 from Frankfurt), on its first visit. The final diversion was also a first visit, with Alitalia Airbus A.300 I-BUSF at 1201 (AZ282 from Rome), landing under a bright blue sky.

24th Air UK BAC 1-11 G-AXMU operated an outbound charter to Strasbourg (UK2863), before returning on the 26th, possibly in connection with the European Parliament.

25th RAF Dominies that actually land at Manchester are very rare indeed, but XS729 diverted in at 1713 today (FYN50 from Finningley), after declaring an emergency with low fuel.

27th February 1982 – Included in this morning line up of various diversions is Air Mauritius B.707 3B-NAE, which went on to serve with the airline until 1988. British Caledonian merged with British Airways and Air Florida ceased trading in July 1984. (Geoff Ball)

27th February 1982 – One of several diversions this morning was Eagle Air Boeing 707F TF-VLJ. Operating a freight flight on behalf Libyan Arab, it was the first visit by the airline since its inception in 1965. This aircraft was operated by Libyan Arab until 1984, when it returned to Eagle Air. It was sold to Boeing in 1986 for spares, as part of the USAF KC-135 programme. (Geoff Ball)

27th Having seen last night's weather forecast, as I did every evening, there was no indication that anything exciting might happen, so I wasn't expecting twenty-two airliners to divert in from Heathrow and Gatwick before midday! Three British Airways flights were B.747 G-BDXD at 1125 (BA010 from Bombay) and two B.737s which were low on fuel: G-BGJG at 0952 (BA5603 from Aberdeen) & G-BGDL at 0959 (BA373 from Brussels) making its first visit. Four British Caledonian DC-10 flights were G-BGAT at 1104 (BR246 from Houston), G-BHDH at 0921 (BR254 from Dallas), G-BHDJ at 0942 (BR676 from San Juan) & G-DCIO at 1116 (BR232 from Atlanta). Lufthansa went mad when three Heathrow flights ventured North: B.727s D-ABCI at 1004 (LH040 from Hamburg) & D-ABKJ at 1027 (LH050 from Dusseldorf) and B.737 D-ABFW at 1104 (LH046 from Bremen). Other arrivals included Cathay Pacific B.747 VR-HIB at 0946 (CX201) on its first visit, Air Florida DC-10 N102TV at 0935 (QH200 from Miami), Finnair DC-9-51 OH-LYW at 1118 (AY831 from Helsinki), the colourful Air Mauritius B.707 3B-NAE at 1152 (MK042 from Rome), which was the first Mauritius registered aircraft to visit Manchester and Eagle Air B.707F TF-VLJ making its first visit at 1017 (LN2600 from Tripoli) in full Libyan Arab colours. Also making its first visit was BWIA L.1011-500 9Y-TGN at 1024 (BW900 from Bridgetown). A former airport employee recalls the events surrounding the arrival of this aircraft 'It followed the usual procedure as any diversion, the airline deciding whether to fuel and return for an approach at destination, or if absolutely necessary terminate at Manchester. The usual factors were considered under the 'fuel and go' scenario, such as crew duty hours and the weather at the destination, a decision often influenced by ATC flow control, which slowed up departures. If as in this case, the airline terminated the flight at Manchester, it was put in the queue for a baggage handling crew and coaches to transport the passengers by road to London. Until these were in place with accurate time estimates, the passengers had to remain onboard. Allocating a baggage crew was a critical factor, as offloading passengers into the reclaim area without knowing when their bags would be delivered, would cause huge congestion around the carousels. Similarly, if they reclaimed their bags but then had a long wait for coaches, the arrivals hall would become a hot spot, so the simple solution was to keep the passengers onboard until everything was in place. On this day the airline took quite a while to decide what to do. Experienced in these scenarios and anticipating the airline may decide to terminate, the ground handling company put the flight in the 'potential offload and coaches' queue, subject to confirmation, which was eventually received. In those days all baggage handling was provided by Manchester Airport Authority loaders and usually they were able to muster excellent resources to handle significant numbers of diversions within a reasonable timescale, but on this particular flight something went wrong. As the ground handling company were advised that a baggage crew was en route to offload the bags, the passengers began to deplane and make their way to baggage reclaim, but at the last minute the loading crew were sent to another flight. This left the BWIA passengers in the reclaim area with no sign of their bags. Understandably, tempers frayed very quickly, after a long flight and an extended period of sitting onboard at the gate and now the unfortunate passengers were left waiting for their bags. In these situations there is often a 'ringleader' amongst the passengers, who serves to wind everybody up and in this case one lady did this with ease, along with a large group of her fellow passengers. She was shrieking at the top of her voice at the reclaim area staff and the situation was becoming very unpleasant, with the all-female passenger handling team being physically threatened by the angry group. The police were called, but prior to their arrival help arrived from an unlikely source. Musician Paul McCartney was a passenger onboard the flight and he calmly stepped forward into the fray and stood on a seat to address his fellow travellers. He said, "Please all stop shouting at the staff. They are doing their best; you can see how busy the place is today.

There's lots of aircraft that should be in Heathrow". He then turned to the ringleader and simply said, "Lady, lady, just calm down, it's a bad situation, but it's not their fault". Amazingly, everybody went quiet and for few minutes Paul McCartney acted as the go-between, relaying information to the passengers. The police arrived, but they weren't needed and the bags arrived shortly afterwards'.

27th Eagle Air PA-31 TF-VLH, arrived at 1235 today (VL620/1 from/to Reykjavik), with a fresh crew to operate B.707F TF-VLJ back to Tripoli as LN2601.

March 1982

The Government put forward a £70m extension plan for Stansted Airport, which would make it London's third airport, capable of handling 15m passengers by 1992. Meanwhile, the ongoing Public Enquiry by the North of England Regional Consortium, consisting of eleven County Councils, six City Councils and eight Regional Authorities, claim it's a direct threat to the regeneration of the North West and Northern regions. They say if the money was spent on the North instead, an extra 15,000 jobs would be created by the region's airports, including Manchester. It was also stressed that the Stansted development, ultimately costing more than £100m, would undermine the role and potential of regional airports, especially Manchester and would further widen the North/South divide. They added it could prove to be the costliest 'white elephant' ever constructed, if the national economic recovery was as slow as its forecast. The consortium, due to be heard on 21st September, recommends the Public Enquiry Inspector informs the Government of the following:

a) There should be no new major facility in the South East.

b) Foreseeable passenger demand in the South East can be met by the construction of a fourth terminal at Heathrow and a second at Gatwick.

c) Work should only go ahead if the potential for growth at regionally-based air services is acknowledged and encouraged.

d) Strong regionally-based carriers should be developed.

e) Commitment of major public resources for the development of a new major airport in the South East is not in the best interests of the nation and redressing the gap between the North and South should have a higher priority.

f) Regional airports should be allowed to use their own revenues and make capital investment in themselves without official restraint.

g) All regional airports should have access to EEC regional development fund money.

The brewers, Greenall Whitley, have bought Arrowsmith Holidays, who were part of the Laker Group. They have paid all the outstanding debts and as soon as existing bookings are reconfirmed, they will start taking new business. If they hadn't have stepped in, Arrowsmith Holidays would have been boycotted by Spanish hoteliers, over uncertainty of payment.

From the 1st April, passengers can make a free telephone call to book their car parking space at the airport. The scheme which is available until 30th November, will apply to surface car parks F & G for a minimum stay of seven days, with the fee being paid on exit. The airport will also provide a recommended price list of taxi fares to prevent overcharging. Leaflets available from the airport and travel agents will detail prices within the City and up to a 4-mile radius outside. Greater Manchester City charges are at meter rates only, but journeys outside of this are negotiable, but subject to a recommended maximum fare plus a third.

The airport has succeeded in recapturing most of the Laker Airways business due to be operated in the summer, except for the Los Angeles and New York flights. British

Caledonian will base a DC-10 for IT operations at Manchester between Wednesday-Sunday, Monarch Airlines will increase weekly flights from 4 to 24, with the additional flights using a based B.720, Orion Airways will add an extra 50 weekly flights and Britannia Airway's 110 weekly movements will increase to 150, with extra B.737s being based.

Air Manchester has been formed by Sureway Travel to rescue thousands of holidays in jeopardy since Laker's collapse. The new airline, who were able to purchase a BAC 1-11 at a knockdown price of £1.2m, are planning to add a second aircraft by the end of next month. Before Laker's crash, Sureway who only set up in January, were projected to turn over £7m in their first summer of trading.

Following on from last year's announcement by Olympic Airway's regarding new three-times-weekly flights to Athens via Brussels with Boeing 727s, they have been put back until 1983 at least.

Equipment changes on scheduled flights included Air France sub-chartering (AF964/3) a couple of times due to a cockpit crew dispute, using Eagle Air Boeing 720 TF-VLB (28th) & Tunis-Air Boeing 727 TS-JHT which was on its first visit (29th). Lufthansa's new Boeing 737-200ADVs are now regular visitors and the B.727s used were D-ABKA (6th), D-ABRI (26th), D-ABKJ (29th) & D-ABKT (30th/31st). SAS used their DC-9-21s again on numerous occasions: LN-RLO (3rd), SE-DBO (23rd/24th), SE-DBP (4th), SE-DBR (1st/11th) & SE-DBS (2nd/9th/25th) and Swissair used MD-80 HB-INE (3rd) and shorter DC-9-32, HB-IFK (30th).

RAF ILS traffic identified included Hawks XX162 (25th), XX165 (4th), XX223 (3rd/23rd), XX296 (30th) & XX299 (2nd); C-130 XV177 (15th); Vulcan XM603 (12th); Jetstreams XX482 (23rd), XX493 (18th) & XX494 (23rd) and an unidentified RAF Jaguar overshot at 1311 as EMQ39 (2nd). Civil ILS traffic were Corvette F-BTTU (23rd), Lufthansa Beech 90 D-ILHC (24th) & Guernsey Airlines SD-330 G-BITV (20th).

2nd Cessna Citation 500 G-BHTT made its first visit today, arriving at 1151 on a flight from Leeds. Based at Birmingham, it's operated on behalf of Lucas Industries, who are well known in the motor and aerospace industry for producing spark plugs.

4th This month's only cattle flight was operated by Air Bridge Carriers Merchantman G-APEJ, which positioned down from Glasgow today, before departing outbound to Milan at 1114 as AK140.

7th Spantax operated Britannia Airways BY421B/A from/to Malaga rotation during the month, with CV-990 EC-CNH today and DC-8 EC-CCG (14th/21st/28th).

9th A short flurry of morning fog diversions from Heathrow and Gatwick, produced plenty of first visits. British Airways B.747 G-BDXI at 0752 (BA020 from Muscat), British Caledonian DC-10 G-BGAT at 0837 (BR246 from Houston), Qantas B.747 VH-EBR at 0749 (QF001 from Bahrain), Air Rhodesia B.707 VP-WKR at 0812 (RH122 from Frankfurt) which was a new airline to Manchester and Bangladesh Biman B.707 S2-ACF at 0841 (BG001 from Dubai). Others arrivals were TWA B.747 N53116 at 0844 (TW704 from New York), South African B.747 ZS-SAP at 0848 (SA220 from Sal Island), Cathay Pacific B.747 VR-HKG (CX201 from Bahrain) and completing a busy hour was KLM DC-9 PH-DNL at 0900 (KL115 from Amsterdam). A deterioration in the evening weather provided Manchester with two diversions from East Midlands: Air Bridge Viscount G-BFMW at 2228 (AK554 from Aberdeen) and Air Bridge Argosy G-APRL at 2313 (AK445 from Belfast).

11th The only interesting military visitor this month was French Air Force Noratlas 150/64-IU, arriving at 1035 today on a training flight (FM0402 Edinburgh-Bournemouth).

12th Executive Express Cessna 421, registration unknown, was en-route as EX612 from Luton-Dublin, when the pilot decided to divert into Manchester due to high winds at Dublin. After making three failed approaches due to strong winds between 0312 and 0328, he returned to Luton where he also failed to land, before eventually touching down at Heathrow.

12th Air Atlantique DC-3 G-AMPY positioned in from Blackpool at 0821 today, to operate an outbound charter to Dublin. It was the aircrafts first visit to Manchester since 17th May 1978, when it diverted in from East Midlands, operating a British Midland cargo flight.

12th Vulcan XM603 overshot at 1213 today (Avro 10 from RAF Waddington), prior to its retirement from RAF service and ultimate preservation at Woodford, where it was built in 1964.

13th PA-28 Cherokee OY-CBG arrived at 1222 today from Newtonards, for Air Kilroe to take up British marks. It became G-BJXW and returned to Newtonards on the 1st July.

13th The second of British Caledonian's recently acquired BAC 1-11s, G-BJRU, visited Manchester this evening, operating BR952 Edinburgh/Gatwick. As mentioned last year, the airline sold all seven of their BAC 1-11-200s to American airline, Pacific Express. These aircraft were delivered brand new to British United in 1965, before eventually passing over to Caledonian when the airlines merged in 1970. The last to visit Manchester was G-ASJE on 19th March 1982 and a full breakdown of their final visits are detailed below:

G-ASJC, 09/09/81, sold as N101EX 12/81	G-ASJC, 09/09/81, sold as N101EX 12/81
G-ASJE, 19/03/82, became N102EX 06/82	G-ASJF, 26/02/82, became N103EX 04/82
G-ASJG, 19/01/82, became N104EX 03/82	G-ASJH, 20/12/81, became N105EX 02/82
G-ASJI, 10/01/82, became N106EX 01/82	G-AST, 09/08/81, became N107EX 10/81

14th Braathens Boeing 737 LN-SUS, which had last visited Manchester on 16th December 1973, positioned in from Gothenburg today to operate an outbound charter to Oslo.

15th Today's arrival of OH-LSG as KR3371/2, was a first visit and the first of three businessmen's charters during the month, from/to Helsinki. Operated by Finnair SE.210s on behalf of Kar-Air, the others were OH-LSD as KR3373/4 (17th) & OH-LSG again as KR3375/6 (19th).

16th Another type on the endangered species list, is the Beagle 206. Although most British registered examples are being snapped up in the United States, Manchester saw the first visit of Halfpenny-Green based G-BCIU at 0818 today. It was operating a flight to Malmo, before returning from Hamburg at 1738 on the 18th. Formerly XS780 with the RAF until its sale to a private owner in 1974, it too was snapped up by an American buyer in June 1983 and sold as N3947L.

16th Corse Air SE.210 F-BVSF, arriving at 1400 today to night-stop, was operating a return charter from/to Paris-Orly (CS232/3). It had visited Ringway previously in 1980 as an Aerotour aircraft.

17th The Shorts SD-330 demonstrator, G-BDBS, called in from Gatwick at 1721 today to pick up a passenger, whilst en-route to Belfast Harbour.

18th The second Cessna Citation making its first visit to Manchester this month, was Citation 501 D-IANO at 0958 today, from/to Heathrow.

18th New corporate BAe.125 G-BHSU, owned and operated by Shell UK, made its first visit today, routing from Liverpool to Amsterdam. On the subject of BAe.125s, there have been no visits for customs clearance en-route from/to Hawarden so far this year.

20th Condor Boeing 737 D-ABHD arriving at 1432 today (DF481 from Rome), was operating the flight on behalf of Britannia Airways, before positioning out to Frankfurt later.

20th C-130 XV203 arriving at 2108 (RR4405 Gibraltar-Lyneham) was the first of two trooping flights this month. The second was XV196 (RR4418 Gibraltar- Lyneham) on the 21st.

23rd Fairflight Charter's new Citation 551, G-BJVP, made its first visit today arriving from Biggin Hill at 1837, to operate to Aberdeen the next morning. Delivered new earlier this month, its life on the UK register was short-lived, as it was sold in the USA the following year.

24th Three Heathrow diversions arriving at Manchester due to fog were Qantas B.747 VH-EBM at 0726 (QF001 from Bahrain), TWA B.747 N17125 at 0737 (TW700 from New York) on its first visit since its purchase from British Airways and Lufthansa B.737 D-ABHH at 0819 (LH062 from Stuttgart).

24th Turbo-Islander G-BJOH arrived from Leicester at 0852 today, to operate a couple of demonstration flights from the South Side, before returning to Leicester at 1439.

24th BAC 1-11 HZ-MAM made its first visit today, arriving from Le Bourget to pick up its owner, Sheikh Al Midani and take him to the USA. The same multi-millionaire also owns BAe.125 HZ-MMM, which has visited Manchester on several occasions.

26th As well as Lufthansa Beech 90 D-ILHC making an ILS approach on the 24th, another D-ILHA, appearing at 1058 today from Dublin, stayed a mere ten minutes before departing for Stansted.

27th On a very windy Saturday morning, four diversions arrived from Dublin, where the wind was even stronger. Three were Aer Lingus B.737 flights: EI-ASB at 0446 (EI6377 from Palma), EI-BEB at 0311 (EI6583 from Malaga) & EI-BCR at 0309 (EI6515 from Rome) and the fourth was Lufthansa B.737 D-ABFL at 1129 (LH078 from Frankfurt).

27th SAS have ceased operating Fred Olsen Electra's on their Copenhagen freight flight. LN-FOI operated the last one today and when the flights recommenced on the 30th, they reverted to operating their own DC-9s again.

27th Ex-resident PA-30 Twin Comanche G-AVPS arrived at 1116 today, with passengers for the afternoons Manchester Utd v Sunderland match.

27th British Airways Trident 1 G-ARPK operated its final flight this evening, arriving as Shuttle back flight BA4524 at 2221. It will now be used by the Airport Authority for fire practice.

28th Iberia commenced a new Manchester-Malaga/Madrid service today, three-times weekly on Wed/Fri/Sun at 1640/1730. The first flight was operated by Douglas DC-9 EC-BPG, which was still in the airline's old colours. To commemorate the new service, the Chairman of the Manchester Airport Authority was presented with a replica of El Cid's sword.

28th Sterling SE.210 OY-STI arrived on a passenger charter from Gothenburg today. It night-stopped, then positioned out to Paris-Orly the following afternoon.

29th Metropolitan Airways have taken over the Inter-City operation from Dan-Air. The route, which still links Manchester to Newcastle, Birmingham, Cardiff & Bournemouth, will now be operated by ex-Loganair Twin Otters G-BHFD & G-BIEM. It's hoped the use of the smaller 20-seat aircraft will return the City-Link operation to profit.

30th Air Europe's latest aircraft, B.737 G-BRJP, due to be based at Gatwick for the summer, made its first appearance at Manchester today operating AE511/0 from/to Malaga.

30th NLM operated an outbound passenger charter to Amsterdam with Fokker F.27 PH-KFE, departing at 1838 today as HN4407.

31st Air India Boeing 707 VT-DSI, arriving at 0048 today (AI515 from Moscow), diverted into Manchester due to Birmingham's night-time closures for runway engineering work.

31st Another Citation making its first visit this month was Citation 550 I-ARIB, arriving at 1713 today from Milan-Malpensa.

April 1982

There were further British Airways Trident withdrawals towards the end of last month. Details of their last visits to Manchester and ultimate fates are as follows:
G-ARPH 25/03/82, last serv. 26/03/82 (BA4952 LHR-Glasgow), preserved Cosford 04/82
G-ARPK 27/03/82, last serv. 27/03/82 (BA4524P LHR-MAN), w'drawn MAN 03/82
G-ARPL 24/03/82, last serv. 26/03/82 (BA4814 LHR-Edinburgh), w'drawn Edinburgh 03/82
G-ARPN 16/03/82, last serv. 26/03/82 (BA4940 LHR-Glasgow), w'drawn Aberdeen 03/82
G-ARPW 19/03/82, last serv. 26/03/82 (BA4651 Belfast-LHR), w'drawn Teeside 03/82
G-AVFB 27/03/82, last serv. 26/03/82 (BA4525P MAN-LHR), preserved Cosford 06/82
G-AVFD 20/02/82, last serv. 22/03/82 (BA379 Brussels-LHR), w'drawn 03/82
G-AVFJ 18/02/81, last serv. 26/03/82 (BA711 Moscow-LHR), w'drawn 03/82

Despite the collapse of Laker Airways, more passengers used Manchester last month than March last year. The figures showed an increase in movements of 18% and a 1% increase in passengers, but the freight figures showed a 9% decrease.

The idea of a cargo village, first mooted in 1972, was shelved years ago when the economic recession stunted any growth in air cargo worldwide. However, it's been resurrected and while plans are only at the discussion stage, its hoped work will start next year. The airport's keen to build the necessary roads and the first cargo building, so to speed things up private investment has been invited to fund the village piece by piece, as more space is needed. As the first phase is estimated to cost £5m, cargo firms wanting accommodation in the complex are expected to invest in the project by paying for the buildings they plan to occupy.

Several airlines made changes to their summer schedules. Air Ecosse will operate two weekday flights to Aberdeen/Dundee and a third (WG752/3) on Mon/Wed/Fri. Air Malta will operate twice-weekly and add a third flight between June-October, as well as numerous charter flights. Austrian Airlines flights will increase to three-weekly again. Air Portugal's twice-weekly flight to Lisbon now serves Oporto. Air UK will add three-weekly flights to Jersey between April-October, complimenting their existing Ronaldsway flights. British Airways added Nice again for the summer and Toronto operates twice-weekly via Heathrow (BA073/2) until 11th May, when it becomes once-weekly with Tristars (BA083/2). Cyprus Airways will operate twice-weekly to Larnaca, peaking at three flights between June-September. Guernsey Airlines will operate up to nine-weekly, mainly with SD-330s. SAS are reverting to operating DC-9s on their five-weekly cargo flights, via Heathrow on the outward leg and two of the six-weekly passenger flights will now precede onwards to/from Dublin.

Equipment changes on scheduled flights include Austrian Airlines DC-9-51 OE-LDK (22nd); Lufthansa B.727 D-ABKC (1st); SAS DC-9-21 OY-KGF (8th) and Swissair DC-9-32 HB-IFK (1st).

RAF ILS traffic identified included Hawks XX168 (5th) & XX250 (7th); C-130 XV203 (23rd); Dominies XS710 (28th) & XS733 (13th/26th); Jetstreams XX482 (15th), XX492 (28th) & XX494 (7th); Devon VP957 (8th) and Andover XS596 (16th). Civil ILS traffic noted included Citation 500 G-BHTT from/to Birmingham (16th) & CAA BAe.125 G-AVDX Stansted/Stornaway (30th) as well as several Cessna 152s/172s from Barton (2nd/3rd).

1st Swissair DC-9-32 HB-IFK made its final flight into Manchester today, operating SR842/3. Its final service was on the 12th, before being sold to Spantax later in the month as EC-DQP.
2nd Metroliner OO-JPI (BC603) arrived at 1543 today from Glasgow, in full Sabena colours, before departing later for Maastricht.
2nd NLM operated Fokker F.27 PH-KFE on an inbound charter from Amsterdam, which arrived at 1723 today as HN4407.

3rd April 1982 - DDR-STE, which served with the airline until 1989, is seen here making its first visit today. It's returning an orchestra home that had travelled from Newcastle. It was the first of four visits by the airline this year, who operated five different IL-18s through Manchester between 1977 and 1982. It was also the first visit of an Interflug IL-18 since October 1977. (Geoff Ball)

10th The only Gulfstream 2 making its first visit to Manchester this year, was today's arrival of N111AC at 1134, which departed later for Frobisher Bay.
10th Spantax CV-990 EC-CNH positioned in from Palma to operate flight AE556/7 from/to Palma today, on behalf of Air Europe.
11th Volkswagen GB now operates a Cessna 404 as their corporate run-around, which made its first visit to Manchester today with the arrival of G-VWGB. Dove G-ARYM, which was a regular visited in the late-1960s/early-1970s, was operated by the company from 1975 to 1978.
12th British Airways transferred two L.1011 Tristars to British Airtours, which both made first visits to Manchester for their new owners during the month. Round-trips from/to Tarbes were operated by G-BEAM today and G-BBAJ (18th). British Airtours will also operate a summer Sunday flight from/to Palma, with L.1011 Tristars (KT657/6).
14th Making a first visit of type today, was Sikorsky S-76 G-BIAV. Operated by British Airways Helicopters, it arrived from their Head Office at Beccles, Suffolk, to collect a crewman off an Aberdeen flight and transport him to Blackpool.
15th Turbo Islander G-BPBN made two visits during the month. The first today was to night-stop from Great Yarmouth to Bournemouth and the second was on the 27th. The aircraft, in a

part-military colour scheme with Fishery Patrol titles, is the Turbo Islander prototype, with a radar nose and extra fuel tanks under each wing.

17th Another new helicopter type to visit, was the Aerospatiale AS.355 Twin Squirrel. Operated by McAlpine Aviation, G-MCAH was transporting printing plates for the Sunday Mail newspaper from London heliport to Salford, before calling in at Manchester for refuel and returning to its base at Hayes, Middlesex. This operation became a regular feature throughout the summer.

19th Two British Airways B.737s making their first visits to Manchester was G-BGDT operating BA901/6 from/to Paris & Amsterdam flight BA922/3 today and G-BGDF (21st) which operated Jersey flight BA5217/6.

20th Two unusual ILS visitors today were German Air Force Bell UH-1 72+17, routing from RAF Shawbury to Edinburgh as DCN2847 observed at 1110 and Dutch Air Force Neptune 204/V, a maritime patrol aircraft. The crew of the Neptune had flown from their base at Valkenburg to give a talk to the Manchester branch of Air Britain. When the aircraft was inbound to Woodford, the pilot was persuaded to make a practice ILS approach and overshoot at 1141.

21st Two Cessna Citations making their first visits today were Citation 501 I-ROST at 0930 from/to Venice, which had been in previously as N445CC in November 1978 and Martinair Citation 550 PH-MBX, arriving at 1037 as MP3627 from Norwich to Stansted.

24th The first foreign BAe.125 to arrive at Manchester so far this year was the Nigerian Government's 5N-ANG, calling in at 1024 today to clear customs, en route for Hawarden.

25th The first of three Canadian Air Force CC-130Es this month was 130322, arriving as CAM515 today. The others were 130320 (CAM516-27th)& 130317 (CAM517-29th).

27th Of the three diversions into Manchester this month, the only one of interest was McDermott Construction's Beech 200 N84MD at 0814 today from Brussels, originally intended for Blackpool.

30th British Caledonian will operate a summer IT programme for the first time since 1976, using two ex-Laker Douglas DC-10s, G-BJZD & G-BJZE. An aircraft will be based at Manchester, although today's first flight, was a 'w' pattern operated by G-BJZE as BR5622/1 from/to Malaga.

May 1982

The following airlines have summer IT programmes from Manchester: Air Malta, Air Portugal, Aviaco, Aviogenex, Balkan, EL AL, Inex-Adria, JAT, Royal Air Maroc, Spantax & Tarom; as do UK operators: Air Europe, Air Manchester, Air UK, Britannia Airways, British Air Ferries, British Airtours, British Airways, British Caledonian, Dan-Air, Monarch Airlines & Orion Airways. There is a huge void in Manchester's transatlantic programme since the collapse of Laker Airways, although the following airlines will operate to the USA/Canada: Air Florida will have a weekly Monday flight to Miami; British Airways are operating to New York, Los Angeles & Orlando; CP Air to Montreal, Toronto & Vancouver and Wardair to Calgary, Edmonton, Ottawa, Toronto, Vancouver & Winnipeg.

Equipment changes on scheduled flights included <u>Air Portugal (TP458/9)</u>: B.727-200 CS-TBS (29th); <u>Austrian Airlines (OS471)</u>: DC-9-51 OE-LDO (13th); <u>Lufthansa's</u> new Boeing 737-200 D-ABHK made its first visit (23rd) and Boeing 727s D-ABKP (7th) & D-ABKR (6th). Due increased demand at the start of the summer, <u>SAS</u> used DC-9-41s on all flights, <u>Air</u>

Malta used a weekly B.720 and Sabena used pure passenger aircraft Sobelair B.737 OO-SBT (5th), rather than a Combi.

RAF ILS traffic identified included C-130 XV297 (13th); Dominie XS711 (11th); Jetstreams XX491 (14th) & XX495 (6th); Vulcan XM569 (10th) overshot as 'NAG81' at 1347 from/to Waddington; Gazelle XW906 (10th) overshot as 'SYN52' at 1512 from/to Shawbury and a pair of Lightning's, XR727 & XS903 (27th), turned up at 1435 from RAF Valley on a warm afternoon to perform a practice ILS, before departing back to their base at RAF Binbrook in true Lighting style - fast and rapid climb - with plenty of after-burner applied! Civil ILS traffic noted included BAe.125-700 7T-VCW (4th); Beech F.90 G-BIED (5th) overshot at 1633; CAA BAe.748 G-AVXJ (7th) from/to Stansted and a couple of Cessna's from Barton were G-BEUX (7th) & G-BHRB (20th/24th). Finally Spitfire PM631 (9th), owned and operated by the Battle of Britain Memorial Flight, performed an overshoot at 0923 en route from RAF Coningsby to Blackpool.

1st Spantax recently acquired two second-hand Douglas DC-9s, the first of which made its first visit to Manchester today, when EC-DQP (ex HB-IFK) operated BX717/8 from/to Palma. The second, EC-DQQ (ex OE-LDE), was used by the airline until April 1983, but it never visited Manchester.

1st Lear Jet N1976L made its first visit today on a flight from Luton, night-stopping before departing to Dublin the following morning. This aircraft was written-off at Seattle in June 1983.

1st The airport was contacted in the early hours by Wilmslow Police, asking why PA-28 Cherokee G-AVWD was parked in the grounds of the Wilmslow Rugby Club. After a telephone conversion with the Director of the Manchester School of Flying, it transpired that the aircraft had been in a non-airworthy condition for a while, since the collapse of the North West Flying School in 1980 and wouldn't be going anywhere!

2nd British Airways operated the first flight of their summer transatlantic programme today, on behalf of Jetsave. L.1011 Tristar G-BHBP will be used exclusively this month on flights to New York, Los Angeles & Orlando.

2nd Transavia B.737 PH-TVD paid its first visit, since being leased by Britannia Airways and based at Glasgow. Arriving at 1509 today (BY518B from Jersey), its colour scheme consisted of a basic white frame, red stripe along the fuselage and Britannia titles and tail emblem. Its last appearance as such at Manchester was on the 4th June, before becoming G-BKBT and making its first visit on the 21st June. By the end of the summer, it had reverted back to PH-TVD and was leased to Air Malta.

2nd EL AL B.707 4X-ATR, which regularly operated the Manchester-Tel Aviv IT flights, has been replaced by B.707 4X-ATY. It's painted in the new Sun D'or colours of a dark blue cheatline/tail and horizontal rainbow stripe, with Sun D'or International Airways in red letters on the fuselage.

2nd As if the lease of four extra aircraft this summer wasn't enough, Britannia Airways have also taken delivery of two brand new Boeing 737s. First visits were made by G-BJCU today and G-BJCV (23rd).

3rd Also on lease to Britannia Airways is a second B.737, PH-TVR, which positioned in from Amsterdam today to operate BY610A/B to/from Corfu. It also operated BY721A/B to/from Heraklion the following day, before positioning to Glasgow later that evening. It was used until the middle of the month, when it was replaced with Air Florida B.737 N37AF.

3rd Air Florida commenced their weekly flight to Miami today, with DC-10 N1035F, but from the 17th it was operated by Martinair DC-10s. Aircraft used this month were PH-MBT (17th) & PH-MBP on its first visit (24th).

3rd The first direct air service between the UK and Orlando began today, when G-BHBP operated the first flight (BA8213). British Airways will operate a series of flights from Manchester throughout the summer on behalf of tour operator Jetsave, with L.1011 Tristars. With return fares starting at £249, Jetsave have already sold 95% of their capacity.

4th Italian Falcon 20 I-EDIS made its first visit to Manchester today, arriving at 0940 from Milan, before its departure for Rome at 1355.

4th Three RAF Gazelles arriving within twenty minutes of each other this afternoon, were XW866 at 1439 (SYN48), XW910 at 1517 (SYN49) & XZ933 at 1456 (SYN50). They were on training flights from RAF Shawbury and departed later for Hawarden.

5th Diversions were thin on the ground again this month, but three early morning arrivals due to fog were British Airways G-BEAL at 0615 (BA128A from Dhahran) & Finnair DC-9F OH-LYH at 0800 (AY032 from Helsinki) both from Heathrow and British Caledonian DC-10 G-BHDI at 0641 (BR381 from Dubai) from Gatwick. The only other diversion of interest during the month was another British Caledonian DC-10, G-BHDH, (as BR381 again) on the 28th.

5th Two British military visitors today were Royal Navy Sea Heron XR441 (Navy718) from/to Yeovilton and Queens Flight BAe.748 XS790 (Kitty1) routing Benson-Heathrow, which was carrying HM Queen Elizabeth II.

6th Champion Spark Plugs F.27 N1823G made the first of several visits this year, arriving from/to Rotterdam today to night-stop. The crew were observed wearing the company's laboratory coats!

11th Icelandic-registered aircraft are very rare to Manchester. PA-31 TF-VLH had visited earlier in the year on 27th February and today, Rockwell 690 TF-ERR arrived at 1659 from Reykjavik, operating as a photo-survey aircraft.

12th The other VC-130H operated by the Royal Saudi Air Force, No.111, made its second visit today. It was on its way for modification at the Lockheed factory at Marietta, when it arrived at 1353 from Jeddah, before departing on the 14th.

13th Britannia Airways are also leasing two B.737s from Canadian airline, Quebecair. The aircraft are in basic Quebecair colours of all-blue with Britannia Airways titles and tail emblems and have been British registered as G-BJZV (which made its first visit today) & G-BJZW, which arrived on the 16th. The recent spate of aircraft leasing is due to their increased summer programme, particularly from Manchester & Gatwick following the collapse of Laker Airways.

13th American giant Braniff Airlines ceased trading today, after one of their creditors called in the debt. Their last visit to Manchester was earlier in the year on 24th January, when Boeing 747 N601BN diverted in from Gatwick as BN602. Their Gatwick-Dallas service has been taken over by American Airlines, who commenced services on the 20th.

14th Royal Saudi Air Force C130H 467 arrived at 0952 today (RSF908 from Gander) and stayed until the 16th, before departing to Cambridge for an engine change. It returned on the 17th, before departing for Milan/Jeddah the following morning.

15th Aviaco now operate three ex-Iberia Douglas DC-9-32s, two of which made their first visits during the month. The first, EC-BIQ, arrived from/to Palma as AO1060/1 today, the second, EC-BIK (20th), operated AO1212/1617 and the third, EC-BIP, made its first visit back in April 1981. The airline is also leasing EC-DQT (ex OH-LNF), which made its first visit operating AO1018/9 from/to Palma in basic Finnair colours on the 18th.

15th RAF Jaguar XX748 arrived from Lossiemouth at 1406 today to night-stop, ahead of the following day's Barton Air Show. It left for the event at 1354, but after developing a fault on the right hand stabiliser during its performance, the display was cut short and an emergency landing was made at Manchester. The aircraft remained until the 18th, before finally flying back to Lossiemouth.

15th Busy Bee Fokker F.27 LN-SUE arrived at 1513 today from Oslo, operating an inbound freight charter. The airline made its second visit of the month on the 29th, when F.27 LN-SUF operated passenger charter BS301/2 from/to Bergen.

16th Not strictly arrivals or ILS visitors, the following aircraft were vectored over the airport as part of the flying display at this year's Barton Air Show. USAF A-10 Thunderbolt 79-0131 from/to Bentwaters, USAF C-141 Starlifter 64-0623 Frankfurt/Dover AFB, RAF Vulcan XM569 Waddington/Biggin Hill & Grumman Bearcat NX700H from/to Biggin Hill.

16th May 1982 – A fine shot of XX260, one of the brand new Hawks operated by the Red Arrows, on their first visit since being re-equipped. The team arrived from Shawbury at 1613 for brief stop, before heading off for their display at the Barton Air Show. They returned to Manchester at 1722 and stayed overnight, before departing back to their Kemble base at 1030 the following morning. (Geoff Ball)

17th Air Atlantique DC-3 G-AMPY positioned in at 0849 today from Wellesbourne, to operate an outbound charter to Jersey, before returning at 2004.

17th Two Nord 262s, F-BPNS & F-BPNX, arrived on a training exercise from Le Touquet today and stayed for sixty minutes, before departing for Dublin.

17th RAF Jaguar XX834 came down from Leuchars at 1439 today, with the 'man with the tool-box', needed to fix fellow Jaguar XX748. It returned again the following day, when both Jaguars left together for Lossiemouth.

17th Air Florida B.737 N37AF, operating for Britannia Airways, made its first visit today arriving from Glasgow as BY636A and then onwards to Rhodes. In basic Air Florida colours with Britannia titles, it will be based at Glasgow for the summer.

18th Newly based airline, Air Manchester, was set up by Sureway Holidays, following the demise of Laker Airways who had flown most of their operating programme. They made their first appearance at Manchester today, when hush-kitted BAC 1-11 G-SURE arrived from Bournemouth. Formerly G-AVOE with British Airways, this aircraft still hadn't entered commercial service by the end of the month, although it undertook a test flight to/from Shannon on the 23rd. Due to the unavailability of G-SURE, flights were operated on their behalf by Orion Airways & British Airways and from the 25th, British Air Ferries Viscount G-AVJB operated all their flights until the 3rd June.

19th Guernsey Airline's Manchester-Guernsey schedules are firmly established as a Shorts SD-330 operation, except for today when a Viscount was used for the only time this summer, when G-BDRC operated GE1725/4.

21st Cessna Citation 550 G-MINE made its first visit to Manchester, arriving at 0909 today from Gamston to operate a round trip to Aberdeen, before positioning back there. This aircraft was sold in the USA less than twelve months later.

21st Aviaco flight AO1056/7 from/to Palma, was operated by Iberia DC-9 EC-BQX today and by DC-8-50 EC-AUM the following week, which was the last visit of one of their 'short' DC-8s.

23rd The once-weekly Manchester-Toronto service (BA073) operated by British Airways B.747s, has been changed to Tristars, usually G-BHBP operating twice-weekly; but the change was short-lived as it reverted to once-weekly again with L.1011s from the 6th June.

26th May 1982 – Prior to the launch of Air Manchester's services, British Air Ferries Viscount G-AVJB was used on a number of flights, due the unavailability of their BAC 1-11. It was delivered new to PIA in 1959, UK registered in 1967 and acquired by BAF in 1980. It served them until October 1986, when it was sold to Baltic Aviation as SE-IVY, who operated it as a cargo aircraft until December 1987, when it was withdrawn. (Geoff Ball)

24th To round up a busy month of aircraft leasing, Air Europe leased two Air Florida B.737s for the summer, to be based at Gatwick. Registered as G-BJXL & G-BJXM in basic Air

Florida colours with Air Europe titles, G-BJXL made its first visit today and G-BJXM on 24th August. Both aircraft returned to Air Florida on the 27th & 29th October respectively.

25th Executive-type, the Aerospatiale Corvette, is not often seen at Manchester except for the French trainers F-BVPK, BVPT & F-BTTU, but this morning EC-DQE arrived at 1056 from Santander to night-stop, before its departure for Southampton the following morning.

25th The biggest executive arrival this month was first-time visitor BAC 1-11 HZ-RH1 today, from/to Heathrow, which parked on Stand 1 of the International Pier.

27th May 1982 – British Caledonian Helicopters Sikorsky S-61s G-BFPF & G-BHPU called in for fuel at 1927 today, en route Aberdeen-Gatwick in connection with Pope John Paul II's UK visit from the 28th May - 2nd June. Both were to be used as transport for the Pope. (Geoff Ball)

28th IGN (Institute Geographic National) Falcon 20 F-BMSS made its first visit today, arriving at 1615 from Creil. It performed a local flight and departed for Exeter on the 30th. It's used for the production and maintenance of geographical information within France.

29th Citation 550 F-GBTL owned by French-airline Euralair, made its first visit to Manchester today, operating from/to Le Bourget, before departing on the 31st.

30th British Caledonian purchased four ex-Laker Airways BAC 1-11s, now registered as G-BKAU, G-BKAW, G-BKAV & G-BKAX. The first of these, G-BKAX (BR985/992 from/to Gatwick), made its first visit today. They complement the two BAC 1-1-500s, G-BJRT & G-BJRU, already purchased from Hapag-Lloyd earlier in the year, which are all replacements due to the sale of seven BAC 1-11-200s to Pacific Express.

30th 1966-vintage helicopter Aerospatiale Alouette G-AWAP called in from Coventry today for fuel, before departing for the Middleton area of Manchester. It was on a security patrol near Heaton Park, in connection with the Pope's visit the following day.

31st Pope John Paul II performed mass and ordained twelve men in front of more than 200,000 people in Heaton Park, Manchester today.

June 1982

New domestic carrier Manx Airlines, set up jointly by Air UK and British Midland will commence operations in November. They will take over existing services between the UK & Isle of Man, as well as the British Midland flights between Liverpool-Belfast.

Equipment changes on scheduled flights included Air France (AF964): MEA B.720 OD-AFQ was used due to their mid-month strike (17th); Air Portugal used two B.707s: CS-TBF (5th) & CS-TBG (30th). Lufthansa's new B.737-200s D-ABFU (19th) & D-ABHU (20th) made their first visits and they also used B.727s D-ABSI (4th) & D-ABPI (24th). SAS used DC-9-21s LN-RLL (7th/17th), SE-DBP (21st/24th) & SE-DBS (28th) and finally Swissair used DC-9-32 HB-IFH (10th).

RAF ILS traffic identified included Hawks XX173 (17th), XX176 (21st), XX184 (28th), XX224 (10th/11th), XX225 (15th/25th) & XX311 (25th); C-130s XV207 (15th) & XV214 (16th); Jetstreams XX491 (17th) & XX496 (24th) and Bulldog XX685 as WVK09 at 1317 from/to Woodvale (4th). Two unidentified RAF Hawks overshot in formation at 1355, using call-sign 'Bird Formation' (25th). Civil ILS traffic noted included BAe.125-700s G-5-18 as 'Newpin 44' (16th) & G-5-20 as 'Newpin 44' (30th) on test flights out of Hawarden, CAA BAe.748 G-AVXJ from/to Stansted (10th) and Genair EMB-110 G-BHYT popped over from Liverpool on a quiet Thursday afternoon to perform an ILS approach and overshoot before its return (17th).

2nd Falcon 20 I-DKET was on its first visit, arriving from Turin during the evening. Owned and operated by the Fiat Motor Company, it was carrying the American tennis champion, John McEnroe.

6th June 1982 - Air Manchester finally took to the skies today, when BAC 1-11 G-SURE departed to Ibiza as VF8012 at 0814. It was carrying just eight passengers and the return at 1415 had only five. Their other flights fared much better during the week, but by the second week, several were cancelled and the passengers were transferred to other airlines. By the end of the month however, the flights were running near normal again. (Rick Ward)

4th Metropolitan Airways, who took over the Dan-Air City-Link operation at the end of March, now operate under their own flight prefix of 'MPL'. Due to the increase in airlines worldwide, from November 1987 all IATA airlines will operate under the new three-letter flight prefix, instead of the current two-lettered system, in order to stop duplication.

4th Aviaco flight AO1056/7 from/to Palma, is regularly operated by an Iberia DC-9. Used during the month were EC-BIS (today/11th), EC-BIJ (18th) & EC-BPG (25th).

5th For the second week running, Busy Bee Fokker F.27 LN-SUF operated passenger charter BS301/2 from/to Bergen today.

5th The first of two trooping flights through Manchester this month operated by C-130 XV303, arrived at 1043 today (RR4405 Lyneham-Wildenrath). The return flight operated as RR5452 Wildenrath-Lyneham on the 18th.

6th Iberia Douglas DC-9-32 EC-BIJ, which operated IB346/7 this afternoon, is currently sporting Aviaco colours on one side and Iberia's on the other.

7th The weekly Miami flight continues to provide interest. It was operated by Martinair DC-10 PH-MBP today and the following week by British Airways Rolls-Royce powered B.747 G-BDXG. British Airways stepped in following Jetsave's dissatisfaction with the late departure of the Miami flight at 2130, but after two weeks the flight reverted back to an Air Florida aircraft again. N103TV operated the flight on the 21st in full Air Florida colours and N1035F operated the flight on the 28th.

7th June 1982 – Fokker F.27 N1823G, owned by Champion Spark Plugs, made several visits during the year, transporting personnel to their factory in Oldham. It arrived from Malmo today to night-stop, before departing the following day at 1018 for Brussels. This aircraft was operated from 1965-1984 and future visits by their other aircraft included Citation 550 N1823B & Falcon 20 N1823F in 1983 and Gulfstream 2 N1823D in 1984. (Geoff Ball)

10th British Caledonian used Air UK BAC 1-11 G-AXOX on this evening's BR985/992 from/to Gatwick. The second of their recently acquired BAC 1-11s, G-BKAW, made its first visit on the 12th (BR952 Edinburgh-Gatwick).

11th British Midland Boeing 707 G-BFLD arrived from East Midlands at 0819 today, to operate Orion Airways flight KG1011/2 to/from Athens.

12th A new type, the Piper T-1041, made its first visit to Manchester today, when N2605Y arrived after an extensive demonstration tour. It's basically an updated version of the PA-31 Cheyenne and this aircraft is the current company demonstrator.

13th Britannia Airways are leasing yet another Boeing 737, in the form of TF-VLM from Eagle Air, which in turn is leased from Aer Lingus. It made its first visit today, before departing for Rhodes the following morning as BY809A and becoming a regular visitor until 16th August.

13th British Air Ferries BAe.125 G-FIVE, arriving at 1845 today from Southend, was formerly G-ASEC. This early production model from 1962 became a Manchester resident between July and October this year and was still operated by British Air Ferries.

14th Goodyear Airship N2A drifted over the airport around 0930 today, on its way from Barton heading southwards.

15th Another early production aircraft, this time Falcon 10 F-BJLH, arrived at 1949 today on an ambulance flight from Corfu, before departing for Le Bourget later on. Although it's a first visit, it's been into Manchester before as F-BSQU & PH-ILT.

16th Due to the unavailability of regular G-BHBP, British Airways used two different L.1011 Tristars during the month. Tristar 200 G-BHBL positioned up from Heathrow to operate outbound BA8201 to Bangor/Los Angeles today, but as G-BHBP has been specially converted to carry up to 393 passengers and G-BHBL only carries 313, the first passengers to check-in at Manchester were shuttled down to Heathrow, to catch a direct Los Angeles flight.

17th Air France had another strike, which meant sub-chartering other aircraft and as a result this evenings Paris flight was operated by MEA Boeing 720 OD-AFQ. Incidentally, MEA's entire operations are currently centred on Paris, due to the conflict in the Lebanon.

21st The North-American Sabreliner, which is quite a rare corporate type, appeared at Manchester today, when N228LS arrived at 0801 routing Stansted-Newcastle.

21st Interflug Tupolev TU-134 DDR-SDC made its first visit to Manchester today, arriving at 1227 (IF7440/1 Berlin/Leipzig).

22nd As far as diversions were concerned, it was another quiet month when nothing much of interest appeared. Three diversions from Birmingham arrived at Manchester today, but the only one of any note was NLM F.27 PH-KFI at 0905 (HN495 from Amsterdam).

23rd Mitsubishi MU-2 D-IFMU, arriving at 1905 today from Bristol as a Leeds diversion, is the only MU-2 on the German register.

24th French Navy Nord 262 No.63 performed a touch-and-go at 0854 today, en-route Amsterdam-Dublin as FA057.

24th Manchester saw an invasion of six Squirrel helicopters in close formation today! They were Aerospatiale AS.355 Twin Squirrels to be precise, arriving from Grimsby on a charter on behalf of Ciba-Geigy. They landed on Runway 10/28 to be refuelled, prior to their departure. Those involved as 'Squirrel Formation' were G-BGCV, G-BGIM, G-BMAV, G-GINA, G-MAGI & G-MCAH. They all left for Hayes, except for G-MAGI, which departed to Wimbledon for the tennis at 1820.

26th Although several longer Boeing 727-200s are operated, the shorter B.727-100s are still dominating Dan-Air's operations out of Manchester. Old-time regulars G-BAEF, G-BAFZ & G-BCDA and less-regular G-BFGM, have been around during the month, along with G-BKCG which made its first visit today operating DA2619/8 from/to Palma.

28th British Airways used an alternative L.1011 Tristar for the second time this month, when L.1011 Tristar 500 G-BFCD arrived at 1111 today. It was on its first visit operating BA8226 from New York, due to G-BHBP going tech in New York.

28th The executive update of the Gulfstream 2, the Gulfstream 3, made its first visit when American Can Company's N130A arrived at 1836 from White Plains, en route to Le Bourget.
29th Cessna Citation 550 G-GAIL arrived at 1215 today from Teeside, on its only visit to Manchester. This was another Citation with a short life on the UK register, as it was sold in the USA by the end of the year.
30th Sir Clive Sinclair, pioneer of the digital watch and home computer, seems to have purchased a new executive toy on the proceeds of his new SX81 computer! His aircraft, Cessna 425 G-BHNY, arrived from Little Staughton at 0917 today, before departing for Dundee.

July 1982

New company Sunrise Airlines, intend starting a low cost Laker-type charter operation between Stansted, Manchester & Orlando by the end of the month. Permission is yet to be granted by the Department of Trade, but they've established offices at Stansted and recruited staff. The Civil Aviation Authority say they are yet to hear from the airline, who plan to operate two ex-Laker B.707s, N500JJ & N600JJ and are negotiating for a third aircraft from Pan American.

2nd July 1982 – Altair, a new Italian airline to Manchester, made their first visit operating a short programme of weekly flights to Naples (SM512/3), with their SE.210 Caravelle's. I-GISA operated today's (SM512/3) and all flights for the rest of the month. Although the airline operated until 1985, this year saw their only flight programme from Manchester. (Geoff Ball)

Equipment changes on scheduled flights included Air France (AF964): Airbus A.300s F-GBEC (28th) & F-BVGO (29th) both first visits; Air Portugal B.727-200 CS-TBW (24th); SAS DC-9-21s LN-RLL (1st/5th), OY-KGF (25th), SE-DBP (4th) & SE-DBS (24th) and Swissair MD-81 HB-INI (25th).

RAF ILS traffic identified included Hawks XX182 (2nd) & XX349 (13th); Dominies XS712 (16th), XS714 (21st), XS727 (8th), XS731 (6th), XS733 (19th) & XS735 (6th); Andovers XS639 (5th) & XS643 (2nd); Jetstream XX491 (13th); Gazelle XW862 as 'SYN'45' at 1314 from/to Shawbury (14th) and Royal Navy Sea King XZ597 as 'SHW72' (29th). Civil ILS traffic was plentiful and varied, with numerous light aircraft ranging from Cessna's to PA-39 Twin Comanche's. Other civil aircraft included British Midland F.27 G-BDDH from/to Liverpool (2nd), Genair EMB-110 G-RLAY from/to Liverpool (4th) and BAe Jetstream 31 G-TALL from/to Hawarden (11th).

2nd The first of three Swiss-registered biz-jets making their first visits this month, was Lear Jet 36 HB-VHF at 0150 today, on an ambulance flight from Corfu. The second, Lear Jet 55 HB-VGZ (12th), a new slightly longer variant than previous models, arrived from Geneva at 1248 with the actor Richard Burton onboard, who was filming in Yorkshire and the third, Lear Jet 35 HB-VFK (30th) arrived at 2238 from Nice.

3rd Interflug IL-18 DDR-STP, arriving at 1402 today (IF7442 from Leipzig), was operating the return flight of the outbound IF7441 to Leipzig on the 21st June.

3rd Busy Bee Fokker F.27 LN-SUF made another visit to Manchester today, operating passenger charter BS301/2 Newcastle/Bergen.

5th Braathens Boeing 737 LN-SUI operated an inbound charter to Tromso today as BU459E, before positioning out later to Oslo. The return flight was operated by the same aircraft on the 12th, before departing back to Tromso as BU460.

5th The weekly Miami charter has finally settled down, after being operated by a variety of airlines at various times. British Airways will operate the weekly flights from today until October and aircraft used this month were G-AWNA today, G-AWNB (12th), G-AWNE (19th) & G-AWNJ (26th).

6th Today saw the first of two visits this year by US Army Beech C-12 73-22261, arriving at 1010 on a round-trip from Hanau, Germany, base of the 104th Area Support Group. The second visit on the 9th was also from/to Hanau.

6th The Fisheries Protection Turbo Islander G-BPBN made another visit today, night-stopping from Cardiff, before departing for Humberside the following day.

7th Mooney C-GMWJ, which visited Manchester on 19th May 1980, is now British registered and made its first visit as such today as G-BIGI, from/to Halfpenny Green.

11th July 1982 – G-BOAF is seen here on short finals, making its first visit to Manchester today on a positioning flight from Heathrow. It departed at 1457 an outbound charter to Madrid (BA9076) for the World-Cup Final. This was the fourth different British Airways Concorde to visit and the first on a charter flight, rather than a diversion, although Air France had already beaten them to that 'first'! (Geoff Ball)

8th There were only two of the customary three Canadian Air Force flights this month. CC-130E 130322 operated as CAM516 today and 130325 (CAM517-11th), but CAM515 was cancelled. An extra flight saw the first visit to Manchester of a Canadian Air Force C-130H, with 130314 (CAM409 from Goose Bay) on the 26th.

8th Executive visitor Boeing 727 C-GQBE arrived at 1133 today, with a party of VIP's for a game of golf at the Mere Country Club.

10th Only the second IAI Westwind visit to Manchester was today, when N793JR arrived at 1145, from Stansted to Munich. The other was YV-388CP on 14th December 1980.

12th Another new airline to Manchester this month was Royal Air Maroc, operating a weekly IT flight from/to Agadir until 30th August, with Boeing 727s. Today's first flight was operated by CN-CCH and by CN-CCW (19th), which were both first visits.

13th RAF Hawk XX349 performed a barrel roll on its departure back to RAF Valley today, after carrying out an ILS approach and overshoot at 1045 as VYT55.

13th A new type to visit Manchester was the Socata TB-20 Trinidad, when G-TBXX operated from/to White Waltham today. It's a light single piston engine aircraft, manufactured in France and the 'TB' stands for Tarbes, where they are built.

14th An unidentified RAF Gazelle called in at the South Side today, when SYN47 arrived at 1220 and stayed for a mere four minutes!

15th The ATC Watch Log recorded the following at 1820 today. 'In amazement we watched a British Airways Tristar being pushed back and towed from Stand 26 to the West Apron. No clearance was requested'. The BA tugs supervisor was spoken to and various excuses were given, such as radio problems and not realising clearance was needed. A telephone call to ATC later on, confirmed there were communication problems on their part.

16th An unusual visitor today was Lockheed's own C-130 Hercules N4206M, night-stopping en route Gander-Athens, ultimately bound for a demonstration tour in the Middle East.

17th July 1982 – Two contrasting Britannia Airways liveries, shows the aircraft in the foreground is clearly wearing the temporary one. The airline leased two very distinctive Boeing 737s, G-BJZV & G-BJZW, from Canadian airline Quebecair for the summer season, in their basic colours with Britannia titles. Also note that Britannia also caught the bug of dropping 'Airways' from their titles, similar to British (Airways). (Geoff Ball)

17th Lufthansa used Boeing 707 D-ABUA on freight flight LH4072/3 today.

18th Tarom started a weekly BAC 1-11 IT flight, from/to Constanta today (RO783/4), until the 25th September. It's the first time they've used the type on a regular basis and the first aircraft used was YR-BCM. Their only other weekly flight (RO733/4) is operated exclusively by Tupolev TU-154s.

25th July 1982 – Boeing 707 N651TF, operated by JET24 Aviation, started with Northwest Orient in 1963, before operating for Cathay Pacific for a further seven years. (Geoff Ball)

27th July 1982 – Flying Tigers, a major US cargo airline serving all the major cities throughout the world, is seen occasionally at Manchester operating freight charters. There were strong rumours they would start services from Manchester around 1980, but it never happened. DC-8 N776FT seen here, was also in connection with the Rolling Stones concert in Leeds, on the 25th. It positioned in from Frankfurt to collect the equipment and transport it to Chicago at 0514 on the 28th as FT5368. It was the fourth of five different Flying Tiger DC-8s to visit Manchester, before being taken over by Federal Express in 1988. (Geoff Ball)

21st The Ford Motor Company (UK) are operating a third Gulfstream 1, G-BRAL, which made its first visit today on an outbound flight to Olbia as FD958.

23rd The latest of BCAL's second-hand BAC 1-11s, G-BKAU, made its first visit today (BR981/8). It was due to be delivered to Air Manchester during the month, but when they weren't forthcoming with the finance, British Caledonian used it themselves for a short time. It made four visits up until the 2nd August in basic Air Manchester colours, but with no titles.

24th The largest executive visitor of the month, was Boeing 707 N651TF, arriving at 2236 today from Dublin. It brought the Rolling Stones in for their concert in Leeds the following day, due to the runway at Leeds being too short for the aircraft to land. It stayed at Manchester until the 26th, when it departed for Stansted.

24th Spantax CV-990 EC-CNF operated from/to Palma as DA2091/0 today, due to tech problems with a Dan-Air BAC 1-11 in Palma. It was the aircraft's final visit to Manchester, as it was withdrawn from service at Palma by December.

25th Air France A.300 F-GBEC was used to operate a charter from/to Paris-CDG today, as AF9932/3, which was the first of three visits this month by Air France Airbus A.300s.

25th Sikorsky S-76 G-BIEH, operated by North Scottish Helicopters, made a fuel-stop at Manchester today from Lands End to Aberdeen.

August 1982

British Airways boasted a 17% increase in passengers on their European and International services from Manchester for April-July, compared to the same months last year. Last month's two-week rail strike helped boost sales to London, Glasgow & Aberdeen by up to 50%. Significant increases were also recorded to other destinations such as Amsterdam up by 24%, Paris by 11% and Toronto by 10%.

Sunrise Airlines who were set up in July, planned flights to Orlando from Stansted via Manchester this month, which they did and in spectacular style - just once! Due to not finalising their own aircraft when they were ready to operate, Jet Charter Services were involved in the short-tem lease of a B.707 (ex Sabena OO-SJL) on their behalf. As the first flight didn't call at Manchester, the passengers were coached to Stansted, where further delays took place due to the late delivery of this aircraft. They eventually left, but on arrival at Orlando, the aircraft was impounded by the FAA for not being licensed to carry passengers and not having the proper navigation equipment - even though they made it across the Atlantic! The 130 passengers were offloaded, until arrangements were made with another tour operator. Sunrise have every intention of recommencing operations, but Jet Charter Services won't have anything more to do with them, as they and several others, are taking legal advice on matters regarding the airline.

Equipment changes on scheduled flights included Air Portugal (TP458): B.707 CS-TBD (25th); Lufthansa (LH074): B.727 D-ABKT (25th) and Sabena all-passenger B.737 OO-SDN (2nd).

RAF ILS traffic identified included Hawks XX165 (3rd), XX180 (4th), XX235 (5th), & XX314 (4th); C-130s XV179 (31st) & XV202 (12th); Dominies XS728 (12th) & XS736 (16th); Jetstream XX500 (16th) and finally the first ever ILS overshoot by a RAF Jet Provost, with XW326 as CFR05 at 1558 (3rd). The type, which has been in use by the RAF since 1969, is used for training pilots. Civil ILS traffic included numerous light aircraft, as well as Genair EMB-110 G-RVIP from/to Liverpool (8th) & British Midland F.27 G-BLGW from/to Liverpool (17th).

1st Aer Lingus used B.737 EI-BMY on this evening's EI214/5 and again on the 29th as EI204/5. The aircraft, in an all-white colour scheme, is owned by leasing company Air Tara.

3rd Executive B.727 HZ-DA5 operated by Dallah Avco, arrived from Jeddah at the unearthly time of 0253, before departing at 0444 for Miami via Bangor, to be fitted out with a new executive interior. This aircraft was formerly operated by Singapore Airlines.

4th Early morning fog at Gatwick produced two diversions: Air Florida DC-10 N102TV at 0841 (QH200 from Gatwick) & CP Air DC-10 C-GCPI at 0958 (CP822 from Toronto).

6th In a repeat of last August, early morning fog affected the South East. As a result Manchester received ten Heathrow diversions up until lunch-time, amongst which were six B.747s, including a pair from Qantas: VH-EBD at 0637 (QF007 from Bahrain) & VH-EBM at 0801 (QF001 from Bahrain). It was the first time two Qantas 747s had been on the ground at Manchester at the same time. Qantas are now handled by Servisair at Manchester, following a disagreement with British Airways last year. The three remaining B.747s were British Airways G-AWND at 0735 (BA174 from New York), G-AWNN at 0730 (BA072 from Toronto) & G-BDPV at 0726 (BA256 from Bridgetown) plus Pan American N657PA at 1112 (PA104 from New York) diverting in for fuel. Other aircraft were two B.707s: EL AL 4X-ATD at 0836 (LY315 from Tel Aviv) on its first visit & Cyprus Airways 5B-DAP at 0839 (CY332 from Larnaca). Air Canada DC-8 C-FTJZ arrived at 0803 (AC860 from Halifax), which incredibly was the first time the airline had diverted a Heathrow flight into Manchester since 17th October 1968, as they would normally divert to Prestwick. Nigeria Airways DC-10 5N-ANR at 0833 (WT804 from Kano) also had also had a disagreement with their handling company, British Airways, with each accusing the other of being rude on the company frequency!

6th A new cocktail/buffet bar and duty-free situated on Pier C were opened today, which turned out to be perfect timing as they were descended upon by weary Heathrow bound passengers, having diverted in due to the London weather.

7th Three more Lear Jets made their first visits this month. Lear Jet 35 D-CDAX arriving at 1109 today was the first and Lear Jet 35 D-CCAX arriving from Nuremberg at 1521 on the 12th was the second.

8th August 1982 – Dan-Air B.727 G-BIUR, seen here in a revised livery, was leased from Arian Afghan for the summers of 1981/82. Mainly operating at Gatwick, it only made the occasional visit to Manchester. (Geoff Ball)

8th Vintage Army Air Corps Beaver XP769 arriving at 0828 today (Army 351 from/to Belfast), visited twice this year and another Beaver, Army XV271, arrived on 8th October.

9th Irish Air Corps Beech 200 No.240 made its first visit at 1101 today, routing Baldonnel-Hawarden, to pick equipment. It made further visits on the 26th & 27th, operating crew training flights.

9th A first visit of type was Jetstream 31 G-TALL, arriving from Prestwick at 1133 today, on demonstration to Air Kilroe. After undertaking a local flight, it departed later for Liverpool.

10th CAA BAe.125 G-AVDX arrived at 1433 today, with CAA officials for the commissioning of the 24ILS, which has been relocated following the recent runway extension.

11th Kar-Air used Finnair SE.210 Caravelle OH-LSG to operate KR3011/2 from/to Helsinki today and again on the 25th.

12th The second RAF Pembroke to visit this year, was XL929 arriving at 1249 today (RR8015A from Wildenrath), before departing later for Woodford. The type continued serving No.60 squadron at RAF Wildenrath, Germany and there was to be one more Pembroke visit to Manchester, before the type was phased out in 1989.

14th Vintage-pair Meteor WF791 & Vampire XH304 called in at 1459 today from Alconbury, en route to Ronaldsway, before returning the next afternoon at 1511 from Ronaldsway to Coventry.

15th Cessna 210 OY-TRT made the last of three visits to Manchester today, arriving at 2037 from Rotterdam. It stayed overnight, before proceeding to Halfpenny Green the following morning. Unfortunately, this aircraft was written-off later this year in October.

17th Manchester Airport took a step into the big league today, when the runway extension from 9,200ft to 10,000ft was finally opened. There was no ceremony, as the official opening will take place on the 7th October, when HRH Princess Anne will attend. Until now, the restricted length of the runway meant either a loss in range of around 500 miles, or the reduction of a hundred passengers for a typical Boeing 747 long-haul flight.

23rd The third and final Lear Jet making its first visit this month, was N111RF arriving from Miami/Gander at 0944 today on an ambulance flight, before returning stateside the following afternoon at 1317. This aircraft is based in Florida and operated by healthcare company, New Creations Incorporated.

28th Spantax used CV-990 EC-BZP, rather than the scheduled DC-9, on today's BX717/8.

30th Lufthansa operated an outbound charter to Munich today, with Airbus A.300 D-AIAD making its first visit to Manchester.

September 1982

The month saw the beginning of the end for short-lived airline Air Manchester, when their BAC 1-11 G-SURE arrived back at Manchester on the 1st in British Air Ferries colours, having just been re-sprayed at Cardiff. It was repainted because the Spanish authorities wouldn't accept the aircraft, as the AOC (Air Operating Certificate) they were using was in British Air Ferries name. The certificate is proof that approval has been granted from the National Aviation Authority for an operator to use their aircraft for commercial purposes. On its arrival back at Manchester after its re-spray, the aircraft was impounded by the Airport Authorities, until its outstanding bills were paid. A further BAC 1-11 purchased by Air Manchester, G-AVOF, was briefly re-registered G-BMAN on the 10th, but it never saw service with the airline.

With the co-operation of British Airways and other airlines, the airport will run a series of courses from next month for those with phobia's, such as fear of flying and claustrophobia. Small group's of sufferers will be shown around the airport and then taken behind the scenes to view the ATC/operational safety systems.

After many years of resistance by the Airport Committee, fruit machines have finally been allowed into the International Departure Lounge, albeit on a six-month trial basis.

The go-ahead has been given for a major shakeup in the airports concessions. Trust House Forte owned by Air Catering Services, lost the catering contract generating an annual turnover of £1m after twenty years and Finnegan's, who run a department store in Wilmslow lost the duty-free concession generating an annual turnover of £6m, held since 1963. Air Catering Services were also told they had won the duty-free concession and the catering concession went to SAS Catering (Scandinavian Airlines), with both companies receiving seven-year contracts. The catering contract award was based on the level of capital investment the applicants were prepared to make and SAS were prepared to fully re-vamp the restaurant, as well as the catering facilities. Also working in their favour were excellent labour relations and a good reputation with the unions.

Twelve months after announcing that all ninety British Airways engineers will be made redundant at Manchester's maintenance facility, a further hundred jobs will go this year under a plan to streamline staff. The airline hopes to turn a £2m loss into a £4m profit within twelve months, under the new British Airways Manchester Division, responsible for stricter financial control by cutting out loss-making flights and investing in more charters.

Equipment changes on scheduled flights included Austrian Airlines (OS471): using their MD-80s on two separate occasions and which were both were first visits, OE-LDV (10th) & OE-LDT (26th); Dan-Air used Loganair Twin Otter G-BGEN on their City-Link flights from 1st-10th; Lufthansa (LH074): B.727s D-ABPI (21st) & D-ABKQ (30th); SAS (SK539): DC-9-21s LN-RLO (27th), SE-DBP (30th), & SE-DBR (29th) and finally Swissair (SR842): MD-80s HB-INL (13th) & HB-INN (15th) were both first visits.

RAF ILS traffic identified included Dominies XS713 (9th), XS726 (8th) & XS731 (23rd); Jetstreams XX492 (29th), XX495 (22nd/23rd/30th), XX496 (28th), XX497 (9th) & XX500 (24th); Vulcan XJ782 (4th); Gazelle XZ933 as 'SYN56' at 1133 (23rd); another Jet Provost XW419 as 'CFJ14' at 1235 (30th) and RAF Jaguar XX146 as UZY94 at 1439 (also 30th). There was also an unidentified RAF Puma as OIJ60 at 1350 (7th). A varied selection of civil ILS traffic included Genair SD-330 G-OCAS (1st); Fords Gulfstream 1 G-AWYF (7th); CAA BAe.748 G-AVXI (10th); Lufthansa Beech 90 D-ILHB (17th); Corvette's F-BTTU (23rd) & F-BVPT (28th); Air Atlantique DC-3 G-AMPO (24th); a variety of light aircraft and finally the first appearance at Manchester of the new British-Aerospace BAE.146, when G-SSCH overshot at 1239 as 'Tibbet 37' in full Dan-Air colours (30th). Both the Genair SD-330 and the Gulf 1 were on Instrument Renewal flights from/to Liverpool.

1st A RAF type making its first visit to Manchester was the Jet Provost, although it wasn't a visit in the true sense of the word! The unidentified aircraft was performing a practice ILS from/to RAF Church Fenton as CFJ56, when it happened to touch the runway at 0922 with its wheels and as this constitutes as a landing, the airport was able to pursue a landing fee!

1st Lufthansa A.300 D-AIAD made its second visit to Manchester, arriving as LH5076 at 1706 today, operating the return flight from last month's Munich charter.

2nd French-airline TAT (Touraine Air Transport) operated Beech 90 F-GDMM from/to Dinard today, in the airlines full gaudy mustard colours and titles. It made further visits on round trips from Dinard, arriving twice on the 27th and again on the 28th. Another Beech 90, F-GBRD, also arrived on the 27th from/to Dinard.

2nd French Navy Nord 262 No.53 was the last of three visiting this year, arriving at 1557 today from Le Touquet, on its way to RAF Finningley for the air show.

3rd Cessna 303 Crusader G-BJZK made a first visit of type today, arriving from Sunderland to Ronaldsway.

3rd The number of USAF C-141 Starlifter visits to Manchester remains at one, after a flight due in this afternoon was cancelled and re-routed through RAF Valley!

3rd Venezuelan aircraft are very rare aircraft in the UK, let alone Ringway, but Beech 55 YV-1120P became the first to land at Manchester. It arrived at 2055 today from Keflavik, before continuing its journey to Bremen the following morning.

4th RAF Vulcan XJ782 was on its final flight, when it overshot at 1611 today as UMA62, routing from Waddington to Finningley for preservation.

5th There were a few early morning diversions today, due fog in the South and Midlands, starting with British Caledonian DC-10 G-BJZE at 0439 (BR5058 from Malaga). Brize Norton was also suffering with poor visibility, when RAF VC-10 XV108 (RR2875 from Dacca) arrived at 0810. A new airline to Manchester was Nigerian-outfit Intercontinental Airlines, when Douglas DC-8 RP-C830 diverted in at 0724 from Lagos as a Stansted diversion, but this wasn't the end of the story! The DC-8 had hit a Flying Tigers DC-8 on the ground at Stansted, whilst overshooting due to the weather and had made it to Manchester with leaking hydraulic fluid, after suffering a damaged starboard and trailing edge flap, which looked like someone had taken a lump hammer to it! Fortunately, it made a safe landing without the use of flaps, but lost its hydraulics soon afterwards. The aircraft is registered in the Philippines, the pilot was Malaysian and the airline currently operates regular flights into Stansted. After leaving the aircraft one passenger was caught by customs with 6lb of cannabis in his case, a second had a fake passport and a third passenger had bogus stamps in a valid passport! Stories were going round that the crew were 'ready to disappear', rather than be questioned by the Accident Investigation Board. On reflection those onboard were extremely lucky to have survived the incident, as a couple of feet lower and the leading edge could have been severely damaged and a few feet to the left or right, the undercarriage could have been sheared off completely! Similarly, if the aircraft was climbing away when it hit the tail of the Flying Tigers DC-8, how close to the ground did it get and why was it so far from the runway centreline? By way of repair the aircraft had been fitted with second-hand flaps by the 24th, courtesy of DC-8 5A-DGK, currently derelict at Tripoli. Since then it's had a CAA writ served on it and it now sits on the apron, behind a large block of concrete placed in front of the nosewheel!

5th The death of Sir Douglas Bader was announced today, aged 72. He flew his own Beech 95, G-APUB, from 1974-1979 which was serviced by Fairey at Manchester. When he was no longer fit to fly, the aircraft was sold in the USA in September 1981. It made the long trip stateside the following month on the 12th October 1981, via various points.

5th Air India B.707 VT-DVB arriving at 1944 today (AI515 from Moscow), would have normally operated from Birmingham, but it elected to use Manchester as it was running late and by the time it was ready to depart, Birmingham would have been closed for night-time runway work.

9th Falcon 20 F-BTML owned by the French Cognac company Hennessy, makers of one of world's best Cognacs, arrived at 1144 today to transport a group of local golfers to a tournament they were sponsoring at Ferndown, near Bournemouth.

11th The Saturday evening flights transporting printing plates for the Mail on Sunday, operated by AS.350 Squirrels of McAlpine Aviation, have been replaced by Business Air Travel aircraft. The flights, which continued throughout the month, were operated exclusively by P.68 G-BJOF. A second flight operated occasionally, with PA-34 Seneca G-BCID being used on the 18th & 25th.

12th The flights transporting Airbus wings to Germany recommenced from Manchester for the first time since April, when Guppy F-BPPA operated today's flight out to Bremen. The Aeromaritime Guppy's had been operating from Liverpool, because of road works on the section of the M56 motorway which links Chester to Manchester Airport. All three aircraft, F-BPPA, F-BTGV & F-GDSG, have been repainted with a rainbow stripe and 'Airbus Skylink' written on the fuselage, as well as a giant fleet number on the tail and nose, rather like the Thunderbirds! For the record, F-BTGV is '1', F-BPPA is '2' & F-GDSG is '3'.

13th Wardair used British Midland B.707 G-BFLD to transport passengers to/from Prestwick today, due to Toronto flight WD810/1 terminating there.

13th Today was the first time that a non-based helicopter had arrived at the South Side for minor work, when Bell 47 G-BGXP appeared from Bangor, North Wales, before returning there later in the day. As Air Kilroe operates their own Bell 206 Jet Ranger, G-MKAN, from Manchester, they must feel confident enough to let their engineers loose on someone else's helicopter!

15th Aer Lingus operated an extra freight flight, EI9210/1 and unlike the scheduled flights, this one arrived in daylight hours. It was sub-charted and operated by Aer Turas CL-44 EI-BGO, which didn't appear at Manchester again until 1985.

15th Manchester Utd is playing European football again this season, by way of the UEFA Cup. They had drawn Spanish side Valencia over two legs and the first to be played was today in Valencia, but the European return turned sour when the game ended in a 2-1 defeat. On the return match on the 29th, United were dumped out of the competition at the first hurdle, after being held to a 0-0 draw at Old Trafford, meaning they lost 2-1 on aggregate.

16th The US Army operated a further Beech C-12 flight today, when 78-23128 arrived at 1019 from Northolt as 'Duke 22B'.

17th This week's warm weather led to some very strange atmospheric conditions, when for several days it was possible to hear southern-based ATC base-stations, as well as aircraft transmissions from the South not normally heard. Heathrow was very foggy in the morning and to a lesser extent, so was Gatwick. As Manchester was also contending with fog, only five diversions were received, the first of which was Heathrow bound Falcon 50 HB-IER from Washington, calling in for fuel on its first visit. The next four arriving over 2½ hours were all Boeing 747s. Three from British Airways were G-AWNB at 1024 (BA176 from New York), G-AWNM at 0809 (BA072 from Toronto) & G-BDPV at 0811 (BA052 from Harare) and the fourth from Pan American, was N740PA at 0858 (PA002 from New York). Several more tried to divert to Manchester, but weren't able to, including South African B.747 ZS-SAM. It held for a while pending an improvement in the weather, but when it wasn't forthcoming it diverted to East Midlands instead. Also intending to divert in was American Airlines flight AA050 (Dallas-Gatwick), but again the weather was reluctant to improve. This was also the day the writer went down to Heathrow for a few days spotting. I'd travelled down by train the previous morning to spend a few days at the airport and was booked into a B&B at Hayes, run by a Heathrow spotter and his wife. I'd taken the tube from Euston to Heathrow and spent a sunny afternoon logging away before heading off for the B&B. Early the next morning (today), I was on the bus to Heathrow and although it was misty, it wasn't too bad, but by the time I got there it was a real 'pea-souper'. I persevered for an hour, during which time I could hear aircraft taking-off in the fog, but not landing, probably because nothing was! I made a rash decision and caught a GreenLine coach to Gatwick hoping for better weather, but not long into the journey the fog started to clear and brilliant sunshine shone through. I wondered if I'd been too hasty, as Gatwick may also be affected, but my fears were groundless as it was clear. I spent an hour there before returning to Heathrow, where I stayed from late-morning until 8pm, in pleasant sunshine on top of the Terminal 3 Car Park.

17th Pan American DC-10 N83NA, originally destined for Shannon, diverted in at 0039 (PA8129 from Istanbul). There were several more visits by the airline towards the end of the month. DC-10 N83NA operated PA8120 New York-Gatwick (18th) and they also operated the Jetsave Miami flights for a couple of weeks, before they reverted back to British Airways again. First visits were made by DC-10 N80NA operating PA8521 Gatwick-Boston/Miami (20th) & DC-10 N84NA as PA8520 on the following days return. N81NA operated PA8521 Gatwick-Shannon/Miami (27th) & DC-10 N83NA operated the return as PA8520 (28th).

17th Wardair used Worldways Canada B.707 C-GRYN to operate inbound WD810 from Toronto, departing as WD251 to Edmonton and returning the next day as WD250.

18th September 1982 – Worldways Canada was born out of Ontario World, which only operated for a very short time. Boeing 707 C-GRYN seen here, was operated by the original airline and transferred to the new airline along with a further two Boeing 707s, C-GFLG & C-GGAB, which were added during the year. They have also purchased a number of ex-CP Air DC-8s. (Geoff Ball)

18th Cessna 414 N5372C is the current UK company demonstrator. Operated by Leeds based Northair Aviation, it diverted into Manchester at 1123 today, due to the Leeds weather.

19th The third Guppy operated by Aerospatiale, F-GDSG, made its first visit this morning, operating outbound to Bremen with more Airbus wings.

18th September 1982 - Two shots of Intercontinental DC-8 RP-C830, the aircraft that caused a whole lot of trouble! It's seen here still parked at Manchester, thirteen days after its arrival! The second picture shows the damage sustained to its leading edge, after its aborted attempt to land in fog at Stansted. (Geoff Ball)

20th The last of British Caledonian's recently purchased second-hand BAC 1-11s made its first visit today, when G-BKAV operated no less than three Gatwick rotations.

22nd The second of two American-registered BAe.125s to visit this year, was BAe.125-700 N60TN, arriving at 1536 today on its first visit. It called in from Milan to night-stop, before continuing its journey stateside the following day.

24th Instone Airlines Bristol 170 G-BISU made its first visit to Manchester today, but as it arrived from Luton at 0037 and departed for Stansted at 0109, very few witnessed it!

24th Spantax CV-990 EC-BZP made its final visit to Manchester, substituting for a Douglas DC-8 on today's BX795/6. It was withdrawn from use by September 1984.
24th Bristow Helicopters new executive BAe.125, G-BFVI, operated a round-trip to Aberdeen today.
28th The French Air Force operated two MS.760 Paris flights through Manchester this year. The first was No.36, arriving at 1119 today (FM0739 from Bournemouth), before departing the following afternoon for Lyneham.
29th The first of three Canadian Air Force C-130 flights to Manchester, was today's arrival of 130322 as CAM515 at 0840. The others were 130323 (CAM516-1st Oct) & 130326 (CAM517-3rd Oct), which all night-stopped.

October 1982

The Air Manchester story continued this month, when BAC 1-11 G-SURE departed Manchester on the 18th, operated an outbound flight from/to Palma on the 23rd and returned the following week. It then moved to Liverpool Airport, after negotiating cheaper landing charges and drastically cutting down on staff.

Intercontinental DC-8 RP-C830 remained parked at Manchester during the month. Three writs are currently served on it, one each from the CAA, Manchester Airport and Dan-Air. It was moved from the North Side Apron, over to a remote parking spot south of Runway 28.

An important piece of the airport's landscape and history disappeared this month. After remaining empty for several years, the former Fairey hangar was demolished, before it fell down of its own accord!

Lear Jet G-LEAR operated by Northern Executive, gained the company much publicity this month as the national media focused their attentions on the return of British pop singer Sheila Rossall, former lead-singer in the 1970's pop group, Pickettywitch. She was returning from the USA after life prolonging treatment, following her diagnosis of Total Allergy Syndrome after exhibiting severe reactions to perfume, man-made fibres and processed foods in 1978. It was thought to be a straight forward allergy, until her body reacted catastrophically and by 1982 she was forced to live as a recluse. Her condition headlined for weeks and stories emerged of her bubble-like existence and dramatic weight-loss, leaving her too weak to even raise her head. She lived in a ceramic-tiled room, slept in a cotton cloth and could only drink natural spring water and eat organic vegetables or wild game. After returning from the US and the media scrum abated, little more was heard of her and she was left to live out her remaining days with as much dignity as the illness allowed.

British Airways withdrew the following routes from Manchester: Edinburgh (22nd) & Zurich (23rd); Edinburgh was taken over by Loganair in November, while another destination, Geneva, was reduced to once-weekly for the winter before being withdrawn altogether in April. Also announced was the withdrawal of their code-share operation on the Malta & Larnaca services, but the flights flown by Air Malta & Cyprus Airways will continue. Air Europe have already shown interest in operating scheduled flights of their own to these destinations, as well as applying for a new route from Manchester to Gibraltar next year. British Airways are expected to start Boeing 757 operations on the Manchester-London Shuttle flights from next March and Monarch Airlines will also start B.757 operations with a based aircraft, operating various IT flights to numerous destinations.

Olympic Airways may finally start operations from Manchester next year and it's rumoured that Royal Air Maroc will begin scheduled operations in 1984. Qantas are looking into possible flights from next April, since acquiring the rights to operate from Manchester to Australia and Pakistan International are hoping to transfer one of their flights from Heathrow to Manchester next year.

Equipment changes on scheduled flights included Austrian Airlines (OS471): using Douglas DC-9-51s OE-LDN (8th) & OE-LDM (31st) with OE-LDM operating the very final Vienna flight following their withdrawal from the route. British Airways reverted to a once-weekly B.747 Saturday service to Toronto with Rolls-Royce powered G-BDXI (9th), but L.1011 Tristars took over from the 30th. Lufthansa (LH074): B.727 D-ABKA (12th); Sabena used Sobelair B.737s OO-SBS (22nd) & OO-SBT (26th) and finally Swissair (SR842): used Douglas DC-9-32s HB-IDP (21st) & HB-IFU (30th).

RAF ILS traffic identified included Hawk XX225 (19th), Dominie XS738 (4th), Jetstream XX495 (18th), Jet Provost XW419 (8th), Gazelle XX374 (25th) and Andovers XS640 (26th) & XS643 (25th). Civil traffic using the ILS only provided Cessna 172s G-BEUX (2nd) & G-MALK (12th), PA-28 G-ARVW (28th) and CAA BAe.748 G-AVXJ (27th), which rounded off a very uninspiring month!

1st SAS DC-9 OY-KGK (SK541) went tech on arrival and was unable to depart until the following afternoon. In the meantime, DC-9F LN-RLW arrived just before midnight as SK9200 with a spare engine, while DC-9 SE-DAO was flown in from Copenhagen to operate the outbound SK540.

2nd Worldways Canada operated an outbound Toronto flight with B.707 C-GFLG (WB301) on behalf of Wardair, which was also making its first visit. A further Wardair sub-charter took place on the 9th, with B.707 C-GRYN operating WD811 to Toronto.

2nd From today, SAS will operate their Copenhagen freight service (SK059/8) on Saturday's only (down from five flights a week at the start of the year), with Fred Olsen Electra's.

3rd Aeroflot rounded off their summer IT programme the way they started, with a Tupolev TU-134, when CCCP-65851 operated as SU1637/8 from/to Leningrad today.

4th The Belgian Air Force operated their first BAe.748 flight through Manchester since 1980, when CS-02 night-stopped, from/to RAF Wyton today.

5th RAF Devon WB531, which joined the RAF in July 1949 and served them until October 1984, made its final visit to Manchester today, operating as RR1789 Northolt-Warton. It was eventually sold to a private owner as G-BLRN.

6th British Airways routed outbound Heathrow-Los Angeles flight BA283 via Manchester today. It was operated by B.747 G-BDXB, in connection with the wind down of Jetsave's programme to California. Up until now it was direct from Manchester, operated by L.1011-200 G-BHBP, but from today and for the remaining two weeks of the programme, the outbound service will operate with flight BA283 calling at Manchester. The return Los Angeles-Heathrow BA282 flight on Thursday's, also routed via Manchester throughout the month.

7th Queens Flight Wessex XV732 arriving at 1016 today (Kitty5), had HRH Princess Anne onboard to officially open the runway extension. The helicopter landed on the extension itself and off-loaded its royal passenger, before positioning up to the terminal. After performing the ribbon-cutting ceremony, she was transported to the main terminal to the switch on the 1,770 high-intensity red and white lights along the 10,000 ft runway. She then cut a 22ft long cake, an exact replica of the runway and its lighting system, containing 450lb of rich fruit, topped with marzipan and icing.

8th Army Air Corps Beaver XV271 (Army351 from/to Belfast) was the third of three visits by Army Beavers this year, with the other two being made by XP769.

8th Spantax used a CV-990 twice during the month, instead of the usual Douglas DC-8 on BX795/6. EC-BZO was used on today's flight and EC-CNH on the 22nd.

10th EL AL temporarily ceased operations today, due to ongoing action by 400 cabin crew. Their aircraft were destined for storage, but this measure was averted at the eleventh hour, when a deal was struck between the strikers and the Israeli Government. The airlines been using non EL AL aircraft since last month and today's Tel Aviv flight, LY5317/8, was operated by Monarch B.720 G-AZKM and again on the 17th/31st. On the 24th, it was operated by B.707 N778PA, which is no stranger to Manchester, as it's visited over the years in two other guises as 9G-ACJ & G-TJAA.

11th Morning fog in Merseyside, Cheshire & North Midlands was the reason for Manchester receiving twelve diversions from 0459-1210. They were mostly ordinary, with the most interesting arriving from Liverpool: British Midland F.27 G-BLGW at 1017 (BD582 from Heathrow), Jersey European Twin Otter G-OJEA at 1117 (JE312 from Dublin) & Genair SD-330 G-BKDO at 1029 G-BKDO (ZA402 from Gatwick).

12th British Airways Aberdeen-Heathrow flight BA5617 routed via Manchester today, operated by B.737 G-BGDN, which also operated Aberdeen-Manchester BA5699 (21st).

12th A short burst of Leeds diversions arriving at Manchester within twelve minutes of each other were Cessna 414 G-JGCL at 1035 (from Bristol), Air UK F.27s G-BCDN at 1038 (UK582 from Belfast) & G-BHMW at 1043 (UK825 from Amsterdam) and Dan-Air BAe.748 G-ARAY at 1047 (DA061 from Glasgow).

18th BAe.125 G-OJOY arriving from Birmingham at 1804 today, made its first visit bringing Intasun Chairman, Sir Harry Goodman to attend the launch of their 1983 summer programme from Manchester. Another BAe.125 today was G-BBEP, on its last visit operating from/to Heathrow, before being sold in Nigeria the following month. Two more BAe.125s also leaving the UK Register during the month was G-ASSI (last visit 16th June 1976) which was sold as 5N-AWD & G-BACI (last visit 14th September 1978) which was sold as XA-LOV.

19th French Air Force Transall F.11/61-MF, arriving at 1254 today as FM0195, was on a training flight from Hanover to Orleans.

21st Air Bridge Carriers started the weekly cattle charters to Milan again, when Merchantman G-APES positioned in from Glasgow in the early hours, before departing as AK140 at 1203.

21st The first British Airways Trident 3 to be withdrawn, G-AWZA, made its last visit to Manchester today, arriving at 1916 (BA4512 from Heathrow). It operated back to Heathrow as BA4413 at 0832 the following morning and was withdrawn on the 23rd. This aircraft was handed over to BEA in May 1971, after spending several months prior to delivery carrying out extensive training exercises. In January 1971, whilst on a training detail, it struck RAE Comet XP915 whilst landing at Bedford, luckily no significant damage was incurred by either aircraft.

22nd PA-23 Aztecs N142143 & N40375 passed through Manchester today, on their way from Spain back to the USA, initially via Reykjavik.

23rd The second British Airways Trident making its final visit to Manchester this month was Trident 1 G-ARPX. Arriving at 0937 (BA4424 from Heathrow), it stayed until the 25th when it positioned to Heathrow as BA4515P at 1834, which was its final flight before withdrawal.

23rd Passing through Manchester on delivery this afternoon was Beech 58 N23712, en route from Reykjavik to Saragossa.

23rd Manchester saw the fine sight of three RAF VC-10s on the ground at the same time this morning. The first, VC-10 XV106, was a Brize Norton diversion (RR2097 from Washington) and the others, XV103 & XV108, made two round trips each returning troops from Hanover. BAe.125 XX507 also arrived from Brize Norton as RR1520, to pick up a senior military official off diverted VC-10 XV106 and transport him onwards to Brussels.

23rd October 1982 – Fred Olsen Electra's have been regular visitors to Manchester since 1971, operating cargo flights to Copenhagen for SAS; which were five-weekly at their peak, but are now down to just a single Saturday flight. Electra LN-FOI is seen here about to touchdown, operating SK057. (Geoff Ball)

24th Manchester received seven diversions today due to fog in the South, all B.747s from Heathrow, apart from Stansted diversion Flying Tigers DC-8 N781FT (FT5452 from Cincinnati) at 0939. Another Flying Tigers aircraft, B.747 N805FT at 0524 (FT010 from Boston), was the first of only two Flying Tiger B.747 visits to Manchester and incidentally, today was the only time the airline had used Manchester as a diversionary airport. The other five B.747 arrivals were Qantas B.747 VH-EBH at 0541 (QF007 from Bahrain), Pan American N652PA at 0548 (PA104 from New York), first time visitor N655PA at 0929 (PA106 from Washington) and British Airways examples G-AWNE at 0545 (BA174 from New York) & G-BDXA at 0929 (BA054 from Nairobi). There could have been so many more, had the ADO not refused them, due to there being thirty-nine on the ground already. Amongst the flights turned away were Air Canada L.1011-500 C-GAGK (AC856 Toronto-Heathrow) & British Airways B.747 G-AWNG (BA020 Abu Dhabi-Heathrow).

24th Tunis Air began a series of weekly Sunday IT flights, from/to Monastir (TU8794/5), with B.737s. First visits were made by TS-IOC operating the first flight today and TS-IOD (31st).

25th Thirty passengers enjoyed champagne 9,000ft above the Lake District onboard SD-330 G-BGNA, on Loganair's inaugural Manchester-Edinburgh flight. They were greeted at Manchester by a lone piper, in celebration of the three-times-weekday operation.

26th Britannia Airways inbound flight BY636B from Rhodes was operated by Transavia B.737 PH-TVS this morning. It originates as a Glasgow flight, but routes via Manchester outward and return. Leased B.737 N37AF, which operated the flight throughout the summer, has returned to Air Florida.

28th Cessna Citation 550 G-FERY, operated by European Ferries, arrived at 0947 on a round trip from its Manston base. Although it was a first visit, it's been in before as G-DJBI.

28th French Air Force Transall F.88/61-ZF, arriving at 1502 (FM9948 from Landivisiau), was on an operational mission, en route to Lossiemouth. It landed straight after another French Air Force aircraft, Nord 262 No.78, had just departed operating Glasgow-Brize Norton (FM0730) in connection with 'Exercise Priory' in Scotland, attended by numerous Air Forces.

29th PA-34 Seneca G-FLYI operated a round-trip from Elstree today. Its arrival at Manchester was unusual, as it's deployed exclusively in the South East, used by London-based radio station Capital Radio as their 'eye in the sky', reporting on traffic jams and hold-ups.

31st Air UK operated the Isle of Man route for the last time today, before being taken over by Manx Airlines. The final flight, UK564/5, was entrusted to Fokker F.27 G-BHMY.

November 1982

The airport has been given the go-ahead to spend £1m on the installation of new baggage handling equipment, as the current ten-year old system frequently breaks down. An additional eleven men will be required by the time its operating early next summer, as it's capable of handling up to 6,000 bags an hour, compared to the current 3,500.

Manchester-based tour operators, Sureways Holidays and its in-house airline, Air Manchester, are up for sale after just one year of trading. Their sole aircraft, BAC 1-11 G-SURE, is currently on lease but will be sold by Pennine Commercial Holdings, the parent company of both concerns. Sureways have no outstanding flight commitments and although their 1983 brochure has been produced, it's yet to be distributed.

Airlines making changes this month included Air Malta operating twice-weekly with B.737s (Fri/Sun), Air Portugal will operate Lisbon twice-weekly, with Weds flight routing via Oporto. British Airways permanently dropped Edinburgh & Zurich, ended Nice for the winter and will operate Toronto (BA073/2) with L.1011-200s. Cyprus Airways reverted to a once-weekly flight again for the winter. Finnair will operate a four-weekly cargo schedule, including a new Sunday morning flight. Guernsey Airlines will operate twice-weekly (Fri/Sun) from/to Guernsey. KLM will reduce the morning Amsterdam (KL153/4) to daily except Sundays. Manx Airlines will start a twice-daily weekday Manchester-Isle of Man operation replacing Air UK. SAS will operate three-weekly from/to Copenhagen (SK539/40) with DC-9-21s, with further flights onwards to/from Dublin (SK541/0) operated by DC-9-41s. Winter IT flights will be operated by Air Europe, Air Malta, Aviaco, Britannia Airways, British Airtours, British Airways, Dan-Air, EL AL & Orion Airways and transatlantic flights by CP Air (Toronto & Vancouver) and Wardair (Toronto).

Equipment changes included Lufthansa B.727s D-ABKM (3rd) & D-ABKA (25th); Metropolitan Airways used Islander G-BEOC on DA056 (16th) and Sabena (SN617): used passenger only-version B.737 OO-SDG (3rd).

RAF ILS traffic identified included Hawk XX312 (25th); Dominie XS712 (18th); Jetstreams XX482 (18th/29th), XX491 (22nd/25th), XX493 (26th/30th), XX494 (23rd), XX497 (25th) & XX498 (18th/26th) and Gazelle XW913 as 'SYN47' at 1300 (11th). ILS movements were dominated by the RAF Jetstream, when Finningley sent in twelve training flights (18th-30th). An unidentified F-4 Phantom overshot in the dark from/to RAF Valley as 'K3P42' at 1831 (11th), as did an unidentified Jaguar as 'NOJ58' at 1501 (30th). Civil traffic included BAe

Dove G-ARHW (2nd), BAe.748 Coastguarder G-BDVH (4th), the second appearance of the new BAe.146 when G-SCHH overshot as 'Tibbet 33' at 1356 (9th) and finally Beagle Pup G-AVLN operated by the head of BAe Woodford, Charles Masefield, overshot at 1207 (28th).

1st Dan-Air is basing a Boeing 737 at Manchester for the first time and the first, G-BKAP, operated out to Tenerife as DA1042 at 0857 today. This aircraft complements the two BAC 1-11s and the single Boeing 727 already based for the winter IT season.

1st Manx Airlines began operations on the Manchester-Ronaldsway, route with twice-daily flights MNX321/2 0845/0915 & MNX325/6 1845/1915. Viscount G-BFZL operated both flights today and subsequent flights until the 12th. From the 13th Fokker F.27s G-IOMA & G-OMAN and Viscount G-AZNA were all used. They also operate a Saturday lunchtime flight (MNX323/4) with EMB-110s G-BGCS & G-RLAY. Curiously, rather than using flight numbers, the aircrafts registrations were used for ATC purposes.

2nd The final Jetsave Miami flight was operated by Pan American DC-10 N81NA today (PA8420 from Miami).

3rd Of last night's five diversions, four from Birmingham and one from East Midlands, there was nothing of excitement. Sixteen more arriving from a variety of airports this morning, but mainly from the Midlands, weren't of much interest either, apart from NLM F.27 PH-KFL, diverting in at 0841 from a foggy Birmingham (HN495 from Amsterdam). The morning also produced a single Gatwick diversion, with Cathay Pacific B.747 VR-HIE at 1129 (CX201 from Bahrain). Leeds was affected by fog all day and diversions from there started with Dan-Air BAe.748 G-ARAY, arriving at 1213 (DA061 from Cardiff). Further arrivals continued sporadically until late evening, amongst which were two Air UK F.27 flights: G-BCDN at 2235 (UK588 from Belfast) & G-BCDO at 2228 (UK829 from Amsterdam) and another Air UK flight, EMB-110 G-BGYV diverting in from Humberside at 2123 (UK575 from Amsterdam).

3rd The second of two visits this year by a French Air Force MS.760 Paris, was No. 36, arriving at 1154 today (FM0731 from Brest), before departing to Lyneham at 1514.

4th British Airways B.747 G-BDXG, arriving at 1207 today as BA286 from San Francisco, was clearing up the remainder of the Jetsave USA programme. Another flight on the 11th was operated by G-BDXB, again as BA286 en route from San Francisco to Heathrow.

7th Scanbee CV-580 SE-IEY arriving at 1410 today from Palma via Gatwick was making its first visit, operating an air ambulance flight before departing later for Stockholm.

8th Loganair used EMB-110 G-BIBE on this morning's Edinburgh LC562/3, but for the rest of the month the flights were operated by their two SD-330s, G-BGNA & G-BIRN.

8th A humorous twist to the annual race bringing in the first bottle of Beaujolais Nouveau to the UK, was organised by Warrington based Vodka producers, Vladivar, with their 'Vladivar Nouveau' race. In a reversal of what usually happens, the aim was to get a bottle of Vladivar Vodka to Villefranche, in Southern France! PA-34 Seneca G-AZON was one of the aircraft involved with the competition, offering various prizes for the fastest time, silliest costume etc. A number of passengers departing for the event on G-AZON had arrived at Manchester earlier on Agusta 109 G-HELY, already in fancy dress. One as a witch, complete with a broomstick and another as Count Dracula. 'Biggles' was also spotted rushing for the evening British Airways BAC 1-11 flight to Paris, after arranging transport to Villefranche on his arrival.

9th Norwegian executive jets aren't too common to Manchester, but Citation 550 LN-HOT arrived from Oslo at 0821 this morning, on its first visit. It was carrying the Norwegian directors of a local company, Manchester Steel, to discuss the future of the company.

10th Skyvan G-BJDC, operating from/to Belfast Harbour today as Short 6, is the company's military demonstration aircraft.

10th The Intercontinental DC-8 saga drew to a close today, when it finally departed at 1203 for Stansted (VS1001A). Impounded since the CAA, Manchester Airport & Dan-Air all served writs on it, things started to happen on the 4th, when it was re-registered from RP-C830 to 5N-AVY. It carried out taxiing trials from its parking place on Runway 28, along the runway and back to the Western Apron on the 8th. On the 9th, it carried out a test flight as VS688 departing at 1309 and returning at 1402, before being moved from the North Side apron over to a remote parking spot just south of Runway 28.

11th Air Malta, who already use Transavia Boeing 737s PH-TVC & PH-TVP, have leased a third, PH-TVD, for the short-term. In an all-white scheme with Air Malta stickers, it operated into Manchester as such for the first time today, on charter flight KM820/1.

13th RAF C-130 XV210 operated an outbound trooping flight today (RR4439 Lyneham-Gutersloh) & C-130 XV182 (Gutersloh-Lyneham) operated the return on the 27th.

14th German-built light aircraft Grob G.109 G-LULU was a first visit of type to Manchester, arriving from Bicester, before departing later for Booker. The type, a two-seat self launching motor glider, has been in production since 1980.

15th ATC were advised at 1309 today that Cessna 182 G-CBIL, on a photo survey in the Mobberley area had just lost a window, which had fluttered down to the ground. After deciding the incident wasn't serious enough to terminate his work, the pilot continued on!

16th The airport was given the go-ahead for airlines to carry freight on passenger flights to Canada. All freight bound for North America from Manchester is currently roaded to London, but from next April airlines such as CP Air and Wardair will also be able to carry cargo.

17th Islander G-BESG routing from Fairoaks to Bristol, is a variation of the standard Islander, but with non-standard turbo engines and STOL (Short Takeoff & Landing) capabilities.

19th East German airline Interflug made two visits this month, both with Ilyushin IL-18 aircraft. DDR-STN arriving at 1402 today (IF1452/3 Berlin/Dresden) was bringing in East German TV personnel, whilst the outbound took tourists out for a short-break. The return flight on the 25th was operated by DDR-STC (IF7454/5 from/to Leipzig).

20th British Airways weekly Toronto flight BA073/2 is now scheduled to be operated by L.1011-200s, which provided first visits by G-BGBB today and G-BHBR on the 27th.

21st British Caledonian BAC 1-11 G-BJRT shed a wheel whilst on departure to Gatwick as BR984 today, but continued onwards and made a safe landing at its destination. The ATC Watch Log recorded at 1226 that the aircraft had lost one, or possibly two wheels on takeoff and vehicles had been dispatched to investigate. At 1255 a wheel was found close to the Air Kilroe hangar and at 1315 it was positively identified as belonging to a BAC 1-11. The axle was sheared and the hub and brake assembly were missing, possibly observed flying off the aircraft in a north westerly direction!

23rd Laura Ashley traded in their Beech 100, G-BBVM operated since 1977, for a bigger and newer Beech 200. G-BJBP made its first appearance at Manchester for its new owners today, arriving from Bournemouth, before departing later for Eindhoven.

24th The biggest helicopter visitor of the month, was British Airways Helicopters Sikorsky S-61 G-BEIC at 1203 today, en route from Aberdeen to Penzance as 'Speedbird 3A'.

24th Dan-Air BAe.748 G-BIUV arrived during the afternoon, having declared a full emergency after shutting down its left engine, en route from Belfast to Gatwick. It departed at 1849 for Gatwick, but returned soon afterwards with the same engine malfunction!

27th November 1982 – Air Zimbabwe Boeing 707 VP-WKR is seen here on its second visit to Manchester. It was one of three different Boeing 707s visits by the airline during the decade, all of which were diversions. It served the airline until 1991, when it was sold to Seagreen Air Transport. (Geoff Ball)

27th November 1982 - South African ZS-SPE was the second of only eight B.747SP (Short-Performance) aircraft to visit Manchester. The idea for the 747SP came in 1975, from a joint request between Pan American & Iran Air, who were looking for a high-capacity airliner with enough range to cover Pan American's New York–Middle Eastern routes and Iran Air's Tehran–New York route. When the latter was launched in 1976, it was the longest non-stop commercial flight in the world. (Geoff Ball)

25th British Air Ferries undertook a number of flights, using Viscounts to transport copies of the Daily Telegraph south. G-AOHV (VF6036/7 from/to Southend) & G-AOYS (VF6038/9 Southend-Gatwick) operated today, G-AOHV (VF6040/1 from/to Southend) & G-AOYS (VF6042/3 Southend-Gatwick-both 26th) and G-AOYS (VF6044/5 Southend-Gatwick) &

Herald G-BCWE (VF2310/1 from/to Southend-both 27th). Viscount G-APEY also operated two charter flights from/to Jersey, VF5992/3 (22nd) & VF5994/5 (24th).

25th Queens Flight BAe.748 XS789 (Kitty4), brought the Duke of Kent into Manchester for a local engagement.

26th KLM DC-9-15 PH-DNB made its last visit today, operating KL155/6. It was sold in January 1983 to British Midland as G-BMAG.

27th Since the last batch on the 4th, there had been few weather diversions, due to a consistent run of wet and windy weather. Once the thin layer of high cloud had dissipated, Saturday dawned to a quiet, calm and sunny winter's morning, perfect conditions for another one of those major diversion days! It all started at 0543 when RAF VC-10 diverted in from Brize Norton as RR2102 from Washington. The first from Heathrow/Gatwick was British Airways B.747 G-AWNM at 0739, which started a steady flow throughout the morning, twenty-three in fact! Wide-bodied flights included British Airways B.747s G-AWNF at 0757 (BA174 from New York), G-AWNM at 0739 (BA274 from Boston) & G-BDPV at 0846 (BA276 from Washington); Pan American B.747s N741PA at 0948 (PA102 from New York) & N753PA at 0909 (PA098 from Miami); TWA B.747 N53110 at 0750 (TW754 from Boston); Cathay Pacific B.747 VR-HID at 0912 (CX201 from Bahrain); Air India B.747 VT-EBO at 0753 (AI110 from New York) and South African B.747SP ZS-SPE at 1043 (SA230 from Las Palmas), the second B.747SP to visit Manchester. British Caledonian diverted in three DC-10s: G-BGAT at 0940 (BR246 from Houston), G-BHDI at 0955 (BR662 from Rio) & G-BHDJ at 1010 (BR232 from Atlanta). Others arrivals were Air Florida DC-10 N102TV at 0933 (QH200 from Miami), BWIA Tristar 500 9Y-TGN at 0914 (BW900 from Bridgetown) & Wardair DC-10 C-GXRB at 1039 (WD800 from Ottawa). Most welcome during the morning, were three Boeing 707s: Air Rhodesia VP-WKR at 1021 (RH124 from Harare), Zambian 9J-AEB at 0936 (QZ704 from Lusaka/Milan) and private N600JJ at 1134 from Newark. This aircraft was previously operated by Laker Airways and made numerous visits to Manchester as G-AWDG. British Airways B.737 G-BGDU at 0808 (BA5441 from Newcastle) diverted in to qualify the crew with the ability to land in Category 3 weather conditions. After landing it turned around for departure to Heathrow, only to find their visibility had fallen below Cat.3 limitations, so it diverted for a second time, this time ending up at Birmingham! The morning also saw a number of European diversions. Lufthansa sent two flights northwards: D-ABFU at 1053 (LH068 from Munich) & D-ABHN at 1100 (LH050 from Dusseldorf) and Air Portugal B.727 CS-TBY, arriving at 1210 (TP472 from Lisbon), was the last of this particular session. A lull followed, due to a temporary weather improvement at Heathrow and Gatwick, just as Manchester had cleared more taxiways for extra diversion parking. The first of another eleven diversions arriving between 1709 and 2308 was British Airways B.747 G-AWNM, which had already left Manchester for Heathrow, only to return due to the rapid deterioration in their weather. It was closely followed by BWIA Tristar 500 9Y-TGN, arriving for the same reason as the BA B.747. The next in chronological order were Alitalia DC-9s I-DIKW at 1745 (AZ266 from Milan) & I-DIKL at 1748 (AZ280 from Rome); Air Portugal B.707F CS-TBJ at 1751 (TP030 from Lisbon) and British Caledonian DC-10 G-BHDI at 1818 (BR662), another flight failing in its attempt to return. Nigeria Airways B.747 LN-AEO at 1823 (WT800 from Kano) was making its first visit and two British Caledonian B.707s: G-AYEX at 1834 (BR216 from Lusaka) & G-AXRS at 1901 (BR334 from Tripoli), were on their very last visits to Manchester as they were sold soon afterwards. Next was another Wardair flight, DC-10 C-GFHX at 1922 (WD410 from Calgary) and the last diversion on a very busy day that saw a total of thirty-seven arrivals, was Dan-Air BAC 1-11 G-BDAE at 2308 (DA1883 from Malaga).

27th In amongst today's big-boy weather diversions, was PA-22 Tri-Pacer G-ARYH. After giving up trying to land at Crossland Moor, near Huddersfield, it came to Manchester instead.

27th November 1982 – Another diversion during the day was early production B.707, N600JJ. This former Laker aircraft was sold to a Saudi Sheik in June 1981, who operated it until August 1987. (Geoff Ball)

28th November 1982 – One of the many highlights from yesterday's diversions was B.747 LN-AEO, operating a Nigeria Airways flight in full colours. On lease from SAS from April 1982 to June 1983, it was eventually UK-registered as G-BMGS and operated with British Airways, British Airtours & British Caledonian. In 1990, it was sold to Virgin Atlantic as G-VOYG. (Geoff Ball)

30th Bad weather affected flights at various airports again and more diversions arrived during the day. Birmingham was affected by fog all day and of the thirteen diversions from there, most were British except for Sobelair B.737 OO-SBS at 1051 (OO2109 from Brussels), Aviaco DC-9 EC-DGC at 1236 (AO1792 from Tenerife) & Air India B.707 VT-DXT at 1651 (AI503 from Moscow) on its first visit. Three from East Midlands during the evening were Britannia Airways B.737 G-AVRO, Alidair Viscount G-ARIR & Orion Airways B.737 G-BJBJ. The RAF diverted stretched C-130 XV212 (RR5033 from Akrotiri) in from a foggy Lyneham and DC-8 N910CL diverting in from Mildenhall early morning on a USAF passenger charter from McGuire AFB, was the first visit from the American-airline Capitol since 1979. Finally, although Heathrow operations were hit from mid-morning to mid-afternoon, the only three diversions were Aer Lingus B.737 EI-BEE at 1109 (EI710 from Cork), Air India B.747 VT-EBO at 1151 (AI103 from Dubai) & JAT B.727 YU-AKG at 1207 (JU210 from Zagreb), as the majority of Heathrow flights diverted to Gatwick and Stansted.

30th RAF Rescue Wessex XR497, which diverted into Manchester with technical trouble today whilst routing from RAF Leconfield, was unable to depart until the 2nd December.

December 1982

Qantas announced the commencement of a twice-weekly service from Manchester next April, after estimates showed 20% of their customers originated from Northern England. Flights operating Fri/Sun, will route Melbourne-Sydney–Bangkok–Bahrain–Amsterdam-Manchester and return. As well as offering Sydney and Melbourne as direct destinations from Manchester for the first time, they will also have Full Traffic Rights, meaning they can sell tickets for any part of the trip. Qantas are the oldest airline in the world and the safest on record.

Work on Phase II of the £2m extension of the West Apron started last month. The eighteen month project will provide services for three new stands for B.747s and one for B.727 aircraft, all equipped with air bridges. Extension work on Pier C, due to start February next should be ready by June 1985. The extra 1,000sq metres of passenger holding space will be linked to the existing Gate 28 by a connecting corridor. A new link taxiway, currently under construction joining the South Bay and Taxiway 2, will provide more direct access to the 06 end of the runway. There will also be increased car parking and a new bus and coach station.

The £1m transformation of the airports catering facilities starting this month, will take nine months to complete. A temporary café will open at the end of the month and a temporary bar in the International Lounge will open on 1st January. The new Manchester Welcome Bar and Cafeteria will open on 1st March and SAS catering, who recently took over the catering contract, have promised a new concept 'free-flow' cafeteria will replace the existing one by next April. The 220-seat Brabazon Suite will also be completely refurbished and promoted as one of the finest restaurants in the region.

Equipment changes on scheduled flights included Iberia operating first visit B.727 EC-CID on IB346/7 (3rd); Lufthansa used B.727s D-ABLI (1st), D-ABDI (2nd) & D-ABKN (8th) and Swissair (SR842): used MD-81 HB-INA, which was another first visit (6th).

RAF ILS traffic identified included Hawk XX250 (16th); C-130s XV183 (10th) & XV222 (30th); Dominies XS726 (21st), XS734 (14th) & XS736 (17th); Jetstreams XX491 (1st) & XX482 (8th) and Andover XS643 (8th). The only aircraft of interest was an unidentified German Air Force Bell UH-1. Although it wasn't an ILS participant, it overflew the airport around 1200, routing Finningley-Shawbury (7th). Civil traffic consisted of Cessna 172 G-BEUX (10th), Cessna 152 G-BHRB (29th) and BAe.125-700 7T-VCW overshooting at 1555 on a test flight out of Hawarden (22nd).

1st PA-22 Tri-Pacer G-ARYH, which diverted in on 27th November whilst trying to land at Crossland Moor, near Huddersfield made another attempt today; only to return to Manchester an hour later, when its efforts to land there were once again thwarted by the weather!

1st The month saw three Sea King visits and today's arrival of Royal Navy XZ598 at 1550, was bringing in spares from RAF Finningley for Wessex XR497. Further visits for fuel and passenger transfer purposes were XZ597 (18th) & XZ599 (21st).

1st Saudi BAe.125 HZ-FMA made its first visit at 1614 today, before departing for Heathrow at 1835, although it had been into Manchester many times before as G-AYRY with McAlpine Aviation.

3rd Yemen Airways B.727 4W-ACF (IY7444 from Rome), arriving at 1036 today as a Gatwick diversion, was on its first visit. The evening also saw five diversions from Leeds: Dan-Air BAe.748 G-ARRW at 1732 (DA'B6ER from Cardiff), Air Malta B.737 PH-TVC at 1832 (KM806 from Malta) and three Air UK F.27 flights - G-BHMW twice at 1754/2237 (UK203 from Cardiff/UK588 from Belfast) & G-STAN at 2233 (UK829 from Amsterdam).

4th BAe.125 G-AVVB suffered a bird-strike on departure to Inverness. The right engine was shut down, but no emergency was declared as the pilot managed to restart the engine.

5th The biggest helicopter visitor for the second month running was another British Airways Helicopters Sikorsky S-61, with the arrival of G-BFFK from Dundee at 1515 today as 'Speedbird 3G', before departing later to Aberdeen.

6th Lear Jet D-CARL was an interesting arrival and a first visit. On a day when the airport was affected by low visibility severely affecting operations, the Lear Jet succeeded in landing at 1755 in 100m visibility, which was more than most aircraft had seen all day!

6th A late East Midlands diversion at 2335 tonight, was British Midland F.27 G-BAUR (BD706A from Ostend).

7th The severity of fog affecting the UK today moved around the country throughout the day. When the Midlands were affected in the early hours, diversions received from the East Midlands and Birmingham were two each from Orion Airways and British Airways. Heathrow was also affected for a short time in the early hours, but their only diversion was the first visit of Saudia L.1011 HZ-AHG at 0538 (SV047 from Jeddah). By mid-afternoon it was Yorkshires turn to be affected, when two arrived from Leeds, as well as Partenavia P68 G-BGXJ from Humberside. When Birmingham was affected by high winds briefly during in the evening, Air India B.707 VT-DXT arrived at 1750 (AI503 from Moscow).

7th US Army VIP Beech C-12 VIP 76-22250 arriving at 1432 today from Stuttgart as 'Clue 32A', was operated by HQUSEUCOM (HQ US European Command).

11th British Airways Toronto flight BA073/2 provided Manchester with two more first visits this month, with L.1011-200 G-BHBN today and L.1011-500 G-BFCE on the 18th.

12th An old friend diverted into Manchester today, due to Stansted's weather. Intercontinental DC-8 5N-AVY, formerly RP-C830, arriving at 0718 (VS802 from Lagos) came and went without incident this time! Another Air India flight diverting in was B.707 VT-DVA at 2102 (AI515 from Moscow).

12th A new airline to Manchester, Air Express International, made their debut today when their first once-weekly freight flight routing New York-Stansted-MAN-Gander-New York, was operated by CL-44 N121AE (formerly G-AZHL). The following week on the 19th, the service was unable to operate through Manchester, due to the aircraft going tech, so the 16 tonnes of cargo had to be trucked to Stansted.

12th An interesting afternoon diversion was Lake LA-4 G-BASO. This single engine amphibious aircraft was bound for Birmingham from Newtonards, when it diverted into Manchester due to the weather. Upon arrival it cleared security and then promptly returned to its base at Newtonards.

13th The three Canadian Air Force CC-130E flights this month were 130321 as CAM515 at 0731 today, 130323 (CAM516-17th) & 130321 (CAM517-19th).

14th The last diversions of note this month were two from Heathrow: Qantas B.747 VH-EBO at 0813 (QF001 from Bahrain) and South African Airways B.747 ZS-SAO at 0940 (SA220 from Sal Island).

19th December 1982 - Two Nord 262s passing through Manchester today were F-GBEG & F-GBEK, routing Keflavik-Toulouse on delivery from Ransome Airlines of Philadelphia to the French Government. F-GBEG arrived at 1357 in an all-white scheme carrying 'Marine' titles & F-GBEK arriving at 1403 was in ex-Ransome Airlines colours. (Geoff Ball)

15th RAE BAC 1-11 XX919 arrived at 1036 today from Farnborough, for a major overhaul with Dan-Air Engineering and Devon VP958 appeared at 1213 as the crew-ferry.

16th Another milestone in the successful history of Manchester Airport was achieved today, when the 5-millionth passenger passed through. A champagne and flowers celebration was held in honour of the lucky passenger, stepping off a Paris flight.

17th RAE Andover XS646 operated a return trip from/to Farnborough today, possibly in connection with the overhaul of BAC 1-11 XX919. Although the aircraft's cargo was well covered, numerous lumps and bumps could be seen, which must have been of a secretive and sensitive nature, as the crew were quite insistent that photographers should be discouraged from taking any pictures!

17th VIP Saudi Air Force VC-130H 111, arriving at 0309 today (RSF122), was on its way back to Jeddah from the Lockheed factory at Marietta after protracted modification work; having originally made its way there as far back as the 12th May!

20th Kar-Air operated SE.210 OH-LSF on a pre-Christmas charter today, from/to Helsinki (KR3011/2).

21st The last RAF Vulcan squadron disbanded at RAF Waddington today, ending 25 years of the country's V-force deterrent, originally consisting of the Vulcan, Valiant & Victor. The Valiant was phased out in the 1960's and most of the RAF Victors were converted to tankers. The last Vulcan to 'visit' Manchester was XJ782 overshooting at 1611 on 4th September this year and the last Vulcan to actually land was XM610 on 24th January 1964!

23rd British Airways Manchester-Aberdeen flight BA5690, originating at Birmingham, made two failed attempts to land at Manchester due to fog, before proceeding to Aberdeen; so B.737 G-BGJG called in en route Aberdeen-Heathrow as BA5608 to collect the stranded passengers.

24th Aviaco used Iberia B.727 EC-CFH on Tenerife flight AO1760/1. It was the second Iberia B.727 this month and only the third to ever visit Manchester. Prior to these two, the last one to visit was EC-CFB as a tech diversion, en route Madrid-Dublin on 19th May 1974!

30th The ATC Watch Log made several references towards the end of the month and at the beginning of the New Year, regarding flocks of birds in and around the airfield causing problems for departing aircraft. It records several bird-strikes in the first few days of January and an entry made in today's log at 1430 typifies the problem. 'Bird scaring tactics by Manfire Charlie have succeeded in arousing a flock of birds, previously settled on the International Apron by Pier C, into a frenzied orbit over the middle of the main runway where they remained for the last five minutes, before eventually returning to their original parking area where they were upsetting no-one'.

First/Last Arrivals & Departures 1982

First arrival:	B.737 G-BGTW/KG730 from Malta at 0055 (Diversion)
First departure:	B.737 G-AZNZ/BY640A to Wildenrath at 0812
Last arrival:	B.737 G-BMHG/AE649 from Malaga at 2151
Last departure:	Cessna 172 G-AZTS on a local flight, at 2357

Airport Stats 1982 (+/- % on Previous Year)		
Scheduled Passengers	5,155,961	+6%
Freight & Mail (Tonnes)	27,210	-3%
Movements	89,002	+8%

4
Airport Diary 1983

January 1983

A report issued by the Department of Trade regarded an incident on the 21st November 1982, when British Caledonian BAC 1-11 G-BJRT lost a wheel on takeoff from Manchester. It concluded that the aircraft had been fitted with a Boeing 707 mainwheel bearing by mistake during a routine maintenance check at Gatwick last October and that the error had gone unchecked for 259 landings, before November's incident. The aircraft had departed Manchester as normal, but the airport was soon alerted to the emergency. When the pilot arrived at Gatwick he made a low pass over the Tower, so ATC could observe how many wheels were missing. Thankfully only one of the two starboard main wheels had fallen off and the aircraft made a safe landing, but the main undercarriage wheel and axle were damaged beyond economic repair. Following the report an engineering supervisor was severely reprimanded over the matter.

Following on from Manchester Airport's successful appeal in having the rules banning charter flights from carrying freight relaxed, they have requested the Aviation Minister adopts an open skies policy and removes the constraints on airlines wishing to operate from Manchester. However, it's been made known that applications for possible new route licences to countries such as Singapore and Pakistan could be blocked, even by UK airlines with no intention of operating the routes themselves. A recent award for Qantas to operate to Sydney/Melbourne from Manchester was only agreed after the Australian Government offered British Airways the right to operate between Heathrow-Adelaide, but when the arrangements failed, airlines such as British Airways simply objected to the new services, in order to maintain their share of passengers who have to fly via London.

The proposed £37m link, connecting Manchester Airport to the inter-city network hangs on the outcome of the ongoing Public Enquiry, into the possible expansion of Stansted Airport. The northern consortium of local authorities campaigning to scrap the development of Stansted as London's third airport, have consistently argued it would rob the rest of the country of investment upwards of £1billion. The proposed link would run from the Styal line in a loop, to a new airport station between the existing terminal and the proposed second terminal, but due to the uncertainty, no firm date has been set for the link's construction.

After less than four years service with the airline, British Airways has sold all six of their Tristar 500s to the RAF, for conversion to airborne tankers over the next three years.

Equipment changes included Air Portugal operating Boeing 707s twice on their Lisbon service: CS-TBG (15th) & CS-TBF (22nd); Loganair operating Twin Otter G-BIEM on Edinburgh LC562/3 rather than the usual SD-330 (17th); Lufthansa (LH074): B.727s D-ABGI (15th), D-ABHI (12th), D-ABKH (4th), D-ABKQ (6th), D-ABKR (18th), D-ABQI (14th) & D-ABSI (17th) and Swissair used DC-9-32 HB-IFH (20th).

RAF ILS traffic identified included Hawk XX250 (16th); C-130 XV182 (12th); Dominies XS709 (11th), XS711 (26th) & XS731 (12th); Jetstream XX494 (19th/28th); Andover XS639 overshot twice during the morning as RR701 whilst undertaking an Instrument Rating flight (24th) and Gazelle XX382 made a very low pass along the runway at 1525 as 'SYN43' (26th). Other military ILS visitors were RAE Comet XS235 as 'MPRHM' at 1434 from/to Boscombe Down (17th) and Queens Flight BAe.748 XS789 (27th). Civil traffic included the following Lancashire Aero Club aircraft: Cessna 152s G-BLAC & G-BHUP (29th) and Cessna 172s G-BEUX & G-MALC (29th) & G-WPUI (8th); Woodford-based Beagle Pup G-AZEW (20th/29th); both of the CAA's BAe.748s: G-AVXI (11th) & G-AVXJ (27th) and BAe.125-700 5N-AVK overshot at 1129 on a test flight out of Hawarden (28th).

3rd A round-trip from Helsinki operated by Kar-Air OH-LSD today (KR3011/2), was the final visit to Manchester of a Finnair SE.210 Caravelle. The last two still remaining in service, OH-LSD & OH-LSF, were sold to Italian charter airline Altair. All subsequent Helsinki charter flights by Kar-Air will be operated by Douglas DC-9s.

4th Today was the first visit to Manchester of a BAE.146, with the arrival of British Air Ferries G-OBAF at 0800 from Southend, operating a return flight to Munich for BAe employees. The type entered commercial service on the 27th May this year, when Dan-Air operated a Gatwick-Berne return flight with G-BKMN, which had been handed over to them just four days earlier.

6th Lear Jet 55 D-CARX, arriving at 2018 today on a flight from Keflavik to Nuremberg, was the only biz-jet making its first visit this month.

10th French Navy Nord 262 No.53 arrived at 1516 today as FA056, on a training flight from Cardiff to Edinburgh and again on the 12th, routing Glasgow-Groningen. A second aircraft, No.68 operating as FM0545, routed Villacoublay-Amsterdam (14th).

11th Few Army Air Corps Scout helicopters have landed at Manchester, but an unidentified example arrived at 1421 from Carlisle, before departing to Hereford at 1554.

14th Andover XS607 operated by the Royal Aircraft Establishment (RAE) based at Farnborough, arrived with a spare crew to take BAC 1-11 XX919 back to Farnborough, after being with Dan-Air for maintenance since the 15th December last year.

16th A rare visit was made today by a US Army Beech U-21, when 67-18013 arrived at 1153 operating as 'Nite 32B/C' from/to its base at Coleman Barracks, Western Germany.

17th The new weekly cargo service operated by Air Express International had a very patchy month! The first two flights were cancelled and today's was over 24-hours late. The following week it was diverted direct into Manchester due to bad weather at Stansted, so the freight had to be roaded up and loaded onto the flight, which left direct to New York. The flight on the 30th was also cancelled, this time due to industrial action at the airport.

17th The first visit of a Westland Lynx helicopter took place at 1211 today, when Royal Navy example XZ736 arrived off HMS Manchester, moored in Brocklebank Dock in Liverpool. Painted in low visibility grey colours, it brought the ship's Captain in for lunch at the airports VIP lounge, before returning from whence it came at 1459.

20th Swissair used DC-9-32 HB-IFH today, which unfortunately is the shape of things to come this summer, when flight SR842/3 will be regularly operated by the smaller DC-9-32. Due to a recent UK/Swiss agreement restricting the number of seats offered between the two countries, the majority will be allocated for Heathrow flights, which leaves Manchester with only enough capacity to operate the smaller Douglas DC-9-32.

21st PA-34 Seneca G-BOSS arrived from Elstree today on demonstration to Eddie Shah, the Messenger Newspapers proprietor and current owner of PA-32R Cherokee G-BHNN. He was obviously smitten, as G-BOSS became a Manchester resident the following month!

23rd British Airways operated a series of Tristar flights to/from Malaga, on behalf of Vauxhall-Opel agents, all aircraft positioned from/to Heathrow, G-BBAF today, G-BBAH (25th) & G-BBAI (27th). Three inbound flights were operated by G-BBAH (25th) & G-BBAI (27th/ 31st).

25th Another car-dealership related flight was former Laker Airways BAC 1-11 G-ATPK, arriving from Gatwick today to operate a flight to Valencia on behalf of BMW agents, before returning on the 27th. It's now privately operated by Heathrow-based Bryan Aviation, specialists in business charter flights, who set up last year and also operate BAe.125s G-BBEP & G-OJOY.

28th The airport was brought to a standstill by a lightning strike by firemen, just three months after the Airport Authority signed a local pay agreement with the unions, hailed as a new era in industrial relations! The action, taken at the start of the annual pay negotiations, involved firemen belonging to the Transport Workers Union walking out at 0943 over a roster mix-up, which left the Watchtower without any fire cover. Although flights were cancelled and others operated from Liverpool and Birmingham, passengers were advised to check in as normal.

29th On a quiet afternoon when the airport remained closed due to the strike action, several Barton aircraft took the opportunity to have a go on the ILS of an International Airport. Cessna 152s G-BLAC & G-BHUP and Cessna 172s G-MALC & G-BEUX, all performed touch-and-goes.

31st The four-day strike paralysing Manchester Airport ended at 1500 today, following a meeting of a thousand TGWU manual workers. They accepted a peace formula after the management agreed to negotiate on pay and the union's assured changes in working practices would be discussed.

31st The last of the ILS traffic this month was an unidentified BAe.125-700, on an early evening test flight out of Hawarden, overshooting three times in the dark.

February 1983

Manchester Airport's hush-money scheme rewarding quieter aircraft with rebates on landing fees is hailed as a great success! Since its introduction, the number of noise infringements has fallen by 18% and noisier aircraft such as British Airways Tridents are gradually being replaced by Boeing 757s and as Monarch Airlines are also introducing the type, this year will be even quieter!

Equipment changes on scheduled flights included Air France (AF964): Britannia Airways B.737 G-BECG (18th); Air Portugal (TP458): B.727-200s CS-TBX (19th/26th) & CS-TBY (12th); Loganair operated EMB-110 G-BIBE on all three Edinburgh flights (14th) & Guernsey Airlines SD-330 G-BITV (16th) plus Twin Otter G-BIEM on LC562/3 (17th) and Lufthansa (LH074): B.727s D-ABKC (9th), D-ABKI (15th) & D-ABKR (16th).

RAF ILS traffic identified were C-130s XV204 (11th), XV207 (16th) & XV290 (10th); Dominie XS733 (7th/8th) and Canberra WK111 overshooting at 1601 as 'Trident 3' (23rd). Civil traffic were Corvette F-BVPT (2nd/3rd), Lancashire Aero Club Cessna 152 G-BHRB (17th), Cessna 172s G-BAXY (13th/26th) & G-BEUX (13th) and Air Hanson Sikorsky S-76 G-OHTL at 1225 (26th).

1st Weathermen said the country may have seen the last of yesterday's strong winds, gusting up to 92mph in some parts, but they were wrong as the UK was affected again today. At 0800 the Manchester Met Office recorded a wind speed of 66mph in the City Centre and although most services operated normally, several flights were cancelled.

1st Manx Airlines were a Fokker F.27 down whilst G-OMAN was on maintenance, so Air UK Fokker F.27 G-BDVS was drafted in to operate this evening's MNX329/330. The same aircraft made further appearances on the 2nd & 3rd.

2nd Corvette F-BVPT overshot this afternoon and again the next day at 1624. It was one of only fifteen of the type to visit Manchester since the first, F-BVPS, on the 31st May 1975.

4th Reckitt & Coleman, who formed in 1856, are best known for their mustard but they spent their first nine years in business selling starch. Nowadays they manufacture food, household products, pharmaceuticals and toiletries. They have owned their own aircraft since 1970s, which up until recently was Beech 90 G-RCCL, but it's been sold in the USA and replaced with another Beech 90, G-BKIP, which made its first visit today from/to Norwich where the company and aircraft are based.

6th February 1983 – Air Express operated a short-lived weekly cargo service to New York with two ex-British Canadair CL-44s from December 1982 to March 1983. N121AE, seen here with its unique swing-tail design, is ready to take its outward load. (Geoff Ball)

7th This evening's Air Ecosse Dundee flight (WG778/9) was operated by C.404 G-WTVC.

8th Today saw the first Jetstar to visit Manchester since September 1981, when Emerson Electrics N8300E made a brief first visit at 1410, on a round-trip from Brussels.

10th Cessna Citation 550 D-IMTM, arriving at 0939 today on a round trip from Munich, was the first of two biz-jet first visits this month. The second was another Citation 550, when EI-BJL arrived from Luton at 1619 for an overnight stay (27th).

10th Snow and low cloud were responsible for the arrival of sixteen diversions into Manchester, from a variety of airports. Included during the evening were five British Airways flights from Heathrow and the following three Air UK F.27 flights from Leeds: G-BHMX at 1538 (UK734 from Dublin), G-BAKL at 1754 (UK203 from Edinburgh) & G-BCDO at 1948 (UK210 from Norwich).

13th Liverpool-based Genair started a newspaper run to Leuchars. Two late evening flights operate nightly except for Saturdays, transporting the Scottish edition of the Daily Mirror, which is printed in Manchester. From the 27th, they were scaled down to one flight and aircraft used so far are SD-330s G-BKDO, G-EASI, G-NICE & G-OCAS and EMB-110 G-BGYT (22nd-24th).

14th Loganair utilised EMB-110 G-BIBE on all of today's Edinburgh flights, but due to the reduced capacity offered in comparison to the normal SD-330, an extra flight was added during the morning, operated by Twin Otter G-BHXG (LC562A/563A).
14th French Air Force Nord 262 No.68/F-RBAC, arriving at 0856 today as FM0545, was on a training flight from Villacoublay to Amsterdam.
15th The only Lear Jet this month was Lear Jet 35 I-FLYC, arriving at 1758 today to night-stop, from/to Turin. Another Italian executive movement was Beech 60 I-ENMA on the 22nd.
18th RAE Devon VP975 made two visits today. Initially arriving from Farnborough at 0939, it was present for less than ten minutes, before operating a round trip to West Freugh and departing back to Farnborough again. West Freugh, which is located to the south of Stranraer, is mainly used as an armaments training school.
18th Another military visitor today was all-white RAF BAe.748 XS792, operating as RR1402. It was returning the Prime Minister, Margaret Thatcher, back to London after a tour of the North West.

19th February 1983 – Aerocenter Fairchild F.27 SE-IEG is seen here on departure having arrived two days ago. It was operating from/to Billund in an all-white scheme, with Nile Delta titles on the nose. Although it operated for the airline from 1980-86, it spent considerable time during that period on lease to other airlines and is showing signs of its recent lease to Egyptian operator, Nile Delta Air Services. (Geoff Ball)

21st British Airways Trident 1 G-ARPP made its last visit to Manchester today, as Shuttle back-up flight BA4424 at 1026, before departing as BA4491 at 1606 the following day. It was withdrawn after operating its last service (BA4962 Heathrow-Glasgow) on the 23rd.
24th Amongst the pick of four weather diversions today, was the second appearance of Heavylift Belfast G-BEPS (NP152 from Lisbon) originally bound for Stansted, arriving at 2136 with a consignment of tomatoes. Gatwick was affected by fog well into the afternoon, but bizarrely Manchester only received one diversion from there, which was Boeing 727 G-BCDA at 1606 (DA1485 from Malaga), whereas Heathrow received at least eighteen and Birmingham at least eight.
25th Another weather affected day saw fourteen more diversions, mainly from the Midlands. Those of interest were NLM F.27 PH-KFK at 0947 (HN495 from Amsterdam) and Centreline EMB-110 G-CTLN (twice), operating City-link flights on behalf of Dan-Air.

22nd February 1983 – The new Boeing 757 entered commercial service on 1st January with Eastern Airlines and operated its first commercial service for British Airways on 9th February, when G-BIKB operated a Heathrow-Belfast Shuttle flight, having been delivered on 25th January. It's certain to be sold in large quantities worldwide, as British Airways alone have ordered nineteen. The above named 'Windsor Castle', is seen making its first appearance at Manchester at 1043 today on a Shuttle back-up flight, departing on a 1-hour demonstration flight via the Isle of Man for the management and various civil dignitaries, prior to landing and performing a fast wheels-up pass on Runway 06. The B.757 will be fully introduced onto their Shuttle network on the 16th March, later than planned due to the lack of trained aircrew and from April they will operate twice-daily from Manchester. Of the four ordered by Monarch Airlines, one will be based at Manchester, operating IT flights from May. Boeing claims the £22m aircraft, powered by the redeveloped and quieter Rolls-Royce RB211 engines, is the most fuel efficient short to medium range twin-jet aeroplane on the market. (Geoff Ball)

25th British Airways flight BA072 (Toronto-Heathrow), made an extra stop at Manchester today, when Tristar 500 G-BFCA made its first visit to offload the Toronto Symphony Orchestra and their equipment. This leaves two British Airways Tristars yet to visit, L.1011-200 G-BHBM & L.1011-500 G-BFCB. One that hasn't visited and won't be is G-BFCF, which operated its last service for British Airways on 28th February and has been sold to the RAF, along with the airlines other Tristar 500s.

25th British Airways B.747 G-BDXB diverted in at 2245 today, with one engine shut down, en route Heathrow-Nairobi (BA055). The aircraft chose not to return to Heathrow, due to their weather being marginal.

26th British Airways B.747 G-BDXE, arriving at 0926 today (BA9532 from Heathrow) to operate the delayed BA055 to Nairobi direct, was also a first visit. This means all of the current Rolls-Royce powered British Airways B.747s, G-BDXA-BDXJ, have visited. Showing what a desperate start to the year it's been, this was only the third Boeing 747 movement at Manchester so far!

27th Air Express International's second CL-44, N122AE, finally put in an appearance today. It's distinguishable from its sister-ship, N121AE, by its black tail, as '122' has a brown tail. Operations were more settled this month, apart from an inbound flight that should have operated on the 13th being delayed for two days, due to heavy snow in New York.

28th Today was the first visit of Shorts big brother, the SD-360, capable of carrying thirty-six passengers, compared to thirty by the smaller SD-330. The first of two ordered by Air Ecosse was G-DASI, which arrived on this evenings WG916 Datapost flight, in their full red colours. These aircraft are quickly converted from passenger to mail operation configuration and vice-versa. The stories behind the two registrations are that the very first contract the Post Office signed with Air Ecosse for their mail flights was Contract D.AS1 (Datapost Air Service 1), hence G-DASI and G-RMSS was registered after the Royal Mail's Special Services.

March 1983

Poor exchange rates resulted in many transatlantic summer services being cancelled, including the entire Jetsave programme from Manchester, which would have been operated by British Airways. Transamerica's programme from Gatwick and Manchester are also cancelled, as are a number of flights due to be operated by the American-airline, Arrow Air. There will be no Air Florida flights to Miami this year, Monarch Airlines who are basing a B.757 from Manchester, have drastically reduced flights due to poor bookings and Air Europe have cancelled their plans to base a B.757 for the summer season.

It was revealed during a conference organised by the Manchester Chamber of Commerce, that Manchester Airport was pricing itself out of the air freight market, losing out to road hauliers and the London airports, which were all cheaper. Bringing Manchester's cargo rates in line with Heathrow and Gatwick would not solve the problem though, as the freight forwarding agents are currently sending down smaller individual loads from their customers and consolidating them in London, which makes it a lot cheaper than Manchester's standard rates on International flights. A freight transport lecturer at Manchester Polytechnic told the conference that the airport's share of the market had fallen dramatically since 1970, when 10% of the UK's air cargo flew out of Manchester. The figure now is now around 3-4%, even though a third of Britain's trade originates from the North.

The proposed rail-link to Manchester Airport moved a step nearer reality this month, when the British Rail Bill was given an unopposed second reading by MP's in the Houses of Parliament.

A 20 tonne granite boulder erected at the airport on the 16th, was in memory of paratroopers based there during the Second World War. The 15ft high rock, found at Dolgarrog in the Conwy Valley, has been sited outside the main entrance. Once sand-blasted, it will be inscribed, before the official unveiling ceremony some time after Easter.

Locally based air-taxi operator, Grosvenor Aviation, has applied to the CAA to operate services between Birmingham, Manchester & Belfast Harbour. Four daily services are planned for this autumn, with Shorts SD-360s capable of carrying thirty-six passengers.

Equipment changes/notes on scheduled flights included Air Malta (KM106): brand new B.737, 9H-ABA, on its first visit; KLM (KL157): NLM F.28 PH-CHD (6th); Loganair operated newly-delivered SD-360 G-BKMX (from 28th); Lufthansa (LH074): B.727s D-ABKA (8th) & D-ABLI (11th); Manx Airlines used Viscount G-AZNA on MNX323/4 (26th); Swissair (SR842): used DC-9-32 HB-IFH (11th/21st) and SAS DC-9-21s OY-KGD & OY-KGE made their first visits for several years, as both have been on lease since 1981 to French-airline Touraine Air Transport.

IT flights slowly increased as the month developed. EL AL's weekly Tel Aviv IT flight, operated throughout the winter by a Monarch Airlines B.737, reverted to an EL AL aircraft on the 27th when B.707 4X-ATY operated LY5317/8. Wardair started their summer programme, with DC-10 C-GFHX operating WD810/1 from/to Toronto, via Prestwick (30th).

RAF ILS traffic identified included Hawks XX173 (11th), XX177 (1st), XX180 (15th), XX242 (3rd), XX249 (14th) & XX297 (10th); C-130 XV177 (25th); Jetstreams XX494 (9th/30th) & XX498 (14th); Dominies XS710 (24th), XS712 (10th), XS727 (17th), XS738 (9th) and Vulcan XL426 (29th). Two unidentified aircraft were a RAF Andover overshooting at 1328 (RR802-7th) and a RAF Bulldog as (WVY08-19th). Civil traffic were Lancashire Aero Club Cessna 152 G-BHRB (7th/17th/20th) and Cessna 172s G-BHNU (1st/3rd) & G-BEWR (7th); Genair SD-330 G-OCAS (1st) and CAA BAe.748 G-AVXI (30th).

2nd Two more US Army Beech C-12 visits this month were 76-22254 on its first visit operating from/to Heidelberg today and 78-23128 from/to Hiedelberg on the 6th.

2nd SE.210 Caravelle F-BJTU, which first flew in 1964, made its first visit to Manchester arriving at 0922 today, from/to Paris-Orly as SF205/6. It spent most of its life operating for Finnair as OH-LSE, before being sold to Air Charter in January 1981.

3rd An interesting helicopter visitor today, was Bolkow 105 G-BFYA from Stalybridge. It was on a pipe-line detail, carrying a large golf-ball type device, attached to the port side. The device is a Heli-Tele stabilized reconnaissance platform, configured for the infra-red surveillance of power lines.

5th PA-23 Aztec G-AXZP arriving from RAF Alconbury today, was transporting a heart transplant patient back to Alconbury, for onward transportation to Papworth Hospital, Cambridge.

6th Balair operated a return charter from/to Zurich today (BB808/9), with ex-Swissair DC-9 HB-IFZ.

8th Shorts are currently using Simmons Airways SD-360 N361MQ as their company liaison aircraft, which called in as 'Short 1' at 1315 today, from/to Belfast Harbour.

8th British Airways Trident 1 G-ARPO, the first of three withdrawn from service this month, made its last visit at 1724 today as Shuttle back-up flight BA4494, before departing as BA4515 at 1841 on the 10th. It was withdrawn after its final service (BA4903 Glasgow-Heathrow) on the 16th March.

9th Transamerica Douglas DC-8 N4868T positioned in from Orlando at 0717 today, to operate a passenger flight out to Las Vegas, via Bangor.

9th PA-31T Cheyenne G-BJIZ, arriving from Tatenhill today for demonstration to NEA the following day, stayed overnight in the South Side hangars.

9th The ATC Watch Log recorded that the airport was put on standby to receive diversions from RAF Waddington and would accept up to four Vulcans.

10th PA-23 Aztec G-BJBU, operated by Harvest Air of Southend, was carrying spraying equipment for the disbursement of oil slicks.

11th This afternoons British Airways Jersey flight BA5217/6, was operated by Boeing 737 G-BGDJ on its first visit to Manchester.

12th Braathens B.737 LN-SUI diverted in at 1651 today, en route from Trondheim to Lanzarote (BU895), with a sick passenger suffering from a heart attack. Sadly, the patient died soon after arriving at Manchester.

14th The French Air Force operated a training flight this morning, with Nord 262 No.89 arriving at 0847 (FM0523 Villacoublay-Amsterdam).

14th Nothing for seventeen months, then two Jetstar's in two months! Privately-owned HZ-FNA, arriving at 1120 today from Hamburg with a Saudi Prince onboard, departed for Warton on the 16th.
15th Seasonal weather has been lacking this winter, but early morning fog sent five Heathrow diversions northwards. They were Qantas B.747 VH-EBP at 0703 (QF001 from Bahrain) on its first visit, TWA B.747 N93104 at 0707 (TW700 from New York), Pan American B.747 N770PA at 0711 (PA002 from New York), Kenya Airways B.707 5Y-BBI at 0730 (KQ104 from Mombasa) & British Airways B.747 G-AWNB at 0753 (BA174 from New York).
16th Two military diversions today were RAF VC-10 XV101 at 1948 (RR2160 from Ascension Island) & RAF C-130 XV307 at 1959 (RR5628 from Bardufoss), diverting from Brize Norton & Lyneham respectively.
17th Custom clearance flights for Hawarden are not too common through Manchester these days, but one passed through today when BAe.125 9Q-CCF arrived from Brussels at 0811, before its 1030 departure bound for Hawarden.
17th RAF Gazelle ZA803 made its first visit to Manchester today. Arriving at 1258 from RAF Shawbury, it stayed for all of seven minutes, before departing for Liverpool.
18th US Army Chinook 68-15838 was noted overflying the airport this afternoon.
21st One American military visitor that didn't make it was C-130H 50962 out of Woodbridge AFB as King 62. When he called Manchester approach for assistance through the zone, he was invited to perform an ILS, but said he was too busy and promised to return the next day which he did, but after getting a different approach controller who incorrectly told him he'd be charged, he declined the offer!
21st A type more familiar with not landing at Manchester is the RAF Dominie, but XS732 which arrived at 1545 today on a round trip from Finningley, stayed just short of two hours.
23rd Royal Navy Sea Heron XR445 (Navy 737) was on the first of three visits to Manchester this year, arriving at 1139 today on a round trip from RAF Yeovilton.
23rd Falcon 20 OO-DOK made its first visit today, arriving at 1523 from Southend. Currently operated by executive air-taxi operator BFS International, it's been into Manchester previously as OO-WTB.
24th Orion Airways have acquired ex-Manchester regular B.737 TF-VLK, which made its first visit today operating flight KG5225. It's been re-registered as G-BKMS and has a very broad red and yellow cheatline.
25th Kar-Air operated a round-trip from/to Helsinki as KR3011/2 today, with Finnair Douglas DC-9-41 OH-LNE and another DC-9-41, OH-LND, operated the return flight on the 8th April. They were making their first visits to Manchester and both are ex-Japanese aircraft.
25th British Airways Trident 2 G-AVFA made its last visit today, arriving at 1231 operating Shuttle back-up flight BA4444, before departing on another back-up flight (BA4495) at 1727. It was withdrawn after operating its final service, Frankfurt-Heathrow, on the 29th.
27th A new outfit to Manchester was Israeli charter airline MAOF, with the arrival of Boeing 720 4X-BMB in the early hours, operating an extra Tel Aviv charter as MG135/6. Formerly G-BCBB with Monarch Airlines, this aircraft operated alongside B.707 N778PA and another ex-Monarch B.720, 4X-BMA. The airline made another visit on 10th April, with all-white B.720 G-AZKM leased from Monarch, but by 1984 they had ceased trading.

27th Air Express International's brief flirtation with Manchester ended today, when CL-44 N122AE operated the final New York cargo flight. They have decided to road the freight to Stansted in future, as they find it too expensive to operate through Ringway.

27th The second 'termination' today was the very last transatlantic scheduled service from Manchester by British Airways. The final BA072 Toronto-Manchester-Heathrow flight, operated by Tristar G-BHBL, completed their withdrawal from the USA/Canada market. Their North American cargo flights were withdrawn in May 1977, passenger flights to Montreal in December 1980 and New York in October 1981. During the airlines peak in the summer of 1971 when they were BOAC, they flew daily flights to Chicago & New York; double-daily to Montreal & Toronto and in the winter, the daily New York flight went onwards to various points in the Caribbean.

27th A new helicopter, the Westland WG-30, made its first appearance at Manchester today, with the arrival of G-BKGD from Cambridge. Operated by British Airways Helicopters, it was carrying a Chinese delegation on a tour of the Manchester area, including the airport. The type is a medium-sized helicopter, based on the military Westland Lynx, capable of carrying up to twenty-two passengers. The three already delivered to British Airways Helicopters to support gas rigs in the North Sea, will be used later on scheduled flights between Penzance and the Isles of Scilly. However, the helicopter was unsuccessful and production stopped in 1987, after just forty had been built.

28th The second RAE Devon to visit Manchester this year was VP959 at 1148 today. It was on a flight from/to Farnborough and stayed for thirteen minutes.

28th Metropolitan Airways, who operate Dan-Air's City-Link operation, supplemented their existing flights today with a lunchtime weekday service from/to Newcastle, with Twin Otters.

28th Inter-City Airlines commenced a lunchtime flight from/to Aberdeen on behalf of British Airways with SD-330s, but so far only G-BITV has operated the service.

29th RAF Andover XS791, arriving at 0953 today (RR1546 from Northolt), brought in various dignitaries for the opening of the Air & Space Museum in Manchester City Centre.

29th Of the numerous ILS visitors this month, the highlight was RAF Vulcan B.2 XL426, overshooting twice during the morning as AHP56. The only remaining RAF squadron still flying the type is No.50, but they will stop using them next year. The ILS and overfly was also in connection with the opening of the Air & Space Museum.

29th British Airways Trident 1 G-ARPZ made its last visit today, positioning in at 1727 from Heathrow, to operate a Shuttle back-up flight (BA4495) at 1700 the following evening. Its last service and the final Trident 1 flight (BA4853 Glasgow-Heathrow) took place on the 2nd April, before being flown to Dunsfold later in the month to be used by RFD Ltd, specialists in training personnel to operate pneumatic elevators and other aircraft recovery systems.

31st A rare helicopter type visiting Manchester today was the Hughes 369, when G-BFYJ made a fuel stop, en route from Rossendale to a private site in Dorset.

April 1983

Manchester Airport's biggest customer, Britannia Airways, marked their 21st year in the holiday flights business this month. Their first flight from Manchester was 5th May 1962, when L-049 Constellation G-ARVP operated an IT flight to Palma, via Perpignan. Today they fly over 1m passengers annually and next year they will take delivery of two brand new B.767s.

The British Airways Shuttle service between Heathrow-Manchester had the best percentage gain of passengers last year, up 13% to 440,000, compared with their other

Shuttle destinations to Belfast, Edinburgh & Glasgow. However, it was announced in Parliament recently that the airline had cut their work-force down from 58,000 in August 1979 to the current figure of just over 39,000.

British Midland lodged an application with the CAA to serve New York, as there have been no scheduled flights since Laker's collapse in February 1982. A decision is expected next month and if successful, the flights would start in April 1984.

The Excelsior Hotel is offering £100 weekends to budding pilots, in conjunction with the Manchester School of Flying, which includes aircraft tours and flying lessons in PA-38 Tomahawks.

Following a Public Enquiry, the go-ahead's been given for a 170-bedroom hotel with 240 parking spaces on a 5-acre site at Outwood Lane, subject to planning permission.

Monarch Airlines sold their last three remaining Boeing 720s in March. The final B.720 flight was operated by G-AZNX (OM347 Naples-Luton) on the 2nd January and their final visits to Manchester and subsequent fates are as follows:

G-AZFB 23/10/82, became N2464C with Jet Charter Service
G-AZKM 10/04/83, became N2464K with Jet Charter Service
G-AZNX 29/10/82, became N24446 with Jet Charter Service

This summer's transatlantic services have been rescued – slightly! Pan American will operate weekly on Sundays to Orlando with Douglas DC-10s and British Airtours will operate three-weekly charters to Los Angeles and New York with Boeing 707s and to Orlando with Tristar 500 G-BFCB. British Midland will also operate a weekly Toronto flight via Belfast on Mondays commencing 22nd May, along with extensive programmes by regulars CP Air and Wardair.

The following airlines made changes to their summer schedules: Air Malta will operate twice-weekly and add a third flight between July-September, as well as numerous charter flights. British Airways added Nice for the summer again, but terminated flights to Geneva and Toronto. Cyprus Airways will operate twice-weekly flights to Larnaca, peaking at three flights between May-September. Finnair reduced their Helsinki freight flights to three-weekly. Guernsey Airlines will operate up to seven-weekly flights, with a mix of SD-330/Viscounts. KLM morning flight (KL153/4) is now daily and the lunchtime flight (KL155/6) operates daily except for Sundays. Manx Airlines will operate three-times daily to Ronaldsway. Qantas began twice-weekly operations during the month to Sydney/Melbourne via Amsterdam/Bahrain/Bangkok & Singapore. SAS continue to operate a once-weekly cargo flight to Copenhagen via Heathrow with Electras and of the six-weekly passenger flights operating from/to Copenhagen; two proceed onwards to/from Dublin.

Equipment changes/notes on scheduled flights included Air Malta (KM106): B.737 9H-ABB on its first visit (3rd); Loganair operated EMB-110 G-BIBE on all three Edinburgh flights (1st); KLM (KL157): NLM F.28 PH-CHD (6th); Lufthansa (LH074): B.727 D-ABQI (17th); Manx Airlines used Guernsey Airlines Herald G-ASVO on flight MNX329/30 (1st) and Swissair used DC-9-32 HB-IFH (2nd/11th).

RAF ILS traffic identified included Hawks XX225 (25th) XX231 (13th), XX297 (22nd); C-130s XV188 (7th), XV212 (26th) & XV217 (12th); Jetstreams XX494 (9th/30th) & XX498 (14th); Dominies XS711 (25th), XS713 (18th) & XS726 (29th) plus Andovers XS603 (22nd) & XS610 (21st). Civil ILS traffic included various Cessna's from Barton, but more noteworthy were the appearances of Citation 500 PH-CTC (11th), Bell 206 Jet Ranger G-AWLL from Blackpool

(12th), Lufthansa Beech 90 D-ILHD routing Shannon-Gatwick as LH1191 (29th) and two BAe.748s from Woodford in Bouraq of Indonesia colours, G-BKLG (18th) & G-BKLI (21st).

1st Qantas operated their first scheduled flight to Manchester, when B.747 VH-EBM arrived at 0931 today (QF009) from Melbourne/Sydney/Bangkok/Bahrain & Amsterdam, with 131 passengers and 5 tonnes of freight. Aircraft used this month were VH-EBB/EBC/EBE/EBG/EBK & EBM and apart from VH-EBB on its first visit on the 10th, they had all been into Manchester before as diversions.

1st After many years of exclusively operating Russian-built Tupolev TU-134s, Aviogenex have just acquired two ex-Government B.727s to supplement their fleet. The first, YU-AKD, which made its first visit today for the airline (JJ101/2), has operated for JAT in previous years. The second, VIP aircraft YU-AKH, which has never been to Manchester, made its first visit (JJ103/4) on 8th May.

1st Aerospatiale AS.350 Ecureuil G-MORR operated by Colt Cars, arrived from Evesham with the double-act, Rod Hull and his bird-puppet Emu. After initially landing on the Freight Apron, it then flew to Stand 26 to see the passengers off on the first Qantas flight. Incidentally this helicopter was sold to Noel Edmonds in January 1984 as G-NOEI, who operated it until 1986.

1st The pilot of Cessna 172 G-BGRO operating from/to Humberside, didn't ingratiate himself with Manchester ATC, after appearing poorly briefed on the airfield's layout and zone procedures!

2nd British Airways L.1011-200 G-BGBB operated an outbound charter on behalf of British Airtours today (KT672 to Palma).

5th BAe.125 7T-VCW arriving from Algiers at 1223 today for customs clearance, ultimately bound for Hawarden, was the first Algerian registered executive jet into Manchester. It's appeared as an ILS visitor before, but this is the first time it's actually landed.

6th The year saw three visits by Army Air Corps Beavers, the same number as in 1982. The first today, was XP769 at 1541 as 'Army 351' (Coventry/Belfast).

6th Midlands-based engineering company GKN had their own executive BAe.125, G-BGKN, from 1976-1981, but it made very few visits to Manchester. They now operate Beech 200 G-GKNB, which is likely to visit as rarely as its predecessor, although it did make its first appearance today, positioning in from Birmingham to operate a round trip to Zurich.

9th Air Europe operated their first Boeing 757 flight into Manchester today, when G-BKRM arrived at 1125. It was originally destined to go from Gatwick to Ostend for crew-training, but instead it was sent to Manchester with a replacement windscreen for a Boeing 737. It also made numerous crew training flights into Manchester for the rest of the month.

10th The first of this year's batch of the three Canadian Air Force CC-130Es, was today's arrival of 130325 (CAM515). The others were 130313 (CAM516-12th) & 130317 (CAM517-14th), which all night-stopped routing Trenton-Lahr. For the first time there was to be a fourth flight on the 16th (CAM 518), but it didn't operate due to airport being closed.

10th Canadian airline Worldways operated a weekly outbound Gatwick-Manchester-Toronto flight as WB901 during the month. The first today was flown by B.707 C-GFLG and later flights were operated by Douglas DC-8s formerly owned by CP Air: C-FCPP (a day late-18th) & C-FCPQ (24th/31st). The airline also operates ex-CP Air DC-8s C-FCPO & C-FCPS.

12th Champion Spark Plugs Fokker F.27 N1823G was a regular last year, but it made no visits this year as their flights were operated by biz-jets instead, starting with Falcon

N1823F making its first visit today at 1049 from Helsinki. It departed later to Luxembourg and made a further visit on the 28th, diverting in due to fog at Hawarden.

12th Swedish light aircraft are not too common at Manchester, but there were three this month. The first today was TB-10 Tobago SE-GFO, arriving all the way from Groningen to night-stop, before departing for Blackpool the following day. The others were Cessna 402 SE-GGU (21st) & PA-28 Cherokee SE-GDB (27th), diverting in due to lack of customs at their ultimate destination, Blackpool.

13th This month's award for 'the one that got away', went to USAF C-141 Starlifter 59412. Inbound from McGuire AFB around midday, it was leaving the Barton beacon when the pilot discovered he had a flap malfunction. He held level at 3,500ft and appeared through the clouds occasionally running a course between Buxton and Oldham, before diverting to Mildenhall. Other US military flights during the month were two more US Army Beech C-12s: 78-23126 from/to Heidelberg as Duke 36A/B (18th) & 73-22262 from/to Heidelberg as Duke 22A/B (19th).

14th Beech 90 G-BIFS, which arrived on the 29th March for NEA, was sold in the USA and left for its new home today as N222BJ.

15th Due to a dispute involving airport cleaners, that's been simmering since the start of the month over a pay reduction by their new employers, the airport was closed today for 24-hours from 2300. A number of contract cleaners had already been on strike since the 2nd, but it hadn't affected operations until last night, when 1,300 members of the TGWU walked out in support. The action ended late on the 16th, when all sides agreed to go to arbitration.

15th Cimber Air Nord 262 OY-BDD called in for fuel at 1714 today, routing Sonderborg-Cork. Although there have been several military visits, this was only the third civil Nord 262 to Manchester since Dan-Air regular G-AYFR last arrived in 1972.

20th April 1983 - Worldways C-130 C-FDSX arrived at 1352 today from Frobisher Bay. It was collecting a 10½ tonne generator from Perkins Diesels, based at Trafford Park, before departing back to Canada the following day, via Keflavik. Amongst its previous identities, this aircraft was formerly RP-C98 of the Philippine Government. It was sold to Transamerica as N39ST in December 1984 and then sold to Transafrik as S9-NAI in November 1988, but it crashed in Angola in April 1989. (Geoff Ball)

19th A type making its first visit as a military version, was the EMB-121 Xingu. Sabena operate them through Manchester occasionally on training flights, but it was French Navy Xingu No.69 (FA015 Luton-Edinburgh) that arrived at 0938 today.

19th Braathens B.737 LN-SUD, operating as BU569 today, was the first of three charter flights to Oslo on behalf of ICI. The others were LN-SUI as BU571/0 (24th) & LN-SUH as BU572 on its first visit to Manchester (28th).

21st The only Queens Flight aircraft this month was today's arrival BAe.748 XS793 (Kitty 2) at 1053 from RAF Northolt, with HRH the Duchess of Gloucester onboard. She was undertaking a series of local engagements, including the opening of the airports new £700,000 Police Station

23rd Air Ecosse SD-360 G-RMSS was operating mail flight WG917 from Stansted today, when it was struck by lightning on its descent into Manchester, which caused a small fire.

24th SAS Douglas DC-9-41 LN-RLD operating today's SK539/540, was noted in a new, slightly revised colour scheme, of a number of blue, yellow and red stripes on the nose.

28th Rolls-Royce recently acquired a Gulfstream 1, G-BKJZ. Although it operated for the company until 1988, today was its one and only visit to Manchester, on a flight from Glasgow to East Midlands.

29th Lufthansa operated their first training flight of the year through Manchester, when Beech 90 D-ILHD overshot at 1212 today as LH1191 (Shannon-Gatwick), using a flight number for the first time.

29th Skyvan G-BJDC, the company's military demonstration aircraft, made its second visit to Manchester today, operating from/to Belfast Harbour.

29th British Air Ferries Viscount G-AOYP operated a return flight to Jersey this afternoon, as VF6006/7. It was in basic BAF colours, with Jersey Air Ferries titles consisting of a red lion on the tail and 'Isle of Jersey' which was also in red, written inside a black box on the left of the nose.

29th Monarch Airlines B.757 G-MONC positioned in from Luton for the start of the airlines Boeing 757 operations from Manchester the following day. Their three other aircraft, G-MONB, G-MOND & G-MONE had all visited by early July.

30th Loganair sold SD-330 G-BGNA to Manx Airlines, which made its first visit as such today, from/to Ronaldsway as MNX325/6.

30th JAT will operate a number of IT flights this summer, as well as their scheduled weekly Pula and Dubrovnik flights. The first of these charter flights commenced today, with YU-AKB (JR1550/5 Split/Pula), YU-AKB (JR1554/1 Pula/Split) & YU-AKA (JR1552/3 from/to Dubrovnik). A Sunday flight will also start next month (JR2220/1 from/to Dubrovnik).

May 1983

Thomson will offer 76,000 holidays from Manchester this winter, including Thailand as a direct destination for the first time, with prices starting at £574. They will also run a two/three week Far East tour, calling at Bangkok, Hong Kong and the beach resort of Pattaya; as well as a Central Asia tour, taking in Leningrad, Tashkent, Bukhara, Samarkand & Moscow, with prices starting at £302.

Manchester Airport's reputation for its high priced duty-free shop is now misplaced, as it's selling the cheapest alcohol in Britain! At £2.75 for a standard sized bottle of spirits, Manchester's prices are 20p below those at Heathrow. The newly expanded duty-free shop was officially opened by television broadcaster Cliff Michelmore, after more than £500,000 was spent on doubling the size and re-designing it to be more like a department store.

British Airways have started naming their Super 1-11 fleet and the honour of being the first aircraft named was G-AVMR, as 'County of Tyne & Wear'. On the subject of their BAC 1-11s, the hush-kitted ones, G-BGKE/F/G, are not scheduled through Manchester during the summer. Meanwhile, British Airtours are leasing two Air Europe B.737s, G-BMEC & G-BMOR, for the summer. They will be based at Manchester, operating in basic Air Europe colours, with British Airtours titles. They have also leased another L.1011 Tristar, G-BEAL, from British Airways, for the summer period. To offset the temporary gap of the two B.737s, Air Europe have in turn leased two aircraft, all-white G-BKRO (formerly EI-BMY with Air Tara) & G-BJXL, which is operating in basic Air Florida colours.

The UK's oldest air-taxi operator, which just happens to be Manchester-based Northern Executive Aviation, celebrated their 21st birthday during the month. They began operations in 1962, with PA-28 Cherokee G-ARVS.

The following airlines have summer IT programmes from Manchester: Air Malta, Air Portugal, Aviaco, Aviogenex, Balkan, EL AL, Hispania, Inex-Adria, JAT, Spantax, Tarom & Tunis Air; as do a variety of UK operators: Air Europe, Air UK, Britannia Airways, British Air Ferries, British Airtours, British Airways, British Midland, Dan-Air, Monarch Airlines & Orion Airways. Airlines operating regular flights to the USA/Canada this summer are British Airtours (Los Angeles, Newark & Orlando), British Midland (Toronto), CP Air (Toronto & Vancouver), Pan American (New York & Orlando) and Wardair (Calgary, Edmonton, Ottawa, Toronto, Vancouver & Winnipeg).

Equipment changes/notes on scheduled flights included Air Ecosse (WG700/778): Cessna 404 G-WTVB (1st/11th); Air France (AF964): used one of their newly delivered Boeing 737s, F-GBYA (1st); Air Portugal (TP488): B.727-200 CS-TBS (25th); Loganair operated EMB-110 G-BIBE again on their Edinburgh flights (2nd/27th); Lufthansa (LH074): operated just one Boeing 727 again this month, D-ABKJ (18th); Qantas used B.747s: VH-EBC/EBG/EBI/EBJ/EBK and VH-EBA on its only ever appearance operating QF009/010 (1st). Finally Manx Airlines used Guernsey Airlines Herald G-ASVO on flight MNX329/30 (1st).

RAF ILS traffic identified included Hawks XX177 (19th) & XX226 (19th); C-130s XV184 (4th) & XV214 (19th) and Jetstream XX482 (10th). An unidentified RAF Gazelle overshot as SYN53 at 1546 (18th). Civil ILS traffic consisted of the usual light Cessna's from Barton.

2nd PA-23 Aztec G-BBSR, en route from Elstree to Glasgow, was forced to land at Manchester today, due to one of the passengers requiring an urgent call of nature!

3rd Four US Army Bell UH-1s overflew the airfield during the month. They were all US based aircraft, on temporary attachment to RAF Sculthorpe for the annual Flintlock exercises, designed to give a number of the US military's Special Forces experience of fighting on foreign soil. The first was 22436 today and the rest were 22435 (2nd), 15342 (16th) & 59823 (17th).

3rd B.737 TS-IOD operated the first flight of Tunis Air's summer programme from Manchester today (TU8794/5 from/to Monastir). Also starting this month is a weekly Friday flight on the 20th (TU8800/1 from/to Monastir) and a fortnightly Tuesday flight on the 31st (TU8810/1 from/to Monastir).

6th Former NEA resident PA-31 Navajo G-AYLJ began its long journey today, routing Bournemouth-Glasgow-Reykjavik, after being sold in the USA.

6th Inex Adria MD-81 YU-ANB (JP554/5 from/to Pula) made its first visit to Manchester today, declaring an emergency whilst on descent, with part of its undercarriage door coming loose. Following this aircrafts delivery in September 1981, it immediately went on lease to Martinair and only returned to the airline earlier in the year in February.

6th British Midland is operating an IT programme from Manchester for the first time since 1973, with a based B.707. In addition to the various IT destinations, there is also a weekly flight to Toronto, via Belfast. Today's first flight was operated by B.707 G-BMAZ as BD7341 to Tenerife and their other two B.707s, G-BFLD & G-BFLE, also operated during the month.

6th British Island Airways are operating BAC 1-11 G-AVOF on a six-month lease from British Aerospace, which made its first appearance as such today, in basic Air Manchester colours (KD3284/3 from/to Tarbes). It was leased to British Caledonian in November until February 1984 and made its last visit as such on 29th January 1984, operating BR987/990.

8th May 1983 – Work on the Western Apron is in full swing. Pan American DC-10 N82NA, seen here on push-back for its flight to Orlando via Bangor (PA8225), is the first of a short series of charters, ending on the 6th June. A weekly flight from/to New York via Prestwick started on the 18th June. The airline visited Manchester over many years, on diversion or operating transatlantic charters and by this time they had taken over another American carrier, National Airlines and were using their DC-10s primarily on charter flights. (Geoff Ball)

10th French Air Force Noratlas No.54/63-WX, arriving at 1312 today on a training flight (FM0760 Newcastle-Lyneham), was the first Noratlas to Manchester since 11th March 1982. Another French Air Force flight, Nord 262 No.61, performed a touch-and-go as FA055, routing Beauvais-Edinburgh (17th).

10th Viscount G-AOHT returned to British Air Ferries after a short-term operation by short-lived Teeside-based airline, Polar Airways. It arrived at Manchester at 2313 today from Maastricht, in full BAF colours and titles.

11th Beech 200 N80GA passed through Manchester this morning, on a flight from Leavesden to Reykjavik. Formerly G-BFEA with Executive Express, it was on its way to new owners in the USA.

11th Falcon 50 D-BDWO made its first visit today, arriving at 1716 from Nice. It's been German registered only recently, after spending a period in the USA.

12th BAe.748 demonstrator G-BGJV, diverted into Manchester from Hatfield today, due to the lack of fire-cover at Woodford. It stayed overnight and was noted wearing Air Sinai titles.

13th Privately-owned Hawker Hunter G-HUNT, arriving at 1003 today from Bournemouth, was the first visit of a Hunter since the 1950s. It was taking part in a press preview of the weekends Barton Air Show, before departing later for Biggin Hill. It returned to the region on Sunday the 15th to take part in the air show. The pilot was planning to use Manchester prior to his display at Barton, but he was forced to overshoot twice due to undercarriage problems. He then went into the hold, by which time the airport was busy with a number of other arrivals, so he diverted to Liverpool instead.

13th Mustang G-BEFU, arriving at 1036 today from Coventry for the Barton Air Show press review, is a replica version of the original WW2 fighter, the P-51 Mustang. In a full military colour scheme, it appeared at Manchester again on the 15th to uplift fuel, prior to its display at Barton, but tragically it crashed during its performance when the engine appeared to cut out during a barrel roll.

13th Other aircraft arriving for the Barton Air Show press review included Chipmunk G-BCSL, Mosquito RR299 and a 1935-vintage Hawk Speed Six, G-ADGP. This two-seat light monoplane has the same owner as former Manchester residents Chipmunk G-BFAW & Harvard G-BDAM.

13th Sabena B.737 OO-SDK (SN617 from Brussels) was all set for touchdown, 1,000ft from the runway, when the pilot realised something was wrong, which was confirmed when ATC made contact and told him he was making an approach at Woodford! A spokesman for British Aerospace explained that the pilot was making a visual approach, when he mistook Manchester for Woodford. The runway was more than long enough to handle the aircraft, so there was never any danger. Had he have landed, he would have simply taxied around and departed for Manchester, but the airline refused to comment over the incident.

14th An unusual aircraft for maintenance at Manchester today was Supermarine 379 Spitfire G-FIRE from Barton, resplendent in red. It had a leak in its port side radiator, which prevented its performance in the following days show. After an engine run it was pushed back into the Air Kilroe hangar and PA-39 Twin Comanche G-SIGN arrived from Elstree to pick up the pilot, Peter Anthorn. The Spitfire departed back to Elstree on the 20th, after temporary repairs. Its history reveals the RAF sold it to the Belgian Air Force in 1951, it returned to the UK in 1966 and was restored to flying condition in 1981. In 1989, it was shipped to the Palm Springs Air Museum, California.

14th Swissair DC-9-51 HB-ISR operated SR842/3 for the final time this evening, as it was sold in September to American-airline Muse Air as N671MC.

15th British Airtours Tristar 500 G-BFCB, arriving at 1148 today from Gatwick, was on its first visit. As well as a weekly Sunday flight to Orlando (KT221/2), they will also operate flights during the week to Newark and Los Angeles, with Boeing 707s.

15th Arriving from Biggin Hill today were 1950's built Anson WD413 at 1700, prior to its display at Barton and RAF C-130 XV299, before departing for Barton to drop the Falcons aerobatic team.

16th New UK airline, Birmingham Executive Airways, will commence operations next month from Birmingham with Jetstream 31s. They undertook extensive crew training throughout the month and Jetstream G-OBEA called in en route Teeside-Birmingham today and the 20th.

15th May 1983 – RAF Lightning XP753 is seen here having just got airborne, on one of the few visits of the type to Manchester, which served with the RAF from 1960-1988. There were many variants of the Lightning, which first flew in 1954 and saw service with the Kuwait & Royal Saudi Air Force. RAF Lightning's XP751 & XP753 arrived yesterday to night-stop for the air show. Operated by the Lightning Training Flight at RAF Binbrook, it was actually XP753 in a two tone grey scheme that gave the performance, with XP741 in standard camouflage as the back-up. Both performed a 'mini' display at Manchester before their arrivals and departures. (Geoff Ball)

16th Metropolitan Airways, who only introduced a new lunchtime-weekday service from/to Newcastle on the 28th March, operated it for the final time today, with Twin Otter G-BHFD.

17th Royal Navy Lynx XZ736, arriving at 1706 today from RAF Cottesmore to night-stop before departing for Shawbury the following day, is currently based aboard HMS Manchester. Another uncommon RAF visitor is the Bulldog, but XX616 also arrived today, from/to RAF Woodvale and parked up for an hour on Stand 41.

18th Bell 206 Long Ranger G-LRII operated by Castle Helicopters, arrived from Wrexham today. It's currently being used by Channel 4 as the star of their TV programme, Treasure Hunt.

18th Shell UK's latest BAe.125, G-BHSW, arrived at 2038 from Rotterdam on its first visit.

19th Today was notable for the appearance of seven biz-jets: Citation 551 G-BJVP (0445 from Almeria), Lear Jet 35 G-JJSG (0857 from Dublin), first visit Falcon 10 D-CMAN (1231 from Dusseldorf), Lear Jet 35 G-GAYL (1437 from Bologna), Falcon 20 F-BVPN (1529 from Clermont-Ferrand), BAe.125 G-BAZA (1704 from Hatfield) and Citation 500 N15AW (1737 from Blackpool).

20th Transavia B.737 PH-TVI, which is on short-term lease to Britannia Airways, operated a return flight to Tarbes today (BY591A/B), in an all-white scheme with a Transavia tail. Another all-white Transavia aircraft, PH-TVP, which is also leased to Britannia Airways, can be seen at Manchester most weekends operating various flights for Britannia until the 8th October.

20th The second British Airways Trident 3 to be withdrawn from service was G-AWZE, after its final service (BA4673P Belfast-Heathrow) on the 22nd. Its last visit to Manchester was at 1216 today (BA4442 from Heathrow), before operating back to Heathrow as BA4463 at 1328. Delivered new to BEA in April 1971, it made its first visit on the 10th June 1971.

21st Due to fog, a short burst of morning diversions were all from Heathrow, except for British Caledonian B.747 G-BJXN at 0614 (BR362 from Lagos) from Gatwick, on the first visit of their newly acquired type. The four from Heathrow included three Boeing 707s, an event unlikely to happen in the future, as they are certainly in their twilight years in terms of operating for national carriers and are gradually being replaced by newer aircraft. In chronological order of arrival they were British Airways B.747 G-BDXF at 0626 (BA020 from Bahrain), Zambia Airways B.707 9J-AEL at 0719 (QZ704 from Lusaka), Bangladesh Biman B.707 S2-ACE at 0727 (BG005 from Rome) & Air Mauritius B.707 3B-NAE (MK042 from Rome).

23rd BAe.125 N125GP arriving at 0937 today on a return flight to Luton, was making its first visit to Manchester. It's currently owned and operated by Garrett Industries, who make turbochargers and various types of engines for the automotive and aero industry.

23rd Turbo Islander G-OTVS operated by TV South, arrived from Rochester with a crew to film Manchester United's preparations for their FA Cup Final replay with Brighton on the 26th. Formerly Britten-Norman's Turbo Islander company demonstrator G-BPBN, it also saw service on fishery protection duties in 1982 and further back it was the company's military demonstrator, the Defender, registered as G-BCMY.

26th A very rare visitor to Manchester was Dove G-AVVF, arriving at 0937 today on a round trip from Chalgrove. This aircraft was operated from 1968-1984 by Martin-Baker, a company producing ejector seats and assorted crew safety equipment. It made a second visit later in the year on the 28th July, having last visited on the 23rd December 1978.

26th Today also saw the first visit of a RAF Harrier. Two of these aircraft were on a low level flying sortie in the area, when ZB601 suffered a bird-strike and was forced to make a full emergency diversion to Manchester. The second, a GR.3 variant which remains unidentified, flew past to check his colleague had landed safely, before setting course back to RAF Wittering. As the broken T.4 Harrier was armed, it was asked to park facing an appropriate direction until it was deemed as safe, so it parked facing the Tower! It eventually departed back to RAF Wittering the next morning.

28th Not strictly a Manchester movement, but landing nearby at the Valley Lodge Hotel was Bell 206 Jet Ranger G-NOEL, flown by Noel Edmonds of course!

28th Hispania, a new Spanish airline, made its first visit to Manchester today with SE.210 Caravelle EC-CIZ (HI202/3 from/to Palma). They operated sporadically until July, before settling into a weekly operation with flights to Alicante & Malaga. The aircraft is ex-Transeuropa and they also operate with two others, EC-CPI & EC-CYI, from the same source.

29th Aeroflot operated the first of this year's fortnightly summer flights today, with TU-154 CCCP-85287 (SU1639/40 from/to Moscow), which will continue until the 4th September.

June 1983

In addition to naming their entire BAC 1-11 fleet, British Airways are also making improvements to the interiors, with brighter lighting and co-ordinated decor of uniform red upholstery, blue carpets and cream walls. New comfort increasing features include larger overhead storage lockers, air conditioning and new seats and toilets.

The airport is planning an extensive improvement programme, to give it the necessary breathing space until work commences on a second passenger terminal, possibly towards the end of the decade. It includes adding seventeen more check-in desks to the existing forty, relocated against the walls of the Booking Hall, to provide increased capacity in the queuing area and a domestic module, separating outward bound domestic passengers from those on international flights. International Departures will be extended, with facilities to transfer passengers by bus to remote parking stands. Pier C will be expanded and the International Arrivals Hall improved.

Equipment changes/notes on scheduled flights included Air Ecosse (WG778): Cessna 404 G-WTVB (6th); Air France (AF964): used another two Boeing 737s, both first visits - F-GBYC (3rd) & F-GBYD (10th); Air Malta (KM106): B.720 9H-AAL (3rd/24th); Air Portugal (TP488): B.727-200 CS-TBW (1st) & first visit B.737 CS-TEK (22nd); Lufthansa (LH074): B.727 D-ABKR (9th) & first visit B.737 D-ABFB (18th); Manx Airlines (MNX329): Viscount G-AZNA (3rd) and Sabena (SN617): passenger B.737 OO-SDE (4th).

RAF ILS traffic identified included Hawks XX238 (21st) & XX314 (29th); C-130s XV177 (17th), XV183 (6th), XV186 (29th) & XV221 (2nd) and Jetstreams XX482 (17th), XX490 (15th), XX498 (17th). RAE BAC 1-11 XX105 overshot at 1111 as 'Nugget 82' (8th), as did an unidentified RAF Jaguar at 1454 as 'SGH77' (1st). Civil traffic included BAe.125s HZ-BO1 from/to Hawarden which was formerly G-ATWH (2nd) & Rolls-Royce G-BARR (3rd); CAA BAe.748 G-AVXI (3rd) and Lancashire Aero Club Cessna 172 G-MALK appeared on nine separate dates.

4th Birmingham Executive Airways operated another crew training flight today, when Jetstream G-OBEA landed at 1206. It taxied around and took off at 1218, bound for Gloucester-Staverton.

5th June 1983 – Arrow Air B.707 N707SH is seen here making a first visit of both the aircraft and the airline, arriving at 1659 today from Gatwick as JW851A, before departing later for New York. In a basic gold and blue livery, it shows clear evidence of its previous owner, Singapore Airlines. It operated for Arrow Air from 1981-1984, before being sold as B-2422 to Shanghai Airlines in December 1984. (Geoff Ball)

4th British Midland B.707 G-BMAZ went tech after its arrival from Athens (BD9746). Another of their B.707s, G-BFLD, was also temporarily out of service due to sustaining damage on takeoff at Gatwick on the 31st May. This meant that the airline had to sub-charter the following flights today: British Airways B.757 G-BIKC (BD9241/2 from/to Palma) & Finnair DC-9 OH-LYD (BD7143/4 from/to Rimini), which was also a first visit.

5th PA-23 Aztec G-FADS, which arrived at NEA last year on the 30th December, finally departed to its new owners in the USA today. It was formerly operated by FADS, 'The paint and paper people', as their advertisement went!

6th All CP Air flights through Manchester will be operated by Douglas DC-10s, after today's last B.747 flight, with C-FCRE operating CP802/3 from/to Vancouver.

6th SD-330 G-BDBS operated as 'Short 4' from/to Belfast Harbour today, eight years after its first flight. It's still the company's demonstrator and operated in this role right up until its retirement in 1992, although its last visit to Manchester was on 15th October 1984.

6th Today saw the first visit of an updated version of the Douglas DC-8, known as the Douglas DC-8-70 series. Company demonstrator N2547R arrived at 1055 on a round trip demo flight from/to Gatwick, operated by Cammacorp. The major feature of the revamp is the fitting of much larger and quieter high performance engines.

6th Company demonstrator PA-31T N9174C, arriving at 1746 today from Glasgow, was paying a brief visit to the South Side.

7th June 1983 – An exceptional visitor to Manchester this year was NASA B.747 N905NA, with Space Shuttle Enterprise on its back. They are seen here on the climb-out, having just performed an ILS and overshoot at 1046 on a very grey morning. En route back to the USA, via Keflavik after their appearance at the Paris Air Show, they also performed overshoots at Birmingham and Glasgow on their way home. (Geoff Ball)

7th Woodford-based Beagle Pup G-AVLN, flown by Sir Charles Masefield, Managing Director of BAe Systems at Woodford, flew in to watch the overshoot of NASA B.747 + Space Shuttle.

7th Beech 200 PH-SLG, arriving at 0116 today, was operating a freight flight from/to Amsterdam.

7th It was a good month for American biz-jet movements, with no less than four first visits. Citation 550 N1823B was operated by Champion Spark Plugs (1608 from Luxembourg) today, Lear Jet 35 N35AK arrived at 1154 (13th), Falcon 50 N50BX at 2051 (19th) and Gulfstream 3 N75RP at 2051, routing Heathrow-La Guardia (22nd). Also during the month was another Champion Spark Plugs run-around, Falcon 20 N1823B (9th/14th/27th) and IBM Falcon 50 N131WT (13th).

9th RAF Devon VP965 made its final visit today, arriving at 1348 (RR7652 from/to Wyton). It entered service in May 1949 and served until 1984, when it was donated to RAF Manston.

10th Due to an increased load, Lufthansa cargo flight LH4072/3 was operated by German Cargo B.707F D-ABUA, which was also the last visit of a Lufthansa/German Cargo B.707 since the first, D-ABUI, arrived on 1st October 1967 (LH971R). The remaining aircraft were sold in 1984/85, when the airline replaced them with five Douglas DC-8-73s.

10th Vecta Geronimo N4422P made its first visit to Manchester since October 1981, arriving at 2109 today from Newtonards. Converted from a standard 1960 Piper PA-23 Apache, it's owned by the Cork based McWilliams Company, manufacturers of windsocks and wind sails. Other geriatric Pipers during the month were two 1963 PA-23 Aztec's, with G-ASHH routing from Newcastle back to its Leicester base (9th) and G-ASMY which has been operated by Thurston Aviation of Stapleford since 1967 (17th).

11th LOT began a fortnightly series of flights from/to Warsaw today, with SP-LSF as LO3183/4, which continued until 3rd September. These are the airlines first flights from Manchester, since withdrawing their Warsaw schedule in October 1981.

12th June 1983 – A warm welcome back to an old friend - in a different coat! Arrow Air DC-10 N902CL, seen here about to depart for New York as JW851, is ex-Laker Airways G-AZZC, a regular visitor to Manchester from 1972-1982. (Geoff Ball)

12th The Red Arrows arrived at 1119 today to clear customs, prior to performing a display at RAF Cosford. They appeared again after their performance, before departing for Church Fenton, accompanied by their support aircraft, C-130 XV219 (RR5986).

12th Balkan's latest Tupolev TU-154, LZ-BTV, made its first visit to Manchester today, operating LZ917/8. From the 26th they will also operate a TU-134 on their fortnightly Bourgas flight (LZ923/4), with LZ-TUL being the first to be used.

14th British Airways B.747 G-BDXK made its first visit today, operating Gutersloh-Calgary as BA9087C, taking an outbound load of troops as part of 'Exercise Medicine Man'. It made further visits on the same routing on the 23rd/24th/25th and in the opposite direction on the 24th/25th. This aircraft has been stored with Boeing since 1981 and was only delivered last month. It was kept with another aircraft, G-BDXM, which is still in storage.

17th Cambridge-based Cecil Aviation brought both of their aircraft into Manchester today. After landing, Cessna 402 G-BLCE & Cessna 421 G-BLST eventually parked on the West Apron, so they could be photographed in front of Qantas B.747 VH-EBI!

18th Lufthansa B.737-230ADV D-ABFB finally made its first visit to Manchester today, operating LH074/5. It's the last of the new batch of Lufthansa B.737s to visit, as it's remained with Boeing up until recently undergoing various tests.

20th Britannia Airways sub-chartered TEA Boeing 737 OO-TEN to operate BY592A/B to/from Tarbes today, which was also a first visit.

21st Two French Military Nord 262s made their first visits during the month. French Navy No.52 arrived at 0944 today (FA056 Amsterdam-Edinburgh) and French Air Force No.89 arrived at 1045 (FM0545 Newquay-RAF Northolt) on the 28th.

25th The Vintage Pair, Meteor WF791 & XH304, arrived at Manchester for fuel, after their participation in the Woodford Air Show, before departing later for RAF Leeming.

26th RAF C-130 XV297 arrived at 1506 today, having been the transport for the Falcons Display Team, who performed a parachute drop near Sheffield.

27th Falcon 10 F-BYCC arrived at 0028 today (BL028), on an ambulance flight from Algiers.

28th Luton-based McAlpine Aviation had operated a growing fleet of BAe.125s since the early 1970's, but recently they've branched out and are using types such as the PA-42 Cheyenne. Although their BAe.125s visited Manchester regularly over the years, they haven't been too common of late and today's arrival of the prototype BAe.125-600, G-BEWW, was the first visit by McAlpine this year.

28th The last of three Swissair DC-9-51s making their last visits to Manchester this year, was HB-ISS operating SR842/3 for the final time. It was sold in January 1984 to American-airline, Muse Air, as N672MC.

29th Finnair have also started a fortnightly series of flights, operating with Douglas DC-9-51s, from/to Helsinki as KR3011/2. The first today was operated by OH-LYX and although the flights continued until the 24th August, they didn't produce any first visits.

29th Ex-Eastern Airways Douglas DC-3 G-AMRA, now operated by Air Atlantique, positioned in from Blackpool at 1603 today to transport car parts to Cologne on behalf of Ford. Another Ford charter operating the following day was Air Atlantique DC-3 G-AMPY, departing at 1923 for Saarbrucken.

30th Genair SD-330 G-BKIE, arriving at 1409 today (EN6552 from Prestwick), was ferrying a number of passengers to catch Wardair flight WD801 to Toronto.

July 1983

Qantas made a slight amendment to their operation this month, flights now route Manchester-Amsterdam-Athens and onwards to Sydney/Melbourne, with Athens replacing the Bahrain stop. All but one of their earlier B.747-238s, VH-EBF, has now visited Manchester.

The marathon Stansted Airport Inquiry closed on the 5th, after 258 days of deliberations. The Inspector heard the final summing up from the British Airports Authority before closing the hearing. The inquiry has considered BAA's application for expansion at Stansted, as well as proposals for developing regional airports such as Manchester. It's hoped the Inspectors Report will be submitted to the Government by January next year, when a decision will be made on whether or not to endorse the recommendations from Britain's longest ever Public Inquiry.

Announced this month was Air Malta and Air Portugal's intentions to withdraw their scheduled services from Manchester in October, but continue operating IT flights. On the positive side, Iberia will operate daily from July next year, Olympic are planning services at some point and Singapore Airlines and Air Lanka are looking to start services from Manchester in the near future.

Professional US-golfer Bobby Clampett, will attempt to win a place in the Guinness Book of Records, by playing on three of the world's top golf courses in 24-hours. He will tee-off at St. Andrews in Scotland at 0430 on the 18th and play an 18-hole game, before boarding Citation 550 G-FERY at RAF Leuchars to fly to Manchester to board BA Concorde G-BOAB bound for New York. On arrival he will be flown by helicopter to the Winged Foot course for another18-holes, before jetting off to Los Angeles to play the Riviera course, arriving on the green by 2010 and due to time differences, this will still be on the 18th!

Equipment changes/notes on scheduled flights included Air Malta (KM106): B.720s 9H-AAK (1st/7th/8th), 9H-AAL (15th), 9H-AAN (21st) & 9H-AAO (22nd/28th/29th); Air Portugal (TP458/488): B.707 CS-TBT (23rd) plus first visit B.737s CS-TEL (6th) & CS-TEN (27th); Lufthansa (LH074): B.727 D-ABHI (9th) & Condor B.737 (7th) and Swissair (SR842): MD-81 HB-INI (2nd), who also operated with DC-9-32s from the 13th.

RAF ILS traffic identified included C-130s XV200 (28th), XV209 (15th) & XV299 (27th); Jetstreams XX491 (26th), XX493 (21st), XX494 (20th) & XX497 (5th); Andover XS640 (4th) plus Canberra WJ986 which overshot at 1606 as 'CGM55' (11th). The only civil traffic was Lancashire Aero Club Cessna 172 G-MALK (4th/5th) & Jodel G-AVOA (19th).

1st Rockwell 690 EC-DFY arrived at 0140 today on a car parts flight, from/to Valencia.

2nd Cessna 172B Skyhawk G-ARID paid a visit from Barton today. Built in 1960 and used for parachute drops, this aircraft divides its time between Tilstock Farm, Shropshire and Barton.

2nd The latest Monarch Airlines B.757, G-MOND, made its first visit today (OM761 from Alicante). Later in the month on the 23rd, B.757 G-MONC had a complete computer system failure, which resulted in Alicante flight OM760/1 being operated by Spantax CV-990 EC-CNH (OM761A/760A) & Douglas DC-9 EC-CGZ (OM761B/760B). EC-CNH was also making its final visit to Manchester, as it was withdrawn from service by September.

3rd Manchester was blessed by three Italian light aircraft visits this month – which weren't exactly 'spring chickens'! Procaer Picchio I-SPID arrived at 1442 today from Le Bourget, before departing for Halfpenny Green on the 6th and PA-23 Aztec I-ARMT arrived at 1502 from Aberdeen on the 15th. A second PA-23, I-ANGI, arrived from Southend at 1608 on the 29th and stayed until the 6th August. Another vintage-1960's aircraft was UK registered PA-23 Aztec G-ARYF, calling in en route from Valley to Stansted on the 26th.

3rd The only biz-jet making its first visit during the month, was Lear Jet 36 HB-VFD, arriving at 1538 today from/to Geneva.

3rd Swissair DC-9-51 HB-ISP operated SR842/3 for the final time this evening, as it was sold in September to American-airline, Muse Air, as N670MC.

4th Aviaco DC-8 EC-BMY arrived at 0040 today on a student charter (AO8448/9 from/to Madrid). It was also the last visit to Manchester of an Aviaco DC-8, nearly eleven years after the first, EC-ARB, arrived on 9th November 1972.

4th TEA Boeing 737 OO-TEH made its first visit today, positioning in from Brussels to operate Britannia Airways flight BY592A/B to/from Tarbes. Two more B.737s making their first visits to Manchester this month were Air Portugal B.737 CS-TEM & Dan-Air B.737 G-BKNH as a Newcastle diversion, both on the 10th.

5th Today's visit of Balkan Ilyushin IL-18 LZ-BEO (LZ5609/10 from/to Sofia) and again on the 10th (LZ5611/2 from/to Sofia), were in connection with the annual Eisteddfod, a Welsh festival of literature, music and performance, taking place this year at Llangefni.

5th Bristow Helicopters Sikorsky SK.76 G-BJVZ arrived to night-stop from North Denes. It picked up passengers from B.727 N505T and whisked them off on a tour of Yorkshire, before returning later in the day.

6th Former TWA machine Boeing 727 N505T now operated by Tenneco, made its first visit arriving from Bangor at 0712 today, before departing later to Dusseldorf.

6th The French Air Force excelled this month, by operating two Noratlas flights through Manchester. The first, 142/64-KP arriving at 1056 (FM0159 Villacoublay-Evereux), departed with actual passengers rather than the usual training flight and the second, operated by 156/47-BJ (27th) in full camouflage colours, was returning the passengers that went out today.

7th The morning saw a number of early morning diversions from Heathrow, but due a lack of parking space, only four were accepted, none of which were of particular interest. They were British Airways flights L.1011 G-BEAK at 0049 (BA134 from Jeddah), B.747 G-AWNE at 0652 (BA128 from Dhahran) & Trident 2 G-AVFG at 1047 (Shuttle 7V from Glasgow) and Lufthansa B.737 D-ABCE at 0740 (LH4060 from Frankfurt).

7th The latest batch of the three Canadian Air Force CC-130Es to arrive this month were 130325 as (CAM515-today), 130323 (CAM516-9th) & 130320 (CAM517-11th). They all stayed overnight routing Trenton-Brize Norton, except for 130325, which routed Trenton-Lahr.

8th Britannia Airways continued operating Transavia B.737 PH-TVP during the month, mainly Thursday-Monday, but they also used another Transavia B.737, PH-TVH, on BY591A/B to/from Tarbes.

9th Dan-Air BAe.146 G-BKHT, arriving at 0527 today on diversion from Teeside (DA2113 from Palma), was the aircrafts first visit and the second BAe.146 appearing at Manchester so far.

11th An unidentified RAF Gazelle landing at 1223 today (SYN44 from Shawbury), departed four minutes later for Liverpool.

11th American-built Cessna 182 G-ROBK diverted into Manchester today due to the Leeds weather, only to be impounded. The CAA contacted the Airport Authority after their flight plan revealed that the operator was a well known aircraft ferry company, Globe Air, who owed them money! The action was duly carried out and the American pilot left on a Heathrow Shuttle to catch a flight back home, but it later transpired that the aircraft was actually owned by Northair Aviation of Leeds, who sent a pilot the following day to fly the aircraft back to Leeds.

12th After an engine caught fire on British Airtours Tristar G-BEAM whilst on stand this morning, there was a war of words between British Airways, who look after the aircraft at Manchester and the firemen's union. The airline said the flames were a routine occurrence from residual vapour, usually combated by starting the engine to blow it through, but a senior spokesman for the firemen said the flames were licking over the wings and considerable applications of foam were needed after a gas chemical agent had failed to extinguish the fire. After an eventual engine change, the Tristar finally departed on the 14th.

12th There were several ambulance flights during the month. Citation 551 G-BJVP arrived at 0220 today from Mahon and again at 0023 from Rimini (21st) and Lear Jet 35 G-ZONE arrived from Malaga at 1659 (25th).

12th Air Atlantique DC-3 G-AMPY operated another Ford car-parts charter this month, positioning in from Blackpool at 1803 today, before departing to Cologne as DG124.

12th The five-times nightly newspaper flights to Leuchars continued, mainly operated by Genair EMB-110 Bandeirantes, although other aircraft were used occasionally. This evening however it was operated by two aircraft, Metropolitan Airways Twin Otter G-BHFD & Euroair EMB-110 G-HGGS. Other flights were operated by Metropolitan Airways Twin Otters G-BELS (19th/20th/21st) & G-BHFD (24th-29th) and Loganair Twin Otter G-BGEN (31st).

13th British Airways Helicopters Sikorsky Sk.61 G-BEWM, arriving at 1508 today from Beccles, was based at Manchester until its return on the 18th. It was operating up to seven round trips a day, ferrying golf enthusiasts to RAF Woodvale, who were then transported by bus to the Open Golf Championship at Royal Birkdale. The helicopter, capable of carrying twenty-six, could make the trip in twenty minutes. Single fares ranged from £26 for a bookable seat, to £20 depending on the times. The flights recall an historic link between Manchester and Southport, as on the 24th May 1919 the first daily air service in Britain was started by Avro Civil Aviation Services, from Alexandra Park, Manchester to Birkdale Sands, Southport. Fares cost £5 single and £9 for a return ticket, but the service only lasted for four months.

14th There were various other private helicopter movements in connection with the golf, mostly arriving for fuel, having originated from the Alderley Edge/Wilmslow area. Included were Hughes 269 G-BIOA & Bell 206 G-BCWM today, Bell 206s G-AZZB & G-LONG (15th), AS.350 Squirrel G-MARC & Bell 206 G-AYMX (16th) and Bell 206s G-AWMK, G-AYCM & G-AYMX (17th). Bell 206 G-AWMK was operated by Bristow's, who also operated numerous flights to the golf from Tatton Park.

17th British Airways Concorde G-BOAB made its first visit today, arriving at 2149 for a night-stop. It departed the following morning to New York as BA9099C, returning a number of well-known participants from the recent Open Golf Championship at Royal Birkdale. Famous golfers such as Tom Watson, Jack Nicklaus, Hale Irwin and Arnold Palmer were all onboard, along with record breaker Bobby Clampett. During the flight the US golfers attempted to make the longest putt in history, by stroking the ball down the central aisle of the aircraft, as Concorde flew at 2½ times the speed of sound! As if this wasn't newsworthy enough, it was also the first transatlantic Concorde flight from Manchester, which left just G-BOAC/BOAF/BOAG still to visit.

18th C-130 CH-09, arriving at 1406 today to night-stop from/to RAF Binbrook, was the first Belgian Air Force Hercules since CH-12 visited on 15th March 1977.

21st Today saw the second of three visits during the year by Army Air Corps Beavers, when XP769 arrived at 1245, on a round-trip from Belfast (Army 339).

22nd July 1983 – British Midland operated summer IT programmes from Manchester this year and next, with their three Boeing 707s. They were granted a licence for a scheduled service to New York, but British Airways operated the service instead from April 1985. (Geoff Ball)

23rd Today's Tarom Constanta flight RO761/2 operated by Ilyushin IL-62 YR-IRB, was the first visit of a Tarom IL-62 since the 28th September 1981.

24th Due to regular EL AL B.707 4X-ATY, which operates the weekly Manchester-Tel Aviv flight LY5317/8, possibly going tech in Tel Aviv, veteran B.707 4X-ATA operated the delayed flight. Before its withdrawal in 1984, this aircraft had served the airline continuously since 1961.

24th The first and only RAF Jet Provost to land at Manchester took place at 1548 today, when XW372 arrived on a round trip from RAF Greenham Common and stayed for a mere nine minutes.

25th Dash-7 OE-HLS arrived on a one-off charter from/to Innsbruck today (TQ4705/6). Operated by Tyrolean Air Services, it was only the second Dash-7 to visit Manchester.

25th Lear Jet 35 G-ZONE arrived from Malaga at 1659 today, on an ambulance flight.

29th Alan Mann Helicopters Agusta 109 G-OAMH was on a heart transplant flight, operating from/to Harefield Hospital.

29th BAC 1-11 HZ-MAM, arriving on a round trip from Luton, was unusual as it wasn't bound for Dan-Air Engineering! The same Saudi owner had it registered as LX-MAM in December 1985.

August 1983

Despite the onset of the Boeing 757, the Trident still dominated the British Airways Manchester-Heathrow Shuttle services. Of the 185 round trips during the month, only 30 were operated by B.757s.

Dan-Air has applied to the Civil Aviation Authority to compete with British Airways on the Manchester-Heathrow route. If successful, they plan to operate up to five flights a day in each direction, serving in-flight food and drinks at cheaper rates than British Airways. Already operating scheduled services to London from the likes of Aberdeen, Inverness, Newcastle & Cork, they hope to compete on one of the major domestic routes, following British Midlands success in winning licences to compete with British Airways' existing Shuttle routes from Heathrow to Glasgow, Edinburgh & Belfast. They may also start BAe.146 operations from Manchester to various Scandinavian destinations, in addition to the recently approved Manchester-Zurich route in 1984.

Alidair, trading as Inter City Airlines these days, went into receivership last month. As they were the owners and operators of flights on behalf of Guernsey Airlines, there was a knock-on effect as regards to operations at Manchester. Guernsey Airlines were taken over by the owners of British Air Ferries, Jadepoint Ltd, who operated the three-times-weekly Viscount flights from/to Guernsey (GE1721/1725). The afternoon flight (GE725/4) continues to be operated mainly by SD-330s, although Herald G-ASVO was used for several flights (14th/21st/28th). Inter City Airlines also had a direct commitment with Manchester as their aircraft, SD-330s G-BITV & G-BITX, operated the lunchtime Aberdeen service (BA5691/4). Air Ecosse aircraft operated the service until the 19th and from the 22nd they were operated by Genair SD-330s G-EASI & G-OCAS.

Equipment changes/notes on scheduled flights included Air Malta (KM106): B.720s 9H-AAK (5th/11th/12th), 9H-AAL (18th) & 9H-AAO (4th/19th/25th/26th); Air Portugal (TP458/488): with further first visits by B.737s CS-TEN (3rd) & CS-TEO (24th) and Swissair (SR842): DC-9-51 HB-ISM (27th).

RAF ILS traffic identified included Hawk XX308 (8th); Dominies XS738 (23rd) & XS739 (26th); Jetstreams XX482 (30th), XX494 (23rd), XX498 (24th/31st) & XX500 (22nd) plus RAE Comet XS235 (18th) and Nimrod XV235 as Avro 2 on a test flight out of Woodford at 1816 (30th). Civil ILS traffic included CAA BAe.748 G-AVXI (2nd), Cessna 172 G-BAXY (6th), Cessna 152 G-BHRB (7th/22nd), TAT Beech 90 F-GDMM (15th), an unidentified Lufthansa Beech 90 (20th) and BAe.125 G-5-16 overshot at 1336 as 'Newpin 44' (24th).

1st According to the ATC Watch Log, the airport was put on standby as No.2 airfield for RAF Waddington and could accept up to three Vulcans.

1st RAE BAC 1-11 XX919 arrived from Farnborough for attention with Dan-Air Engineering today, before departing back on the 22nd, with Devon VP959 acting as crew ferry on each occasion.

6th Arrow Air made their third appearance at Manchester today, when Douglas DC-8 N6162A arrived from New York at 0423. This aircraft had visited previously on the 4th February 1974, operating for Airlift International.

6th Tarom produced another IL-62 on today's Constanta flight RO761/2. It was YR-IRB again, but the flight on the 20th was operated by Tupolev TU-154 YR-TPJ.

7th The only UK military flights this month were RAF C-130 XV196 (RR4996 from/to RAF Brize Norton) today, Vintage Pair Meteor WF791 & Vampire XH304 routing Ronaldsway-Coventry (14th) and RAF Wessex XT607 routing Barton-Stafford (21st).

9th The French Air Force operated two Noratlas flights again this month, both passenger flights. The first, 154/64-KJ arrived at 1108 today (FM01209 Villacoublay-Evereux). The second operated by 132/64-KP as FM1216 Evereux-Villacoublay, arriving at 1103 on the

30th, was the very final Noratlas to land at Manchester, although there would be one more appearance by the type as an ILS visitor on the 20th February 1985.

6th August 1983 – Seen here is the only visit to Manchester of a SAS Airbus A.300, when SE-DFL arrived at 1829 today from Copenhagen. It was operating an Air Portugal flight (TP6035), picking up seventy-five passengers before flying onwards to Lisbon. SAS DC-9 OY-KGL (TP6045) operated the return flight the next morning. The airline only operated the type from 1980-1983, before transferring them to their subsidiary airline, Scanair. (Geoff Ball)

10th Finnish Citation OH-CIT made it first visit to Manchester today, arriving at 1123 on a night-stopping flight from Helsinki. Other biz-jet first visits during the month were Lear Jet 55s D-CARP (4th) & F-GDHR on an ambulance flight (13th), Citation 550 SE-DEV (19th) and Lear Jet 35 OY-ASO, operated by Sterling in full colours minus titles (24th).

12th A seven day fuel strike affecting Irish airports resulted in a number of Aer Lingus flights calling in for fuel. Also making fuel stops were four Iberia flights: DC-9s EC-BYJ (IB743 Dublin-Malaga-13th) & EC-BYF (IB5745 Dublin-Malaga-13th) and two B.727s making their first visits: EC-CIE (IB5741 Dublin-Malaga-13th) & EC-CFC (IB741 Dublin-Madrid–14th).

13th British Airways used Boeing 737 G-BGDN on today's Jersey flight BA5221/16.

19th For the second month running, Monarch B.757 G-MONC caused considerable difficulties, this time with an engine generator problem. It should have departed at 0900 to Faro (OM800), but as it didn't leave until the following morning, 214 passengers were stuck at the airport for more than eighteen hours. They were provided with morning refreshments, lunch at the airport's Lancaster Restaurant and dinner at the Excelsior Hotel. When the aircraft finally departed, they were also given free drinks throughout the flight. The passengers waiting at Faro were provided with lunch and dinner, but they complained about the lack of information.

20th Due to Monarch Airlines B.757 G-MONC running late due to the previous days problems, British Airtours B.707 G-AVPB was sub-chartered to operate OM752 to Malaga, which positioned in from Gatwick at 2352 today as OM752P.

21st August 1983 – Herald G-ASVO is seen here on a sunny Sunday afternoon, in basic BAF colours with Guernsey Airlines titles, in an overall yellow and blue scheme, rather than the customary white and blue. (Geoff Ball)

23rd A major diversion session could have taken place today, as Heathrow, Gatwick & Stansted were all shut to traffic by 0700 due to dense fog, but unfortunately Manchester also suffered from low visibility and lack of parking stands. The net result was just four diversions received: Lufthansa B.737 D-ABFE at 0617 (LH4060 from Frankfurt), two British Airways B.747s: G-AWNM at 0742 (BA072 from Toronto) & G-BDXC at 0736 (BA174 from New York) and British Caledonian DC-10 G-BHDH at 0810 (BR381 from Dubai). To give an idea of how much traffic went elsewhere, Prestwick took two Northwest B.747s, N609US & N620US, Air Canada B.747 C-FTOE, People Express B.747 N602PE and Qantas B.747 VH-EBN. Shannon did even better with Saudia B.747 HZ-AIC, two Pan American B.747s, four TWA B.747s and two L.1011s!

23rd Partenavia P.68 Victor N4432M, arriving at 1707 today from Amsterdam to night-stop before proceeding onto Shannon, was on delivery to its new owners in the USA. Formerly PH-RVU, it had last visited Manchester on 6th October 1979. The pilot, a former Transamerica Station Manager at Manchester, had stopped off for some liquid refreshment! When he eventually left, he lost the use of some navigational equipment on departure. This led to an extended routing bound for Shannon, to be fitted with long range tanks, which enabled him to continue his routing of Reykjavik-Gander-Bangor-Charlotte-Tampa-Lakeland, Florida.

24th Herald G-AYMG diverted into Manchester at 0541 today (SKD003 from Belfast). Purchased by Skyguard Aviation from Air UK earlier this year in May, it operated nightly mail services out of Birmingham until March 1989, when it was sold to Channel Express Air Services until its withdrawal in 1992.

24th The fourth Guppy to be operated by Aerospatiale, F-GEAI, made its first visit to Manchester this morning, operating outbound to Bremen with more Airbus wings.

26th Interflug TU-134 DDR-SCS made its first visit today, positioning in from Gatwick as IF7113P to operate an outbound charter to Dresden. The return leg of this flight, operated on 6th September by TU-134 DDR-SCN (IF7120), was another first visit.

31st Three more Heathrow diversions were British Airways B.747s G-AWNA at 1021 (BA072 from Toronto) & G-AWNF at 0908 (BA020 from Abu Dhabi) and Kenya Airways Boeing 707 5Y-BBK at 0859 (KQ154 from Athens). Also this morning was the first visit of an RAF L.1011 Tristar, when ZD948 arrived at 1044 as a Brize Norton diversion (RR3716 from Winnipeg). This aircraft was formerly British Airways G-BFCA and had seen less than three years service with the airline. It was still in basic BA colours with no titles, a white tail and 'CA' on the nose and nose-wheel door.

September 1983

Singapore Airlines are planning to launch a Manchester-Singapore service, but so far talks between British Airways and the Governments of both countries have failed to reach an agreement. The British believe that the present economic climate couldn't sustain the introduction of the three-weekly service from next year.

British Airways currently operate the Boeing 757 on three-daily Shuttle flights, but from next month they will be cut back to once-daily. November will also see the launch of the Super Shuttle service, which includes new features such as hot breakfasts, a free bar and seating selection, which should end the current bun-fight for the no-smoking seats! Also announced was the acquisition of fourteen new Boeing 737-200s, due for delivery towards the end of next year. They will replace the Trident fleet, operating on Super Shuttle routes and to major European destinations.

An application by Monarch Airlines to operate a once-weekly Manchester-Toronto winter service has been turned down by the CAA, due to their reluctance to allow twin-engined commercial aircraft to fly across the Atlantic.

Equipment changes/notes on scheduled flights included Air Malta (KM106): B.720s 9H-AAK (9th), 9H-AAN (16th/23rd) & 9H-AAO (2nd/30th); Air Portugal (TP488): B.727 CS-TBP (21st/28th); KLM (KL153): DC-8 PH-DEC (27th) & NLM F.28 PH-CHF (28th); Lufthansa (LH074): B.727 D-ABKC (8th/30th); Manx Airlines (MNX329): Viscount G-AZNA (9th/30th) and Sabena (SN617): B.737 passenger versions OO-SDC (12th) & OO-SDF (3rd).

RAF ILS traffic was numerous, but mostly unidentified except for Hawk XX177 (29th), Dominie XS736 (23rd) and Finningley-based Wessex XR518 at 1629 as 'SHW76' on a test flight out of Woodford (19th). Civil ILS traffic included CAA BAe.748s G-AVXI (2nd) & G-AVXJ (30th); British Aerospace BAe.748 G-BGJV (3rd); Cessna 152 G-BHRB (2nd/5th) and BAe.125 G-5-11 overshooting twice as 'Newpin 43', firstly en route Hawarden-Woodford and secondly on a local flight out of Woodford (30th).

1st Probably the most dramatic event of the year took place today, when Korean Air Boeing 747 HL-7442 (KE007) was shot down by Soviet National Air Defence Forces. According to investigations, the aircraft had strayed off course and into Russian airspace. The Soviet pilots claimed their warnings were ignored, before shooting it down and killing all 269 onboard.

4th Danish-airline Maersk operated two charters, which were both first visits. The first, B.737 OY-APP arrived at 0924 today from Copenhagen, before departing for Karlstad transporting a number of Volvo representatives to their factory in Sweden and the second, B.737 OY-MBZ, operated the return flight from Karlstad (7th).

4th Two more Russian aircraft making their first visits this month were Aeroflot TU-154 CCCP-85092 today (SU1639/40) & Balkan TU-134 LZ-TUE (18th).

5th A sad day in the airports history and major blow to enthusiasts, was today's closure of the public terraces on top of Piers A & B for 'security reasons', which sadly became a permanent feature. They were without doubt the best aviation viewing facilities anywhere in the country. The only official viewing spots still remaining are on the Central Terrace and the top of Pier C.

5th Douglas DC-3 G-APML, operated by Air Atlantique since 1981, made two round trips from Blackpool today and a further and final visit on the 14th. Previously operated by Martin-Baker as a company liaison aircraft since 1958, it's still in their basic corporate colours. It was withdrawn permanently towards the end of the decade.

5th September 1983 – Cessna's latest business jet, the Citation 650, is seen here having recently arrived from Gander. HZ-AAA, on its delivery flight for its new Saudi Arabian owners, was a first visit of type and one of fifty-three biz-jets making their first visits this year. Development began in 1978, the first prototype's maiden flight was on 30th May 1979 and the second on 2nd May 1980. After a flight testing program, its FAA type certification was received on 30th April 1982. Flown by a crew of two, its typical corporate interior seats six, but in a high-density configuration up to nine passengers can be seated. Shortly after the first aircraft were delivered to customers this year, the Citation 650 set several class records, including an overall speed record of 5-hours 13-minutes for a flight from Gander to Paris Le Bourget. Production continued until 1992, after 202 had been built. (Geoff Ball)

7th The first of two Falcon 50s this month, was Ingersoll-Rand N1871R from White Plains, which eventually returned on the 10th. The second, N83FJ, made its first visit arriving from Pescara at 1141 on the 13th, before departing two days later for Bangor.

9th Only thirteen Corvettes have ever visited Manchester and the fourteenth, F-BVPB, arrived at 0958 today from Le Bourget. Other Corvettes during the month were F-BTTU (8th) & F-BVPG (19th).

9th EAS SE.210 F-GDJU positioned in from Stansted at 1835, to operate the following morning as EY4142 to Nuremburg. New to the EAS fleet, it was making its first visit to Manchester as such, having just spent eleven years with Syrian Arab as YK-AFC.

12th BAe.125-700 G-BJDJ which was new in 1981, made its first visit today on a flight from/to Hatfield, where it's currently based. Another BAe.125 first visit was Irish Air Corps No.238, making a very brief stop, en route Brize Norton-Dublin (18th). Other BAe.125 visits were Short Brothers G-BAZB & G-AVRF on the 20th, the latter of which had been in continuous service with BAe up until last year and was a very elusive visitor to Manchester and finally a McAlpine example, G-BEWW, from/to Stansted (28th).

14th Racal-Decca Navigator Handley-Page Jetstream G-AWVK, made a brief stop from Norwich, before departing for Stornaway and returning later in the day. It also operated the same flight details on the following two Wednesdays (21st/28th).

14th Earlier in the year in May, when Manchester Utd beat Brighton 4-0 in the FA Cup final replay, it meant the return of European football to Manchester the following season. As an entrant in the European Cup-Winners Cup, their opponents in the first round were Czech-side Dukla Prague, who arrived at 0953 yesterday onboard TU-134 OK-DFI (OK1269/70 from/to Prague), the first CSA jet aircraft to visit Manchester. The score after today's match was a 1-1 draw.

14th Two Lear Jets making their first visits this month were Lear Jet 35 D-CCAD arriving at 1615 today from/to Dusseldorf and Lear Jet 35 HB-VGU on the 21st.

15th CSA TU-134 OK-DFI made another appearance, arriving at 1034 today (OK1270 from/to Prague), to collect the Dukla Prague team. As Manchester Utd managed a 2-2 draw on the return leg played in Prague on the 28th, it meant the aggregate score was 3-3 and Utd were through to the second round, under the away goals rule.

18th September 1983 – Today saw the third CSA aircraft to Manchester in six days and the first of only two CSA Ilyushin Il-62s to visit. OK-ABD, arriving at 1233 was operating OK1283/4 from/to Prague on behalf of Aeroflot, as following the shooting down by the Russians of Korean Airlines B.747 HL-7442 earlier this month, Aeroflot were banned from UK airspace for fourteen days. OK-ABD was in service with CSA from 1971-1986. (Geoff Ball)

16th The second biz-jet type making its debut at Manchester was the Mitsubishi MU-300 Diamond, when OH-KNE arrived at 1022 today from Helsinki. Delivered in May, it's the only one of its type currently based in Europe. The type first flew on 29th August 1978, but after Beechcraft bought the production rights in 1986 and manufactured it as their own model, it was re-designated as the Beechjet 400.

18th An interesting visitor this afternoon, was Air Guadeloupe Fairchild F.27 F-OGJB at 1505 from Keflavik. It was returning from its base to Toulouse, presumably for maintenance.

20th Air Ecosse operated a Euroair EMB-110 Bandeirante on their Dundee flight WG778/9 twice this month, G-LATC today and G-HGGS (26th). Euroair have also purchased Viscount G-AOHV from the defunct Polar Airways, which made its first visit to Manchester as such on the 17th.

20th British Airport Authority Rockwell 690 G-BXYZ arrived on a night-stop from Prestwick, before returning there the following morning.

23rd Aer Lingus took delivery of their first Shorts SD-330 in May, to operate some of their low-density routes. EI-BEH made its first visit today, operating an extra Dublin flight, EI2216/7, but it only served the airline until November 1984, when it was replaced with two of the larger Shorts SD-360s and sold to Fairflight Charter as G-BKMU.

24th PA-23 Aztec G-AYLY, arriving in full British Island Airways titles, was operated by Peter Villa, owner of British Island Airways and former head of Air UK. This aircraft was operated by the company until its sale in 1990.

27th Air France Concorde F-BVFB, which operated the first Concorde charter into Manchester in 1980, arrived from Paris-CDG at 1212 today (AF4864) on a round trip from Paris as part of the airlines 50th Anniversary celebrations.

27th Two late evening Birmingham diversions were Britannia Airways B.737 G-BJCT at 2321 (BY135B from Palma) and Birmingham Executive Jetstream G-CBEA at 2341, on its first visit to Manchester.

28th It was proving to be a good month for executive visitors to Manchester. Canadair CL-600 Challenger N600KC, arriving at 1701 today from Le Havre, was the third new biz-jet type this month. Another CL-600, TAG Aviation HZ-TAG, arrived two days later at 1006, from/to Le Bourget. The type was an independent design by Bill Lear, who resigned as Chairman of Lear Jet in 1976. Originally dubbed the Lear Star 600, Lear sold exclusive the rights to produce and develop the design to Canadair, who renamed it the CL-600 Challenger. The first prototype took off on 8th November 1978 and was certified in 1980, despite a fatal crash to prototype No.3 in April 1980.

28th The first of the latest batch of Canadian Air Force CC-130Es arrived today, but there were two rather than the usual three, which both night-stopped. 130326 (CAM515) routed Trenton-Brize Norton today and 130325 (CAM516-30th) routed Trenton-Lahr.

29th The month had been mainly devoid of weather diversions, but there were two interesting arrivals today. British Caledonian B.747 G-BJXN diverted in at 0631 (BR362 from Lagos) on its second visit and Gulfstream 2 N45Y, arriving at 1222 from Frankfurt due to the Leeds weather, was the only one of its type making its first visit to Manchester this year.

October 1983

TV ads promoting British Airways Super Shuttle services, with just one passenger onboard, are attracting a fair amount of comment! To keep on the right side of the Advertising Standards Authority, they have to operate at least one flight with just one passenger, but the only time this appears to have happened was during the filming of the advert! They say if a flight is full, another will be provided even for one person, but in practice they are put on British Midland flights and refunded for the difference. British Midland operate the same Heathrow-Belfast/Edinburgh/Glasgow routes as British Airways, except for the Manchester flights which only BA operate, so in those cases the system doesn't work.

The first phase of the new Pier C apron extension was opened on the 5th, but for the time being the area will only be used as a taxiway, to enable aircraft to park on Stands 22, 24 & 26. This is due to work starting on the second phase, involving the removal of the grass island between Pier C and the Western Apron. Once completed, extra parking space will be available for seven narrow-bodied aircraft or up to three Boeing 747s.

Britannia Airways B.737 G-BHWE was unveiled as the first aircraft in their new colour scheme, consisting of a dark blue underside with white/red stripes, a dark blue upper half to the fin with a white Britannia logo and a dark blue logo on the fuselage, with their name in dark blue lettering.

Air Europe will base a Boeing 757 at Manchester for their 1984 summer operations and LOT, who have no plans to recommence their Manchester-Warsaw scheduled service, will operate a weekly charter flight into Manchester again next year.

Equipment changes/notes on scheduled flights included Air Malta (KM106): B.720s 9H-AAK (7th/14th) 9H-AAN (2nd) & 9H-AAO (21st); Air Portugal (TP458): B.707 CS-TBU (1st); KLM (KL153): NLM F.28s PH-CHB (2nd/24th), PH-CHD (16th), PH-CHF (29th), PH-CHN (8th/9th/15th/22nd/23rd); Lufthansa (LH074): B.727 D-ABKC (8th/30th); Manx Airlines used Viscount G-BFZL (8th/20th/28th); Sabena (SN617): B.737 passenger version OO-SDA (22nd) and Swissair (SR842): DC-9-51s HB-ISK (16th), HB-ISM (12th/31st) & HB-ISW (11th).

RAF ILS traffic identified included Hawks XX165 (7th), XX182 (5th) & XX226 (31st); C-130s XV183 (10th) & XV298 (6th); Jetstream XX482 (26th); Dominies XS726 (5th), XS731 (19th), XS734 (3rd) plus Andover XS643 (18th/24th/25th/26th). Civil ILS traffic included Cessna 172 G-BEUX (7th), Lufthansa Beech 90 D-ILHD (15th), Cessna 152 G-BHRB (25th) and BAe.125 G-BGGS (26th).

1st Pan American operated their final charter through Manchester today, when Douglas DC-10 N84NA arrived at 1018 (PA8128 from New York). From now on their only visits would be on diversion. Their summer programme was finished off by Arrow Air Douglas DC-8 N6162A (8th) and first visit Boeing 707 N707ME (15th/22nd).

1st IDS Fanjets Citation 550 G-JETD, arriving at 1146 today from/to Heathrow, was one of four biz-jets making their first visits this month. The others were Citation 501 SE-DES (27th), newly registered Falcon 10 SE-DEK (8th) and two BAe.125s: Rank-Xerox owned G-BGTD (19th) and the CAA's new aircraft, G-CCAA (31st).

2nd KLM suffered from crew shortages this month, which meant numerous visits by NLM Fokker F.28s, the first of which, PH-CHB, operated today.

2nd Air Malta B.720 9H-AAN made its last visit to Manchester this evening, operating KM106/7 from/to Malta. It was withdrawn towards the end of the month and eventually made its way to the USA as a spares aircraft for the military J-Stars program.

3rd PA-31 Navajo N62992 arriving at 2255 today from Madrid, night-stopped before proceeding onwards to Reykjavik the following morning. It was returning to the USA after being based in Spain for the summer. Another aircraft based in Spain and returning to the States was PA-23 Aztec N40375 (13th), which followed the same routing.

5th Frankfurt-based Beech 100 N331GB arrived from Frankfurt at 1804 to night-stop.

7th The cattle flights to Milan re-started today after an eight-month break, with Air Bridge Carriers operating Merchantman G-APEK. Further flights were operated by G-APEK on 12th/14th/19th/20th/31st and by G-APES on the 29th.

8th Air Atlantique Douglas DC-3 G-AMCA operated from/to Blackpool today, on a crew training flight. Formerly operated by Manchester-based Fairey Surveys, this aircraft last visited Manchester on 21st October 1980.

8th The latest British Airways Trident 3 destined to be withdrawn from service, G-AWYZ, made its last visit to Manchester today. Arriving from Heathrow at 1530, it was on a back-up flight (BA4490), before operating another back-up flight (BA4511) to Heathrow at 1653. Delivered new to BEA in March 1972, it made its first visit on 29th April 1972 and was withdrawn after its last flight (BA4833 Edinburgh-Heathrow) on the 16th of this month.

8th Cyprus Airways B.707 5B-DAK, a regular visitor since the airline recommenced services to Manchester in 1979, made its last visit today (CY358/9), before being withdrawn on the 31st.

9th British Airtours Boeing 707 G-AVPB made its final visit today, operating KT294/5 from/to Newark. It was withdrawn from service after operating its final flight (KT284 Vancouver-Gatwick) on the 15th, before being sold later to ZAS Airline of Egypt as SU-DAC. This left just one Boeing 707, G-AXXY, still being operated by British Airtours.

10th October 1983 – This month's highlight was almost certainly today's arrival of Tarom Antonov 24 YR-BMN (RO601/2) at 2351. Another first visit of type this year, it would be 17 more years before another AN-26 would visit Manchester. The Romanian football team had the pleasure of flying on this aircraft from/to Bucharest, via Budapest, for a friendly match with Wales at Wrexham's Racecourse Ground. It was parked on the West Apron until the 13th, when it returned the team home after a resounding 5-1 defeat. As with the inbound flight, the return had to route via Budapest to refuel as Hungary is an Eastern bloc country and they prefer making transactions in their own currencies, rather than in hard Western currency. (Geoff Ball)

10th British Midland DC-9 G-BMAH positioned in from East Midlands to operate an outbound charter to Milan today. DC-9 G-BMAA operated a further flight on the 14th and both were first visits.
11th Another Royal Saudi Air Force flight was C-130H 1605, arriving as 'RSF1002' from Milan-Malpensa today. There was nothing unusual about this, except that until its departure back to Milan on the 13th, it was parked on the South Side of Runway 28, well away from the airport rather than its customary spot on the Freight Apron.
11th The third CL-600 Challenger to visit Manchester arrived this afternoon, when VR-CKK operated from/to Madrid.
13th The third and final visit of an Army Beaver this year was XP769, arriving at 0102 today, from/to Belfast (Army 338).
15th Royal Saudi Air Force C-130H 466 attempted to depart for Gander (RSF918), only to return to Manchester an hour later with an engine feathered, before eventually leaving the following morning.
16th Qantas offered up B.747 VH-EBL for a pleasure flight today. All 433 seats were filled at £24 each, for the 45-minute demonstration flight over the Lake District and Isle of Man.
16th Loganair BN-2 Islander G-BFNV was en route from Wyton-Glasgow, when it diverted into Manchester for fuel, due to strong headwinds.
16th All-white Boeing 737 G-BKRO, which has been leased to Air Europe for the summer, operated its last flight today (AE5643 from Alicante), before departing to Lasham in preparation for its lease to Air Lanka as 4R-ALC.
18th PA-32R Cherokee OO-VIP arrived at 1202 today, on an ambulance flight from Charleroi.
18th The airport played host to 8th Squadron RAF Shackleton WL747, arriving at 1225 today on a round-trip from Lossiemouth. It brought the Squadron's Commanding Officer into Manchester for a local engagement and stayed for twenty-five minutes before departing via Woodford for some ILS approaches. It appeared again the following day, before returning him back to Lossiemouth.
20th Balkan IL-18 LZ-BEA arrived in the early hours, returning Manchester Utd fans from Varna after their recent second-round first leg European Cup-Winners Cup tie with Spartak Varna of Bulgaria, ending in a 2-1 away for United.
21st British Airways Concorde G-BOAB, arriving from Heathrow to operate a charter to Majorca (BA9065C), became the first Concorde to land at Palma.
23rd The writer was up bright and early on this glorious morning, in anticipation of last night's weather forecast predicting fog across the country, but the net result was disappointing. The first of four Gatwick diversions was People Express B.747 N602PE, a new airline to Manchester arriving at 0643 (PE002 from Newark). Earlier in the year on the 26th July, this American airline began a non-stop service from Newark to Gatwick, with leased B.747 N602PE, previously operated by Braniff International as N602BN, which had visited Manchester as such on 21st November 1979. Fares were initially $149 each way and the airline was an instant success, with all flights being sold out for several months within 24-hours of being launched. All seats were the same price, with slight differences between peak/off-peak fares and overseas flights, which offered Premium & Economy Class. Fares were paid in cash onboard the aircraft early in the flight and passengers were permitted one carry-on bag free of charge, but checked-in bags cost $3.00 each. They were the first airline in the USA to charge for checked-in bags and modest amounts were also charged for in-flight refreshments.

Sodas, honey-roasted peanuts and brownies were 50 cents each and a People Express 'snak-pak' of assorted cheeses/crackers/salami cost $2. Next to follow was Monarch Airlines B.757 G-MONC at 0653 (OM899 from Ibiza), then another airline first visit from American Airlines with DC-10 N137AA at 0753 (AA050 from Dallas). They had taken over the Gatwick-Dallas service on 20th May 1982, previously operated by Braniff International. Cathay Pacific produced their first visit of the year, with B.747 VR-HIC at 0827 (CX201 from Hong Kong/Bahrain) and the last diversion of the morning was the only one from Heathrow, with Kuwait Airways B.747 9K-ADC arriving at 0955 (KU102 from New York).

23rd October 1983 – The first new airline into Manchester today was US-carrier People Express, introducers of low cost flights to the US from Gatwick. N602PE operated with the airline until 1985, when it was purchased by Northwest Airlines as N635US. (Geoff Ball)

25th A flying instructor and his pupil had a lucky escape today, during a training flight in the Peak District, when Manchester resident Cessna 150 G-BFRP was caught by a freak downdraught and went into a steep dive. The aircraft was working Manchester Approach 119.4 at 1940, when he reported the downdraft and lost contact. The pilot applied full power to attempt a climb, but the aircraft flew straight into the mountainside. Miraculously, both men walked away from the wreckage and travelled on foot for two miles, before eventually reaching the Nags Head public house in Edale for help. Last year in July, the same aircraft had to make a forced landing in a field near Holmes Chapel, after running out of fuel.

26th Another weather affected morning, particularly in the South East, produced just two diversions into Manchester. First visit Kuwait Airways B.747 9K-ADD arriving at 0846 (KU102 from New York), was followed an hour later by British Caledonian DC-10 G-DCIO (BR232 from Atlanta).

27th A single diversion was the highlight of today's movements, when Delta L.1011 Tristar 500 N753DA arrived at 0700 (DL010 from Atlanta), on its first visit to Manchester. Today and the last two diversion days seemed to have followed a pattern as far as Heathrow was concerned, as when one runway fell below limits, the second remained above and saved the airport from any major disruption.

23rd October 1983 – The second US airline making its debut today was American Airlines with DC-10 N137AA. Purchased from Air New Zealand in July 1982, it was one of six to visit Manchester from 1983-1988, which were all diversions. (Geoff Ball)

23rd October 1983 – B.727 9V-WGA (formerly 9V-SGH), is seen here in basic Singapore Airlines colours arriving from Helsinki. Operated by The Age of Enlightenment based in Jersey, the organisation brought the Maharishi (of Beatles fame) into Manchester, along with his followers and the press for a spiritual meeting in Skelmersdale, where he was expanding their operations. (Geoff Ball)

27th Another aircraft operating its last flight prior to return after lease, was Dan-Air B.727 G-BHVT at 0512 today (DA1773 from Malaga), before its eventual departure for Lasham. It was returned to LACSA as TI-LRR the following month, but would return again next April.

28th The second British Airways Trident making its final visit this month, was Trident 2 G-AVFM. Arriving at 1120 today from Heathrow as back-up flight BA4424, it operated another back-up flight, BA4465, back to Heathrow at 1354. This aircraft, which was delivered new to BEA in April 1969, was withdrawn next month on the 28th November, after its final service.

30th Qantas held another open day at the airport, this time giving the general public the chance to walk inside one of their Boeing 747s. The ticket-only event was over-subscribed within two weeks of the airline announcing the event. Over 5,000 people turned up on a wet and windy Sunday afternoon, for the privilege of looking inside B.747 VH-EBL.

30th American airline TWA retired their last four Boeing 707s from scheduled service today, with the final B.707 operating New-York-Miami flight as TW5. Thirty-eight different TWA B.707s visited Manchester from 1967-1979. B.707-331B N18708 was the first on 9th June 1967 & B.707-331B N28726 was the last on 15th January 1979.

November 1983

Britannia Airways returned two Boeing 737s to their leasing companies at the end of last month. The first, G-BOSL, which was sold to Dan-Air as G-ILFC, made its first appearance at Manchester on 21st May 1984 and the second, G-OSLA, was sold to America West as N138AW.

Following encouraging signs of an upturn in the economy, British Airways are considering reintroducing a Manchester-New York service in 1985, possibly three flights a week. They ran an all-year round service, until withdrawing from the route in October 1981. Their sudden interest in reviving the service follows British Midland's intent to operate the route with five-weekly flights in the summer and four-weekly in the winter, assuming their CAA application is successful. Manchester welcomed the news from both airlines and sees no reason why they can't compete on the route.

The Airport Authority has given the go-ahead for the new £6m cargo centre, which should be operational by May 1985.

Iberia will increase their Manchester services from next year, with four-weekly flights to Barcelona and Madrid. As the extra flights will operate alongside the three-weekly to Malaga and Madrid, it means Madrid will become a daily service.

The new £2.14m link taxiway from the South Bay to Taxiway 2 opened on the 25th. At 1,500 metres long, it provides an alternative route to a very busy section of Taxiway 2, increasing total taxiway capacity. During particularly busy periods of up to thirty-six movements an hour, aircraft can be held on the taxiway, whilst others proceed to meet their takeoff slot time. For landing aircraft it provides an additional approach to route to the stands and serves as extra parking when required.

Scheduled services were ended by Air Malta on 28th October, when the last KM106/7 flight was operated by B.737 9H-ABA and by Air Portugal on 29th October, when their last (TP458/9) was operated by B.737 CS-TEL. Cyprus Airways reverted to once-weekly for the winter, Finnair will operate a three-weekly cargo schedule (AY032) including the Saturday afternoon (AY034) and Guernsey Airlines will operate twice-weekly (Fri/Sun) from/to Guernsey. KLM reduced the morning Amsterdam (KL153/4) to six-weekly and the lunchtime service (KL155/6) to weekdays, but will operate Sat/Sun mornings as KL157/8 and from the 14th, the five-weekly cargo flight (KL911) will be operated by leased Transavia B.737s. Loganair introduced a twice week-day flight from/to Belfast Harbour from the 21st, but reduced Edinburgh flights from three to two each weekday. Manx Airlines will operate twice-daily between Manchester-Isle of Man. SAS continue three-weekly flights from/to Copenhagen

(SK539/40), with a further flight onwards to/from Dublin (SK541/2), whilst maintaining their weekly Saturday freight flight and Swissair continue to operate Douglas DC-9-32s.

Winter IT flights are being operated by Air Europe, Air Malta, Aviaco, Britannia Airways, British Airtours, British Airways, Dan-Air, EL AL, Monarch Airlines & Orion Airways. Transatlantic flights are being operated by Wardair (Toronto) and by CP Air (Toronto) until 15th December, but they will withdraw from the charter market completely in January.

Equipment changes/notes on scheduled flights included Iberia (IB346): first visit B.727 EC-CBF (4th); KLM (KL157): NLM F.28s PH-CHB (12th) & PH-CHD (5th); Loganair operated British Midland F.27 G-BMAE on all three Edinburgh flights (4th/7th); Lufthansa (LH074): B.727s D-ABGI (26th), D-ABKA (23rd), D-ABKJ (11th) & D-ABRI (1st); Manx Airlines used Air UK F.27 G-BDVS (24th-28th); Sabena (SN617): B.737 passenger version OO-SDB (14th) & OO-SDL (7th) and Swissair (SR842): DC-9-51 HB-ISN (7th).

On a quiet month for ILS traffic, RAF aircraft identified included C-130 XV209 (14th) and Dominies XS709 (4th) & XS739 (4th). No Civil ILS traffic was noted.

1st Bulgarian side Spartak Varna landed in Manchester today, in preparation for the following day's European Cup-Winners Cup match at Old Trafford. Arriving onboard first time visitor Balkan Tupolev TU-134 LZ-TUD at 1221 (LZ5703 from Varna), they stayed until the 3rd. Manchester Utd won the game 2-0, so with an overall aggregate score of 4-1, they were now drawn to play Barcelona in the quarter-finals next March.

4th Of the eleven weather diversions during the day, nine were from Heathrow. An increasingly familiar phrase applying to certain diversions days seems to be 'What might have been'! Heathrow was affected by fog for most of the day, apart from a temporary lifting from mid-afternoon to mid-evening, but unfortunately for most of the morning Manchester was affected by low visibility as well, which precluded a number of aircraft from diverting in, but having said this some good numbers arrived! The first two, British Airways B.747 G-AWNC at 0433 (BA006 from Anchorage) & Saudia L.1011 Tristar 200 HZ-AHD at 0458 (SV045 from Jeddah) arrived when our visibility wasn't too bad, but it had certainly deteriorated by the time Qantas B.747 VH-EBN came in at 0620 (QF001 from Bahrain), when further diversions were deterred for another three hours. The fog started to lift into low cloud around 0930 and the next arrival was South African Airways B.747-300 ZS-SAT making its first visit at 0948 (SA220 from Sal Island), which was also technically a first visit of type as the B.747-300 differed from the standard Boeing 747-100/200 series due to its upper deck being stretched by an extra 23ft. The arrival of ZS-SAT and a clearance in Manchester's weather raised hopes for more diversions, but in the end only three more arrived during the morning: British Airways B.747 G-AWNG at 1009 (BA295 from Miami), Kuwait Airways B.747 9K-ADB at 1027 (KU102 from New York) & B.707F 9K-ACJ at 1130 (KU2103 from Kuwait). One more arrived after another short deterioration in Heathrow's weather, when Pan American B.747SP N606BN made its first visit at 2138 (PA100 from Heathrow). Formerly operated by Braniff and purchased by Pan American in September 1983, this aircraft was actually allocated the registration N529PA, but this wasn't carried until January 1984.

7th Air Bridge Carriers cattle flights to Milan continued during the month, with Merchantman G-APEK today, G-APEK (9th) & G-APES (14th/17th/18th/24th).

8th The Trident withdrawals are gathering pace with three last visits this month, starting with Trident 3 G-AWZL at 2104 today as BA4532. Having gone tech, it was parked up until the 24th, when it positioned down on a two-engine ferry flight to Heathrow for subsequent withdrawal. Delivered new to BEA in November 1971, it made its first visit to Manchester on the 30th January 1972.

9th Thirteen more diversions arrived today and another seven the following day, mainly from Leeds. There was nothing much of interest over the two days, when the only two non-British arrivals were Avair Beech 200 EI-BFT at 1006 today (WV072 from Dublin) & Lego Beech F.90 OY-BEL (10th), both from East Midlands. Air UK Herald G-BBXI made its last visit to Manchester today, diverting in from Leeds at 1257 (UK204 from Norwich). This aircraft was damaged beyond economical repair, when it was struck by a lorry in June 1984, whilst parked up at Bournemouth.

13th November 1983 – Cayman Airways BAe.748 VR-CBH has just returned off an 18-month lease to the airline. After an extensive overhaul, it emerged from Dan-Air's hangar in the livery of a new UK airline, Air Venture, registered as G-VAJK. (Geoff Ball)

13th Another football charter involving Balkan was Tupolev TU-154 LZ-BTL, arriving to take Wales out to Bulgaria for an important Euro 84 qualifying match on the 16th. After Wales were beaten 1-0, they returned to Cardiff via Manchester onboard Balkan TU-154 LZ-BTD.

13th Aeroflot TU-154 CCCP-85551, arriving at 1807 today on a one-off charter from/to Moscow as SU1245/6, was also a first visit.

14th Delta Air Transport Fairchild FH-227 OO-DTC operated the first of three flights through Manchester this month, transferring CP Air passengers from/to Amsterdam. The same aircraft also operated on the 28th, OO-DTE operated on the 21st and both were first visits.

14th KLM's nightly cargo flight, KL911, is now operated by a leased Transavia B.737. PH-TVE operated the first flight today and for the remainder of the month and a second aircraft, PH-TVD, was also used the following month.

17th The fifth and final Boeing 707 making its first visit this year, was Korean Airlines B.707F HL-7431, arriving at 0718 today (KE9159 from Seoul/Anchorage). It was bringing 28 tonnes of clothing into Manchester, before returning to Seoul, via Ostend and Anchorage.

17th The first BAe.125 customs flight passing through Manchester in quite a while, was F-BYFB on its first visit, arriving from Hawarden en route to Le Bourget. The only other biz-jets making their debuts this month were Lear Jet 35 D-CCAY (10th) & RAF BAe.125 ZD704 (21st).

21st Loganair started a second service from Manchester today, operating two weekday return flights and one Sat/Sun return flight to Belfast Harbour Airport, ten minutes from the City Centre. Tickets for today's first flight operated by SD-330 G-BIRN cost £44 one-way, or £82 for a day-return.

22nd RAF C-130 XV212, (RR5865 Leuchars-Akrotiri) diverted into Manchester at 0523 today, having declared an emergency with fumes in the cockpit. After landing it came to a halt on the runway and eventually closed down both engines, but the situation was worse than it first appeared due to its dangerous cargo. The airport was closed until 0640, when the aircraft was finally cleared off the runway.

22nd Former Sterling Boeing 727 OY-SBD made its first visit today, after being sold to Dan-Air and re-registered as G-BHNE. It replaces the airlines Manchester-based Boeing 727, G-BHNF, which has gone on a winter lease to American-airline, Sun Country.

23rd Seven Boeing 747s arriving due to fog at Heathrow were Qantas VH-EBN at 0656 (QF001 from Bahrain); Pan American N739PA at 0749 (PA002 from New York) on its first visit in addition to being the 148th B.747 to Manchester; TWA N93104 at 0756 (TW700 from New York); British Airways G-AWNO at 0942 (BA174 from New York); Kuwait Airways 9K-ADC at 0956 (KU102 from New York); TWA N93119 at 1042 (TW770 from Chicago) & British Airways G-AWNH at 1228 (BA295 from Miami). As the fog only affected Heathrow, the southern airports took most of the diversions; but when the forecast predicted more extensive fog in the south by the evening, preparations were made at Manchester by clearing aircraft already parked on the stands to make way for possible diversions, but in the end this proved to be a red herring as the deterioration didn't materialise.

23rd Trident 3 G-AWZW made its last visit today, arriving at 1047 (BA4422 from Heathrow), before departing at 1140 (BA4443 to Heathrow) and being withdrawn from service later in the month. Delivered new in November 1972, it made its first visit to Manchester on its first operational flight for BEA on 9th December 1972 (BE4092 from Heathrow).

25th British Airways Trident 3 G-AWZB was the third and final Trident making its last visit to Manchester this month, arriving at 1729 today (BA4492 from Heathrow) and departing at 1826 (BA4513 to Heathrow) on its very last flight. Delivered in February 1971, it was the first of two Trident 3s making their first visits on the 18th May 1971, with the second being G-AWZF.

28th The second Belgian Air Force C-130 to visit Manchester this year, was CH-07 arriving at 1033 today, from/to Brussels.

29th The ATC Watch Log recorded that BAe Hatfield had put in a request for a 4-hour Cat.II ILS training detail at Manchester this afternoon with a BAe.146, but the request was refused due to the length of the detail and the interference it would cause to normal traffic, so the training was carried out at Liverpool instead. Although Manchester approved the aircraft for a couple of ILS approaches, BAe declined the offer.

December 1983

Although British Midland was granted a licence to operate a Manchester-New York service on the 22nd, they will only commence if the licence still held by British Airways is revoked, even though BA pulled off the route in October 1981.

According to the Chief Executive, Gil Thompson, the airport had high hopes for next year, following ongoing talks with various airlines over possible flights to Islamabad, Tel Aviv,

Dubai, Lagos, Tripoli, Hong Kong & Singapore. However, there was a setback earlier in the year, when Singapore Airlines applied for a licence for the route and the British Government pointed out that under an agreement between Singapore Airlines and British Airways that they must have an equal number of flights between the two countries, Singapore Airlines were told they could have the two-weekly flights they wanted, if they withdrew two flights from Heathrow. When faced with disrupting their successful daily service to Heathrow, Singapore Airlines decided not to operate from Manchester after all. In view of this, Manchester Airport and local MP's are hoping to persuade the Government to reconsider their decision.

The Government's go-ahead for further improvements to Manchester Airport paves the way for work to be carried out on the operational control centre, splitter island surfacing, auto-docking, covered West Apron accommodation and the airport-link road.

Equipment changes/notes on scheduled flights included British Caledonian using Dan-Air BAC 1-11 G-AXCP to operate BR983/4 & BR985/992 and Iberia (IB346): B.727 EC-CAJ (25th). Due to the crash landing of Fokker F.27 G-IOMA, Loganair operated the following on Edinburgh flights LC562/3 & LC568/1: Dan-Air BAe.748s G-ATMI (16th), G-ARRW (12th) & G-BIUV (13th) and British Air Ferries Viscounts G-AOHM (30th-31st) & G-AOHV (17th-27th). Lufthansa (LH074): B.727s D-ABFI (29th), D-ABQI (17th), D-ABKD (12th), D-ABKE (13th), D-ABKH (10th) & D-ABKR (9th); SAS flight SK539 continues to be exclusively operated by DC-9-21s and Swissair (SR842): DC-9-51s HB-ISL (10th/31st) HB-ISM (30th) & HB-ISU (12th).

It was another quiet month for ILS traffic. RAF aircraft identified included Hawk XX312 (14th); Jetstreams XX482 (20th), XX491 (13th), XX496 (15th) & XX497 (14th) and RAE BAC 1-11 XX105 (7th) overshooting at 1437 as 'Nugget 82'.

1st Canadian Air Force CC-130E 130315 arrived at 0915 today (CAM6409 from Trenton) on a navigation exercise.

2nd Irish airline Aer Arran, the former operators of two BN-2 Islanders, now lease EMB-110 Bandeirante G-BHJY from Jersey European, which operated an early charter (EH801/2 from/to Dublin). Their other EMB-110, G-BHJZ, operated GE725/4 from/to Guernsey (4th).

2nd A trio of noteworthy elderly British aircraft during the month started with today's arrival of 1967 PA-24 Comanche G-AVJU (from/to East Midlands), followed by 1965 PA-30 Twin Comanche G-ATFK (Bembridge-Redhill-4th) and 1966 PA-28 Cherokee G-ATOP (Halfpenny Green-Popham-31st).

5th British Midland have no winter programme from Manchester, but B.707 G-BFLE arrived from East Midlands today to operate BD800 to Nassau & B.707 G-BMAZ operated BD6412/1 from/to Toronto on the 19th.

8th Irish Air Corps Beech 200 made the first of two training flights during the month, routing Birmingham-Liverpool at 1319 today and again at 1256 on the 15th.

9th In a month lacking of typical December weather, four weather diversions arrived at Manchester today. Aer Lingus SD-330 EI-BEH made the first of four visits this month, diverting in from Leeds at 1234 (EI334 from Dublin) and two British Airways Trident flights from Heathrow were G-AVFN at 1956 (BA4515 from Manchester) & G-AWZS at 1957 (Shuttle 7P from Glasgow). The fourth, Heavylift CL-44-0 EI-BND arriving at 2307 (NP700 from Milan) from Teeside, was formerly N447T with Transmeridian/British Cargo.

13th Cessna 310 OY-DRH called in for fuel today, en route from Skive to Shannon.

7th December 1983 - BAe.125 G-AYER, arriving at 2001 today from Heathrow, acquired the marks 'IAF125' the following day for its part in a film called 'The Glory Boys'. On the 9th, it was parked on a remote stand, surrounded by armed soldiers and a number of armoured cars. The actress Joanne Lumley was also noted! After some uncooperative weather, the filming was extended and the aircraft took part in some flying shots on the 11th, before eventually departing for Heathrow on the 12th. Manufactured in 1970, this aircraft made its first visit to Manchester on 5th April 1971, before spending four years in Kuwait. It returned to the UK in 1978 and was eventually re-registered as G-TOPF in July 1984. (Geoff Ball)

13th The first of the latest batch of Canadian Air Force CC-130Es, 130325 as CAM515, arrived today. There should have been four flights this month rather than three, but the one due to operate on the 15th (CAM516) was cancelled. The other flights were 130317 (CAM517-17th) & 130327 (CAM518-18th), which all night-stopped after their arrival from Trenton. CAM515 departed to Brize Norton and the other two flights departed for Lahr.

15th The fourth different Falcon 50 to visit Manchester this year was HB-ITH, arriving at 0832 today on a round trip from Heathrow.

17th The most interesting twin prop arrival during the month, was Cessna 421 TF-ELT, arriving from Reykjavik today as a Leeds diversion.

19th Former Laker Airways BAC 1-11 G-ATPK, now operated by Bryan Aviation, night-stopped from Gatwick before departing for Nice the following day. After being in private hands until 1985, the aircraft had a new lease of life back in front-line service with Dan-Air for another six years, before being sold to Okada Air of Nigeria in 1991 as 5N-OMO.

20th As CP Air will not be operating into Manchester after Christmas, today's movements of B.747 C-FCRA warrant a mention, as out of their four Boeing 747s, this aircraft was always the rarest this side of the Atlantic. Arriving at 1034 (CP800 from Vancouver), it departed to Gatwick, returned at 1736 and departed again this time at 2054 (CP823 to Toronto). It appeared again in the early hours of the 23rd, operating CP822/801 Toronto/Vancouver.

20th Queens Flight BAe.748 XS789, arriving at 1056 today as 'Kitty 4', was dropping Prince Charles off for a local engagement. When it returned from Northolt at 1455, Princess Diana was onboard on her first visit to Manchester.
22nd Hapag-Lloyd B.737 D-AHLI positioned in from Tenerife at 1917 today, to operate for Britannia Airways the following morning as BY293A to Munich.
23rd The last biz-jet movement this year was former resident BAe.125 G-AZVS, at 0814 today from Coventry. It spent Christmas parked on the South Side, before departing for Gerona on the 27th.
23rd Another two Hapag-Lloyd aircraft today were both Boeing 727s and also first visits. D-AHLS (HF996F from Hanover) arrived to operate Britannia Airways flight BY596A/B to/from Munich and then outbound again to Munich (BY246A) & D-AHLU positioned in from Munich to operate BY272A/B to/from Munich and then back again (BY566A).
23rd Avair SD-330 EI-BNM, arriving at 1425 today, brought computer parts in from Dublin.
24th PA-28 Cherokee G-AVNU, originally intended for Barton, was a most reluctant arrival at Manchester. Having been informed that Barton was closed, he replied to ATC, 'I have no option but to come to Manchester!'
25th During the early hours of the morning, B.727 G-BHNE (DA1738 to Malaga) was initially told he was No.20 in the queue to start (ATC joke)! Once taxiing he requested to hold on the runway to rectify a technical snag, so the Tower said that was OK as the next inbound had just taken off from Faro! The Captain of DA1738 replied 'That he would probably have taken off by then, but just in case he hadn't when was the next inbound', to which the Tower replied 'It's you coming back!'
25th The jokes and japes courtesy of Manchester ATC continued, when Qantas B.747 VH-EBL operated Christmas Day's QF009/010 outbound flight with 280 passengers, one of the highest loads this year, on the quietest day of the year. The Captain wasn't amused when he was told to wait for start up whilst they got him a slot!

First/Last Arrivals & Departures 1983

First arrival:	Cessna 172 G-BFTS at 0014 (Local flight)
First departure:	B.737 G-BFVB/BY806A to Palma at 0738
Last arrival:	B.757 G-MONB/OM755 from Palma at 2300
Last departure:	B.727 G-BHNE/DA1738 to Palma at 2359

Airport Stats 1983 (+/- % on Previous Year)		
Scheduled Passengers	5,218,000	+1%
Freight & Mail (Tonnes)	27,800	-2%
Movements	86,300	+1%

5
Airport Diary 1984

January 1984

Manchester recorded a 7% rise in holiday traffic last year, with Palma proving the most popular destination with over 500,000 passengers, almost as many travelling to/from Heathrow. Freight traffic was down 2% to just under 28,000 tonnes, of which 25% was Ireland bound.

Blackpool-based Spacegrand Aviation has applied to operate between Blackpool-Manchester. If successful, they plan a twice-weekday service with PA-31 Navajo Chieftains and weekend flights with the larger Twin Otter.

British Airways are going from strength-to-strength, as far as their Shuttle services are concerned. Since revamping last November, passenger numbers on the Manchester-London route have increased by 12% over the same period last year. Meanwhile, at a travel conference held at Manchester Town Hall, the airline reaffirmed plans to launch a direct New York service in March 1985 and said they were looking into a number of new services, including flights to the Middle East and the Indian sub-continent, which could be in brought into operation over the next twelve to eighteen months.

As well as creating a purpose-built security area specifically for passengers bound for Belfast, Manchester Airport has also purchased new X-ray equipment; which will greatly reduce the labour content of the screening operation currently requiring up to seven security guards for every Belfast flight.

Equipment changes/notes on scheduled flights included British Caledonian using Dan-Air BAC 1-11 G-AXCP to operate BR983/4 & BR985/992 and Iberia (IB346): B.727 EC-CAJ (25th). Due to the crash landing of Fokker F.27 G-IOMA, Loganair operated the following on Edinburgh flights LC562/3 & LC568/1: Dan-Air BAe.748s G-ATMI (16th), G-ARRW (12th) & G-BIUV (13th) and British Air Ferries Viscounts G-AOHM (30th-31st) & G-AOHV (17th-27th). Lufthansa (LH074): B.727s D-ABFI (29th), D-ABQI (17th), D-ABKD (12th), D-ABKE (13th), D-ABKH (10th) & D-ABKR (9th); SAS flight SK539 continues to be exclusively operated by DC-9-21s and Swissair (SR842): DC-9-51s HB-ISL (10th/31st) HB-ISM (30th) & HB-ISU (12th).

RAF ILS traffic identified included C-130s XV183 (26th) & XV207 (16th); Dominie XS732 (11th) and Andover XS643 (12th). Civil ILS traffic included Cessna 152s G-BHRB (8th), G-BHCX (19th) & Cessna 172 G-BEUX (21st).

3rd Canadian Air Force CC-130E 130315 arrived at 0702 today from Trenton, before departing the following morning to Lahr as CAM6409.

3rd CP Air operated their penultimate flight from Manchester with one of their rarer Boeing 747s, when C-FCRA arrived inbound from Gatwick at 1215 today as CP802, before departing later to Toronto as CP837.

5th Today saw the very last operation by Canadian-airline CP Air, when B.747 C-FCRA arrived at 0712 (CP822 from Toronto), before departing for Gatwick as 0824. They will no longer operate charter flights from/to the UK, but will concentrate on their scheduled flights out of Amsterdam. In 1986 they reverted to their original name of Canadian Pacific Air Lines and replaced their trademark orange livery with a new navy blue colour scheme and logo, shortly after taking over another Canadian-airline, Eastern Provincial. The new incarnation proved to be a short-lived affair, as less than a year later in 1987, Canadian Pacific Air Lines was sold along with Nordair to Calgary-based Pacific Western. PWA would assume the airline's debt of $600m and in April 1987 they announced the new name of the merged airline would be Canadian Airlines International.

6th Newly delivered Genair SD-360 G-BKZR was on its first visit today, arriving to operate an outbound load of newspapers to Dublin.

8th British Airtours Boeing 707 G-AXXY made its final visit today, arriving at 1005 operating KT271 Gatwick-Toronto, as the airline had phased out the type by March. From the summer they will operate former British Airways L.1011 Tristars G-BBAI/BBAJ & BEAM and Boeing 747 G-BDXL.

12th Loganair F.27 G-IOMA (LC568 from Edinburgh), blocked the runway for over four hours today, following the collapse of its starboard undercarriage on landing. Damage to the starboard engine and underside of the fuselage was sustained after the aircraft slid 600ft, before finally coming to a stop. Although the flight, with thirty-five passengers and four flight crew was running more than two hours late, disruption to the airport was minimal as the accident happened at night. The aircraft was removed to Dan-Air Engineering for a temporary patch-up, before departing for Norwich on the 24th for further work. The incident affected Loganair's operations for the remainder of the month. Two Dan-Air BAe.748s, G-ATMI & G-BIUV, were used until the 17th, British Air Ferries Viscount G-AOHV arrived from Southend to operate all Edinburgh flights until the 27th and another British Air Ferries Viscount, G-AOHM, was used from the 30th.

13th Lear Jet G-ZIPS, (formerly G-ZONE), made its first visit to Manchester on its way from Leavesden to Stornaway. Arriving with a technical problem, it was attended to by NEA.

15th Two Citations making their first visits to Manchester this month were Citation 550 PH-HET at 0835 today, en route from Rotterdam to Aberdeen and Citation 501 I-CIPA on its delivery flight, routing Gander-Milan Malpensa on the 22nd.

15th Truste House Forte's BAe.125 G-HHOI arrived from Heathrow, with a number of senior managers to celebrate the company's 20th Anniversary.

17th The French military operated two flights through Manchester this month. The first was French Air Force Xingu No.089/F-TEYJ (FA399 from/to Dinard) arriving at 1443 today and the second, French Navy Xingu No.055, operated Edinburgh-Lorient as F-YDAU on the 22nd.

19th Sabreliner N301MC operated by the Millicore Corporation, was the first of three visits by the type this year, arriving at 1448 from Gothenburg, before departing for Heathrow.

24th Air Ecosse used a variety of aircraft from different operators towards the end of the month. Peregrine Air Services Jetstream G-BKHI was used on this evening's WG778/9, backed up by PA-31 G-BGOX operating WG779A, due to a larger load than the Jetstream could handle. Jetstream G-BKHI was used again to operate WG778/9 on the 30th and SD-330 G-BITV was used on the morning WG700/1. On the 31st, both flights were operated by Cessna 404 G-BKUN (WG700/1) & Loganair EMB-110 G-BIBE (WG778/9).

24th British Caledonian BAC 1-11 G-AWYR, inbound from Gatwick as BR991, was forced to carry out an emergency evacuation on landing due to a bomb threat, but nothing was found.

25th Blackpool-based operator Spacegrand Aviation routed Twin Otter G-BGMD through Manchester today, en-route Brussels-Blackpool to clear customs.

26th During the current cold snap, ground staff have been working round the clock keeping one step ahead of the weather. The entire fleet of 27 snow-clearing vehicles have been kept busy over the last five days, keeping the airport's surfaces clear of snow and ice. More than 43,000 tonnes of de-icing fluid, costing £105,000, has already been used.

27th Four morning diversions from Birmingham included NLM F.27 PH-KFL at 0944 (HN495 from Amsterdam). Also arriving was another Genair SD-360, when G-BKKT appeared at 1338 as a Teeside diversion (EN131 from Gatwick).

27th Viscount G-AOHV made its last visit today, operating on behalf of Loganair. Recently owned by Polar Airways and Euroair, it's now re-registered as G-BLNB with British Air Ferries.

27th Two British military BAe.125s also making their first visits to Manchester this month, were RAF ZD620 at 1439 today (RR1697 Teeside-Northolt) & RAE BAe.125 XW930 (Nugget 89 from/to Bedford) on the 31st.

30th RAE Andover XW750 arrived at 1041 today (Nugget 03 from Bedford), to drop off a crew to return BAC 1-11 XX105 to Bedford, after maintenance with Dan-Air Engineering. Although the BAC 1-11 wasn't ready to leave because of a technical fault, the Andover still returned to Bedford within twenty minutes of arrival, leaving the crew behind. Later in the day when it became apparent the BAC 1-11 wouldn't be ready, RAE Viscount XT661 arrived at 1632 to pick up the 'stranded' crew and return them to Bedford. The BAC 1-11 finally left for Bedford the following day, when a third RAE aircraft, BAe.125 XW930, arrived with a fresh crew.

30th The automatic parking of aircraft introduced at Manchester today, was pioneered by the airport's Head of Technology. It's part of a massive computer system known as ADIS (Airport Digital Information System), which includes flight information/scheduling, baggage handling, radar, meteorology, noise monitoring and eventually an automatic routing system. The automated docking is only operating on one stand so far, but it's soon to be installed on a further seventeen parking stands, at a cost of £180,000, which should be recouped over the next two years by reduced operating costs.

February 1984

The next stage in British Midland's battle to operate Manchester–New York will take place in April, when the CAA's inquiry into the application is heard. The airline have been granted a licence, but they will only take it up if British Airways, who also have a licence they haven't used since 1981, are prevented from flying the route as neither airline is prepared to compete with the other on the route.

British Airways chose Manchester as the focus for the biggest transatlantic operation they've ever mounted. Their new budget travel subsidiary, Poundstretcher, announced flights from Manchester to New York, Los Angeles, San Francisco, Orlando & Toronto as well as to sixteen Mediterranean destinations. They hope to carry more than 25,000 passengers during the year.

A bill to end the municipal ownership of the airport, dating back to the day it was opened in 1938, was put before the Houses of Parliament. The plan is that the airport becomes a private company, with the City Council retaining less than their present share. The Conservatives, who want to scrap the Greater Manchester Council, believe their share should be expanded and then floated to employees and the public, but two days after saying this, the bill was defeated at the first hurdle.

During his recent visit to Britain, the President of US-airline People Express was asked by MP's about the possibility of starting flights from Manchester. They currently operate a no-frills Gatwick-New York service and have already held talks with Manchester Airport. A licence would have to be sought and any intention of British Airways and British Midland in starting services on the route would need to be clarified, factors which could prove a deterrent to any interest!

Equipment changes/notes on scheduled flights included Air Ecosse almost exclusively operating all flights with SD-330s G-BGNA, G-BITV & G-BKSV; British Caledonian used Dan-Air BAC 1-11 G-AXYD on various flights (1st/2nd/13th/14th/15th/16th/19th/23rd/26th/27th); Loganair operated British Air Ferries Viscount G-AOHM on all Edinburgh flights during the month; Lufthansa (LH074): B.727s D-ABCI (18th) & D-ABKS (14th) and Swissair (SR842): DC-9-51 HB-ISW (2nd).

RAF ILS traffic identified included Hawks XX171 & XX224 (both-16th); Dominie XS734 (8th); C-130s XV181 (23rd) & XV301 (18th); Dominie XS730 (6th); Andover XS641 (17th) and an unidentified Royal Navy Jetstream as 'Navy 565' at 1012 (9th). Civil ILS traffic included Cessna 152s G-BHCX (5th), G-BHRB (9th); Cessna 172 G-MALK (5th/25th) and two British Aerospace aircraft, Jetstream G-JSSD (7th) & BAe.748 G-BGJV (21st).

3rd The only military visitor in an uninspiring month was UAS Manchester RAF Bulldog XX615, arriving from RAF Woodvale at 1047 today as 'WYY08', before returning later in the day operating in the opposite direction.

4th Beech 200 G-FOOD, recently acquired by the food-chain Tesco, made the first of three visits to Manchester this month, on a return flight from Leavesden.

9th British Airways B.757 G-BIKJ (BA4492 from Heathrow), had trouble with its leading edge controls but managed to land safely, although at 30kts faster than normal!

10th Heavylift Belfast G-BEPE, arriving at 2022 today (NP749 from Montpellier), was on an IBM charter bringing computer equipment into Manchester.

11th Boeings latest airliner the 767 made its first visit today courtesy of Britannia Airways, when G-BKVZ arrived from Teeside on a crew training and familiarisation flight, before departing the following day for Liverpool.

13th The winter hibernation of myself and other enthusiasts was awoken, when the airport sprang to life for the first time in three months, with a number of fog diversions. Forty-one arrived over the next three days, starting with eleven today. Apart from the rare appearance at Manchester of an Air Bridge Carriers Argosy, when G-BEOZ arrived on diversion from Liverpool at 2255 (AK719 from Belfast), there was nothing else of interest today.

14th A couple of diversions worthy of note arrived at Manchester today, when Liverpool was affected by fog for the second day running. Aer Lingus SD-330 EI-BEH arrived at 1943 (EI198) from Liverpool) and Cessna 404 D-IBFL arrived at 1954 from Cologne.

15th Today was the third in a row of weather affected operations at various airports. Manchester handled twenty-two aircraft from airports such as Birmingham, Coventry, East Midlands, Leeds, Liverpool, Luton & Mildenhall! Most weren't noteworthy but amongst the diversions were three first visits: two from East Midlands were Falcon 20 I-EKET at 0849 (from Milan-Malpensa) & Iberia Boeing 727 EC-CBG at 1349 (AO1190 from Palma) and one from Mildenhall, which was probably the best of the bunch, was Jet24 Boeing 707 N3238S (BL27 from McGuire AFB) arriving at 0953 operating a US Forces family flight. This aircraft was ex-Sabena OO-SJN, which was sold to Jet24 in October 1982, before being repossessed by Sabena in 1985. Also diverting in twice during the day was Euroair Viscount G-AOHV, operating a newly launched Coventry-Paris passenger service (CD102 at 1034 & CD104 at 2116). It's a pity the major London airports escaped the worst of today's weather, or Manchester could have seen many more diversions!

16th Cessna 335 F-GCQH, arriving at 0859 today on a round-trip from Pontoise, was also a first visit of type. It's basically an unpressurised version of the already successful Cessna 340. The type was certified in 1979, but only sixty-four were built from 1979-1980.

16th Minerve SE.210 Caravelle F-GATZ arrived from Bordeaux with the French Rugby League team, for their match with England at Headingley, before departing on the 18th.

18th Its going to take a long time to beat today's non-arrival! At 1041 USAF C-5 Galaxy 00464, the world's biggest aircraft type, frightened the life out of the writer in his 14th floor flat and numerous shoppers in Stockport, with its sheer size after performing an ILS and overshoot. Routing from Mildenhall to Prestwick, it was operating at a lower cruising level due to a pressurisation problem and because he was low, ATC asked if the pilot was prepared to carry out a radar approach at Manchester, as not only would this help a controller who was training at the time, it would also give them a 'birds-eye' view of the mighty C-5! Reports in the local press afterwards described people as 'Gazing open-mouthed as the colossal aircraft screamed overhead'. They added that Labour Councillors were said to be furious over the transport plane that "buzzed" Manchester Airport, fearing that the routine ILS approach could have been something more sinister, as it may have been carrying Cruise Missiles.

20th BAe.125s G-AVRG & G-BKUW, currently operated by British Aerospace, arrived during the evening for a company meeting in Manchester. BAE.125-800 G-BKUW is a new variant of the successful corporate jet and was a first visit of type. It differs from earlier models due to an increased wingspan, streamlined nose, tail fin extension, increased fuel capacity and up-rated engines. It's also the first corporate jet with EFIS (Electronic Flight Instrument System), which means the display technology is electronic, rather than the traditional electromechanical display. Another BAE.125 making its first visit this month, was G-BKAJ on the 24th (formerly G-AYNR with McAlpine Aviation), which was also operated by British Aerospace.

21st Beech 55 G-WOOD, arriving from Fairoaks at 0924 today, was formerly G-AYID. In its previous identity, it was the second aircraft to be used by Eric Raffles as 'Raffles One', the first being Beech 95 G-ASZC, a regular visitor to Manchester in the late-1960s/early 1970's. Also today was G-IBLL, a revised Rockwell 690D known as the Jetprop 900D, with improved pressurisation and an internal rear cabin extension. Operated by Imperial Breweries & Leisure, better known as Courage Brewery, it was on a round trip from Fairoaks.

21st This evenings Genair newspaper flight was operated by Blackpool-based Spacegrand Aviation, with Twin Otter G-BGMD until the 24th.

24th British Airways were affected by a 24-hour cabin crew strike, which meant that all Manchester flights were cancelled and several European flights were sub-chartered to other operators. Hapag-Lloyd Boeing 727 D-AHLS operated this evenings Dusseldorf flight, arriving at 1823 as BA1953. TEA Boeing 737 OO-TEN was used on the Brussels flight (BA921/0) and Martinair MD-82 operated the Amsterdam flight (BA931/0), which was also a first visit.

25th Britannia Airways unveiled its newest airliner, when Boeing 767 G-BKVZ arrived at 1432 today (BY282BF from Luton). It made its first revenue flight the following day as BY426A to Faro, departing at 0934 with 264 passengers onboard.

27th French Navy PA-31 No.227 passed through Manchester twice today, arriving at 1131 routing Cherbourg-Kinloss as 'F-YDAZ' and again at 1918, operating in the opposite direction.

March 1984

The airport opened the new £250,000 bus station on the 2nd, providing half-hourly links with Piccadilly Station, Victoria Station and Chorlton St. Bus Station. The eventual plan is to build a rail-link connecting the airport and the London mainline. Further schemes include a £4.1m extension to the Arrivals Lounge, £3.7m on extending the Departure Lounge to include new duty-free areas, improved bussing facilities for passengers, new operations Control Tower, increased check-in desks to 57, a £5.4m extension to Pier C and commencement of the new £7.9m cargo village.

The first two months of the year saw a 21% increase in passenger numbers and a 17% increase in freight over the same period last year.

The CAA gave Loganair the go-ahead to fly services between Glasgow-Manchester, complementing their existing services to Edinburgh Belfast City. The Glasgow-based airline will operate Fokker F.27s on the new route and be in direct competition with British Airways.

Equipment changes/notes on scheduled flights included Air Ecosse operating SD-330s on passenger flights WG700/1 & WG778/9 with G-BITV & BKSV throughout; British Caledonian used Dan-Air BAC 1-11s G-ATTP (25th) & G-AXYD (12th/20th/21st/28th)27th); Guernsey Airlines (GE725): British Air Ferries Herald G-ASVO (2nd/4th) & Viscount G-AOYO (18th); Loganair continued operating British Air Ferries Viscount G-AOHM on all Edinburgh flights this month as well as British Midland SD-360 G-BMAJ on LC256/7 (18th); Lufthansa (LH074): B.727 D-ABGI (15th); Manx Airlines used Viscount G-AZNA (24th) & Air UK Fokker F.27 G-BCDO (4th-11th) and Swissair (SR842): DC-9-51 HB-ISN (20th).

RAF ILS traffic identified included Hawks XX171 (16th) & XX224 (16th); C-130s XV196 (22nd) & XV219 (22nd); Dominies XS710 (14th), XS729 (6th), XS730 (26th) & XS736 (9th); Jetstreams XX493 (14th), XX494 (30th) & XX495 (14th); Tornados ZA320 (23rd/26th) & ZA362 (23rd); Andover XS641 (7th) & French Air Force Transall F.91 FM0103 Lyneham-Edinburgh at 1042 (14th); German Air Force Tornado 43+06 as CTM24 at 1324 (26th) & Italian Air Force Tornado MM55000 as CTM24 at 1118 (27th), both these flights originated from RAF Cottesmore. Civil ILS traffic included PA-28 G-BCGS (3rd), PA-27 G-AYWG (16th), Cessna 152 G-BHRB (10th), Cessna 172s G-BEUX (3rd) & G-MALK (10th) and Sabena Xingu OO-SXC (30th).

1st The arrival from Gatwick of British Airtours L.1011 Tristar G-BBAJ, was the first of numerous publicity flights outbound to Nice, in connection with next month's launch of the Austin Rover Montego. Others during the month were British Airways L.1011 G-BBAG (3rd); British Airtours L.1011s G-BBAJ (7th/9th) & G-BEAM (11th); British Island Airways BAC 1-11 G-AXOX (19th/20th) and British Midland B.707 G-BFLD (23rd/25th).

2nd More than forty staff employed by the handling company, Servisair, who work on the apron carrying out such jobs as aircraft cleaning and towing, walked out today over work being allocated to temporary staff. They are supported by twenty-eight cargo staff, but other Servisair employees, including those on check-in and administration, are still working and flights continued as normal. The strike was finally called off on the 14th.

2nd Ford Motor Co Gulfstream 1 G-BRAL (FD843 from Stansted) landed at Manchester on its second attempt, due to strong crosswinds.

5th Monarch Airlines flight OM781 from Malaga, had the benefit of the Boeing 757s Cat.III capabilities this morning and landed in thick fog. Monarch is the first British independent to be fully approved by the CAA for automatic landing at the UK's airports.

6th CAA BAe.748 made a total of thirty-six ILS runs between 1105 and 1430 today!

6th A new type making its first appearance at Manchester was the Slingsby T67, a two-seat aerobatic training aircraft, which made its first flight in 1974. G-BJXB arrived on a round trip from Barton today and another, G-BJNG, appeared from Blackpool on the 8th. Built in Kirkbymoorside, North Yorkshire, it was originally known as a Fournier RF-6 before the designer, Rene Fournier, sold the rights in 1981.

7th Falcon 50 N299W was the first aircraft to arrive at Manchester from its American namesake, Manchester in New Hampshire. It was also the first of three Falcon 50s making their debuts at Ringway this year.

8th Gulfstream 3 HZ-AFL, arriving at 1128 today (SV7180 from Le Bourget), was in full Saudi colours. It was making its first visit to Manchester, bringing in the Saudi Minister of Finance, who was visiting a colleague undergoing medical treatment at the Alexandra Hospital, Cheadle.

10th The Saturday evening newspaper flights which first started in 1982, are currently being operated by McAlpine Aviation Cessna 441s, with G-BJYB & G-BLCL being used on this evenings flights.

14th In another month devoid of any interesting military visitors, apart from the ILS variety, Army Air Corps Beaver XV270 operated as Army 364, from/to Belfast in the early hours.

14th Despite their age, SE.210 Caravelle's still make occasional visits to Manchester and Air Charter example F-BJEN (ex-Finnair OH-LSC) made its first visit today, operating an outbound flight to Alicante as SF337.

18th March 1984 – Seen here on a pleasant Sunday afternoon, is a diverse collection of British airlines at Manchester. Of note is that British Airways & Britannia Airways had both dropped the 'Airways' part of their titles at this point. (Geoff Ball)

14th Cessna Citation 501 G-GENE, currently operated by Yorkshire-based ABI Caravans, made a return flight from its Humberside base today.

14th An interesting demonstration flight was today's arrival of Singapore Airlines B.747SUD (Stretched Upper Deck) N118KD at 1120 (SQ743 from Heathrow). The airline is still negotiating with the UK and Singapore Governments for permission to operate into Manchester without capacity restrictions. The current stance is that they can operate from Manchester, if they reduce the frequency of their Heathrow flights accordingly, something the airline is not prepared to do!

14th The airport was subjected to a simulated plane crash today, in order to test its rescue services. Thirty-four ambulances were scrambled in response to a practice message that a Trident inbound from Antwerp had crashed on landing. Seven fire engines and thirty-five firemen from nearby stations bolstered the airports own tenders. The 107 passengers and crew, played by Army Cadet Volunteers, were taken to Wythenshawe and Withington hospitals, so they could practice handling large numbers of casualties. The exercise lasted for three hours, ending with a 'casualty' list of 4 killed, 100 hurt, 27 with minor injuries and 3 uninjured.

16th Noel Edmonds arrived from Staverton today in his latest acquisition, AS.350 Squirrel G-NOEI.

19th March 1984 - Spantax CV-990 EC-BZO arrived at 1816 today as BX021, with Spanish side Barcelona FC, before eventually departing on the 22nd as BX022. Having been beaten in Barcelona 2-0 on the 7th, Manchester Utd would face them again for the return leg of the European Cup-Winners Cup on the 21st. In front of more than 58,000 fans, they achieved the improbable, by overcoming the two goal deficit and winning 3-0, therefore advancing into the semi-finals for the first time since 1969, resulting in another two-legged tie, this time with Juventus. This aircraft is now one of only three still operated by the airline, from a peak of twelve in 1979. (Geoff Ball)

22nd BAe.125s clearing customs from/to Hawarden are still relatively rare at Manchester, but today produced a good one and a first visit. Nigerian Petroleum BAe.125-700 5N-AVJ arrived from Hawarden at 1308 on a night-stop, before proceeding for Alicante the next day.

22nd RAF Gazelle XW906 made a brief stop at Manchester today, as SYN52 to undertake a crew change, en route from RAF Shawbury to Liverpool.

23rd British Midland DC-9 G-BMAG operated a round-trip publicity flight to Belfast Harbour today, taking company officials to the Shorts factory where the British Midland Group, which includes Manx Airlines & Loganair, were taking delivery of four new SD-360s: G-ISLE & G-LEGS for Manx Airlines, G-BMAR for BMA and G-BLGB for Loganair.

24th Swissair DC-9F HB-IFW operated its final Manchester-Zurich cargo flight (SR847) today. The aircraft was sold in April to Airborne Express as N931AX.

25th Air Atlantique DC-3 G-AMCA operated from/to Blackpool on a crew training flight.

26th The month saw three charters operated by Finnair from/to Helsinki, with Douglas DC-9-51s. OH-LYP arrived at 0958 today (KR3223/4), OH-LYS as KR3225/6 (28th) & DC-9-51 OH-LYR as KR3227/8 (30th).

27th Air Bridge Carriers took over the Zurich cargo flights previously operated by Swissair, but the timings and frequency of the service remains unchanged. Their first flight today was operated by Merchantman G-APES.

28th The Milk Cup replay at Maine Road, Manchester between Everton and Liverpool generated a football charter this afternoon, when Aer Lingus SD-330 EI-BEH operated as EI4210/1. In keeping with the Wembley final played three days earlier, the replay was just as dour, with Liverpool managing to score the only goal of the game.

31st March 1984 – British Caledonian A.310 G-BKWT is seen here on its first visit to Manchester today, operating BR985/992, resplendent in freshly painted colours. Delivered new on the 20th of this month, this aircraft operated a number of Gatwick schedules until May, but it was used primarily on the airlines services to various African destinations. Its career with British Caledonian was short-lived however, as it was sold to Libyan Arab in August 1986. Their second aircraft, G-BKWU, made its first visit to Manchester on the 14th May. (Ian Barrie)

30th The first diversion session of the year involving Heathrow flights was today, with the arrival of three unremarkable B.747s: British Airways G-AWNB at 0904 (BA072 from Toronto) & G-BDPV at 0707 (BA006 from Anchorage) and TWA B.747 N53110 at 0842 (TW700 from New York).
31st The last RAF unit still flying Avro Vulcan's, No.50 Squadron, was disbanded today at RAF Waddington. The squadron has operated in the tanker role since May 1982 and the last 'appearance' of a Vulcan at Manchester was XL426 on the 29th March 1983.
31st Dan-Air BAE.146 G-BKHT, arriving at 1555 today operating an inbound charter from Nice, was also the first scheduled passenger BAE.146 flight into Manchester. The very first BAE.146 to visit was G-OBAF in January 1983, operating a demonstration flight.

April 1984

Expectations were exceeded when Qantas carried 26,000 passengers between Manchester and Australia in the first year of their twice-weekly operation. Contributing to their success was the amount of freight carried, averaging at 8 tonnes per outbound flight.

The airport approved two schemes for purpose built plane-spotting facilities during the month, subject to several conditions. Enthusiasts are currently using the former Oversley Ford brickworks on the south side of the airport, but now that a property firm has been given the go-ahead for a site with 66 parking spaces, Cheshire County Council have decided they also want to create a viewing park, with a picnic area and room for 150 cars. Which scheme will be successful is down to negotiations between the County Council and the owners of the land.

Equipment changes/notes on scheduled flights included British Caledonian using A.310 G-BKWT (1st/2nd/8th/9th) and Dan-Air BAC 1-11s G-AXYD (1st/4th/5th/27th) & G-TARO (26th) which was also a first visit. Loganair's Edinburgh flights were operated by British Air Ferries Viscount G-AOHM throughout the month, with the following exceptions: British Air Ferries Viscount G-AOYP (18th) & Herald G-ASVO (24th); Lufthansa (LH074): B.727s D-ABFI (27th), D-ABKH (12th) & D-ABKN (6th/10th/15th) and Swissair (SR842): DC-9-51s HB-ISK (1st), HB-ISN (22nd) & HB-ISW (8th).

RAF ILS traffic identified included C-130s XV293 (6th/10th) & XV303 (15th); Dominies XS730 (26th) & XS736 (6th/24th); Jetstream XX493 (27th) plus Andovers XS603 (12th/13th) & XS641 (13th). German Air Force Tornado 43+06 overshot as CTM05 at 1433 (17th) and an unidentified RAF Gazelle overshot at 2243 as SYN 51 (30th). Civil ILS traffic included CAA BAe.748 G-AVXI (9th); PA-28s G-AVSA (3rd) & G-BCGS (14th); PA-23 G-AYWG (14th); PA-32 G-BGFD (3rd); Cessna 152 G-BHRB (5th/12th/15th/25th); Cessna 172s G-BEUX (11th), G-BHNU (21st) & G-MALK (12th/16th) and Jodels G-AWWO (26th) & G-BKOV (22nd).

Airlines making changes to their summer schedules included Air Ecosse adding a fourth weekday Aberdeen flight, with the inbound leg operating via Liverpool and Air Portugal returning to Manchester with a weekly Monday flight to Lisbon/Faro with B.727s. British Caledonian will operate lunchtime flight (BR625/6) from/to Brussels via Gatwick and Cyprus Airways will operate three-weekly to Larnaca, peaking at four in August/September with a mix of A.310 & B.707 aircraft and weekly flight to Paphos on Tuesdays with B.707s. Dan-Air will introduce a weekly Zurich service from 14th May and Guernsey Airlines will operate up to four-weekly flights with Viscounts, which represents a reduction on last year's operation. Iberia will operate six-weekly to Madrid and daily between 20th August-20th September, with three flights via Malaga and four via Barcelona. KLM morning flight (KL153/4) is now daily, as is the lunchtime (KL155/6) except for Saturdays. Loganair will introduce a weekday Glasgow service from the 24th September and Manx Airlines will operate three-times daily to Ronaldsway, with two on Saturdays. SAS no longer operate cargo flights, but the six-weekly passenger flights continue from/to Copenhagen, with two proceeding onwards to/from Dublin. Finally, Swissair's five-weekly cargo operation from/to Zurich has been taken over by Air Bridge Carriers operating as SR847 throughout, with the inbound continuing via Glasgow.

1st April 1984 – Jersey Air Ferries Viscount G-AOYP is seen here operating GE725/4 on behalf of Guernsey Airlines, in revised titles. It was sold in 1989 to British World and re-registered as G-PFBT in 1994. (Geoff Ball)

2nd Hot on the heels of British Caledonian introducing their Airbus A310s into service, Cyprus Airways made first visits this month with their recently delivered aircraft, 5B-DAQ today & 5B-DAR (7th), which will become regular visitors to Manchester.

6th Although British Midland are not uncommon at Manchester, flights by their Douglas DC-9s are, but this evening DC-9 G-BMAG positioned in from Heathrow to operate a charter to Amsterdam as BD8414 the following day, before returning as BD8415 (8th).

7th This month's selection of British oldies included two PA-28 Cherokees. Registered new in 1966, G-ATRR arrived from/to Ronaldsway today and G-ATMW from/to Blackpool on the 15th. Some of the others were 1964 PA-30 Twin Comanche G-ASRH from/to Ronaldsway (17th), 1962 PA-23 Apache G-ARJT from/to Coal Aston (25th) and 1965 PA-24 Comanche G-ATJL White Waltham/Oxford (26th). Staying on the subject of light aircraft, although Fuji 200 G-FUJI was UK-registered in 1979 the type is quite rare, but this aircraft operated a round trip from Luton (29th).

8th Today was the final visit to Manchester of Heron G-ANUO, which had been a regular visitor to Manchester over many years, operated by British Nuclear Fuels. It was sold to Aces High in October 1982 and then to Fairoaks based Topflight Aviation in September 1983, who used it for business and charter work until 1988.

8th The Cessna 180 is a four/six seat, fixed gear light aircraft, produced between 1953 and 1981. Many are still used as personal aircraft and in utility roles, such as bush flying. Some were fitted with floats for landing on water and Cessna 180H G-BKMM, arriving at Manchester today on a flight from Exeter to Dublin, was one such aircraft.

9th Meridiana DC-9-51 I-SMEI made a first visit of both airline and aircraft today, bringing Juventus FC into Manchester.

11th This evenings European Cup-Winners Cup semi-final match at Old Trafford, between Manchester Utd and Juventus, attracted several extra flights. These included Aer Lingus B.707 EI-ASO, arriving at 1346 (EI4208 from Dublin), on the very last visit of an Aer Lingus B.707 to Manchester. Light aircraft visitors were Cessna 337 EI-AVC, Cessna 210 EI-BLJ and Fiat owned Falcon 20 I-EKET, cutting it fine for the start of the match by arriving at 1810. The game proved disappointing for United, ending in a 1-1 draw. The return at Turin two weeks later saw Juventus finishing off the job, beating United 2-1 and ending their European dreams of winning a European title for the first time since 1968. Juventus were to play Portuguese side Porto on the 16th May, which they won 2-1, so maybe it was no disgrace that Manchester Utd lost out to the eventual winners of the trophy!

12th A firemen's dispute at Woodford was the reason for this evening's visit of Shorts SD-330 demonstrator, G-BDBS, which night-stopped before departing for Hawarden the following morning.

13th BAE Dove G-ARBE operated from/to Brough today, due to the lack of fire cover at Woodford. The last time this aircraft visited Manchester was on 31st October 1978. Having operated for the Aerospace manufacturer since 1965, it would continue with them for another two years.

14th Cessna Citation 500 D-ICCC, arriving at 2237 today from Saarbrucken, was the first of three biz-jets making their first visits to Manchester during the month.

14th April 1984 – Transamerica DC-8 N4865T, seen here on departure from Manchester for San Diego via Bangor, has been converted into a -73 series, noticeable by the larger engines. (Geoff Ball)

16th Possibly best known for being a loyal BAe.125 customer over the years, McAlpine Aviation also operate a Citation 500, G-BKSR, which made its first visit to Manchester today on a round trip to Prestwick, before positioning out later to Hatfield.

17th An abundance of Canadian Air Force flights during the month, started with CC-130E 130307 at 1048 today as CAM6590 (Halifax, Nova Scotia/Edinburgh). This month's set of three were 130315 (CAM515-24th), 130320 (CAM516-26th) & 130320 (CAM517-28th), which all night-stopped routing Trenton-Lahr. Also on the 28th was the first Canadian Air Force CC-130H to visit, 130331 at 1104 as CAM6409, in full camouflage colours rather than the regular silver/white/grey scheme, which night-stopped en route Trenton-Lahr.

17th PA-44 Seminole G-BGCO arrived from Dunsfold at 1050 today, due to the continuing fireman's strike at Woodford. Used as a liaison aircraft between the various BAE factories, it departed later for Warton.

17th Lear Jet 35 N37962 arriving at 1913 today from Paris-Orly, was on its only visit to Manchester, night-stopping before departing for Leeds the following day at 1300.

18th Another flight destined for Woodford, RAE Bassett XS765 (Evergreen 16 from Boscombe Down), arrived at 0952 today due the strike. Also this morning was RAE Andover XS606, arriving for a short stay at Dan-Air engineering.

19th Aircraft shortages affecting Britannia Airways seem to be a common occurrence at this time of year. Braathens B.737 LN-SUI was sub-chartered today to operate the following days BY221A/B to/from Rome and first time visitor Air Belgium B.737 OO-PLH was also used on another round trip to Rome, as BY737A/B (23rd).

23rd French operator Minerve started a short series of flights, from/to Tarbes on Mon/Fri. The first today was operated by SE.210 Caravelle F-BRGU and again on the 27th.

25th The only French military flight this month, was French Air Force Xingu No.107/F-SECV (FA397 Dinard/Cambrai). Arriving at 1503 today, it stayed for just over an hour.

26th Dan-Air's new BAC 1-11, G-TARO, made its first visit operating on behalf of British Caledonian. Although it served with Dan-Air for almost eighteen months, it was never based at Manchester, but it could be seen operating for British Caledonian on a 'w' pattern flight for Dan-Air or as a maintenance visitor. In December 1985 it was sold to Tarom as YR-BCO.

29th Today saw the start of a new Manchester-New York cargo service, organised by a consortium of freight forwarders, operated by Transamerica for an initial period of five months. DC-8F N4868T, capable of carrying 42 tonnes of cargo, operated the first flight.

30th The BN-2 Islander is not too common these days, but Manchester received two today! BN-2B G-BLEC operated by LEC Refrigeration arrived from East Midlands and BN-2T G-OPBN, owned and operated by the makers, Pilatus Britten-Norman, routed from/to Bembridge.

May 1984

Passenger figures saw a 16% increase in the first quarter and when freight traffic was up 14% over the same period, the authorities took the opportunity of providing further details of the new cargo village, when Manchester played host to a major air-cargo conference and exhibition.

An extensive review of all routes is being undertaken by the CAA, following pressure from independent's such as British Caledonian, to cream off some of the more successful routes. British Airways have refuted claims that all services from Manchester, including the Shuttle, are at risk.

Equipment changes/notes on scheduled flights included Air Portugal using B.707 CS-TBC to operate TP876/878 (20th); British Caledonian (BR987): A.310s G-BKWT (9th) and first visit G-BKWU (14th/21st), plus British Island Airways BAC 1-11s G-CBIA (1st) & G-AXLN (2nd); Loganair operated BAF Viscounts G-AOHM on all Edinburgh services (1st-4th) & G-AOYR

(8th-11th) and thereafter F.27 G-IOMA returned to service with the airline; Lufthansa (LH074): B.727 D-ABKG (9th); Manx Airlines used Air UK F.27 G-BLGW (18th) and Swissair (SR842): DC-9-51 HB-ISN (27th).

Extensive RAF ILS traffic included Hawks XX175 (1st) & XX179 (22nd); C-130s XV185 (3rd) & XV186 (16th); Dominie XS713 (1st); Jetstreams XX491 (9th), XX492 (4th), XX493 (14th), XX494 (14th) & XX496 (8th/10th) and Royal Navy example XX497 (9th/11th); Andover XS641 (18th) and Gazelle XX406 (31st). Further Tornados also performed ILS manoeuvres, with two from the RAF: ZA362 overshooting at 1015 as CTM24 & ZA365 at 1025 as CTM28 (both-29th). A further RAF example ZA320 overshot at 1011 as CTM25, as did Italian Air Force example MM-5500 at 1917 as CTM28 (both-30th). Civil ILS traffic included CAA BAe.748 G-AVXI (10th), Cessna 152 G-BHRB (4th), Cessna 172 G-MALK (8th), PA-31 Navajo G-BEYY (29th) and Ralleye G-BFMS (31st).

The following airlines have summer IT programmes from Manchester: Aeroflot, Air Malta, Air Portugal, Aviaco, Aviogenex, Balkan, EL AL, Inex-Adria, JAT, LOT, Tarom & Tunis Air; as do a variety of UK operators: Air Europe, Air UK, Britannia Airways, British Air Ferries, British Airtours, British Airways, British Island Airways, British Midland, Dan-Air, Monarch Airlines & Orion Airways. Airlines operating regular summer flights to the USA/Canada are British Airtours (Los Angeles, Newark & Orlando), British Midland (Vancouver), Transamerica (New York), Wardair (Calgary, Edmonton, Toronto & Vancouver) and Worldways (Toronto). Looking closer at some UK operators, Monarch have B.737s G-DGDP & G-DWHH back on-line after their winter lease in Canada and they have also leased ex-Air Florida example N52AF as G-GPAA for the summer. British Airtours operated a number of Air Europe B.737s during the winter, which have been returned and from early this month the Manchester based examples were replaced by British Airtours aircraft again, who also used British Airways Tridents/BAC 1-11s on a number of flights during the month. Finally, having disposed of B.737s G-BOSL & G-OSLA last year, Britannia found themselves short of aircraft, resulting in a number of Manchester flights being sub-chartered by TEA & Air Belgium B.737s.

2nd Cessna 421 Golden Eagle G-AXAW, which has been on the British register since new in 1969, is now owned and operated by Stansted based Heavylift in their full colours.

3rd The French military operated four flights through Manchester this month. Two were Transall flights F.91/F-RAZI FM0131 Lyneham-Brussels today and F.55/F-RAZC FM0109 Lyneham-Edinburgh (28th). The others were French Navy Xingu No.066 operating Cardiff-Aberdeen as FA050 (14th) and French Air Force Xingu No.080/F-TEYF, operating Dinard-Chambery as FA397 (28th).

5th The latest new type making its first visit to Manchester was the Dornier 228, with LN-HPA arriving at 0106 today from Stavanger, on an oil related charter. It's a fourth production example, German built and based on the successful Dornier Do.28 Skyservant. The Do.228 first flew in 1981, entered service in 1982 and is used extensively by the German military.

5th Herald G-AYMG made its first visit today with its new operator, diverting in at 0446 (SKD006 from Stansted). Formerly operated by Air UK, it was sold in May 1983 to Securicor for cargo work based out of Birmingham.

5th American-airline Transamerica will be well represented this month. From today and on each Saturday throughout the summer, they will operate a weekly passenger charter to New York. DC-8 N4865T operated today's, but from the 19th the flight will be upgraded to a Boeing 747. The airline will also operate a weekly cargo flight to New York on Sundays.

5th The Beech 99 has never been a common aircraft at Manchester. Derived from the company's successful models, the King & Queen Air, it has an extended fuselage capable of carrying up to seventeen passengers. It was fully certified in 1968 and deliveries began the same year, with LN-LMT being the first example to visit Manchester on 27th October 1970. This month produced two different examples, starting with today's appearance of Niteflight's G-NIUT, the only one to ever appear on the UK register. It arrived from Luton on a freight flight, but unfortunately the company ceased trading later in the month and the aircraft was soon sold in Germany. The second, D-IEXA, arrived from Gatwick and operated a return freight flight to Dublin (23rd).

6th British Airtours sub-chartered BCAL Charter DC-10 G-BJZD to operate the first Orlando flight of their summer programme, departing at 1314 today as BR5737.

7th May 1984 – Air Europe are basing a B.757 at Manchester for the summer season, after taking delivery of their first last year. Against the back-drop of the work in progress to extend Pier C, G-BKRM is seen being pushed back from Stand 22 for its departure to Las Palmas as AE852. This aircraft was originally destined for British Airways as G-BIKE. (Geoff Ball)

9th Finnair operated two charters this month with DC-9-51 OH-LYN, which arrived at 1102 today as KR3289 (Amsterdam-Geneva) and again on the 12th as KR3292 (Gothenburg-Amsterdam).

11th Today was the start of the Barton Air Show weekend, but visitors to Manchester in connection with the event were well down on previous years. Royal Navy Wasp XS562 popped over from Barton for fuel, before returning there thirty minutes later. Two-seater RAF Jaguar XX143 arrived from RAF Coltishall (12th) in preparation for its participation the following afternoon and returned after its display, before finally leaving for RAF Lossiemouth on the 14th. RAF Harrier XZ967 which also arrived after its display at Barton (13th), refuelled before departing for RAF Kemble. RAF C-130 XV178 arrived at 1348 (13th) transporting the Falcons parachute team and finally vintage-Provost G-AWPH made a return trip from Woodley to take part in the show (13th).

12th RAF Tristar 500 ZD952 arrived at 1942 (RR3852A from Brussels), returning troops back from the Continent. It was making its first visit and the second overall of a RAF Tristar. Other UK military movements were BAe.125s XW788 (RR1872 from/to RAF Cranwell–3rd) & ZD703 (RR1735 Heathrow/Northolt-9th) and Army Air Corps Beaver XP825 (27th).

13th The 150th Boeing 747 to visit Manchester was today's arrival of British Airtours G-BDXL, operating KT201 outbound to Orlando.

14th Dan-Air inaugurated a new service today, with BAC 1-11 G-ATPJ operating the first daily Zurich flight (DA875/6).

15th Today's first visit of Citation 500 D-IMLN, was one of two biz-jets making their debuts at Manchester this month. The other, Gulfstream 2 N289K (16th) routing Birmingham-Prestwick, was operated by Crawford Engineering, owners of a number of factories in the UK.

15th Another regular visitor to Manchester since its registration in 1973 was PA-23 Aztec G-BBST, now operated by Thurston Aviation, but its return flight from Stansted today was its final one. It took part in a mid-air photo-shoot of Beech 1900 N305BH at the annual Hanover Air Show on the 20th, only to be involved in a tragic accident when the aircraft collided. The Beech 1900 managed a safe landing, but the crew onboard the PA-23 were both killed.

16th Lego Industries of Denmark brought their latest corporate aircraft into Manchester today, when Beech 200 OY-BVL arrived at 1706 from/to Billund, for an overnight stay.

17th Dan-Air BAC 1-11 G-BCXR (DA4807 from Faro) declared an emergency today, after shutting down one of its engines whilst on approach.

18th After just two years service with Monarch Airlines, B.737 G-BJSO made its last visit to Manchester today (OM541/0 from/to Naples), before returning to its leasing company. Re-registered G-GPAB and leased to Orion Airways for the summer, it made its first visit as such on the 27th, operating in basic Monarch colours with an Orion tail and titles.

22nd Former British Airways and British Air Ferries Viscount G-AOHT, now operated by commuter operator Euroair, made its first visit as such today from Gatwick as EZ455, before departing later in the day on a charter to Sonderborg. It also operated a flight for Guernsey Airlines on the 26th.

22nd A 'phobia flight' organised by British Airways to help cure the fear of flying was welcomed by jittery travellers, but when it came to the crunch, the mile-high aversion therapy proved to be too scary! When only forty-four brave fliers forked out the £20 fare for the hour-long flight, the first of its kind from Manchester, it was cancelled as a full load was needed to cover the operational costs.

23rd Since SAS withdrew its cargo operation to Copenhagen in December 1983, Fred Olsen Electra's are no longer common visitors to Manchester, but LN-FOI arrived from Stockholm today to operate a one-off cargo flight to Oslo.

23rd Another interesting freight flight was Nigeria Airways B.707F 5N-ABJ (WT762 from Lagos) at 1700. It stayed overnight, before departing back to Lagos as WT763 with spares for the Nigerian Air Force Jaguar fleet. B.707F 5N-ABJ operated a further flight on the 27th (WT766/7 from/to Lagos).

26th RAF C-130 XV299 arrived at 1625 today, in connection with the Falcon Display Team's participation in the Congleton Carnival.

27th Dan-Air commenced a weekly summer BAE.146 charter to Biarritz, which positions in from Teeside to operate DA4582/3, before returning to Newcastle. The first operated by G-BKHT today, was also the first of the season, so there was no return flight.

28th Balkan operated an extra IT flight during the early hours, with first time visitor TU-134 LZ-TUZ (Bourgas/Sofia) as LZ917A/918A.
28th A couple of familiar visitors passing through Manchester, en route for their annual summer stint in warmer climes, were PA-23 Aztec's N40375 & N200RD, routing from Keflavik and onwards to Saragossa the following morning.
31st British Midland DC-9 G-BMAA, arriving at 0340 (BD8514 from Rome), was returning Liverpool fans after bagging yet another European Cup Final, beating FC Roma 4-2 on penalties. The outward bound fans due to depart Manchester the previous morning, were already in the Departure Lounge with their duty-frees, when they were notified that their aircraft had been unable to land due to fog and they were being coached to Liverpool for their flight. Because of this, their duty-free goods had to be returned, but as many had opened their purchases and were busily consuming them, what was left was confiscated without a refund!
31st Rounding off an eventful month for freight charters was former British Caledonian B.707F G-BDEA, now operated by UK cargo airline Anglo Cargo. Operating as ML228/9 from/to Cairo, it was transporting outbound 30 tonnes of cigarettes. This aircraft saw a further eight years of service with the airline and was even named after one of its Captains, 'Keith Hooper', before being sold to Omega Air in 1992 as EL-AKH.

June 1984

The CAA review of UK aviation recommended that amongst other things, British Airways should give up all their International schedules from Manchester and the provinces, something the airline wasn't prepared to accept. The Airport Authority eventually sided with British Airways, following discussions with the other airlines that had showed interest in some of the routes, but then indicated that not all would be taken up.

The Manchester-New York saga took another unexpected twist this month. British Midland planned to operate the route via Prestwick, but the British Airports Authority who runs Prestwick refused permission. British Midland have now asked the CAA for a licence to operate Manchester-New York direct, on condition that the British Airways licence is revoked. Meanwhile, People Express is holding further talks with Manchester officials about a possible Manchester-Newark service.

Rank Travel, whose subsidiaries include Wings, OSL, Ellerman Sunflight & Planefair, will offer free parking at Manchester worth up to £28.50 for the first time, with their winter programme.

The Bill giving Manchester Airport its rail-link to the main-line has finally been given Royal Assent, but British Rail have stated that much work needs to be carried out before it can go ahead. Once the feasibility studies are completed and the remedial work is done, the job would involve laying 1½ miles of track from the south of Heald Green Station round the airport itself underground and then out again in a loop, linking up with the main-line near Styal Station.

More than £900,000 will be spent on a computerised central control system, enabling automatic entry and exit from the airport's car parks and self-service entry to the spectator terraces. In a bid to boost the airport's parking facilities as 'good value for money', a brand new Austin Montego is being offered as the 1st Prize in a free competition for travellers parking their vehicles at the airport for at least seven consecutive days during the summer. Other news is that the airport has been granted a licence to serve alcoholic drinks landside on Sundays between 2pm and 5pm, times currently prohibited under the present law.

Equipment changes/notes on scheduled flights included British Caledonian operating British Island Airways BAC 1-11s G-AXBB & G-CBIA (8th); Lufthansa (LH074): B.727s D-ABCI (1st), D-ABDI (19th), D-ABHI (16th) & D-ABKB (8th); Manx Airlines used Loganair SD-330 G-BIRN (13th); Sabena (SN617): Passenger B.737s OO-SDA (16th) & OO-SDE (12th) and Swissair (SR842): DC-9-51 HB-ISN (27th).

RAF ILS traffic included Hawk XX347 (14th); C-130 XV211 (5th); Dominie XS713 (1st) and Jetstream XX495 (12th); Royal Navy Sea King XZ594 made two overshoots at 1252/1302 as SHW78 (21st); RAE Comet XS235 at 1058 (21st); BAe.748 G-BCDZ at 1319 (26th) and Italian Air Force Tornado MM-5500 at 0938 as CTM28 (8th). Civil ILS traffic included Cessna 150 G-ATMB (2nd), CAA BAe.748 G-AVXJ (11th), Cessna 152 G-BHRB (13th/28th/29th) and Tiger Moth G-BFHH flying low over the airfield after its departure from Woodford Air Show.

1st Gulfstream 2 N924DS, operated by Diamond Shamrock, arrived at 0927 today on a round trip from Heathrow. This aircraft had visited previously in the guise of N24DS.

1st French charters were plentiful this month and today saw the last of the pilgrimage flights from/to Lourdes by Minerve, operated by SE.210 F-BRGU (FQ0043/4). Air Charter operated a couple of SE.210 flights: F-BJTU (19th) & F-GDFZ (26th) both Paris-Orly/Gatwick as SF579/580, the latter being a first visit as such, as it had been in previously as OH-LSH with Finnair. Finally Uni-Air operated a couple of charters from/to Paris-Le Bourget with F.27s F-GAOT (26th) & F-BYAO (29th), which made a change from the more regular F-BIUK.

3rd Lear Jet 55 F-GDHR arrived at 1512 from Naples, operating an air ambulance flight.

4th Finnair operated no less than five charters from/to Helsinki during the month: DC-9-51 OH-LYN KR3263/4 today, DC-9-41s OH-LNC KR3265/6 (6th) & KR3269/70 (10th), OH-LNE KR3267/8 (8th) and DC-9-51 OH-LYS KR3314/3272 (12th).

4th Falcon 50 N283K owned by Kellogg's, made its first visit this evening calling in for fuel en route Gander-Copenhagen. Another Falcon 50 also making its first visit was N731F the following day, routing Waterford-Heathrow.

5th Early morning low cloud which was stubborn to lift, brought in a number of Leeds/Newcastle diversions, including the first visit of Newcastle based Dan-Air Boeing 737 G-BLDE at 0130 (DA2333 from Palma). The others were Aviogenex TU-134 YU-AHY at 1028 (JJ153 from Pula), BIA BAC 1-11 G-CBIA at 1126 (KD7841 from Edinburgh) & SD-330 G-BGNA (MPL061 from Glasgow), now operating for Metropolitan Airways.

6th Norwegian carrier Busy Bee also operated a number of charters from/to Scandinavia with three different Fokker F.27s: LN-NPH today, LN-NPC (14th) & LN-SUE (16th).

6th SE-DEN, arriving at 1633 from Malmo, was the only Corvette making its first visit to Manchester this year. This aircraft had been in previously as OO-MRF and was withdrawn from use next year.

6th Euroair EMB-110 G-BHJY, arriving at 1829 today (EZ848 from Le Havre), was transporting a number of passengers back from the D-Day celebrations at Dunkirk. The airline also operated flights ferrying Wardair crews to/from Frankfurt via Ostend during the month. Their Viscount G-AOHV, which has been re-registered G-BLNB, made its first visit to Manchester as such on the 16th (EZ892 from Stavanger).

9th Transamerica DC-8 N4866T, which has been converted to a DC-8-73 series, diverted in from Gatwick today.

9th June 1984 – Ex-Dan-Air BAe.748 VR-CBH finally left today, having been present since last September. Named 'Lady Godiva' and re-registered as G-VAJK, the aircraft in full Venture Airlines livery, will be used on the airlines new Coventry-Paris service. (Geoff Ball)

10th June 1984 – Mobil Oil Twin Otter 5A-DBH, arriving from Keflavik at 2116 yesterday, was on its return to Libya after attention at the De Havilland factory at Downsview, Ontario. The southward stop at Manchester was probably due to the pilot having friends in the Urmston area. The aircraft departed the following day, bound for Montpellier. (Geoff Ball)

11th Two BAe.125s making their first visits this month were RAF example ZD621 at 0839 today (RR1497 Northolt-Finningley) & BAe.125-800 G-GAEL operated by Heron Property Managements, arriving from Cambridge at 1047 on the 16th. It was operated by Heron until February 1985, when it was purchased by British Aerospace as a company aircraft.

11th Britannia Airways are suffering from aircraft shortages, particularly on Mondays, so TEA B.737 OOTEL (BY592A/B to/from Corfu) & Balair DC-9 HB-IFZ (BY592A/B to/from Tarbes) were used today. TEA B.737 OO-TEL (BY592A/B to/from Tarbes) & Maersk B.737

OY-APP (BY748A/B to/from Corfu) were operated on the 18th and first time visitor Balair MD-81 HB-INB (BY748A/B to/from Corfu) & TEA B.737 OO-TEL (BY592A/B to/from Tarbes) were operated on the 25th. Their weekly Saturday flight, BY830A/B to/from Reus, has been operated by a British Airways Trident 3 on each occasion during the month and will continue throughout the summer, G-AWZG (30th), G-AWZN (16th), G-AWZP (2nd) & G-AWZZ (9th/23rd).

15th Monarch Airlines B.757 G-MONC (OM419 from Gerona) was due to operate OM420 to Athens, but because of a hydraulic leak it was grounded until a part was specially flown in from the Boeing plant in Seattle, as neither the airline nor any of the other European operators had the necessary spare. The airline made two aircraft substitutions, Spantax CV-990 EC-BZO (OM443/2 from/to Alicante) & Spantax DC-8 EC-CCG (OM423/2), all of which delayed more than 400 passengers for at least 24-hours. They were put up at the nearby Valley Lodge Hotel and a similar load waiting at Athens for the return flight were provided with an extra night's accommodation.

16th June 1984 - Transamerica changed days on their New York passenger charter and today's last Saturday flight was operated by B.747 N480GX, on its first visit to Manchester. This aircraft, in basic Egyptair colours with a white tail, was formerly D-ABYA with Lufthansa and would eventually become N780T. These flights are now operated on Fridays with DC-8s. (Geoff Ball)

17th British Midland B.707 G-BFLE (BD6201 to Toronto) was forced to return to Manchester, after spending several hours dumping fuel to reduce the aircrafts landing weight, due to an undercarriage problem. It eventually left for Toronto at 1926, over five hours late.

17th LOT's latest summer programme from Manchester commenced today, with Ilyushin IL-18 SP-LSF. Weekly flights will operate as LO3009/10 from/to Warsaw until 23rd September.

17th Two light aircraft, Cessna F.182 G-BEZM & Cessna FRA.150L G-BANE, arriving at Manchester to clear customs today, were originally destined for Blackpool.

18th Heavylift Belfast G-BEPS, arriving at 1847 today as NP892, was on the second charter this year courtesy of IBM, bringing further computer equipment into Manchester from Montpellier.

19th Citation 501 I-GERA has finally been Italian registered, after operating for several years as N26498 whilst based in Milan, during which time it made many visits to Manchester.

19th Cessna 206 G-STAT made daily visits until the 22nd, whilst involved with parachute drops at Tatton Park.

19th Army Air Corps Lynx XZ172, operating a return flight from RAF Middle Wallop, was only the third Army Lynx to visit Manchester since XZ192 in 1980.

19th Bond Helicopters AS.365 Dauphin G-BKXV, diverted in direct from a gas rig in Morecambe Bay, after bad weather prevented it from landing at Blackpool.

19th RAE BAC 1-11 ZE433 arrived for attention with Dan-Air Engineering today, with RAE Sea King ZB506 acting as its crew ferry. Recently acquired from Air Pacific, it displayed their basic colours with a military roundel and fin flash. It was eventually rolled out in the RAE's raspberry ripple colour scheme, before departing on the 20th July.

21st Beech 90 D-ICPD called in for fuel at 0530 today, on its way back from the USA via Keflavik.

20th Cessna 182 C-GDHU encountered a belt of thunderstorms en route Prestwick-Biggin Hill, so the pilot requested a diversion into an airfield where he could catch a plane to London. As no reservation was required for the Super Shuttle, Manchester was ideal, so the pilot simply parked up and left for Heathrow. Four days later he returned, jumped into his aircraft and returned to Canada!

20th Two French Military visitors today were French Navy Xingu's 081 (FA052) & 083 (FA083), arriving within five minutes of each other, en route Edinburgh-Amsterdam.

21st Comet XS235, which overshot during the morning, has been used by the Royal Aircraft Establishment for testing radio and radar equipment since being delivered straight off the production line at Chester in 1963. Until its retirement in 1997, it was the last remaining flying Comet, having only clocked up 82,000 hours.

21st More problems with their Boeing 707s, resulted in British Midland terminating the BD6026 Vancouver flight at Prestwick this morning, so Viscount G-BMAT brought the Manchester passengers in as BD8002 this afternoon.

23rd RAF Wessex XT669 made a fuel stop at 1713 today, en route from RAF Coltishall to Belfast.

24th The highlight of this month's crop of single-engine visitors, was 1941-built Beech 17 Staggerwing G-BDGK. Following its arrival from Tatenhill, it spent the whole time parked on the Freight Apron, before departing for Biggin Hill.

28th Queens Flight BAe.748 XS789, arriving at 1655 today (Kitty 2 from Northolt), brought The Duchess of Kent into Manchester to view the airport's development schemes and open the new Check-in Hall.

30th BAE Dove G-ARHW arrived from Dunsfold at 1830 today to night-stop, due to the weekend closure of Woodford; but as their air show was taking place, the airfield was technically open!

July 1984

The airports attempt's to persuade British Rail to build the much-delayed airport rail-link came to nothing this month, after BR's feasibility study concluded it was uneconomical!

A national dock strike resulted in Lufthansa using the larger Boeing 727 on its passenger service on nine occasions, as well as operating an additional cargo flight on top of their five-weekly flights. If Manchester airport workers hadn't come out in support of the action, there would have been many additional freight flights during the month.

British Airways will add Larnaca, Malaga & Munich from Manchester next year and New York has been confirmed, following British Midland's failure to revoke their application.

Equipment changes/notes on scheduled flights start with British Caledonian operating Dan-Air BAe.748 G-ARRW (4th); Lufthansa (LH074): B.727s D-ABCI (24th), D-ABKC (23rd), D-ABKH (17th), D-ABKI (26th), D-ABKJ (15th), D-ABKR (16th) D-ABKS (18th), D-ABLI (21st), & D-ABSI (22nd) and Swissair (SR842): DC-9-51's HB-ISK (3rd), HB-ISL (22nd) & HB-IST (28th).

RAF ILS traffic included Hawks XX179 (5th), XX185 (19th), XX310 (13th) & XX349 (10th); C-130s XV215 (11th) & XV293 (18th); Jetstream XX495 (4th); Andovers XS610 (5th), XS639 (4th) & XS643 (9th); Dominie XS728 (20th); Gazelle XX406 (2nd) and Nimrod XZ283, which overshot at 1834 as Avro 3 (21st). Civil ILS traffic included Lufthansa Beech 90 D-ILHA (5th), Cessna 172 G-BEWR (3rd), Cessna 150 G-BDNR (7th), Cessna 150 G-ATMB (30th) and Cessna 152 G-BHRB (14th/16th/18th/20th); but the highlight was Israeli Air Force B.707 4X-JYS (formerly ex-South African ZS-SAH), overshooting at 1000 as IAF969 from/to Frankfurt on its first visit to Manchester (24th). Goodyear Airship N2A overflew the airport (12th), having just spent the previous week based at Barton.

1st Transavia B.737 PH-TVR, arriving at 1407 today (BU317) from Ronaldsway to Bergen, was operating a flight on behalf of Braathens, who were on strike.

2nd Mondays continue to be interesting for Britannia Airways, as regards sub-charters. B.737s used this month were Eagle Air TF-VLT BY748A/B in full colours today, TEA OO-TEL BY592A/B (today/23rd/30th), Braathens B.737 LN-SUD BY748A/B (16th) and Maersk OY-APP (16th) & OY-APS on its first visit (23rd/30th), both operating BY748A/B.

2nd Due to British Midland being a B.707 short, first visit DC-9 G-BMAM & British Island Airways BAC 1-11 G-AXBB combined to operate Faro-flight BD7831. Further problems on the 26th resulted in Air Malta B.720 9H-AAL operating BD7732/1 from/to Malta.

2nd Bell 206 Jet Rangers G-BIZB & G-JMVB arrived from the Belfry Hotel, Handforth for fuel, before departing for Fairoaks and Elstree respectively.

4th Finnair DC-9-51 OH-LYZ made its first visit to Manchester today, operating Kar-Air's latest fortnightly Helsinki charter flight (KR3011/2) and again on the 18th.

4th The first of two corporate jets making their first visit to Manchester this month was Lear Jet F-GDCP, arriving at 1029 today (Luton/Le Bourget).

5th Early morning fog produced the arrivals of Britannia B.737 G-BKHE, diverting in from Newcastle at 0717 (BY286B from Tenerife) and People Express B.747 N602PE, diverting in from Gatwick at 0728 (PE002 from Newark).

5th Piper PA-18 Super Cub G-BIZV made an unexpected arrival at an International Airport this evening! The crew from the West Country were on their way home from holiday, via the PFA Rally, after venturing as far north as Stornaway. They were destined to call at Barton, but by the time they were in the vicinity the airfield had closed and although some of the airfield staff were present, the Piper was still told to go away!

4th July 1984 – CL-600 Challenger HB-VFW, the third different CL-600 Challenger to visit Manchester, arrived from Gatwick at 0447 today, en route to Cape Verde. Seen here on the first of two visits this year, it operated for Swiss Air Ambulance until 1992. (Geoff Ball)

6th Fords BAC 1-11 G-BEJW arrived for a respray with Dan-Air today and BAC 1-11s G-AWWX & G-TARO arrived for attention on the 13th, after being damaged in a severe thunderstorm at Munich.

7th Tarom operated Ilyushin IL-18 YR-IMJ on IT flight RO763/4 today and on the 14th.

8th RAF VC-10 XR807 arrived at 2122 (RR2491 from Newburgh), on a trooping flight.

9th Condor operated an outbound charter to Athens today (DF874) with B.727 D-ABNI. B.737 D-ABHT arrived the following week at 1313 (DF875) to operate the return flight (16th).

10th Businessman Michael Zeal got a surprise today, when he turned up to check-in at Heathrow for his British Airways Shuttle flight to Manchester. As their 2-millionth Super Shuttle customer since the service was re-launched last November, he received 'Champagne VIP treatment', along with the other 123 passengers onboard Trident 3 G-AWZX (BA4442).

13th Air Atlantique DC-3 G-AMSV positioned in from Stansted to operate an outbound freight flight today (DG132 to Le Havre), in connection with the national dock strike.

13th Liverpool-based Genair, who operate two flights through Manchester, the lunchtime Aberdeen flight on behalf of British Airways (BA5691/4) and the midnight Leuchars newspaper flight ceased trading today. SD-330 G-EASI operated the final Aberdeen flight today, Beech 200 G-WWHL operated the flight from 17th-19th and from then on it was operated by Peregrine AS Jetstreams. The last newspaper flight was operated by EMB-110 G-BHYT (EN507) in the early hours and although Casair continued in the short-term, Spacegrand Aviation Twin Otters took over from the 22nd.

15th 'Standard' EL AL B.707 4X-ATD made the first of several visits during the year, operating charter flight LY5317/8, rather than the regular B.707 4X-ATY.

16th US Army Beech C-12 76-22549 arrived at 1007 today (Clue 60B/C Mildenhall-Coleman Barracks) and a second US Army flight, T-39 Sabreliner 61-0685 (Clue 54A from/to Essen), made its first visit at 1115 on the 20th.

16th Air Portugal B.727 CS-TBS had to return to Manchester after blowing an engine on departure today (TP879 to Lisbon). The next day, Air Portugal B.727F CS-TBO arrived at 1502 with a spare engine for CS-TBS and Air Portugal B.737 CS-TEN arrived at 1628 (TP700F) to collect the delayed passengers.

18th The latest trio of Canadian Air Force CC-130Es were 130320 (CAM515-today), 130325 (CAM516-20th) & 130327 (CAM517-22nd), all operating Trenton-Lahr.

18th American-registered Agusta 109 N3983N based at Leavesden, arrived on its first visit from Swadlincote today, before departing again for Sheffield.

19th A magnitude 5.4 earthquake with an epicentre in the Llŷn Peninsula, North Wales was felt throughout the UK around 8.30am. The writer witnessed it from his home on the 14th-floor of a block of flats and was terrified!

19th Another unusual light aircraft visitor to Manchester was Cessna 180 floatplane G-BKMM, from/to Exeter today. It was carrying a very elegant lady passenger, who descended from the aircraft onto the float and then onto the tarmac in great style!

20th RAE BAC 1-11 XX105 arrived at 1144 today (Nugget 86), with a flight crew to take BAC 1-11 ZE433 back to Bedford.

20th Robinson R-22 G-BJBR arrived to night-stop, en route from Shoreham to Cranfield. The two-bladed single-engine light utility helicopter, that's been in production since 1979, was making a first visit of type to Manchester. One of the biggest helicopters around, the Sikorsky S.61 also appeared when British Airways G-BEJL called in for fuel on the 29th, routing Penzance-Aberdeen.

26th July 1984 – A new airline, Airways Cymru Intl, set up earlier this year by leading Welsh tour operator Red Dragon Travel, made their first visit today. BAC 1-11 G-YMRU is seen here having just positioned in from Cardiff to operate outbound British Midland BD7753 to Malta. (Geoff Ball)

23rd Slingsby T-67 G-BJZN was observed doing numerous touch-and-goes today, as part of a free concession for ATC personnel.
24th Austrian Cessna 414 OE-FBF arrived at 1638 today to clear customs, on its way to Fearn, on the West Coast of Scotland. It returned in the opposite direction, to clear customs again on the 27th.
25th Several older Cessna's visiting Manchester during the month were, Cessna 172s G-ARYS today & G-ARIV (26th) and Cessna 150 G-AVEM (15th).
25th Exactly fifty years ago today following a long and bitter debate, Manchester Councillors made one of the city's most important decisions, to build an airport at Ringway - by just one vote! The closeness of the result reflected the anger and frustration felt way back in 1934, when their £30,000 municipal airport at Barton was declared as inadequate for scheduled flights by the Dutch-airline, KLM. The final straw came when the Russian-born KLM Captain, Ivan Smirnoff, hero of First World War air battles over the Russian front, flew into Barton and gave it the 'thumbs-down' by preferring to fly to Hull and Liverpool instead. Following a search for a new airport site, Ringway got the nod over Woodford and Mobberley and was opened for business on the 25th June 1938.
28th GAS Air Cargo B.707F 5N-ARQ, made the first of two visits on consecutive days, arriving at 1849 today to night-stop (GS501 from Lagos). It departed the following morning for Kano and returned for its second visit later the same day at 2334 (WT739 from Kano-29th) to night-stop again.
29th Douglas DC-3 N711TD called in for fuel at 0136 today, en route Reykjavik-Milan, but as the pilot only had dollars and nobody would take them or change them at that time of the morning, he had to wait until the bank opened before finally departing at 0845.

30th July 1984 – B.707F 5N-ARQ was the first of several Nigerian cargo flights this year and one of six Boeing 707s making their first visits to Manchester during the year. (Geoff Ball)

30th Air Portugal B.727 CS-TBS disgraced itself for the second time in two weeks, by going tech when due to operate TP879 to Lisbon and being unable to depart until the following day.

August 1984

For the first time in its history, the airport handled more than 750,000 passengers in a single month. Last month's figures showed a 10% increase over the same month last year, with scheduled service movements up 12% and IT flights up 13%, reflecting a 22% increase for the first seven months.

The airports high-tech projects launched in January as 'revolutionary', have hit a series of major snags, which are sure to cause hold-ups and extra costs. The Airport Authority has been told that the taxiing routing system 'Is still not operating as originally envisaged and will cost more' and that the aircraft docking system 'Needs considerable changes'.

2nd August 1984 - A new transatlantic freight charter by Caribbean Air Cargo started today, with the arrival of B.707F 8P-CAC at 1000 (DC187 from New York). The airline, which operates two former BWIA B.707s, was set up as an all-cargo airline on 28th December 1979, under the joint ownership of the Governments of Barbados and Trinidad & Tobago. The flight was being on behalf of a US-airline called Nortstar, but a whole load of trouble was caused when the Caribbean airline didn't have the proper operating rights. Tradewinds wanted to operate the flight themselves into Gatwick and Flying Tigers & British Airways also objected, so in the end this was their one and only flight, as they scrapped the whole operation shortly afterwards. (Geoff Ball)

Equipment changes on scheduled flights began with British Caledonian operating British Air Ferries Heralds G-ASVO (12th) & G-BAVX (11th) & British Island Airways BAC 1-11 G-AYWB (23rd); Lufthansa (LH074): B.727s D-ABGI (7th/10), D-ABKH (19th), D-ABKI (22nd), D-ABQI (11th) & D-ABKR (27th); Manx Airlines (MNX327): Viscount G-AZNA (13th); Sabena (SN617): passenger B.737 OO-SDC (13th) and Swissair (SR842): DC-9-51s HB-ISL (31st), HB-ISL (20th) & HB-ISM (30th).

RAF ILS traffic included Hawks XX239 (7th) & XX312 (22nd); C-130 XV221 (10th); Jetstreams XX494 (13th/14th), XX495 (9th/29th) & XX497 (9th); two Nimrods: XV241 overshot at 1808 as Avro 5 (1st) & XZ281 at 1934 as Avro 2 (9th) and Jet Provost XW372 at 1126/1411 as CFT78 (9th). Other military visitors were RAE Comet (13th) and another Israeli Air Force B.707 when 4X-JYQ overshot twice during the morning (9th). Civil ILS traffic included

Cessna 152 G-BHRB (4th/11th/17th/18th/21st/24th/25th); PA-28s G-AVGI (5th) & G-BCGS (18th) and Cessna 172s G-BAXY (15th) & G-BEUX (31st). BAe Dove G-ARHW overshot at 1458, en route to Woodford (24th).

5th Aeroflot operated two TU-154 first visits on their weekly SU1639/40, with CCCP-85590 today and CCCP-85441 on the 19th.

5th The weekly New York freight flights operated by Transamerica continued this month with DC-8s N805WA today, N804WA (12th/26th) & N4868T (19th). As the airlines contract to operate the flights expires on the 26th, it's unclear who will operate them afterwards.

6th This month's Britannia Airways B.737 sub-charters were TEA OO-TEL BY592A/B (6th/13th/20th27th) & first visit OO-TEO BY748A/B (6th/13th); first visit Maersk OY-MBV BY748A/B (20th) and Britannia used one of their own aircraft on BY748A/B (27th)!

7th The only interesting activity at Dan-Air was today's arrival of Fords BAC 1-11 G-BFMC at 1802 for a respray, which is replacing G-BEJW.

9th Due to the unavailability of a B.707, British Midland used BIA BAC 1-11s G-AXOX (BD7732) & G-AXLN (BD7732A) inbound from Malta today and Airways Cymru International BAC 1-11 G-YMRU (BD7734) & BIA BAC 1-11 G-AYWB (BD7732) also from Malta (16th).

11th Demonstrator Aerospatiale Dauphin 2 G-DFIN, which operated for McAlpine Helicopters until 1987, called in for fuel today routing from/to Haydock Park.

13th This month's interesting single prop arrival, was Pitts Special G-BOOK at 1734 today, clearing customs en route Dublin-Barton. This aircraft is owned by the world famous aerobatic pilot, Brian Lecomber.

14th Former Transmeridian CL-44-0 N447T has been Irish registered as EI-BND for Heavylift Cargo, after the type experienced problems gaining its airworthiness certificate with the CAA. It made its second visit to Manchester this morning, as a Stansted diversion (NP619 from New York).

15th August 1984 – Balair DC-8-63 HB-IDZ arrived from Zurich to operate British Midland BD6025 to Vancouver, via Keflavik, before its return the next day. This aircraft operated for Balair until it was sold to UPS as N874UP in 1985. (Geoff Ball)

14th Italian PA-23 Aztec I-ANGI returned to Manchester again this year, appearing at 1741 today from Southend. It went off on a round-trip to Ronaldsway on the 19th and departed to Ghent on the 21st.

16th Cessna Citation 650 A4O-SC, arriving at 0110 today, was on its delivery flight. It is operated by Omani Air Services and as the pilot had friends in the area, he elected to stop off at Manchester. Other foreign Citation visits during the month were PH-MBX (7th), D-IAEV (23rd), I-GERA (28th), HB-VGS (29th) and Lego's latest machine, Cessna Citation 650 OY-GKL (28th).

16th This was another year when August produced a stubborn and persistent fog in the South East, resulting in seventeen diversions arriving at Manchester throughout the morning. At this time of year there is usually little parking space available for extra aircraft, so ATC advised any potential diversions of a delay in obtaining a parking stand, as at one stage there were four wide-bodies waiting on a taxiway. Unfortunately this information was interpreted by some London ATC frequencies as 'Manchester was full', so Cathay Pacific B.747 VR-HIF (CX201) diverted to Prestwick & People Express B.747 N602PE (PE002) diverted to Newcastle. Saudia diverted in two L.1011 Tristars: first visit HZ-AHB at 0624 (SV045 from Jeddah) & HZ-AHM (SV037 from Dhahran); Gatwick produced three diversions: British Caledonian B.747 G-BJXN at 0615 (BR362 from Lagos) & DC-10 G-BHDH at 0651 (BR381 from Dubai) and Wardair DC-10 C-FHX at 0807 (WD410 from Vancouver). Heathrow diversions were British Airways B.747s G-BDXG at 0643 (BA020 from Bombay) & G-BDXB at 0813 (BA054 from Nairobi); TWA B.747 N53116 at 0700 (TW708 from New York); Qantas B.747 VH-EBN at 0702 (QF001 from Bahrain); Air France B.737 F-GBYC at 0819 (AF1824 from Lyon) and the last diversion due to ATC delays was Trident 3 G-AWZZ at 1143 (BA4573 from Belfast).

18th Rich International DC-8 N1805 made the American-airlines first visit to Manchester, arriving at 0937 today (RZ805 from Atlanta), due to fog at Stansted. Initially set up as a cargo airline in 1969, they were granted permission to fly passenger charters in 1982.

18th Company demonstrator BAE.146 G-5-146 operated a touch-and-go at 1011 today and a further two ILS approaches (Tibbet 37 from/to Hatfield). Later in the year in October, it went on a six month lease to PSA as N5823B.

18th Tarom continue to provide interest on their weekly IT flight RO763/4. Today's, operated by IL-62 YR-IRC, was the types first visit this year and IL-18 YR-IMF arrived on the 25th.

19th Monarch Airlines sub-chartered TEA B.707 OO-TYC to operate OM698 to Palermo, which was also a first visit. Purchased earlier in May, this aircraft operated for TEA until 1989.

21st The only corporate Gulfstream into Manchester this month was a first visit, when Gulf 3 HZ-MAL from Deauville arrived as a Leeds diversion at 1032 today.

21st The only corporate Gulfstream into Manchester this month was a first visit, when Gulf 3 HZ-MAL arrived at 1032 today from Deauville as a Leeds diversion.

21st RAF Gazelle ZB629, operated by the VIP No.32 squadron based at Northolt, made its first visit to Manchester, arriving at 1830 today (RR1401 Bolton-Northolt).

24th Minerve SE.210 Caravelle F-GATZ operated an outbound charter to Tarbes (FQ0044).

24th Two Bell 206 Jet Rangers, G-BLCA & G-STST, arriving from the Belfry Hotel in Handforth for fuel before departing for Oxford, were both carrying Polycell stickers.

25th Cessna 414 N8359C called in for fuel at 1348 today, en route Munich-Glasgow. Its American registration was crudely painted over its previous German identity and it was still carrying a German flag on the tail. Another American twin was Cessna 310 N4256C, routing Brussels-Nantes (28th).

28th Two more Gatwick arrivals rounded off a good month for diversions. The first, American Airlines DC-10 N136AA arrived at 0912 today (AA050 from Dallas), making its first visit, as its alternate, Amsterdam, was also suffering from fog. The second, B.747 N602PE (PE002 from Newark), arriving a few minutes later at 0918, was another visit by People Express.

28th Shorts SD-330 demonstrator, G-BDBS, operating from Boscombe Down to Belfast Harbour as Short 4 today, stayed for just under two hours.

29th Lear Jet G-GAYL, arriving from Cardiff at 0321 today, is now operated by the Automobile Association. Painted in their yellow and white colour scheme, it's mainly used for air ambulance flights.

September 1984

July's runaway figures were surpassed again, when August became the busiest month ever, with 782,153 passengers handled. Freight traffic was also up 35% on last August.

After just five weeks, considerable progress has been made in constructing the new Cargo Centre, due for completion in twelve months. So far 8,000 cubic metres of topsoil have been removed and retained for landscaping, 10,000 cubic metres of hardcore fill has been brought in from all over the country by a fleet of fifty tippers and the erection of the structural steel work for the first phase of the transit shed will start this month.

British Airways flew two £20 trips from Manchester, taking in the illuminations at Blackpool and Morecambe, by flying at low-level and low-speed up and down the Lancashire coast. The hour long flights designed for timid and first-time flyers, took place with G-AVMM (BA9126C-8th) & G-AVML (BA9125C-15th).

Equipment changes on scheduled flights started with Lufthansa (LH074): B.727s D-ABKB (1st), D-ABKD (7th), D-ABKH (12th), D-ABKQ (11th) & D-ABKS (19th) and Manx Airlines used BAF Herald G-ASVO (19th/20th). Metropolitan also operated their SD-330, G-METO as well as their Twin Otters (from 13th) and Swissair (SR842): DC-9-51 HB-ISU (16th/19th).

RAF ILS traffic included Hawks XX162 (14th) & XX184 (24th/26th); C-130s XV204 (21st) & XV221 (10th) and Dominies XS736 (19th), XS737 (26th) & XS738 (19th). Civil ILS traffic included Cessna 152s G-BHRB (8th/17th/23rd/24th/26th), G-BHCX (15th), G-BHUP (27th) & G-BLAC (28th) and French Beech 90s F-BTCA (17th) & F-BXSF (21st). From Woodford, BAe.748 D-AHSF/G-11-2 overshot at 1725 as Avro 8 (24th) and an unidentified French Navy Xingu overshot at 0700 (21st).

1st Tarom rounded off their summer programme (RO763/4) this month, with further IL-18 visits by YR-IMG today, YR-IMD (22nd) & YR-IMJ (29th).

2nd British Midland F.27 G-BLGW operated an inbound charter from Gothenburg today (BD8906), as the outbound had operated the previous day. Also today was Dan-Air BAe.146 G-BKMN, making its first visit to Manchester, positioning in from Teeside to operate the weekly Ajaccio flight DA4582/3.

3rd This month's Britannia Airways sub-charters were operated by B.737s Sobelair OO-SBT BY592A/B (10th), TEA OO-TEL BY592A/B (17th) & OO-TEO BY592A/B today, Maersk OY-APP BY614A/B (10th) & OY-MBV BY748A/B today and BY614A/B (17th).

3rd Minerve SE.210 Caravelle F-GATZ was present today and also 7th/14th/21st/28th, operating from/to Tarbes.

7th British Air Ferries Viscount G-AOYJ, which has now been re-registered as G-BLOA, made its first visit as such today, operating VF7603/2 from/to Rotterdam.

7th Transamerica returned to using B.747s on their weekly New York flight, operating inbound from New York each Friday or Saturday, finishing off Jetsave's summer programme. N780T formerly N480GX, which was still in basic Egyptair colours and operated throughout, was sold late in 1985 to Tower Air as N603FF.

7th The oldest Beech 90 on the UK register, G-AXFE, operated outbound today to Munich. First registered in 1969, it was operated up until recently by engineering giant, GKN.

8th Air Atlantique was due to operate a couple of charters to Blackbushe, in connection with the Farnborough Air Show, but when DC-3 G-AMPO arrived at 0410 today from Newcastle to operate the first flight, it went tech and didn't leave until 1711. Another DC-3, G-AMSV, commandeered from Stansted, arrived at 0810 and departed at 0853. Also today was a charter by Norwegian-airline Busy Bee, when F.27 LN-NPM made its first visit, before departing for Bergen (BS302).

10th Boeing sent in their company Boeing 737-300 demonstrator, N352AU, on behalf of Orion Airways for publicity purposes following their order for four aircraft, one of which will be based at Manchester from next summer. It arrived at 0910 today from Farnborough, where it had been on display and departed an hour later for Birmingham. Airport chiefs were positively glowing about the aircraft, which was so quiet on departure it didn't even register on the noise monitor. However, as there were no seats fitted and no passengers, the reading was always going to be low; but this was refuted by an airport spokesman who said the aircraft had weighty aircraft monitoring equipment onboard, reflecting the shape of things to come!

13th The first of two Lear Jet's making their first visits this month was today's arrival of N741E at 0945, for brief attention with NEA. The other, N505EE, arriving at 1001 on the 23rd en route Milan-Keflavik, was in a smart red pin-stripe colour scheme.

13th The second visit to Manchester this year of a rare corporate jet was the arrival of Sabreliner HZ-AMN, making its one and only visit, arriving at 1232 today from/to Heathrow.

13th Cargolux B.747F LX-ECV arrived at 1613 today, on its first visit to Manchester. Routing Luxembourg-Seattle via Edmonton, it called in to collect three RB-211 engines for Boeing to fix.

13th 1976-built PA-31 Navajo N62992 called in at 1829 today from Madrid, to clear customs en route to Carlisle. It returned two days later and stayed until the 26th, when it departed Stateside via Prestwick and Keflavik.

15th Manchester Airport was one of eleven UK airports used for the biggest British military mobilisation since the Second World War, when 'Exercise Lionheart' started today with a massive airlift of troops. As well as the RAF, various British airlines were also involved with today's movements and the pick of these was British Airways B.747 G-BDXC, which departed to Gutersloh, while the RAF utilised C-130s XV178/XV303/XV220/XV221 and XV304, all departing to Hanover, Gutersloh or Wildenrath.

16th Today's 'Exercise Lionheart' movements involved RAF C-130s XV192 & XV197, Tristars ZD948 & ZD952 and VC-10s XV105/XV107/XV108 all to Gutersloh or Wildenrath and British Airways B.747s G-BDXC & G-BDXH to Gutersloh.

16th First visit Gulfstream 3 N26L arrived at 1038 today for fuel, en route Frankfurt-Gander.

16th The weekly New York freight flight recommenced today, with first time visitor Arrow Air DC-8 N6161A, which also operated subsequent flights during the month.

17th Air Portugal B.737 CS-TEM (TP8608) brought Porto FC into Manchester to play Wrexham in a European Cup-Winners Cup match two days later, won by Wrexham 1-0. The return game in Portugal two weeks later was a fantastic match, won by Porto 4-3, but it was Wrexham that progressed to the next round on away goals, they were to play Roma in the next phase.

19th The only two diversions of any interest this month were TWA B.747 N93119 at 0753 today (TW754 from Boston), due to long ATC delays at Heathrow after a short period of Cat.3 landings only and Transamerica DC-8 N4865T at 1009 on the 29th (TV302 from New York), due to fog at Shannon.

19th Manchester Utd was also back on the European trail, this time in the UEFA Cup. Tonight's opponents were Hungarian team Gyori, arriving on a Shuttle service without any fans. United won 3-0, having drawn the first leg 2-2, which meant they went through to the next round on aggregate.

22nd Aer Lingus SD-360 EI-BEL made its first visit, arriving at 1215 today (EI4202 from Dublin), bringing in fans for the Manchester Utd v Liverpool match.

22nd Dan-Air B.727 G-BCDA (DA4712) was forced to evacuate prior to its departure to Corfu this evening, when smoke filled up the cabin, but luckily no one was injured.

23rd September 1984 – Rich International DC-8 N1805, arriving at 1052 today (RZ805 from New York), was returning students back to the UK. This former Braniff aircraft served with Rich until 1989. (Geoff Ball)

24th Condor B.737 DABHT made its second visit to Manchester this year, arriving at 1514 today (DF885 from Lisbon).

25th Shorts Skyvan demonstrator G-ASZJ, now 25 years old, paid a visit at 1557 today, from/to Belfast Harbour as Short 6.

26th Not a common light aircraft to Manchester these days, is the unique Cessna 337 Skymaster, but there were two different examples today. German D-ICEP arriving at 1355 from Stuttgart stayed overnight, before departing to Biggin Hill the following afternoon and Lands End based G-BCBZ, which is a STOL conversion, also stayed the night.

28th The mass return of troops from 'Exercise Lionheart' began today, with RAF C-130s XV177 & XV189 plus Tristar ZD952 from Hanover/Gutersloh and B.747 G-AWNN plus Tristars G-BBAH & G-BBAI from Gutersloh.
28th RAF Andover XS596 arriving at 1315 today (RR776 from Manston), was still in brown camouflage colours and BAe.125 XX508 arriving the following day (RR7686 from/to Alconbury), brought in the top military brass who were monitoring the troop movements.
28th Spantax DC-8 EC-CCF operated a much delayed Air Europe flight, AE555/4 from/to Mahon, due to an unserviceable B.737.
29th Queens Flight Wessex XV732 brought Princess Anne into Manchester for the reopening of the Opera House, following its extensive refurbishment.
29th The flights returning troops continued today, with RAF C-130 XV207 & VC-10 XV101 and British Airways Tristars G-BBAF/G-BBAI/G-BHBL. Many flights were also operated by the following civilian airlines: Orion Airways, British Caledonian & Britannia Airways. Approximately 6,000 troops passing through Manchester in each direction on the inbound leg were processed through the terminal in full battle dress, complete with rifles and lots of bags of duty free! A total of 35,000 UK-members of the Territorial Army also took part, alongside 17,000 UK-based regular soldiers and 4,500 reservists.
30th American Transair made their first and only visit to Manchester this year, when DC-10 N183AT arrived at 0946 today (TZ837 New York-Gatwick).

October 1984

Singapore Airlines have reapplied to operate a Manchester-Singapore service, after their application for a twice-weekly service failed, due to their reluctance to relinquish a corresponding number of services from Heathrow, because of an international agreement stating that Singapore Airlines and British Airways must operate the same number of flights. Their second application makes it clear that any Manchester services will be in addition to those already operated from Heathrow.

A Council Health Officer was called to the airport to inspect some interesting foodstuffs! Upon arrival he observed a number of huge snails, 6" long and 4" wide, happily crawling along a Customs Officer's table, after being found in a passenger's hand luggage.

Equipment changes on scheduled flights included Air Ecosse using first visit Brymon Dash-7 G-BRYB (WG778/9). British Airways lunchtime Aberdeen flight (BA5691/4) was operated by BAe Jetstream G-JSBA (29th/31st); British Caledonian used BIA BAC 1-11 G-CBIA (5th); KLM (KL155): NLM F.28 PH-CHD (19th); Lufthansa (LH074): B.727 D-ABKJ (28th); Manx Airlines (MNX329): BAF Viscount G-BLOA (12th) and Air Portugal ended their once-weekly service with Boeing 737 CS-TEO (29th).

RAF ILS traffic identified were Hawk XX294 (15th); Jetstreams XX493 & XX500 (15th) and Andover's XS641 (23rd) & XS643 (24th). Others were Royal Navy Jetstreams XX485 (Culdrose/Woodford-10th) & XX490 (Culdrose/Finningley-4th); RAE Comet XS235 (11th); Beech 200s Irish Air Corps No.240 (19th) & PH-SBK (29th) and finally Canadian Air Force B.707 13705 overshooting at 1243 as CAM737 (31st), was the first to visit since 16th December 1976!
1st The final Britannia Airways sub-charter took place today, when TEA B.737 OO-TEL positioned from Gatwick to operate BY748A/B from/to Corfu.
1st Today's arrival of CAA BAe.125 G-CCAA (Cranfield-Edinburgh), in connection with the CAA securing the contract to run Manchester Air Traffic for another seven years, was the

first of thirty-two corporate jet visits this month. These included first visits by BAe.125s N207PC (4th) & Royal Air Force ZE395 (13th); Citation 550s G-BJIR (11th) & N4209K (16th); Champion Spark Plugs Gulf 2 N1823D (4th) & Gulf 3 N888MC (19th) and Lear Jet N296BS (13th) for attention with NEA.

2nd Dan-Air is leasing three BAe.748s to Philippine Airlines. The first, G-BHCJ, arriving today for attention should have been the first to leave, but technical problems on several occasions prevented its departure until the 26th as RP-C1030. In basic Dan-Air colours with no titles, its registration was written in black on the red stripe on the rear of the fuselage.

5th Minerve SE.210 Caravelle F-GATZ operated the last of a short series of flights from/to Tarbes today. Although this aircraft saw another eight years of service with the airline before its withdrawal, it would not operate into Manchester again.

6th Aeroflot operated a weekly programme this summer with no first time visitors. However, the airline today operated a one-off charter (SU3241/4638 Newcastle-Leningrad) TU-154 CCCP-85397, which was a first visit.

6th October 1984 – BAC 1-11 N111GS, arriving from Gander for attention with Dan-Air today, departed to East Midlands for fitting out on the 17th as A6-RKT. It was on delivery to the Ras Al Khaimah Government and served them until 1988. (Geoff Ball)

7th The next Dan-Air BAe.748 to leave on lease to Philippine Airlines was G-AXVG, which arrived for attention today. It departed on the 17th as RP-C1031, in basic Dan-Air colours with no titles and its registration written in white on the red stripe on the lower fuselage.

7th This month's Royal Saudi Air Force C-130 flights started with 470 (RSF918 Milan/Gander) today, 1604 RSF604 from/to Milan (11th), 470 RSF918 Gander/Cambridge (14th), C-130E 1610 RSF919 Milan/Gander (20th), 465 RSF619 from/to Milan (23rd) and C-130E 1610 RSF919 Gander/Milan (26th).

8th Making a second visit of type, was Colt Cars Mitsubishi MU-300 Diamond G-JMSO, operating outbound to Turin. It was on the UK register for less than twelve months, before being sold in the USA in February 1985.

9th Airways Cymru Intl BAC 1-11 G-YMRU made two further visits during the month. The first was to Faro today (CYM7001) and the second operated the return leg (CYM7002-15th).

10th The latest trio of Canadian Air Force CC-130Es were 130314 CAM515 today, 130321 (CAM516-11th) & 130327 (CAM517-14th), all operating Trenton-Lahr. An extra flight was operated by camouflaged CC-130E 130328 (CAM410A Lahr-Trenton-16th).

14th Rescue Wessex XT602 called in at 1242 today for fuel, on a detail from/to Leconfield.

14th The month saw another three Cessna 337 visits. G-BARD arrived at 1452 today, G-RORO (31st) which had been into Manchester before, but 1969-built G-BJIY (22nd) operating Blackpool-Oban, was a first visit.

14th Nigeria Airways B.707 5N-ABJ, which last visited Manchester on 15th December 1975 as a passenger aircraft, was converted to a cargo aircraft during 1976. It arrived at 1637 today (WT724 from Lagos), to collect Jaguar spares for the Nigerian Air Force.

15th Today was the fourth visit of People Express to Manchester, when B.747 N604PE arrived at 1004 (PE002 from Newark). It was a Gatwick diversion and a first visit.

15th British Airtours used BA L.1011 G-BBAH (KT353 from Malta), as the flight was running over 24-hours late due to Tristar G-BBAJ going tech at Malta, having operated the outbound flight.

15th This month's largest corporate jet was Boeing 727 N727EC, from/to Stansted. Making its first visit today, it stayed for sixteen minutes with its engines running, even when a passenger disembarked via the rear stairs. This aircraft operated for Nigerian Oil Mills from 1984-1988.

16th Another biz-jet rarely seen at Manchester is the MBB Hansa Jet. D-COSA plies its trade each weekday between Munich and Warton on company business, but due to fog at Warton it landed at Manchester at 1137 today, after failing to land at its alternate, Blackpool.

19th Gulfstream 3 N888MC made it first visit to Manchester, arriving from Heathrow at 1044 today. A large inscription on the nose reading 'Here comes Pia', refers to the singer Pia Zadora, onboard to make a recording at Granada Television.

21st The number of serviceable Handley-Page Heralds still in passenger service are slowly dwindling. Air UK G-ASKK, which made its last visit to Manchester today operating UK274/5 from/to Jersey, had been withdrawn at Norwich by March 1985.

22nd Monarch Airlines BAC 1-11 G-AXMG took Wrexham FC out for their latest European Cup-Winners Cup tie with Roma, which proved to be a forgettable match, losing 2-0. Two weeks later on the return leg, Wrexham were beaten again 1-0 and were out of Europe.

23rd The last Dan-Air BAe.748 to leave on lease to Philippine Airlines was G-BEBA. Arriving at 1416 today for attention, it departed on 3rd November as RP-C1032. The three aircraft all left on delivery to the Philippines via Rome.

23rd This month's first visit of type goes to Varga 2150 Kachina G-JLTB, arriving at 1716 today from/to Blackpool. The origin of this low fixed-wing, two-seat light aircraft can be traced back to 1948, when it was originally designed as an all wood and fabric aircraft. This particular plane, one of several imported earlier this year, flew until 1988.

30th British Midland operated the final flight of their summer programme today, when B.707 G-BFLE arrived at 1814 (BD7332 from Tenerife), before positioning out at 1930 to East Midlands. This also marked the final visit of a BMA B.707 to Manchester. The last visits and subsequent fates of all three aircraft are as follows:

G-BFLD 26th October 1984, sold August 1985 as N862BX
G-BFLE 30th October 1984, sold August 1985 as N861BX
G-BMAZ 26th October 1984, sold August 1985 as N863BX

28th October 1984 – Arrow Air continued operating the weekly New York freight flight with regular DC-8 N6161A. Today however, DC-8-63 N2674U was used, but due to technical trouble the return flight operated over 24-hours late. (Geoff Ball)

30th Tunis Air operated their final flight of the season today (TU8798/9 from/to Monastir), with new B.737, TS-IEB, making its first visit.

November 1984

Holiday bookings for next summer are likely to be hit by the knock-on effects of the miners' strike. The gloomy forecast was made by Cosmos Holidays Associate Director, Keith Watson (the writer's boss at the time!), at the company launch of their 1985 summer programme. Despite an expected drop in overall business of 3%-5%, Cosmos still anticipate a 14% increase in holiday traffic from Manchester.

Metropolitan Airways have applied to the CAA to serve Hamburg, Oslo & Stockholm from Manchester. They already operate domestic services between Manchester-Newcastle, Birmingham, Bournemouth & Cardiff and are being encouraged by the Government/EEC with incentives to develop regional services within Europe, which would mean purchasing larger aircraft.

Dan-Air has been granted a licence to compete with British Airways on the Manchester-Heathrow route and will begin flights next April. They also applied to serve Amsterdam, Dublin, Oslo, Dusseldorf & Stockholm.

Air Europe is offering a new Premier Class service on their Tenerife and Madeira flights. For a supplement of £19 one-way or £39 return, passengers get priority check-in, use of an executive lounge, a free bar onboard, a hot meal and warm towels. Free wine is served with the meal, which includes a meat course, fresh fruit and a cheese board, followed by liqueurs. Plastic cups are out, as only the best china is used for the maximum number of eleven passengers per flight, seated in a separate cabin at the front of the aircraft.

British Airways have arranged seventeen 45-minute 'Santa Specials' next month, at £17 a head, operated by a Super 1-11. Their latest brainwave is that shortly after takeoff, the

Captain will announce that the aircraft is flying over the North Pole and at this point (providing all onboard are suitably convinced); Santa will appear and hand out presents to the children.

Airlines making winter schedule changes included Air Ecosse reverting to a three-times weekday Aberdeen service, via Dundee. Air Portugal ceased their Lisbon/Faro schedule last month. British Airways added an extra weekday Heathrow rotation (BA4412/4503) and due to imminent withdrawal of the remaining Trident 2s, they are using BAC 1-11s on Shuttle back-up flights. Cyprus Airways reduced flights to twice-weekly. Dan-Air reduced Zurich flights to five-weekly. Iberia dropped Barcelona and will now operate three-times weekly to Madrid via Malaga. KLM morning flight (KL153/4) and lunchtime (KL155/6) now both operate on weekdays, with KL157/8 at weekends. Manx Airlines maintain a three-times daily service to Ronaldsway, with two flights on Saturdays and three of the six Copenhagen flights operated by SAS proceed onwards to/from Dublin.

The following airlines have winter IT programmes from Manchester: Air Europe, Air Malta, Air Portugal, Britannia Airways, British Airtours, British Airways, Dan-Air, EL AL, JAT, Monarch Airlines, Orion Airways & Wardair, who operate a once-weekly Toronto service via Prestwick.

Equipment changes on scheduled flights included British Airways using the following B.737s on Shuttle services: G-BGDR (4th) & G-BGJJ (15th) and they also used BAe Jetstream G-JSBA again on BA5691/4 (2nd); Lufthansa (LH074): B.727s D-ABDI (18th), D-ABGI (25th), D-ABKB (5th), D-ABKF (1st), D-ABRI (11th) & Condor B.737 D-ABHT (6th/13th) and Swissair (SR842): DC-9-51s HB-ISO (2nd/9th/13th) & HB-ISU (14th/24th/31st) and first visit MD-81 HB-ING (16th).

Very little RAF ILS traffic was identified during the month, with Dominies XS714 (13th) & XS727 (5th) and RAF Honington-based Tornado ZA367 overshooting at 1246 as 'MSC99' (23rd). Others were Royal Navy Sea Devon XK895 (6th); Cessna 152s G-BHRB (7th) & G-BHUP (24th); Cessna 172 G-BEUX (1st/5th) and all-white Jetstream 31 G31-642 overshooting at 1509 as Tennent 4 (29th).

1st Of the few charters operated during the month, EAT Metro OO-JPI arrived at 0952 (BC603 from Amsterdam). Others were British Caledonian DC-10 G-BJZD (BR5738 from Orlando/Bangor-5th), Jersey European Twin Otter G-BKBC (12th) & BAF Herald G-BAVX (20th).

2nd The nightly newspaper flight to Leuchars operated for the final time, this time with Spacegrand Twin Otter G-BFGP. On several occasions during the month an early morning newspaper flight was operated to Dublin, again with Spacegrand Twin Otters.

4th This month's Royal Saudi Air Force C-130 flights started with 469 RSF920 Milan/Gander today & RSF920 Gander/Milan (12th), 1614 RSF620 from/to Milan (6th), 1605 RSF921 Milan/Gander (21st) & RSF921 Gander/Milan (25th) and 464 RSF621 from/to Milan (21st).

5th Another Rescue Wessex, XT674, called in at 0153 today for fuel, en route from Heathrow to RAF Valley (Rescue 22).

6th Transavia B.737 PH-TVH, which stayed until the 8th, brought PSV Eindhoven into Manchester to play Utd in the UEFA Cup. The first leg, played two weeks previously, had ended in a 0-0 draw, but after a very nervy game Manchester Utd scored in the 93rd minute and won 1-0, which put them through to play Dundee Utd.

6th Royal Navy Sea Devon XK895, which overshot as Navy 819 (Culdrose-Leeming) at 1307 today, was making its final visit. This aircraft, along with many others, was phased out by the Royal Navy by 1989, with XK895 becoming G-SDEV and based at Coventry.

7th Of the five diversions this morning, two from East Midlands and three from Leeds, the only one of interest was the second visit of JCB's run-around, BAe.125 G-TJCB at 0958.
7th Today's Man Utd v PSV Eindhoven match produced a couple of supporter specials! PA-42 PH-BDV and PA-42 PH-ALA both arrived from Eindhoven, via Norwich.
7th Christian Salvesen's new executive aircraft, Beech 90 G-SALV, made its first visit to Manchester today.
8th British Airways have leased Air Europe B.757 G-BKRM for the winter, for use on their Shuttle services. The aircraft, in full AE colours except for 'British' on the forward fuselage and 'Air Europe' on the tail, made its first visit as such today, operating BA4462/93.

9th November 1984 – Herald G-AYMG arrived at 0432 today, as a Birmingham weather diversion. This aircraft operated for Securicor Express and later for Channel Express, until its withdrawal from service in July 1992. It made its last visit to Manchester on the 6th December 1991. (Geoff Ball)

11th A short burst of diversions from the South produced first time visitors Saudia L.1011 Tristar 200 HZ-AHR at 0521 (SV047 from Jeddah) & Intercontinental DC-8 5N-AVS at 0830 (VS802 from Lagos). The DC-8s colours weren't unlike those of its previous operator, United Airlines and although the aircraft arrived without incident, it did go tech for a time. Two more diversions of note were British Airways B.747 G-BDXG at 0701 (BA052 from Harare) & British Caledonian DC-10 G-BEBM at 0815 (BR254 from Dallas). The fog cleared before the diversions got fully underway, unlike the next session four days later!
11th Royal Navy Lynx XZ736 arrived at 1432 today, on a round trip from HMS Manchester moored in Liverpool Docks. The Army Air Corps also chipped in with Lynx ZD272, arriving at 1552 (Army 402 from Netheravon) to night-stop. This particular machine had lifted the Met Office radar off the roof of the CIS building, in central Manchester.
11th Company BAe.748 demonstrator G-BDVH arrived from Frankfurt at 1619 today, at the end of a sales tour, due to Woodford being closed for the weekend.
13th BAC 1-11 5N-AOP arrived from Algiers at 0745 today, for attention with Dan-Air before departing on the 11th December. Operated by Nigerian-outfit Okada Air, it's effectively

in basic British Caledonian colours, with Okada titles and a large Chief's head on the tail. This aircraft is ex-Laker Airways G-AVBX & British Caledonian G-BKAV.

13th Three BAe.125s making their first visits during the month, were all re-registrations. G-DBAL formerly G-BSAA, arrived at 0949 today (Heathrow-Newquay) and is now operated by Falcon Jet Centre, based at Heathrow. G-TOPF (27th) formerly 9K-ACR/G-AYER, arrived at 2008 from Le Bourget and lastly G-BXPU formerly G-AXPU, which arrived from Luton (29th), has been re-engined and still operates for McAlpine Aviation.

15th Early morning fog caused problems for the South again. Heathrow was affected for most of the day, but Gatwick was clear from mid-morning. Saudia was the first airline to divert in again, producing two L.1011 Tristar 200s within five minutes of each other: HZ-AHD at 0552 (SV031 from Jeddah) and first visit HZ-AHO at 0557 (SV045 from Riyadh). British Caledonian produced two flights before Gatwick's weather improved: DC-10 G-BHDJ at 0605 (BR381 from Dubai) & B.747 G-BJXN at 0619 (BR362 from Lagos). A selection of the Heathrow diversions on this classically cold, clear and sunny winters day were two TWA B.747s: N53116 at 0711 (TW700 from New York) & N93105 at 0934 (TW704 from New York); two British Airways B.747s: G-AWNM at 0816 (BA292 from Miami) & G-BDXK at 0906 (BA174 from New York); KLM DC-9 PH-DNK at 0931 (KL117 from Amsterdam); Qantas B.747 VH-EBN at 0950 (QF001 from Bahrain); Air Malta B.720 9H-AAL at 1107 (KM100 from Malta); Lufthansa B.727 D-ABKF at 1916 (LH070 from Munich) and the highlight of the day was the first visit by an EL AL B.767, with the arrival of 4X-EAB at 1407 (LY315 from Tel Aviv). Other diversions included Cessna 303 OO-PEN (Leeds), Air Express CL-44 N122AE (Stansted) & RAF VC-10 XR808 (Brize Norton). There could have been many more during the evening, had the visibility not dropped from 10km to 100m in less than thirty minutes, a situation which persisted until mid-afternoon the following day.

16th The majority of this morning's Manchester arrivals were forced to divert elsewhere due to fog, with the exception of all Shuttle flights, which operated normally due to their Cat.3 capability. This was also the day of the last notable diversion this month, with the arrival of British Airways G-BKYA, on its first visit diverting in from Dublin at 2300 (BA830 from Heathrow).

17th A new addition to the UK register, PA-31 Navajo G-ONPA, arrived in bare metal/primer with a crudely applied registration fastened on by tape, to operate a couple of demonstration flights.

19th Other aircraft of note arriving for Dan-Air included BAC 1-11 HZ-MAJ at 1150 today, before its departure on 6th December and another BAC 1-11 for the Royal Aircraft Establishment. ZE432 arrived on the 28th in a pseudo military scheme and basic Air Pacific colours with roundels, before departing on the 4th January 1985, painted in their 'raspberry-ripple' scheme.

22nd Swedish Cessna 404 freight flights were SE-INE today and SE-IRB on the 27th.

22nd British Airways Chairman, Lord King of Warnatby, arrived at 1032 today in the airline's latest executive 'taxi', Beech 200 G-LKOW.

26th The Irish Air Corps brought their two Beech 200s into Manchester today, both operating Glasgow-Luton on a training exercise. No.234 was white with red dayglo hoops and Maritime Squadron titles, whereas No.240 was in an orange and white scheme.

27th Two Gulfstream visits this month, both arriving today to night-stop, were Champion Spark Plugs Gulf 2 N1823D (from/to Dublin) & American Can Gulf 3 N130K (New York-White Plains).

28th The French Navy also operated a training flight, with Nord 262 No.102 arriving at 1109 today as FA071 (Cardiff-Amsterdam), which was the first to land at Manchester since June.
28th RAE Bassett XS770 arriving at 1149 today, was acting as crew ferry for BAC 1-11 ZE432.
29th Super Puma G-PUMH operated by North Scottish Helicopters, was a first visit of type, arriving to pick up some passengers off the 1020 Shuttle flight BA4422, before returning them later in the day to catch BA4513 back to Heathrow.
29th Due to a bomb scare at Liverpool, there were two late evening diversions. Dan-Air BAe.748 G-BEJD arrived at 2157 and Queens Flight BAe.748 XS793 at 2220 (Kitty 2 from Blackpool), which had Princess Anne onboard.

December 1984

A possible third handling agency at Manchester, which is already in the pipeline, has been attacked as a threat to more than a hundred existing jobs. Although it would create jobs initially, it's said they would be at the expense of the present handling companies, British Airways and Servisair. Discussions regarding the proposal have already taken place with the consortium, consisting principally of Dan-Air people.

In addition to the launch of flights to Heathrow next April, Dan-Air will also launch a weekday service to Oslo and Bergen, via Newcastle and a weekly summer service to Montpellier.

Lots of bad weather during the month meant one thing – diversions, although not as many as in previous Decembers. So far this winter, there's been a regular pattern of Heathrow being foggy for long periods, but Gatwick being unaffected at the same time, meaning they could take most of the diverted traffic. Other factors for there being less diversions to Manchester is the increase in Cat.3 aircraft these days and for airlines such as JAL, Air India & Northwest to name but three, being more readily prepared to divert to the Continent.

British Airways unveiled their new livery on the 4th, which took eighteen months to design. It consists of a midnight-blue lower fuselage containing a red speedwing near the top, a pearl-grey upper fuselage and a midnight-blue tail design, similar to their current scheme. The main difference is that the top part of the tail is blue, instead of red and it carries the airline's crest and the British Airways titles are in block blue capitals on the upper forward fuselage. The first aircraft in the new scheme was B.737 G-BKYF, with the rest of the fleet being repainted over a two-year period. A revision of the airline's naming policy will see their Boeing 757s & BAC 1-11s named after counties, Boeing 747s after cities, Boeing 737s & L.1011 Tristars after rivers, but BAe.748s will remain unchanged. They also withdrew a number of Tridents this year and their last visit details and subsequent fates are as follows:
G-AVFF, 29/11/84, last service 30/11/84 (BA4761 Belfast-LHR), withdrawn 11/84
G-AVFL, 30/11/84, last service 05/12/84 (BA4834 LHR-Edinburgh), withdrawn 12/84
G-AVFN, 07/12/84, last service 08/12/84 (BA4493 MAN-LHR), withdrawn 12/84
G-AWZC, 12/10/84, last service 31/10/84 (BA417 Amsterdam-LHR), sold as 9Q-CTM
G-AWZX, 30/09/84, last service 01/10/84 (BA4673 Belfast-LHR), withdrawn 10/84
G-AWZZ, 01/11/84, last service 04/11/84 (BA4753 Edinburgh-LHR), withdrawn 11/84
G-AYVF, 01/02/84, last service 01/02/84 (BA4813 Edinburgh-LHR), withdrawn 02/84

Equipment changes on scheduled flights were Air France (AF964): B.737s F-GBYF (31st) & F-GBYJ (30th); British Airways used the following B.737s on shuttle services: G-BGJJ (7th)

& G-BGDP (27th); Guernsey Airlines (GE725): Viscounts G-AOYG (21st/23rd), G-AOYL (28th) & G-APIM (9th); Lufthansa (LH074): B.727s D-ABDI (16th), D-ABKB (14th/17th), D-ABKD (6th), D-ABKP (28th) & D-ABKR (20th) and Swissair (SR842): DC-9-51s HB-ISO (4th), HB-IST (21st), HB-ISU (28th) & HB-ISV (7th/14th).

Another lean month for ILS traffic, with just the following four aircraft: RAF Jetstream XX492 (4th), Royal Navy Wessex XR524 at 1104 (6th), French Navy Xingu No.90 (3rd) & Cessna 150 G-ATMB (9th).

3rd The only Jetstar visit this year occurred today, with the arrival of N10PN making a first visit at 1045, on a round-trip from/to Luton. Other noteworthy biz-jets were Citation 551 D-IGGK also on its first visit today, Italian Citations I-FLYA (4th) & I-GERA (5th) and another two first visits both BAe.125s, 5H-SMZ (8th) & G-CYII (21st).

5th This month's Royal Saudi Air Force C-130 flights started today with 1618 (RSF622 Milan/Jeddah), which went tech and wasn't able to leave until the 9th. The others were 468 RSF922 Gander/Milan (7th), 460 RSF623 from/to Milan (17th) & 1612 RSF923 Dover AFB/Jeddah (21st).

6th Another flight transporting Jaguar spares to Nigeria brought Nigeria Airways B.707F 5N-ABJ into Manchester at 1451 today (WT754 from Lagos).

6th RAE Bassett XS770 visited Manchester again this month, operating from/to Boscombe Down today, but in-between it also flew a return flight to Warton.

7th Saudia VC-130H HZ-115 brought in spares for 'tech' Saudi Air Force C-130H 1618 today and paid another visit on the 18th, en route Athens-Gander-Marietta.

7th The pick of this month's light aircraft was today's visit of Swiss Mooney HB-DVY at 1202, from/to Basle.

8th Kellogg's Falcon 50 N283K called in for fuel today, en route Strasbourg-Gander. With the exception of the regular Michelin Falcon 20 F-BVPN, this was the only Falcon visit this month.

8th The latest Okada Air BAC 1-11 arriving for attention, was 5N-AOZ at 1710 today from Palma. This crew took BAC 1-11 5N-AOP back to Nigeria, via Madrid and 5N-AOZ remained with Dan-Air until the 11th January next year.

9th Arrow Air's weekly New York freight flight was operated by first time visitor DC-8-62 N941JW today and on the next two Sundays.

11th Today's arrival of thirty-two diversions, from four different airports, was the most since November 1982. Arriving from Heathrow, Gatwick, Birmingham & East Midlands, the session saw the now customary early morning Saudia diversion L.1011 Tristar 200 HZ-AHM at 0505 (SV045 from Jeddah), but the first diversion was British Airways B.747 G-BDXA at 0453 (BA006 from Anchorage), which started the morning's busy session. Next were British Airways B.747 G-BBPU at 0553 (BA012 from Muscat); British Caledonian flights A.310 G-BKWT at 0531 (BR212 from Libreville) and DC-10s G-BHDJ at 0701 (BR381 from Dubai) & G-BGAT at 0839 (BR232 from Atlanta); Qantas B.747 VH-EBP at 0701 (QF001 from Bahrain); the last visit of a Zambia Airways B.707 with the arrival of 9J-AEB at 0708 (QZ7202 from Lusaka); TWA B.747 N93106 at 0722 (TW700 from New York); first visit American Airlines DC-10 N138AA at 0901 (AA050 from Dallas); Pan American B.747 N734PA at 0905 (PA102 from New York; NLM F.28 PH-CHD at 0930 (HN403 from Rotterdam) and two KLM Airbus A.310 first visits: PH-AGD at 0937 (KL117 from Amsterdam) & PH-AGB at 0943 (KL115 from Amsterdam). Once these two aircraft were parked nose-in on the International Pier, it was then realised that the Airport Authority did not have a tow-bar for an A.310, having been incorrectly advised by KLM in Amsterdam that a standard Airbus tow-bar would suffice, so one had to be transported from Amsterdam aboard the lunchtime flight KL155, which ultimately delayed their departure. It's common for winter fog to temporarily improve before the sun goes down, when it thickens up again and although today followed that trend, there were no further Heathrow diversions until mid-evening, mainly due to them diverting elsewhere. Early evening saw seven diversions from the Midlands, with nothing out of the ordinary and the first diversions from Heathrow weren't until 2002 when DC-9 PH-DNC (BD061 from Edinburgh) arrived and eight more followed: Aer Lingus B.737 EI-ASB at 2012 (EI716 from Cork), British Midland DC-9 G-BMAH at 2016 (BD063 from Edinburgh), first time visitor Nigeria Airways B.707 5N-ANO at 2034 (WT802 from Paris), British Airways BAC 1-11s G-AVMV at 2055 (BA737 from Hamburg) & G-BGKF at 2027 (BA357 from Lyon) and finally British Airways B.737s G-BGDF at 2057 (BA761 from Stuttgart) & first visit G-BKYE at 2101 (BA653 from Stockholm). Fog then descended on Manchester and precluded any further arrivals, which may have been a good thing, as there were nearly forty aircraft parked on the International Apron, including fifteen imaginatively parked on Pier C!

11th December 1984 - This relatively quiet scene is giving a false impression! Taken around 10am, the airport had already received fifteen weather diversions, all but three being wide-bodied aircraft. The day would see a total of thirty-two diversions before Manchester itself became a victim of dense fog, spreading in from the River Bollin. (Manchester Airport Archive)

11th Manchester Utd travelled to play their latest European opponents, Dundee Utd, onboard Air Ecosse SD-330 G-BIRN. They returned two days on the same aircraft, having seen off the Scottish side 5-4 on aggregate.

11th The Cup Winners-Cup second leg, played between Celtic and Rapid Vienna at Parkhead on the 7th November, was abandoned after a Rapid player was struck by a missile. It was decided that tomorrow's replay should take place on neutral ground, so Old Trafford was decided upon. The Rapid Vienna team arrived at Manchester at 1321 today, onboard Austrian Airlines MD-81 OE-LDX (OS3611 from Vienna), which was also a first visit.

11th The latest Canadian Air Force CC-130Es to visit were 130315 CAM515 today, camouflage 130328 (CAM516-14th) & 130322 (CAM517-15th), all operating Trenton-Lahr. An extra flight was also operated by CC-130E 130307 (CAM6370 from/to Lahr-17th).

12th Viscount G-AZNA, which recently returned to British Midland after being on lease to Manx Airlines, diverted in at 1350 today from Leeds (BD414 from Heathrow), still in full Manx colours. Other diversions were JCB BAe.125-700 G-TJCB from East Midlands and Birmingham diversion, Birmingham Executive Jetstream G-CBEA at 1221 (BEX5689 from Aberdeen).

12th The Celtic match at Old Trafford produced some extra supporter's traffic, with the arrival of Aer Lingus B.737 EI-BEB (EI4206/7 from/to Dublin) and a number of Scottish originating light-aircraft with PA-31s G-BTHL & G-BPAR and PA-23s G-BBMJ/G-BBSN/G-BFVP.

13th The final RAF visit of the year was BAe.125 XX507 (RR1449 Teeside-Northolt) at 1431 today.

14th Moroccan Beech 200 CN-CDE arrived from Stansted at 2013 today, on a training flight.

15th Birmingham was affected by fog for most of the day, but only produced five diversions. The only one of interest was NLM F.27 PH-KFD at 0827 (HN495 from Amsterdam).

17th Traditionally extra Canadian charters are laid on over Christmas and this year was no exception. They included Wardair B.747 C-FDJC (today/19th), Worldways DC-8 C-FCPQ (19th) & British Caledonian DC-10 G-BJZE as BR5467 (20th).

18th British Air Ferries Viscount G-BBDK arrived at 0345 today, to operate an outbound freight flight to Bergen (VF8074).

20th Air Atlantique Douglas DC-3 G-AMCA, routing Stansted-Glasgow, diverted in today with engine trouble in both engines!

22nd Today saw the only charter of the year by East German-airline Interflug, when TU-134 DDR-SCO arrived at 0719 (IF7168 from Berlin).

26th Another British Airways B.737 making its first visit was G-BGDH, calling in en route as BA5620 Heathrow-Aberdeen, which just leaves G-BGDA/BGDE/BGDS from the original batch yet to visit.

27th Topflight Heron G-ANUO was due in today, but after problems with its nosewheel it diverted to Liverpool, where it blocked the runway for nearly an hour. Manchester had persuaded the aircraft to go to Liverpool, to avoid the prospect of a runway blockage, as evening fog was expected at the London airports.

28th A cold and grey winter's day saw Heathrow affected by long periods of fog, but Manchester saw few diversions. They started with the first visit of Bangladesh Biman DC-10 S2-ACO at 0932 (BG003 from Dubai) and some of the other morning diversions were TWA B.747s N93108 at 0935 (TW754 at Boston) & N17125 at 1107 (TW704 from New York); British Airways B.747 G-AWND at 1020 (BA072 from Toronto) and Kuwait B.747 9K-ADB at 1056 (KU102 from New York). Qantas flight QF001 was also due to divert to Manchester, but it ended up at Frankfurt without telling anyone! BA B.747 G-AWND arrived back at Manchester at 1848 (BA072W), after a failed attempt to return to Heathrow when the visibility dropped again. This was followed by BA B.747 G-AWNB at 1855 (BA274W from East Midlands), arriving for the same reason.

28th Manchester Airport greeted its 6-millionth passenger today, with a bagpiper and Scottish dancers. The lucky recipient was Australian Rugby League star Eric Grothe, who'd just made the 27-hour journey from Sydney onboard Qantas flight QF009. He was also presented with a giant gallon bottle of whisky, a decanter and a life-size koala doll! He'd arrived in Britain to play for Leeds, after being sold by the Australian club, Parramata.

29th Euroair Islander G-BHXI made its first visit to Manchester at 2205 today (EZ141 from Gatwick), arriving on a crew ferry flight.

29th Fog still affecting the South-East produced four wide-bodied early morning arrivals, all within an hour. British Airways B.747 G-AWNE at 0706 (BA012 from Muscat), Qantas B.747 VH-EBP at 0708 (QF001 form Bahrain), British Caledonian DC-10 G-BEBL at 0743 (BR254 from Dallas) and the pick of the four was the first visit of Singapore Airlines B.747-300 N120KF at 0815 (SQ022 from Muscat), on the airlines first diversionary visit since December 1975. Later on Busy Bee F.27 LN-NPH diverted in from Leeds at 1405 (BS2561 from Bergen), on its second visit.

30th The final diversion of 1984 was Iberia B.727 EC-CBE at 1243 today (AO1674 from Malaga), due to fog at Birmingham, which meant that ten different Iberia B.727s have visited Manchester in the last eleven years.

First/Last Arrivals & Departures 1984

First arrival:	BAC 1-11 G-BEKA/DA1255 from Alicante at 0031
First departure:	Cessna 421 G-BAGO to East Midlands at 0722
Last arrival:	BAC 1-11 G-BCXR/DA1553 from Palma at 2143
Last departure:	B.757 G-MONB/OM760 to Palma at 2154

Airport Stats 1984 (+/- % on Previous Year)		
Scheduled Passengers	6,034,928	+16%
Freight & Mail (Tonnes)	31,950	+15%
Movements	92,096	+7%

6
Airlines & Routes 1980-1984
Scheduled Passenger Routes

Aberdeen	Air Ecosse	June 1982-1984
"	British Airways	1980-1984
Amsterdam	British Airways	1980-1984
"	KLM	1980-1984
Athens	Qantas	April 1983-1984
Bangkok	Qantas	April 1983-1984
Barcelona	Iberia	May 1984 onwards
Barrow	Air Ecosse	July 1982-September 1982
Belfast	British Airways	1980-1984
Belfast Harbour	Loganair	November 1982-1984
Berlin	British Airways	1980-March 1982
Birmingham	Dan-Air	1980-March 1982
"	Metropolitan Airways	March 1982-1984
Bournemouth	Dan-Air	1980-March 1982
"	Metropolitan Airways	March 1982-1984
Brussels	British Airways	1980-1984
"	Sabena	1980-1984
Cardiff	Dan-Air	1980-March 1982
"	Metropolitan Airways	March 1982-1984
Copenhagen	British Airways	1980-1984
"	SAS	1980-1984
Cork	Aer Lingus	1980-1984
Dublin	Aer Lingus	1980-1984
"	British Airways	1980-1984
Dubrovnik	JAT	1980-1984 (Summer only)
Dundee	Air Ecosse	June 1980-1984
Dusseldorf	British Airways	1980-1984
Edinburgh	British Airways	1980-October 1982
"	Loganair	October 1982-1984
Faro	Air Portugal	April-October 1984
Frankfurt	British Airways	1980-1984
"	Lufthansa	1980-1984
Geneva	British Airways	1980-March 1983
Glasgow	British Airways	1980-1984
"	Loganair	May 1984 onwards

Guernsey	Guernsey Airlines	April 1980-October 1984
Jersey	Air UK	1980-1984 (Summer only)
"	British Airways	1980-1984
Larnaca	Cyprus Airways	1980-1984
Lisbon	Air Portugal	May 1981-October 1983, April 1984-October 1984
London-Gatwick	British Caledonian	1980-1984
London-Heathrow	British Airways	1980-1984
Ljubljana	JAT	December 1984-March 1985 (Winter only)
Madrid	Iberia	March 1982-1984
"	Iberia	March 1982-October 1984
Malta	Air Malta	1980-October 1983
"	British Airways	1981 (Summer only)
Melbourne	Qantas	April 1983-1984
Milan	British Airways	1980-1984
Montreal	BOAC/British Airways	June 1980-September 1980
Newcastle	Dan-Air	1980-March 1982
"	Metropolitan Airways	March 1982-1984
Newquay	Brymon Airways	1980-1981 (Summer only)
New York	British Airways	1980-October 1981
Nice	British Airways	1980-1984 (Summer only)
Oporto	Air Portugal	April 1982-October 1983
Paphos	Cyprus Airways	1984 (Summer only)
Paris	Air France	1980-1984
"	British Airways	1980-1984
Pula	JAT	1980-1984 (Summer only)
Rome	British Airways	1980-1984
Ronaldsway	Air UK	April 1980-October 1982
"	British Airways	January 1980-March 1980
"	Manx Airlines	November 1982-1984
Shannon	Aer Lingus	October 1982-1984
Split	JAT	1983 (Summer only)
Sydney	Qantas	April 1983-1984
Toronto	British Airways	1980-October 1983
Vienna	Austrian Airlines	April 1980-October 1982
Warsaw	LOT	June 1980-October 1981
Zurich	British Airways	1980-October 1982
"	Dan-Air	May 1984 onwards
"	Swissair	1980-1984

Scheduled Cargo Routes (excludes Datapost/Newspaper flights)

Amsterdam	KLM	1980-1984
Atlanta	British Caledonian	January 1980-February 1980
Brussels	Sabena	January 1980-May 1980
Copenhagen	SAS	1980-December 1983
Dublin	Aer Lingus	1980-1984
"	Clyden Airways	1980-January 1981
Frankfurt	Lufthansa	1980-1984
Helsinki	Finnair	1980-1984
Houston	British Caledonian	January 1980-February 1980
New York	Air Express International	December 1982-March 1983
"	Northwest Orient	1980-September 1981
Zurich	Swissair	1980-1984

Charter/IT Operators

Aeroflot	Summer only destinations: Leningrad (1980-1984) & Moscow (1980-1984).
Air Europe	The airline operated an extensive IT network to various destinations.
Air Florida	Miami (1980-1981) Summer only.
Air Malta	The airline operated IT flights year round.
Air Manchester	Operated IT flights to various destinations from June 1982-October 1982.
Air Portugal	Summer destinations: Faro (1980/1982). Winter destinations: Faro (1984)
Aviaco	Summer destinations: Alicante (1981-1982), Barcelona (1981) Ibiza (1981-1983), Malaga (1980-1983), Palma (1980-1982) & Tenerife (1982, 1984). Winter destinations: Malaga (1980/81, 1982/83) & Tenerife (1981-84).
Aviogenex	Summer only destinations: Dubrovnik (1980-1984), Ljubljana (1980-1984), Pula (1980-1984), Split (1980-1984), Tivat (1984) & Zadar (1980-1982).
Balkan Bulgarian	Summer destinations: Bourgas (1980-1984) & Varna (1980-1984). Winter destinations: Plovdiv (1983/84).
Britannia Airways	The airline operated an extensive IT network to various destinations.
British Airtours	Various European IT destinations were served during the summer (1980-1984) & winter (1981-1984). Also the following long-haul destinations were served: Los Angeles (Summer 1983-1984), Newark (Summer 1983), New York (Summer 1984) & Orlando (Summer 1982-1984).
British Airways	Operated IT flights to various European destinations (Summer 1982-1984) & (Winter 1982-1984). Also the following long-haul destinations were served: Los Angeles (1982) & Orlando (Summer 1982).
British Air Ferries	Jersey (1982-1984) Summer only.
British Caledonian	Operated IT flights to various destinations during Summer 1982.

British Island Airways	Summer destinations: Rotterdam (1983-1984) & Tarbes (1983). Winter destinations: Grenoble (1984/85).
British Midland	Operated a summer programme to various European IT destinations (1982-1983). The following long-haul destinations were also served: Toronto (1983) & Vancouver (1984).
CP Air	Summer destinations: Edmonton (1980-1981), Montreal (1982), Toronto (1980-1983) & Vancouver (1980-1983). Winter destinations: Toronto (1982-1984) & Vancouver (1982/83).
Dan-Air	The airline operated an extensive IT network to various destinations.
EL AL	Tel Aviv (October 1980-January 1981, April 1981-November 1982, April 1983-1984).
Hispania	Summer destinations: Alicante (1983) & Malaga (1983).
Inex-Adria	Summer destinations: Dubrovnik (1980, 1983-1984), Pula (1980-1984) & Split (1980-1984).
JAT	Summer destinations: Dubrovnik (1983-1984), Pula (1984) & Split (1983).
Laker Airways	Operated IT flights to various destinations until February 1982. Also the following long-haul destinations were served: Los Angeles (Summer 1980-1981 & Winter 1981/82), Miami (Summer 1980-1981 & Winter 1980-1982), New York (Summer 1980-1981 & Winter 1981/82) and Toronto (Summer 1980-1981 & Winter 1981/82).
LOT	Summer destinations: Krakow (1980-1981) & Warsaw (1980, 1984).
Monarch Airlines	Operated IT flights to various European destinations (Summer 1980-1984) & (Winter 1983/84).
Nor-Fly	Bergen (1981) Summer only.
Orion Airways	The airline operated an extensive IT network to various destinations.
Royal Air Maroc	Agadir (1982) Summer only.
Spantax	Summer destinations: Las Palmas (1980), Malaga (1981) & Palma (1980-1982).
TAE	Palma (1981) Summer only.
Tarom	Constanta (1980-1984) Summer only.
Transamerica	Summer only destinations: Los Angeles (1980-1981), New York (1980-1981, 1984) & Miami (1981).
Transeuropa	Summer destinations: Malaga (1980) & Palma (1980-1981).
Tunis Air	Monastir (1983-1984) Summer only.
Wardair	Summer destinations: Calgary (1980-1984), Edmonton (1980-1984), Ottawa (1982-1983), Toronto (1980-1984), Vancouver (1980-1984) & Winnipeg (1981-1983). Winter destinations: Edmonton (1981/82), Toronto (1980-1984) & Vancouver (1981/82).
WDL	Dusseldorf (1981) Summer only.
Worldways	Toronto (1984) Summer only.